CAUSES
AND
CONSEQUENCES
OF THE
AMERICAN
REVOLUTION

ESMOND WRIGHT was born in Newcastle on Tyne, England, and studied at King's College (Durham) and the University of Virginia. He is the author of *Washington and the American Revolution, The World Today,* and *Fabric of Freedom, 1763-1800,* as well as numerous articles dealing with American History and the American Revolution in particular. He is at present Professor of Modern History at the University of Glasgow.

CAUSES
AND
CONSEQUENCES
OF THE
AMERICAN
REVOLUTION

EDITED WITH AN INTRODUCTION BY

ESMOND WRIGHT

QUADRANGLE BOOKS

CHICAGO 回

Library of Congress Catalog Card Number: 66-11876

FIFTH PRINTING

PREFACE

In the last sixty years, and with increasing sophistication in the years since 1945, many articles have appeared in historical journals on almost every aspect of the American Revolution. Each generation has brought to the study of the Revolution its own dilemmas, its own vantage points, and an increasingly meticulous scholarship. In quality many of these articles have, of course, been fugitive pieces; but a number of them have proved to be seminal, and some of the most valuable have not always been printed in the most obvious or the most accessible places. Accordingly, I have collected here a number of articles on the causes and consequences of the American Revolution. These pieces, the work of different hands and of different generations, reveal how varied is the "image" and how rich the significance of the American Revolution.

It is unnecessary, I hope, to say that this collection can be neither representative nor comprehensive; it constitutes simply a selection of those articles that seem in the editor's judgment to be particularly important, and some of which are hard to track down. Every scholar will note at once the omissions; but those who are aware of the omissions can congratulate themselves on not needing the book. The articles are preceded by an introductory essay designed to offer a historiographical perspective.

E. W.

Glasgow, Scotland, 1966

CONTENTS

PREFACE   5

I. Introduction

THE SIGNIFICANCE AND PROBLEMS OF THE REVOLUTION   11

HISTORIANS AND THE REVOLUTION   15

A GUIDE TO THE BIBLIOGRAPHY OF THE REVOLUTION   52

II. Causes

THE IMPERIALIST INTERPRETATION   65

   Herbert L. Osgood: *The American Revolution*   65

   Charles M. Andrews: *The American Revolution:
An Interpretation*   77

   Lawrence Henry Gipson: *The American Revolution as
an Aftermath of the Great War for the Empire,
1754-1763*   87

THE PROGRESSIVE INTERPRETATION   103

   Arthur M. Schlesinger: *The American Revolution
Reconsidered*   103

   Louis M. Hacker: *The First American Revolution*   114

THE NEO-WHIG INTERPRETATION   143

   Philip G. Davidson: *Whig Propagandists of the
American Revolution*   143

   Lawrence A. Harper: *Mercantilism and the American
Revolution* (with some comments by O. M. Dickerson)   155

   Edmund S. Morgan: *The American Revolution
Considered as an Intellectual Movement*   172

THE CONSERVATIVE INTERPRETATION   193

   Lewis B. Namier: *King George III: A Study of
Personality*   193

   Esmond Wright: *Parliament: Politics and Policy,
1763-1774*   208

Richard W. Van Alstyne: *Parliamentary Supremacy
versus Independence*   217

III.   Consequences

THE CONFEDERATION PERIOD   233

Richard B. Morris: *The Confederation Period and the
American Historian*   233

CONSEQUENCES FOR THE UNITED STATES   249

Wilbur H. Siebert: *The Dispersion of the American
Tories*   249

Frederick B. Tolles: *The American Revolution
Considered as a Social Movement: A Re-Evaluation*   259

Merrill Jensen: *Democracy and the American Revolution*   267

Clarence L. Ver Steeg: *The American Revolution
Considered as an Economic Movement*   283

CONSEQUENCES FOR THE WORLD   293

Louis Gottschalk: *The Place of the American Revolution
in the Causal Pattern of the French Revolution*   293

W. R. Brock: *The Effect of the Loss of the American
Colonies upon British Policy*   305

I
Introduction

THE SIGNIFICANCE
AND PROBLEMS OF
THE REVOLUTION

The American Revolution is the central event in American history. But, perhaps more accurately than 1453 or 1492, it marks also the beginning of the distinctively modern period in world history. The forces at work for the first time in North America in 1776 thereafter recur elsewhere, until in the twentieth century they seem almost expected: the quest of distinct national groups for separate political identities, the concern with the extension of political power to ever wider electorates, the drafting of written constitutions after public debate, the faith in political solutions and rational arguments—even if the degree of rationality was often greater in the eighteenth than it is in the twentieth century.

The struggles of colonies for independence are not, of course, unfamiliar events in history. "The fruit clings to the tree only until it ripens," Turgot forecast. When the American colonies were ripe for independence, "they would do," he said, "what Carthage did." But what was unusual was the relatively easy victory won by 1783 and the relatively easy survival of the new state after 1783. It survived despite numerous—apparently overwhelming—hazards: despite the problems of territory and distance; despite the threat of Indian or Spanish attack, or of the resumptions of attacks by Britain; despite the risks involved in devising a new constitution of a federal rather than of a unitary sort; despite the dangers of internal dissension and collapse—in 1785-1787, in 1790, in 1797, in 1803, in 1814; and, not least, despite the still greater risks involved in declaring itself a republic rather than a monarchy. The attempt to combine federalism and republicanism in so vast an area seemed, in the eyes of eighteenth-century Europeans, an invitation to catastrophe.

Inevitably the great experiment was accompanied by and the product of a great debate—on the nature of tyranny and the legitimacy of revolt; on the principles on which any new government should be founded; on empire, aristocracy, and democracy; on mixed government and divisions of powers; on slavery and freedom. It was a debate conducted for the most part freely and publicly—though in 1787 it was conducted behind closed doors. Most of the themes of American political mythology—liberty and equality, the open society, the career open to talent, the sanctity of private property, the rights of the individual as against the state, freedom in land ownership, freedom in law, and freedom in the expression of opinion—most of these, derived though they are from a colonial past or a Whig ethic, are in essence products of the experiences of the Revolution of 1776 and of the debate before and after it.

These features and achievements of the Revolution are not contested by historians. They argue about other questions. Were the people of the North American colonies aware of themselves as a nation before they won their independence? Was the revolt genuinely the product of "a history of repeated injuries and usurpations" of authority by Britain, or the product of assertiveness of a new society in an utterly alien environment? If the latter, would it not have come sometime, sooner or later, whatever the character of the government of Britain? Was the Revolution a contest over who should rule at home as well as a struggle for home rule? Was the Constitution a Thermidorian reaction, a defense of colonial merchants' property rights, a conservative "backlash" after the democratic excesses of the Pennsylvania constitution of 1776 or that of Massachusetts in 1780? Was it, in other words, a Revolution not made but prevented— and if prevented, by whom? On these issues there is still much variety of view and as yet no consensus. But these issues, too, are central in any assessment of the place of the American Revolution in world history.

Recent research in the United States has emphasized the American features of the Revolution, its "givenness" in an American environment. However much the product of imperial mishandling, it owed its character and significance to the fact that it was in the end a declaration of American independence from the Old World. There can be little quarrel with this view, and it has been solidly buttressed by almost every contemporary American student of the Revolution. And, given the conflicting and selfish character of the various groups in the Parliaments of the early years of George III's reign, as Sir Lewis Namier has revealed them, imperial policy could hardly fail to have been other than shortsighted and vacillating, and any colonial administration directed from London could hardly have been other than erratic and contradictory.

Yet there remain about the events before and after 1776 some questions for historians, questions not yet answered, and some thus far not yet even asked. And on their answers the true significance of 1776 depends, at least as seen in the perspective of two centuries of subsequent history. If George III's Parliaments were, in policy-making, feeble and anemic, why was there, in areas outside the twelve colonies in revolt, so much evidence of imperial liberalism: in the Quebec Act of 1774, in the handling of Canada in 1776 and afterwards, in Lord North's Regulating Act in India, in the measures enacted for Ireland in 1782? Was it only in the handling of Boston that things went wrong? And since the Floridas stayed loyal, what were the forces that led to the alignment of the Upper South with New England? The contrast between the success of Britain's Indian, West Indian, Canadian, and (for a while) Irish measures and the failure of its North American policy remains unexplained.

Equally, whatever the nature, the genuineness, and the extent of American bitterness against the Mother Country, that bitterness could only "escalate" into a quest for independence if it were allowed some room for maneuver—if there were an adequate newspaper press and full freedom of expression of opinion, if there were opportunities for militia to drill and train, if America were already, in other words, a free society. And, as Robert E. Brown argues, Massachusetts and other colonies were already far more truly property-owning democracies than previous historians have believed. Why, then, after decades of salutary neglect, did Britain decide on repression where Boston was concerned in 1774, and why did she do so with so few troops and so ineptly, and against much influential advice? We still know far too little about the key decisions taken in Britain and in America in the years from 1773 to 1776.

Again, in part because of the recent emphasis on the nationalist aspects of the Revolution, we certainly know too little of its character as a civil war. Despite some recent studies by William H. Nelson, North Callahan, Paul Smith, and Jack Sosin, the role of the Loyalists remains elusive. And not only the Loyalists in the Americas but those who chose to settle in Britain and to influence or try to influence Lord North. For this was a civil war in Britain, too, albeit fought out there politically. How far were Loyalist counsels heeded? Were their optimistic figures of Loyalist numbers responsible for the new thrust to the South in 1779-1780? Why did they play so small a role socially and politically in London? Indeed, where did they go and how far did they stay together as a community? In twentieth-century wars the traitors within the gates have been much more sedulously cultivated than were these unhappy men.

And here too we still await the personal studies of the back-room boys, of the men behind Hillsborough and Dartmouth, Germain and North: the dispatches were read by, the minutes and plans drawn up by, the drafts of parliamentary papers and the instructions to governors and commanders are in the handwriting of William Bollan, the brothers Pownall, Henry Ellis, Maurice Morgann, and William Knox. The colorful John Temple emerges only occasionally from the shadows, though when he does he leaves behind an impression of a Falstaff and/or a Munchausen. It is here, from 1763 through to 1782, that there is a real continuity, not of policies but of personnel. Until we have biographies of these men, and studies of the role of Gage and Hutchinson and Bernard in London in 1775, we shall not be able to see the Revolution as an Anglo-American crisis, a study in mutual confusions.

And, again, if in 1776 a distinct society was asserting that independence in fact should become independence in form, was this a conviction reached slowly and step by step, or was there behind it an element of revolutionary organization and ferment? In this respect the Pennsylvania and Massachusetts constitutions are of major importance. And why and when did the revolutionary spirit in America blow itself out? Whatever might have been the revolutionary forces at work, they were soon tamed. There can be little debate among historians on one point, that by 1787 perhaps, and by 1793 certainly, the Revolution was—whether concluded or not at home—no longer (perhaps never?) meant for export abroad. Whatever the storms in Europe or Latin America after 1789, the United

States would have no part of them. If its own revolution was herald of a new order of things across the world, its leaders were unwilling to assume the role of world crusaders. Not only was this a revolution that acquired an ideology belatedly, but it was a revolution that curbed itself at its own frontiers.

Yet ironically, this relatively smooth and domestic transition from one order of things to another has become both symbol and prototype of the most frequent of political phenomena today. Revolution in all its unpredictability is the most familiar fact of today's world, even more necessary to national pride than its consequence, independence. To assert the rights of man is now to stake a claim to the right to affluence. Every African and almost every Asian country has passed or is passing through social or political changes, many of them violent, that can be traced back in lineal descent to the events of 1776. And the role of world leader enjoyed by, or thrust upon, the United States gives its own Revolution a peculiar importance outside and inside the United States. It was the first true revolution in modern history. Its relative smoothness makes it in some measure an event worthy of emulation. Yet paradoxically, many Americans see it with a certain ambivalence. As Kenneth E. Boulding has said:

> We feel a certain obligation to like revolution on principle, having been born in one ourselves. On the other hand, we are also afraid and suspicious of revolutions. This, no doubt, can be traced back to a suppressed guilt feeling about the treachery to a parent culture which any revolution implies. Our attitude toward revolution, therefore, is a compound feeling of both love and hate, affectionate regard for the infants toddling in our early footsteps and unresolved guilt about our own breakaway.[1]

1. Kenneth E. Boulding, "The United States and Revolution," An Occasional Paper on the Free Society published by the Center for the Study of Democratic Institutions (Santa Barbara, Calif., 1961), p. 4.

HISTORIANS AND
THE REVOLUTION

The "search for consensus" has become a familiar phrase in recent discussions of the American Revolution: many historians and commentators have taken it to be their task to establish a body of agreed interpretation about the causes and significance of the Revolution. But a revolution is in itself a denial of consensus. It is possible to list a chronological table indicating the stages of development of the Revolution, although even about that there can be endless debate over selection, omission, and emphasis. But at no point since 1774 has there been agreement on either the "facts" of the Revolution or on its "causes": everything has depended on the background and standpoint of the teller of the tale. The late Aneurin Bevan was not entirely wrong when he said forthrightly that "history is only a form of gossip": the historiography of the Revolution abounds in gossip, opinion, and the proving of a multitude of contradictory theses. It was so from the start. The viewpoint of George Bancroft was slow to establish itself as a Revolutionary norm.

The Revolutionary Age

It has been fashionable to distinguish in the first generation of Revolutionary writing—the age of the contemporary and the eyewitness—between four approaches: that of the chronicler, the Loyalist, the patriot, and, after 1787, the Federalist. Yet in fact few of the early Revolutionary historians can be thus safely pigeonholed. The chroniclers did not stick to the facts and the record, although they pretended to; they were just as prompt to quote from other historians—usually without acknowledgment—as from the records they industriously collected. And, inevitably, in telling the straight story of American success and British failure, the chroniclers appeared as more patriot than Loyalist. The Loyalists, whether diarists like Jonathan Boucher or pamphleteers like Daniel Leonard, wrote most movingly. And the patriots range from the romanticism of Parson Weems, through the solid storytelling of Federalist John Marshall, to the vivid insider's view of that assiduous chronicler-turned-patriot-turned-Federalist, John Adams. Of him it could be said, as was said of a British patriot turned world statesman, Winston Churchill, that he wrote his autobiography and called it *World Crisis*.

The avowed chroniclers were apt to be, paradoxically, the least valuable, since despite their concern with the collection of documents and with the "facts," they tended in practice to distrust their own evidence and relied heavily on the verdicts of others. Their accounts were derivative and often unashamedly plagiaristic. This is especially true of William Gordon. Although he had left his Southwark charge in 1770 because of his sympathies with the colonial cause, had served for fourteen years as a pastor in Roxbury, Massachusetts, had conducted a vast correspondence, and had traveled widely in the colonies to collect manuscripts, Gordon returned to England in 1786 to write his history.[2] "Should Great Britain mend its constitution by the shock it has rec'd . . . life, liberty, property and character will be safer there than on this side the Atlantic; and an Historian may use the impartial pen there with less danger than here." In fact, once in London Gordon found its atmosphere no more conducive to objectivity. His manuscript was deemed by his friends too favorable to the American cause to be likely to find a publisher. Accordingly he altered both the form and the emphasis of his work and omitted much material for fear of libel. What emerged took the form of an exchange of letters between an English and an American correspondent, but the names of the authors were suppressed and what they had written was doctored; in the end he drew heavily on the *Annual Register*, "without varying the language," as he put it, "except for method and conciseness." Gordon's *History* in its final form was thus a pale and partial derivative of Burke and Dodsley, neither vigorous nor authentic. And the author who had, whatever the merits of the work, tried in life to see and express both sides of the case, died in abject poverty.

A similar indictment of sources can be launched against David Ramsay, the South Carolina doctor and politician, whose *History of the American Revolution* was published in 1789[3] and was for long held in high repute, not only in the United States but in Europe. He too drew heavily on the *Annual Register*, without acknowledgment; he too changed indirect speech to direct; his purposes too were frankly partisan and patriotic.

But the approach and emphasis of Ramsay's *History* is surprisingly modern. If it can be seen as in some respects a precursor of Bancroft and of the neo-Whigs of today, it can also be seen as heralding the mid-Atlantic and neo-imperial viewpoint of Andrews and Gipson. The American Revolution was in Ramsay's eyes the product of geography ("distance . . . generated ideas in the minds of the Colonists favourable to liberty"), of religion ("all Protestantism is founded on a strong claim to natural liberty, and the right of private judgement"), of the absence

2. William Gordon, *The History of the Rise, Progress. and Establishment, of the Independence of the United States of America* (London, 4 vols., 1788). Cf. Orin G. Libby, "A Critical Examination of William Gordon's History of the American Revolution," American Historical Association *Annual Report* 1899 (Washington, 1900), I, 367-388; David D. Van Tassel, *Recording America's Past: An Interpretation of the Development of Historical Studies in America, 1607-1884* (Chicago, 1960), pp. 31-46.

3. David Ramsay, *The History of the American Revolution* (Philadelphia, 2 vols., 1789; London, 1793). Cf. Orin G. Libby, "Ramsay as a Plagiarist," *American Historical Review*, VII (1901-1902), 697-703; Page Smith, "David Ramsay and the Causes of the American Revolution," *William and Mary Quarterly*, XVII (1960), 51-77.

of a strong sense of social inequality ("all of one rank"), and of a considerable measure of actual political freedom ("the prerogatives of loyalty and dependence on the Mother Country were but feebly impressed on the colonial forms of government"). It was not caused by economic grievances, since the colonists greatly benefited from the mercantilist system. Britain treated them "as a judicious mother does her dutiful children . . . The good resulting to the Colonies, from their connection with Great Britain, infinitely outweighed the evil." Nor were George III and his ministers peculiarly malevolent; they were unimaginative, rigid, and shortsighted men caught up in a mounting series of crises which they failed to control. If in the end the crises generated a momentum of their own and produced a situation that was truly revolutionary, this was neither designed nor inevitable; and the motives of the patriots, as Ramsay describes them, were as mixed and often as unheroic as those of the Loyalists. "The very hinge of the controversy," however, was the matter of constitutional principle.

> The absolute unlimited supremacy of the British Parliament both in legislation and taxation, was contended for on one side, while on the other, no farther authority was conceded than such a limited legislation, with regard to external commerce, as would combine the interests of the whole empire. . . . In government as well as in religion there are mysteries from the close investigation of which little advantage can be expected. From the unity of empire it was necessary that some acts should extend over the whole. From the local situation of the Colonies it was equally reasonable that their legislatures should at least in some matters be independent. Where the supremacy of the first ended and the independency of the last began, was to the best informed a puzzling question.[4]

The contemporary Loyalist interpretations of the Revolution were, in all their partiality, also remarkable for their efforts at balance and objectivity.[5] The most vivid and detailed pictures of colonial life before the Revolution come from Loyalist sources. Alexander Hewatt, an Edinburgh graduate who was pastor of the First Presbyterian or Scots Church in Charleston, South Carolina, from 1763 until 1775, wrote *An Historical Account of the Rise and Progress of the Colonies of South Carolina and Georgia* (1779); it was, despite its lack of access to the colonial records, the first history of South Carolina. Robert Proud, the Yorkshire Quaker who became a Philadelphia schoolmaster, wrote the first history of Pennsylvania—*The History of Pennsylvania in North America* (2 vols., 1797, 1798); it contains a useful chapter on the pre-Revolutionary

4. Cf. also the long narrative chapters of straight history of the causes of the Revolution embedded in John Marshall's *Life of George Washington* (Philadelphia, 5 vols., 1804-1807), and William A. Foran, "John Marshall as a Historian," *American Historical Review,* XLIII (1937-1938), 51-64.

5. From this, however, we must exempt Peter Oliver's scurrilous *Origin and Progress of the American Revolution,* ed. by Douglass Adair and John Schutz (San Marino, Calif., 1961).

decade. And especially valuable are ex-Governor Thomas Hutchinson's second and third volumes of his *History of Massachusetts Bay* (1767, 1828). These volumes are particularly praiseworthy, for the original manuscript of Volume II was among his books and papers when the shoemaker Mackintosh and his Stamp Act rioters broke into Hutchinson's Boston home and rifled, destroyed, or scattered his possessions. Ironically, he had until then opposed both the Sugar Act and the Stamp Act, querying the right of Parliament to tax the colonists. Thereafter he became the advocate not of expediency but of authority—overactively so in the dog days of 1770-1773. Volume III was not published until 1828, but both Volumes II and III are, in all their conservatism and in all the vividness of their personal portraiture, curiously cool, accurate, and judicious studies. Hutchinson, in his writing as in his politics, was cautious and conscientious, Loyalist but liberal, proud of Massachusetts but still prouder of being a prerogative man. Like many another Loyalist he suffered in England from a divided allegiance, homesick for his native but rebellious country; and to the last he never gave up hope of laying his "bones in New England." He died and was buried in alien Surrey.

Joseph Galloway, Jonathan Boucher, and Daniel Leonard were too close and too involved to pretend to such objectivity, and, unlike Hutchinson, they did not seek to write history. George Chalmers did. A Scot who had left Edinburgh for Baltimore, he returned to Britain at the outbreak of war. In 1780 he published his *Political Annals of the Present United Colonies, from Their Settlement to the Peace of 1763.* He drew heavily on state papers and the Journals of the Board of Trade and Plantations—as later he drew on the correspondence of colonial governors—and his writing was well buttressed. He was highly critical of Massachusetts—New England, he believed, "has at all times found delight amid scenes of turbulence"—and in all his writing had a certain sympathy with the Southern colonies. He contended that there was neither in law nor in history any basis for the colonists' claims. Although in fact they enjoyed perfect freedom, they had, he argued, no share of sovereignty. When in 1782 Chalmers brought out privately his *Introduction to the History of the Revolt of the American Colonies,* he pushed these views further. The British failure lay in permitting the colonial assemblies to increase their authority. The New England colonists "acted during sixty years rather as the allies than subjects of the state." Despite his sympathies for the South, Chalmers comes close to expressing the viewpoint of the official governing class in London.

At the opposite end of the spectrum, and of value as much for auto-biographical as for historical reasons, is Mercy Otis Warren's three-volume *History of the Rise, Progress and Termination of the American Revolution, interspersed with Biographical, Political and Moral Observations* (3 vols., 1805). Her history reflected the views of one who, as the sister of James Otis, the wife of James Warren, and the beneficiary of the overthrow of Governor Hutchinson (she wrote much of it in the Hutchinson home in Milton which the Warrens had bought in 1781), was at once a laureate of the Revolution and of feminism. Mrs. Warren saw Hutchinson, indeed, as one of the main enemies—he was "dark, intriguing, insinuating, haughty and ambitious." But for all who were similarly "aristocratical" she had a similar contempt. Her writing was lively, frank, unashamedly patriotic, and democratic. Although in her account of the war she ranged widely and saw the struggle in North America as part of a larger conflict, she saw it also as one between heroes and devils. Indeed, John Adams felt far from certain when he read her later pages that he was placed in the proper camp. Mrs. Warren had written that "his passions and prejudices were sometimes too strong for his sagacity and judgment" (III, 392); he was seen, after his stay in London [in the 1780's], as a monarchical man. "It is my opinion," Adams bluntly informed Mrs. Warren, "that your History has been written to the taste of the nineteenth century, and accommodated to gratify the passions, prejudices and feelings of the [Jefferson] party who are now predominant." Mrs. Warren, equally blunt, replied that Adams' opinions were "more like the ravings of a maniac than the cool critique of genius and science." As for her use of the sources, she claimed that she had in fact planned her history long before the party divisions of the nineteenth century and had drawn, *inter aliis,* on the contemporary writings of John Adams himself.

Adams was vulnerable here, for in the midst of the war he had confessed to Mrs. Warren that he planned to spend his leisure in writing a history of the Revolution. "With a hand as severe as Tacitus, I wish to God it was as eloquent," he would, he said, draw the portrait of every Revolutionary character. "But when it is done, I will dig a vault, and bury the manuscript . . . not to be opened till a hundred years after my death." The manuscript, unfortunately, was never written.

Nor were the histories which at one moment or another John Jay and Elbridge Gerry, Thomas McKean and Benjamin Rush claimed to be writing or assembling. For his part, Adams came to doubt whether the task was possible; and if possible, whether the history of this event—as of any—would be the true story. "Who shall write the history of the American Revolution?" he asked McKean in 1815. "Who can write it? Who will ever be able to write it? The most essential documents, the debates and deliberations in Congress, from 1774 to 1783, were all in secret, and are now lost for ever."

Between 1815 and 1826, Adams and Jefferson corresponded with each other and recalled many events in the fantastic story of what was now coming to appear in retrospect not as an erratic and revolutionary course but as a process destined and dedicated from the beginning. By 1826, fifty years after, the pattern had become that of a heroic age. But when they died, within a few hours of each other on July 4, 1826, the two major architects of independence had left the story still unwritten.

But few of the highly professional and detailed studies of the Revolution that have appeared in the 140 years since have caught the vivid argument and immediacy of the accounts that came from this first generation of participants-turned-historians. In their closeness to the time, in their contentiousness, in their realistic mixture of fact and opinion, and in their richness of texture, they are closer to the actuality of the Revolutionary struggle than most subsequent writing.

The Nationalist Interpretation

On that same day of Adams' and Jefferson's death, July 4, 1826, appeared George Bancroft's first major prose writing, appropriately and characteristically a statement of democratic and nationalist principles. And eight years later appeared the first of what were to be the ten volumes of his *History of the United States.*

The Revolutionary debates were over. Isolated from European revolutions and thus for twenty-five years from Europe, the independent country had grown into a radically distinct and powerful society. It looked now to the West, an area now linked to the East by road and (soon) by rail, and no longer potentially separatist. Its most significant political experiment was Henry Clay's attempt to link Southern cotton planters and Northern traders and manufacturers in the development and exploitation of the West: there was a growing awareness of the potential affluence of this vast federal society. Its most peculiar institution was the slave system, anathema to most European observers but in Southern eyes the bedrock of the prosperity not only of the Cotton Kingdom but of the United States as a whole. Its most obvious social and political characteristic, however, was Jacksonian democracy: equality of opportunity and of suffrage, rotation in office, the belief that to the victor belonged the spoils of office, the denial that politics demanded the special skills that in Europe bred the class system and governing elites. From this vantage point 1776 acquired a new meaning. Of this view, George Bancroft became the spokesman: the Revolution was but the final event in a self-determined American progress toward liberty.

Bancroft buttressed this view, however, by a professional familiarity with the facts as conveyed by documents. He was far more fortunate than Ramsay or Gordon, for by the 1820's some valuable collections were available. Hezekiah Niles published his *Principles and Acts of the Revolution in America* in 1822. Between 1827 and 1830 Jonathan Elliot brought out his five volumes of documents, *The Debates in the Several State Conventions on the Adoption of the Federal Constitution.* Publication followed of the *American State Papers: Documents, Legislative and Executive of the Congress of the United States.* In 1822 Peter Force, printer and journalist, began his remarkable collection of documents— "the clay and the straw," as Bancroft described them, "providing everything necessary but the forming hand." Lyman Draper began collecting the sources of Western history. The Library of Congress, founded in 1800 and strengthened by the purchase of the Jefferson and Madison libraries, became more and more important. In 1827 Jared Sparks persuaded Bushrod Washington, nephew of the first President, to allow him to remove the 40,000 Washington letters in eight large boxes from Mount Vernon to Boston for easier study; they too found their way to the Library of Congress. The archives of Britain, Holland, and France were raided for American material by John Romeyn Brodhead, John R. Bartlett, Henry Stevens, Jr., and especially by Sparks. The latter toured American state archives, visited London and Paris in 1828-1829 and again in 1841, talked to survivors of the Revolution, mapped historic sites, and in 1830 followed Arnold's route to Quebec. The Harvard and John Carter Brown collections became conspicuous. Between 1830 and 1850 thirty-five historical societies were founded. In 1815 the *North American Review* was founded; in 1817 Jared Sparks became its managing editor and in 1824 its owner and editor.

Indeed, in many respects Sparks was far more typical of the age than Bancroft. He was, first and last, the editor—*The Diplomatic Correspondence of the American Revolution* (12 vols., 1829-1830), *The Life of Gouverneur Morris* (3 vols., 1832), *The Library of American Biography* (10 vols., 1834-1848), *The Life and Writings of George Washington* (12 vols., 1833-1839), *The Works of Benjamin Franklin* (10 vols., 1836-1840), *The Correspondence of the American Revolution* (4 vols., 1853). In all he produced some hundred volumes. And if, with him as with Bancroft, the sources when used were not always used scrupulously, if only those private letters were published which accorded with the subject's dignity, if many that were published were embellished, if his history was over-rich in biography and thin in social and economic facts, and if his own writing was pedestrian, he yet rendered an immense service as, in Samuel Eliot Morison's phrase, "an explorer and producer of American history." At last a massive, if incomplete, collection of Revolutionary source material was now in print. He had not written as he had planned a Documentary History of the Revolution, but he had rescued Washington from Weems and had begun to transform the prevailing portrait of Franklin.

The nationalist age was conspicuous for its zeal in collecting historical documents; equally conspicuous was its pride in using them to tell a story of national origins that would be a saga of liberty. Sparks the editor was also Sparks the pedagogue: his concern was the story of great men, accounts often more edifying than enlightening, more gentlemanly and pietistic than scientific.[6] It was not only the South but the Northern academics and libraries which took a romantic and proud, but factually informed, view of the past. In the mid-nineteenth century United States, as in Britain, the fabric of rhetoric was closely interwoven with reality, as in the pages of Macaulay, of Prescott, of Motley, and of *Waverley* itself. The age of Sparks and Bancroft was also the age of Sir Walter Scott.

To these now abundant sources Bancroft added his own: while min-

6. Herbert Baxter Adams, *The Life and Writings of Jared Sparks* (New York, 2 vols., 1893); John Spencer Bassett, *The Middle Group of American Historians* (New York, 1917).

ister to Britain from 1846 to 1849 and to Germany from 1867 to 1874, he searched European archives for material—and some of this he used, for example, in his tenth volume published in 1874. He was a friend of Mommsen and Ranke, of Guizot and Thiers, of Hallam and Macaulay, a member of an international literary profession. And as Jacksonian Democrat, politician, Secretary of the Navy in the Polk administration, and twice ambassador in Europe, he brought a sharp sense of high politics to his writing of history.

His ten-volume work is essentially a three-volume (1834, 1837, 1840) study of the process of American colonization, followed—after the first twelve-year period of his public life—by the seven volumes on the Revolutionary period.[7] Despite his assiduity in collecting documents and his pride in bringing to his writing "the freedom of an unbiased mind," Bancroft paraphrased his sources liberally and loosely: he was uncritical in his approach and ran on one speech with another; like his contemporaries he minimized economic forces and was preoccupied with blood and gore; if his chapters on the military aspects of the Revolution are sound—although the descendants of Greene, Schuyler, and Sullivan began a long battle with him over his views of their ancestors— his economic and constitutional chapters are shaky; and he brought to the treatment of them a viewpoint all his own. For him, as for his contemporaries, history was "philosophic" and progressive, its momentum the spirit of freedom. In 1776 Great Britain "made war on human freedom." His three volumes on the colonial period were designed to show the emergence of the movement for independence: in three volumes the British administration is given but three chapters. "The spirit of the Colonies demanded freedom from the beginning." "Tyranny and injustice peopled America with men nurtured in suffering and adversity." "The best Britons migrated in quest of freedom." "When America traces the lineage of her intellectual freedom she acknowledges the benefactions of Wickliffe." George III was a ruthless tyrant with a "hatred of reform, and an antipathy to philosophical freedom and to popular power." The Revolution against him sounded the death knell of "the ages of servitude and inequality" and rang in "those of equality and brotherhood."

There are many errors in his story: some Pilgrims were not heroes but convicts; Puritans were by nature not freedom-worshiping but intolerant; the Navigation Acts, some of which had been in operation for a century before 1776, were not wicked; the reign of George III is not a continuation of Stuart tyranny; and in his telling, the British "case" goes by total default. Two of these errors—the tyranny of George III and the threatening character of the Navigation Acts—became enduring

7. George Bancroft, *History of the United States* (Boston, 10 vols., 1834-1874); Mark A. De Wolfe Howe, *Life and Letters of George Bancroft* (New York, 2 vols., 1908); John Spencer Bassett, "George Bancroft," in Bassett, ed., *The Middle Group of American Historians;* N. H. Dawes and F. T. Nichols, "Revaluing Bancroft," *New England Quarterly,* VI (1933), 278-293; Russell B. Nye, *George Bancroft, Brahmin Rebel* (New York, 1944).

Revolutionary stereotypes. But, beyond the errors, the emphasis is not to twentieth-century taste: the language is one of exaltation—"très democratique," said Guizot; even to Carlyle, who liked its "light and shadow," it was too didactic. Looking back on his country's story and quite unaffected by the Civil War, Bancroft saw it all through a golden haze of success:

> In America a new people had risen up without King or princes or nobles, knowing nothing of titles and little of landlords, the plough being for the most part in the hands of free holders of the soil. They were more sincerely religious, better educated, of serener minds, and of purer morals than the men of any former republic. [Their constitution] excelled every one known before; and . . . secured itself against violence and revolution by providing a peaceful method of every needed reform.

Bancroft's views of George III were given support in the next generation from a distant and at first glance a very alien quarter. The king's role is central to the explanation of the outbreak of the American Revolution, and that role cannot be assessed merely in an American context; the American Revolution is also an event in British history. Until the middle of the nineteenth century, the prevalent British view of George III was still Tory, substantially that of John Adolphus, whose *History of England* (from 1760 to 1783) had appeared in 1802. George III was no tyrant but a constitutionally minded King seeking to liberate himself from the oligarchy which surrounded and frustrated the throne. But in the years from 1838 to 1853 a number of volumes of letters and memoirs appeared that furnished ammunition for the Whig view: the *Chatham Correspondence* (1838-1840), the *Bedford Correspondence* (1842-1846), a six-volume edition of Horace Walpole's letters in 1840, and in 1845 his *Memoirs of the Reign of George III;* in 1844 came the correspondence of Burke, in 1852 the *Rockingham Memoirs,* in 1852-1853 the *Grenville Papers,* and between 1853 and 1857 the *Memorials of Charles James Fox.*[8] At this point, when Fox was seen by twisted irony as an eighteenth-century Lord John Russell—a comparison neither would have welcomed—the writing of British history begins to accord with Bancroft. Erskine May's *Constitutional History* gives the old Whig charges against the King the sanctity not of partisanship but of historical truth. Before 1760, thanks in part to the role of the Russells in 1688, government had been, apparently, ministerial and responsible; George III had set out to overthrow it. W. E. H. Lecky took over some of these views—though not all of them—when he published the third and fourth volumes of his *History of England in the Eighteenth Century.* They reached their climacteric in Trevelyan.

Sir George Otto Trevelyan came to his study of the American Revolution from a dedication to liberty quite as strong as Bancroft's. In style

8. Herbert Butterfield, *George III and the Historians* (London, 1957), p. 97.

he was equally given to rhetoric; "philosophic" history was still in fashion, and in any event he was Macaulay's nephew. And he too brought to his study of the past a concern with contemporary affairs: he served the Government of India, he was a member of Parliament from 1865 to 1897, and he held office as chief Secretary for Ireland and Secretary for Scotland. He had become especially interested in Charles James Fox, whose early life he had recorded in what is still one of the great biographies in English historical writing.[9] Trevelyan found himself unable to complete the life of his hero Fox, especially the years from 1774 to 1782, without studying the American Revolution. From 1899 to 1914 there thus appeared the six volumes of his *The American Revolution,* the last volume of which was subtitled *George III and Charles James Fox.* Vividly written, with masterly portraits of the major British figures and with a heavy preoccupation with political and military developments, Trevelyan brought to his study a passionately liberal bias. And for him liberal meant Liberal. The American Revolution was seen, rightly, as part of a civil struggle; it was a struggle, to adapt Carl Becker's later phrase, over who should rule at home, in Britain. The Bancroft view, the devil theory of history, was confirmed for British, not American, reasons. George III, "formidable," "pertinacious," and "insatiable of power," with his group of yes-men hungry for office, was responsible for the American Revolution. Not only the Revolutionary cause but Charles James Fox's career, Whiggism, and, indeed, British liberalism in general depended on calling a halt to a "system of personal government." For the sake of liberalism in Britain the success of the colonies became essential. This was not an international struggle but a war of ideas in which nationalism was at a discount; the Revolutionary struggle was seen not as an alignment of Britain *versus* France, but of liberalism (Washington plus the Rockingham Whigs plus the France of Louis XVI) against George III and his corrupt placemen. Trevelyan brought passion, preoccupation, and persuasion to his pages: the passion for liberalism of a Gladstonian, the preoccupation of the late nineteenth century with liberalism—as in India, Ireland, and Italy, the causes that always excited the Macaulay and Trevelyan families —and the persuasions of style derived from his uncle. He tells us much about the Liberal party's view of its origins and its mythology, its claim to descent from Burke and Fox and the Rockingham Whigs. He tells us much—though some of that we now know to be erroneous—about the constitutional principles of Burke and Fox. He tells us very little about the domestic American aspects of the Revolution and offers a false picture of its British aspects. Trevelyan's recent republication, however, reveals how far the history written today has moved away from the purple prose of the nineteenth century.

This stylized view of George III became an American stereotype, firmly fixed in the popular imagination. John Fiske, an able and versa-

9. *The Early History of Charles James Fox* (London, 1880).

tile writer but not a profound scholar,[10] gave it the sanction of his quite considerable public reputation in 1891 when he published *The American Revolution*. Fiske ignored the internal revolution in the colonies and made George III the evil genius of the story. "Almost boorishly stiff in his ordinary unstudied manner, he could be smooth as oil whenever he liked." "He had little faith in human honor or rectitude, and in pursuing an end he was seldom deterred by scruples." "It is historically correct to regard him as the person chiefly responsible for the quarrel." Against this mythology almost all recent scholarship has been enlisted. But myths, like old soldiers, are slow to die.

The Imperial School

When Bancroft died in 1891, his work was already being questioned. This criticism began even in his lifetime when Richard Hildreth wrote his six-volume *History of the United States* (1849-1852). He presented his subjects, as he put it, "unbedaubed with patriotic rouge, wrapped up in no finespun cloaks of excuses and apology, without stilts, buskins, tinsel, or bedizenment, in their own proper persons." The pageantry and panoply of Parkman and Prescott—history seen as the martial exploits of heroic men—became suspect. A series of solid histories—but still epic and many-volumed in their scale, and narrative in form—appeared from Justin Winsor and James Schouler, John Bach McMaster and James Ford Rhodes.

The emphasis was tending not toward war and personalities but toward social and economic developments, toward the growth of institutions and the relationship between the colonies and the imperial government. These patterns were still seen as patterns of growth and progress, but the growth could now be scientifically plotted and explained: for there were laws in history. Americans were now studying in considerable numbers in Europe; by 1898 the war with Spain, with its own colonial consequences, brought a new awareness of the reality of empire; by 1900 one of the most striking social phenomena was the extent of intermarriage between American heiresses and members of the financially enfeebled British aristocracy. And the interest in Darwin and Darwinism was paralleled by a concern in America, as in Britain, with the Teutonic origins of British and, therefore, in turn, of American institutions: the germ-and-German theory of constitutional origins. The notions of empire of Sir Charles Dilke and Sir John Seeley, the racist and white-man's-burden themes of John Fiske and John W. Burgess in America and of Kipling in both the United States and Britain, the interest in an Anglo-

---

10. Between 1888 and 1902 Fiske wrote twenty-one volumes on historical topics, as well as other books. And in the five years from 1888 to 1893 he gave no less than 527 lectures on historical subjects, as well as fourteen on philosophy and six on music. J. B. Sanders, "John Fiske," in William T. Hutchinson, ed., *The Marcus W. Jernegan Essays in American Historiography* (Chicago, 1937), pp. 150-151.

American-German accord shared by Joseph Chamberlain and Theodore Roosevelt, the concern with naval power of Mahan in Washington and Fisher in London, the joint origins of British-American policy toward China in the friendship of Lord Charles Beresford and Arthur Hippisley of Britain with Hay, Rockhill, and Straight of the United States: these common diplomatic problems and political and social interests of the early twentieth century made the older nationalist history no longer fashionable, nor tenable. The patrician and the literary stylist, whose works were read by the public, gave way to the professional, whose works were read mainly by other professionals.

The professionals drew their inspiration primarily from Europe and in particular from Germany. The nationalist historians who had been Bancroft's mentors in his youth in Germany, were now being challenged and replaced by a new type of scientific historian exemplified by Leopold von Ranke, who was Herbert Osgood's teacher and model. Each major European country took pride in the opening of its archives and in the publication of collections of source material: the *Monumenta historica Germanica* (1826), the *Documents inédits* (1836), the Rolls Series in Britain (1858). The scientific history of Germany, in which many Americans were trained, became the model, rather than the elegant literary history of a Macaulay or a Michelet. Scientific history made its most delayed impact in Britain—James Froude followed Edward Freeman at Oxford. But in the United States it became dominant. The treatment that Sparks had meted out to Washington's or Franklin's letters was now unthinkable. So was the sweep, *l'histoire à la longue haleine,* of a Bancroft. William Ellery Channing was the last to write a history of America from the beginning and to try to include in it all points of view. In the United States there were now abundant collections of sources, thanks to editors like Hezekiah Niles, Jonathan Elliot, Peter Force, Lyman Draper, and Sparks himself, and splendid research libraries. Active state historical societies were in being—by 1861 there were no less than sixty-five of them—and Massachusetts and New York, Pennsylvania and North Carolina were publishing their colonial records *in extenso.* The Civil War, the spate of books and memoirs provoked by it, not least *The Battles and Leaders* series, the celebration in prose and verse of the centenary of 1776, and the publication of periodicals like *The Historical Magazine* (1857-1875); *The Magazine of American History,* founded in 1877 and edited from 1883 to 1893 by Martha J. Lamb, the historian of New York City; and the *Pennsylvania Magazine of History and Biography,* also founded in 1877: all these provided a firm foundation for a new-style history. But none of these forces would necessarily have made the amateur historian give way to the professional had history not in the 1880's become an established university discipline.

Jared Sparks had accepted a Harvard professorship—the McLean Professorship of Ancient and Modern History—in 1838 on the under-standing that he would teach nothing but history, an advance in itself. He was the first professor of history other than ecclesiastical in any

American university; his first course was on the American Revolution; and he taught only for four months in the year: still more an advance. But these steps led nowhere—except for Sparks: in 1849 he became President of Harvard, and four years later resigned that office for reasons of ill health. His carefully planned and researched study of *The American Revolution* was never completed. Not until Andrew D. White introduced his history courses at Michigan, emphasizing wide reading and the use of sources in teaching, did genuine historical study begin. When White became president of the newly established Cornell University in 1868, and when Daniel Coit Gilman went to Johns Hopkins in 1875, graduate schools built on modern lines came into being, and history became a major subject of university study. The seminar method, with its emphasis on the critical examination of original texts and the challenging of established orthodoxies, with the quest for new theses, rigorous impartiality of description, and a weighty bibliographical apparatus, was imported from Germany. Charles K. Adams, who had been a student under White, began seminar teaching at Michigan in 1869, Henry Adams and his successors at Harvard in 1871, John W. Burgess at Amherst in 1873.

By 1880 there were no less than eleven professors of history in the whole United States. Moses Coit Tyler held the first professorship of American history, established in 1881 at Cornell; and under Herbert Baxter Adams at Johns Hopkins and Burgess at Columbia the history graduate school became a major educational force. From both institutions came historical publications in which scholars could publish specialized monographs on carefully limited topics—the Johns Hopkins University "Studies in Historical and Political Science," initiated by Adams in 1882, and the Columbia University "Studies in History, Economics and Public Law," initiated by Burgess and Dunning. Articles on American history began to appear in the 1870's in the *Revue historique* and the *Historische Zeitschrift*. Charles Adams brought out in 1882 a guide to historical literature, Channing and Hart the first edition of theirs in 1896.[11] Under the stimulus of John Franklin Jameson the Carnegie Institution of Washington became a publisher of historical manuscripts, records, and guides to materials on American history in Europe. With the founding of the American Historical Association in 1884, the establishment of the *Political Science Quarterly* in 1886, and the publication of the *American Historical Review* in 1895, with Jameson as its first editor, American history may be said to have become fully professional. And the professionals, writing often—perhaps too often?—for each other, were not only critical but self-conscious about their activity. Not for them what Henry Adams once called the "commonly unconscious and child-like" assumptions of an earlier day.

Inevitably history changed not only in style but in form and content. It became ethically neutral rather than moralistic, expository rather than

11. *Guide to the Study of American History,* later revised by Frederick Jackson Turner (1912).

pictorial, analytic rather than oracular. It became as much concerned with economic and social forces as with war, politics, and constitutions. General histories could now only appear if they were the work of many specialists in collaboration. In the *American Nation* series (1904-1907), twenty-four authors, each writing a separate volume, were needed. But the major change was that history became social in its emphasis, as in McMaster, and its theme became the idea of social continuity, of progress and growth. This was particularly so where it remained primarily a study of institutions: Comte, Buckle and Spencer, Maine, Stubbs and Fustel de Coulanges were the pacemakers. And American history was no longer seen in isolation, or as absolutely unique.

The American Revolution benefited particularly from all these developments. The origin of the American nation was, after all, an Anglo-American event and could be studied at least as profitably from the vantage point of London as from that of Boston.[12] It had been relatively nonviolent in character, and thus federal institutions as they emerged after independence bore strong traces of their colonial origins. And in one sense the Revolution had always been studied in terms of its colonial roots: all American historians of the Revolution had properly approached it as the logical conclusion of the century and a half of colonial history.[13] The Revolution lent itself to an institutional, administrative, and imperial emphasis.

In the half-century from 1893, when George Louis Beer wrote his master's thesis, to 1943, when Charles M. Andrews died, the Revolution was studied as the *terminus ad quem* of colonial history. Beer, Herbert Osgood, and Andrews agreed in emphasizing that the colonies were English foundations and that London was the center of the empire. Osgood, trained at Amherst and Columbia under Burgess, at Yale under Sumner, and at Berlin under Schmoller, Treitschke, Gneist, and not least Ranke himself, at first taught European and English constitutional history and saw the colonial period "as a natural outgrowth of the history of Europe." Accepting the Burgess-Sumner-Darwinian view of the evolutionary growth of institutions and societies ("it is only through law and political institutions that social forces become in the large sense operative"), familiar with the best German scholarship and with British Public Record Office materials, he made colonial history his life-work. He published no less than thirteen major articles—all but three on colonial history—in the recently founded *Political Science Quarterly*. One of these, "England and the Colonies," published in 1887, may be said to herald the imperial view of the Revolution. "The whole

12. Cf. Andrews: "The years from 1607 to 1703 were Colonial before they were American or national, and our Revolution is a Colonial and not an American problem." Or cf. Herbert L. Osgood: "American Colonial history was a natural outgrowth of the history of Europe."

13. And one historian had been impossible to categorize as nationalist or Revolutionary: Lorenzo Sabine, who in 1864 had published his case-book, *The American Loyalists* (Boston), with its searching—and for its day, unusual—introductory essay examining the nature of colonial society.

struggle," he said, "was but an episode in the development of the English colonial system." In flat contradiction of Bancroft, he denied that there was any proof that Parliament intended to overthrow the constitutional rights of the colonists. "There was nothing that can be called tyrannical or unconstitutional in the plans of Grenville, Townshend or Lord North." When James Harvey Robinson joined the Columbia University staff, Osgood turned exclusively to colonial and Revolutionary history, and in his "investigation course," as it was called, on the "Political History of the Colonies and the American Revolution," he assembled the material of what became his major volumes. From this source also came not only his many articles, the three volumes of *The American Colonies in the Seventeenth Century* (1904-1907), and the four volumes of *The American Colonies in the Eighteenth Century* (1924, published posthumously), but at least fifty dissertations from his students, prominent among whom were Charles A. Beard, Arthur M. Schlesinger, and George Louis Beer.

Osgood was preoccupied with the transformation of British institutions in an American setting. If he minimized the commercial relationship— just as he minimized social and intellectual developments—he was vividly aware that even as the system of royal control grew, so did the psychological gaps between the two worlds. By the end of the seventeenth century, he argued, the colonists "in their large relations . . . were [still] subordinate to Europe," but "their personal and local concerns were as distinct from those of contemporary Europeans as time or space could well make them. In their languages and in the type and traditions of their culture they were Europeans; but they were transplanted upon a new and distant continent, and felt chiefly the pressure of its environment. They had already become colonials in the full sense of the word but had not yet reached a developed American type." His studies of the eighteenth century, unfinished at his death and still perhaps lacking a coherent shape, brought out the development of an "imperial rather than particularist" British policy, the growing maturity of each colony, and the successive attempts at a form of intercolonial union—of which 1776, though the final, was only one. Not until Lawrence H. Gipson in our own day has a historian so skilfully wedded American developments to the history of Britain and Empire. And despite Osgood's balanced and, in places, pedestrian treatment of the British-colonial relationship, it is impossible not to be struck in his pages by the recurrence of colonial complaints and grievances on constitutional issues.

George Louis Beer was to become an important figure in Anglo-American affairs, the leading American expert on colonial questions at the Paris Peace Conference and a member of the mandates commission until the United States failed to join the League of Nations. Both as man of affairs and historian, he made the British colonial system his particular concern. The relationship was less that of imperial master and subject colony than of joint exploiters of a mercantilist system that brought benefit to both. *The Commercial Policy of England Toward the*

American Colonies was the subject of his master's thesis in 1893; after a short but highly profitable career as a tobacco merchant, he worked at the Public Record Office; and in 1907 he published *British Colonial Policy, 1754-1765*. He revealed very clearly the administrative weakness of the Old Colonial System and its need for reform. He contended that in general terms before 1763 the colonies accepted the laws of trade, and that the commercial regulations of 1764-1765 aimed at the encouragement, not the restriction, of colonial industry. Increasingly, however, both in Britain and in the colonies, economic motives became subordinated to political. It was not mercantilism but the tightening up of the colonial system, partly because of the extent of smuggling and partly because of the need for colonial defense, that shattered the old Empire. For their part the colonists showed neither gratitude nor loyalty to the mother country, despite the protection it gave them against France. The colonies moved to independence not because they sought a liberty denied them by a tyrant, but because the Empire no longer brought them visible economic benefits.

Beer struck a very modern note; many of the detailed studies of our own day—studies, particularly those of O. M. Dickerson, that have emphasized the benefits of the mercantilist system to the colonists, the groups that favored the maintenance of the system and the monopoly of the British market they enjoyed—are amplification and developments of his theme. He introduced a highly topical note into his conclusion. He thought it too early to say whether the break-up of the old Empire constituted progress or reaction, or "merely a temporary regression necessary to a further step in advance." It was, he thought, not at all improbable "that the political evolution of the next centuries may take such a course that the American Revolution will lose the great significance that is now attached to it, and will appear merely as the temporary separation of two kindred peoples whose inherent similarity was obscured by superficial differences, resulting from dissimilar economic and social conditions."

Beer then moved back into the earlier period, to write *The Origins of the British Colonial System, 1578-1660* (1908) and *The Old Colonial System, 1660-1754* (1912). He was at work collecting material for a four-volume study of the years from 1688 to 1754 when the First World War began and turned his attention to the current scene.

Like Osgood and Beer, Charles Andrews was primarily a colonial rather than a Revolutionary historian. His knowledge of the British sources for colonial history was unrivaled, and in his guides to them, published by the Carnegie Institution, he gave his successors the tools of the trade. His view of the colonial period is that it is "not American only but Anglo-American." It was only in the fourth volume of his *The Colonial Period of American History* (4 vols., 1934-1938) that he reached the Revolutionary period with a chapter on "England's Commercial and Colonial Policy." Some of his work in this volume, especially that on the Board of Trade, needs modification in the light of the work of Lawrence A. Harper (*The English Navigation Laws,* 1939) and O. M. Dickerson (*The Navigation Act and the American Revolution,* 1951). In 1924 Andrews published a volume of four essays, *The Colonial Background of the American Revolution,* in which he repeated his view that preceding historians had been guilty of judging colonial development in the light of a democracy that came later. It ought, he insisted, to be seen in terms of the ideas and practices of Britain at the time. Andrews insisted that the Revolution was a "colonial" rather than an "American" problem, and that it could only be seen in the context of that imperial policy devised in London for all the British colonies in the West. He gave as much attention to Britain as to the colonies themselves; he was fully aware that the struggle between the British effort to contrive a system of colonial dependence on the one side and the efforts of the colonies for their part to attain self-government, constituted the real tension between them. He was scornful of the super-patriots of the Bancroft type:

> It is an unhappy fact that more errors in the writing of American history have been committed in the name of patriotism than were ever dreamed of in Horatio's philosophy.[14]

He left a major imprint not merely because of the extent and magisterial quality of his own writing, but because of the whole generation of Yale men, and Yale women, who emerged from his seminars. If there is a single archetypal figure dominating the "imperial" school—as Bancroft dominates the "nationalist"—it is Andrews.

Two of his students have been and remain especially important: Lawrence H. Gipson and Leonard W. Labaree. The most detailed description of the colonies in an imperial setting in and just before 1763 is in Gipson's monumental *The British Empire Before the American Revolution,* of which twelve volumes have thus far been published (since 1936). This looks at all the Brtiish colonies, East as well as West; it examines social and economic developments as much as military and political; it tells the story simply but in a superbly rounded fashion. Gipson argues that for its part the British government acquired vast, new, and remote areas on the American continent in 1760 and had to devise a more efficient system of administration for them; that its unprecedented war debt led it justifiably to request a colonial contribution to defense; and that the colonies, relieved in 1763 of the pressure of hostile nations on their borders, were given a new and dangerous freedom. Only in volume 12 does he reach the years of sharpest controversy [15]

14. *American Historical Review,* XXIV (1919), 104.

15. He does, however, give a summary of his views on the years from 1763 to 1775 in his *The Coming of the Revolution, 1763-1775* (New York, 1954), a study of unusual balance of judgment. The Revolution was the product not of a quest for independence as such but of the demand for a position of autonomy within the Empire. For a critical assessment of Gipson, see A. R. M. Lower, "Lawrence H. Gipson and the First British Empire, An Evaluation," *Journal of British Studies,* III (1963), 57-78.

and is thus almost nostalgically imperialist in tone. Labaree, another student of Andrews, has written a definitive study of colonial governors and their repeated clashes with colonial assemblies in his *Royal Government in America* (1930) and supplemented it by editing *Royal Instructions to British Colonial Governors, 1670-1776* (2 vols., 1935). For the development of a colonial aristocracy, see his *Conservatism in Early American History* (1948).

If Osgood, Beer, and Andrews are the major progenitors of the imperial school, other historians have shared similar preoccupations. Sydney George Fisher praised the mildness and conciliatory spirit of Britain. The Revolution was "not a contest between a dragon and a fairy," not "a mere accidental mistake on the part of England" resulting in a war brought on "by the king alone against the wishes of the English people." It was, on the contrary, a path "entered upon by the English nation as deliberately and intelligently as any other imperial expansion they have undertaken and upon principles which for them are still unchangeable."

Clarence Alvord (1868-1928), a New Englander who became an historian of the Midwest, editor of the Collections of the Illinois State Historical Library and of the five-volume centennial history of the state, and in 1914 founder-editor of the *Mississippi Valley Historical Review,* left his mark on Revolutionary studies with his *The Mississippi Valley in British Politics: A Study of the Trade, Land Speculation and Experiments in Imperialism Culminating in the American Revolution* (2 vols., 1917). Alvord was greatly influenced by Turner and chose to concentrate on Illinois and the Old Northwest as a section as well as a colonial frontier. He emphasized the dominant themes of frontier advance and land settlement, deliberately underplayed military and political factors in order to heighten the social and economic, and saw in the fur trader and speculator figures far more significant than the conventional textbook hero. Thus he was always prompt to criticize George Rogers Clark or Daniel Boone, "whom fickle tradition has chosen to apotheosize as the prototype of western state makers of all generations." "Research," he said, "offers no support for his fame, which is a myth, like that of William Tell, conceived in caprice, reared by uncritical history, and perpetuated by popular sentimentality."

But if on the one hand a Turnerian, he was also an imperialist. He boldly asserted in his preface that

> Whenever the British Ministers soberly and seriously discussed the American problem the vital phase to them was not the disturbances of . . . Boston and New York, but the development of that vast transmontane region that was acquired in 1763 by the Treaty of Paris.

These plans for the West formed the warp and woof of British imperial policy. Alvord thought it equally impossible to understand British-American relations without a thorough comprehension of British politics, and he was fully aware that if factions were abundant, "of principles there is almost no sign." He had here a remarkably acute view of British factional politics, for which he was later saluted by Sir Lewis Namier.[16] But if he was right to say that this was an age in which principles were few, his pro-British sentiments and his quest for warmth and unconventionality in his writing of history led him to discover heroes of his own, chief among them Lord Shelburne. Whatever merits there were in the Proclamation of 1763 were due, he believed, to Shelburne; the cession of the Northwest to the United States in 1783 was his, not George Roger Clark's, handiwork. This view, which had much influence and appeal, and in the hands of Vincent Harlow produced a most convincing picture of Anglo-American policy-making in the 1760's,[17] has not stood up to subsequent investigation.[18] But in one respect Alvord was a pioneer and remains unmatched. No one before or since his day has sought with such success to knit the West into the fabric of British policy-making. Its importance as a cause of Revolution, however, is still a subject that challenges the Revolutionary historian.[19] If Alvord's study of it was not definitive or, in a literary sense, particularly graceful, he at least proved that the check given by the Crown to the land speculator was an important cause of the Revolution.

Claude H. Van Tyne, although a more impartial and better disciplined historian than Alvord, properly merits inclusion in the imperial school. So much so indeed that his textbook, written in collaboration with A. C. McLaughlin (*History of the United States for Schools,* 1911), was regarded as at once so liberal and so pro-British that it was positively un-American, and in the 1920's it was banned from use in many states. His best work was certainly done in the Revolutionary field. He wrote five books and four major articles on this topic. His doctoral dissertation on *The Loyalists in the American Revolution* (1902) was at once both his most specialized book and his least satisfactory. It was in structure rather a group of essays than a synthesis; nor did he succeed in establishing the Tories firmly in their American setting. But it was a welcome corrective in 1902 to the century of historical

16. Lewis B. Namier, *England in the Age of the American Revolution* (London, 1930), p. 273.

17. Vincent Harlow, *The Founding of the Second British Empire, 1763-1793* (New York, 1952).

18. Robin Humphreys, "Lord Shelburne and British Colonial Policy, 1766-1768," *English Historical Review,* L (1935), 257-277, and "Lord Shelburne and a Projected Recall of Colonial Governors in 1767," *American Historical Review,* XXXVII (1932), 269-272.

19. It has been well surveyed by Jack M. Sosin, *Whitehall and the Wilderness* (Lincoln, Nebr., 1961), who emphasizes how constant a factor in British policy was the desire to secure the frontier. The colonists evaded their responsibilities, and on both sides the frontier administrators were irresponsible. The rigid curb on colonial expansion westward came largely as a result of the disturbances after 1765. "The final program of the ministry seems a responsible decision in the face of a difficult and complex task."

writing which had with few exceptions neglected the American Tory and his point of view.[20] His second book, *The American Revolution, 1776-1783* (1905) was a terse but lucid survey in the *American Nation* series. His third, *The Causes of the War of Independence* (1922), equally a synthesis, drew heavily on Alvord and on Schlesinger's *Colonial Merchants and the American Revolution, 1763-1776*. In both studies Van Tyne saw the Revolution as a civil war both in Britain and North America; in comparison with other colonies, the Americans were remarkably free before their Revolution from economic and political control; the "freest of people were the first to rebel." The fourth book, *England and America* (1927), was avowedly popular, an elaboration of the Sir George Watson lectures delivered at various British universities (Oxford, Cambridge, London, Glasgow, and Birmingham) in 1927. He used this opportunity to avow a position on the Revolution that was frankly imperial. And his final and most scholarly work, *The War of Independence* (1929), based on the rich resources of the Clements Library in Michigan, told the story of the war to 1778. Alongside— and as "raw material" for his books—Van Tyne wrote four major articles. In these he contended that the states were sovereign during and after the Revolution, and unity was slow to emerge; that religious forces played a major part in causing the Revolution—more important, he believed, than economic; and that the dominant motive for French entry into the war in 1778 was the conviction that war with Britain was, for her, inevitable, but peace between Britain and her colonies possible, and that therefore she should enter the war when she might still have allies. In all, Van Tyne was remarkably successful in marrying a liberal attitude and an interest in economic and social forces to a sympathetic view of imperial—and world—problems of which the Revolution was, at least in part, the consequence. His work on the Revolution, along with Channing's third volume, can still be read with profit as a balanced statement of both the British and the American sides of the case.

The imperial school has great merits. First, it brings back the interpretation of the Revolution to a proper emphasis on the contemporary realities of the eighteenth century; it sees it not only as an assertion of colonial independence but as a failure of statecraft and imagination in London. The Revolution cannot ever again properly be judged except as an Anglo-American phenomenon. As a subject of study it becomes more fascinating and more interesting when seen against the British

20. To this three exceptions should be noted. Sabine had collected in his *American Loyalists* much material, some of it still in raw form. In the second volume, subtitled *Colonies and Nation,* of his five-volume *History of the American People,* Woodrow Wilson gave a sympathetic account of the Loyalist role. And Moses Coit Tyler published both an admirable essay on "The Loyalists" in the *American Historical Review,* I (1895), 26-45, and an excellent assessment of their literature in his *Literary History of the American Revolution, 1763-1783* (New York and London, 1897).

background than when construed as an American problem only. Andrews and Gipson in particular saw it in an Atlantic context, as a theme that was part of a civil and also an international struggle.

Second, the imperialists present the Revolution as the story of the growth of colonial assemblies, which are gradually transformed from the provincial councils that the home government intended them to be into miniature parliaments. In the end they emerge as powerful legislative bodies, increasingly self-conscious, as the House of Commons itself was becoming during the same eventful years.

And third, the British orientation heightens the significance of the Revolution, for this school, strongly rooted though it is in the study of assemblies, does not see the struggle in aridly institutional terms. It sees it as the story of the gradual elimination of those elements, feudal and proprietary, that were foreign to the normal life of a frontier land, and of the gradual adjustment of the colonies to the restraints and restrictions imposed upon them by the commercial policy of the mother country.

All these writers were or are, in all their sympathy with London, liberals: they have made clearer than Bancroft ever did how divergent Britain and the colonies had become, and how impossible it had become for them—for institutional rather than moralistic reasons—to remain in a position of subordination. They see the Revolution as a conflict of sovereignties, and as such, inescapable. The imperial school is not a pro-British school; in his essays of 1924 and his address of 1925, Andrews made his position very clear. But in some members of this school—in Gipson, in Louis B. Wright's studies of the cultural relations across the Atlantic, and in the recent study of Jack Sosin—the references to the Old Empire have a touch of nostalgia that would have had Bancroft reaching for his revolver.

The Progressives

Alongside this London-oriented view of the Revolution arose a new group of historians sometimes broadly called the advocates of the New History. Its early ornaments were Charles A. Beard, James Harvey Robinson, Carl Becker, and Vernon L. Parrington. Product in part of Turner and still more of late nineteenth-century Populism and Progressivism, they were influenced by British Fabianism, by the new interest in the social sciences, and later by the Depression and the New Deal. They were for the most part from the Midwest and identified themselves with it and its rural .values: they believed in social progress, they were suspicious of "interests," often Eastern in their origin, they believed in the natural goodness of the ordinary man. Their values, and their historical preoccupations, were those of Main Street, U.S.A. They saw conflict as a major fact of life in contemporary politics and in history, and progress, in Hegelian-Marxist terms, as a product of the dialectic. They were often, as citizens, *engagés,* and their history reflected this sense of commitment. History, said Turner, should do more than preserve "curios for the . . . Museum"; it should "hold the lamp for conservative reform." These historians were in rebellion against a falsely scientific history, against neo-Rankeism and what they saw as a dangerous historical positivism. They turned away from the older political-military, "drum and triumpet," and even institutional history, in order to tell the story of the common man, to trace social, economic, and cultural forces, to abandon the broad highway for the curious but exotic bypath rutted with problems and puzzles that did not lend themselves to smooth handling. The shift in emphasis was from the continuous to the episodic, from history as tale to history as topic, from description to analysis. The new tools of analysis provided by economics, sociology, and psychology were called into service. History—as publishers have been prompt to realize—is now seen as the study of problems. Mr. Dooley was skeptical about it:

> Historyans is like doctors. They are always lookin' f'r symptoms. Those iv them that writes about their own times, examines th' tongue and feels th' pulse and makes a wrong dygnosis. Th' other kind iv history is a post-mortem exam. It tells ye what a counthry died iv. But I'd like to know what it lived iv.

In Revolutionary studies, the struggle against Britain was taken as given, as was the imperial relationship. The emphasis was now on the colonial scene and on the conflicts within it—creditor versus debtor, eastern seaboard versus frontier, agrarian versus industrial interests. In his *History of Political Parties in the Province of New York, 1760-1776* (1909), Becker, student under Turner at Wisconsin and under Osgood, Burgess, and Robinson at Columbia, wrote a doctoral dissertation which proved to be a seminal work; he said that the politics of New York in the Revolutionary period revolved around two questions, home rule and who should rule at home, and the latter was quite as important as the former. This issue was, of course, especially clear in New York, which was dominated by the Hudson Valley patroonage, the men of the big estates. Although these men had taken the lead ·in opposing Britain on the Stamp Act, they were frightened by the whirlwind they had unleashed, and they drew back. They joined the revolutionary committees in order to try to curb them. Some, like Gilbert Livingston and Peter Van Schaack, became Loyalists. Others, like John Jay and James Duane, for example, joined the Revolution and retained sufficient leadership to fasten a conservative constitution on the new state.

Becker's study can be faulted: he minimized the extent of the postwar depression after the peace of 1763 which was, perhaps, responsible for much of the discontent of these years; and he underplayed also the conflict between Anglicans and Presbyterians in New York politics. But his study was the first thorough analysis of the clash of economic and social forces inside a single province.[21] He did not, however, contend that the Revolution in New York was merely an internal struggle between social classes, nor did he argue that what was true for New York was necessarily true for the other colonies.

An analysis similar to Becker's came from Arthur M. Schlesinger in his *Colonial Merchants and the American Revolution* (1918). The merchants were, he argues, the true causes of British-colonial discontents. Opposing the Sugar and Stamp Acts and later the Tea Act as threats to their profits, as bureaucratic interference, and, where tea was concerned, as a dangerous and alien monopoly, the merchants gave a lead to the Revolutionary forces. But they became alarmed after 1767 at the character and extent of colonial rioting, at the growth of republican feeling and egalitarian sentiment. Some stayed with the radicals hoping to control them from within, but in the end they lost control to "the democratic mechanic class," which Schlesinger described as a "proletarian element," mainly unenfranchised. Once separation from Britain became reality, however much they might have regretted it, the merchants became part of a general conservative reaction. Here too this clash of economic interests was to survive the Revolutionary period. There was, however, no question that, whatever their counterrevolution of 1787, twenty years earlier they were critics of Britain. The Revolution was something more than "a great forensic controversy over abstract governmental rights." It was a conflict of interests, prominent among them the mercantile.

John Franklin Jameson, in four lectures delivered at Princeton in 1925, and subsequently published as *The American Revolution Considered as a Social Movement* (1926), outlined the nature of this broad movement through all the colonies. It tended, he argued, "in the direction of a levelling democracy." It was marked by the abolition of the slave trade and of slavery in many states, the abolition of primogeniture and entail, the confiscation and dispersal of Loyalist estates, the reduction in property qualifications for voting, and the disestablishment of the Anglican Church.

For the Constitution-making in 1787, Charles Beard told a related tale: the Constitution was the work of personal property holders, land speculators and holders of public securities, a small but able group of self-interested men determined to protect their own and to re-establish in their own hands a central authority of the kind formerly exercised by Britain. They too, like the Hudson Valley aristos and the merchants of Boston and Philadelphia, were "reluctant revolutionaries." Beard's findings were drawn from data on the public security holdings of the framers in 1791, but he projected backward from them, assuming that

21. Subsequent studies of New York politics, such as Irving Mark, *Agrarian Conflicts in Colonial New York, 1711-1775* (New York and London, 1940), and E. W. Spaulding, *New York in the Critical Period, 1783-1789* (New York, 1932), confirm the accuracy of this diagnosis. But contrast Milton Klein, "Democracy and Politics in Colonial New York," *New York History,* XL (1959).

they were approximately applicable also to 1787. Additional local data existed, including information on other property and on holdings in 1787, but, as Beard correctly observed, such data would require "years of research" to unearth. He dug no further, and his own data seemed massive enough to silence the doubtful and to awe more than a generation of historians. The logic of Beard was spelled out for the years between 1783 and 1787 by Merrill Jensen, and for the Revolution itself by Louis Hacker in his article "The First American Revolution." [22]

Beard's viewpoint met heavy attack. In his own day it was called not only deterministic but subversive, impious, Marxist. Today, though Beard still has his followers,[23] the criticism of his work has become devastating. Robert E. Brown, in *Charles Beard and the Constitution* (1956), reviewed Beard step by step. He denied that the Constitution was the work of a selfish minority, "put over undemocratically in an undemocratic society." In his *Middle Class Democracy and the Revolution in Massachusetts, 1691-1780* (1955), he demonstrates that the great majority of adult males in Massachusetts at least enjoyed the right to vote; and Western farmers were as fully represented in the legislature as Eastern merchants. Massachusetts, he contends, was "democratic" before the Revolution. It was precisely because the people of Massachusetts enjoyed political, economic, and social democracy that they so bitterly resented British imperial policies. If there is as yet little evidence that this thesis can be sustained for other States,[24] there was certainly in "undemocratic" Virginia at least a strong sense of participation in elections, and in other states there was no evidence of any strong demand for social change.[25]

Forrest McDonald, having worked in the local records on a scale which to Beard seemed impossible, proves even more conclusively that Beard's hypothesis does not fit the facts. He demonstrates first that the men who framed the Constitution at Philadelphia and those who ratified it in the states were not predominantly creditors and security holders of the economic class to which Beard assigned them, and insofar as such men participated, a good half of them opposed the Constitution. There was no "consolidated economic interest" at work. McDonald's second major achievement is to provide new and more revealing light on the positive question why various states and various interests *did* support the Constitution. In general, he shows that such states as Georgia, which feared hostilities with the Indians, New Jersey, which had no port of its own, and others, which were dependent on cooperation between the states, favored ratification, while such

22. *Columbia University Quarterly*, XXVII (1935), 259-295.

23. Merrill Jensen, *The Articles of Confederation* (Madison, Wis., 1940) and *The New Nation* (New York, 1950); Elisha P. Douglass, *Rebels and Democrats* (Chapel Hill, 1955); Jackson Turner Main, *The Antifederalists* (Chapel Hill, 1961); and E. James Ferguson, *The Power of the Purse* (Chapel Hill, 1961).

24. For the contrary view, see Douglass, *Rebels and Democrats*.

25. Cf. Robert E. and B. Katherine Brown, *Virginia, 1705-1786: Democracy or Aristocracy?* (East Lansing, Mich., 1964).

potentially self-sufficient states as New York, Virginia, and North Carolina were most reluctant. He also shows that where economic motivation was involved, the question of the status of confiscated Tory estates may have been more important than the question of paper money or public securities.[26]

It can be argued that McDonald refuted Beard's use of a deterministic theory rather than the theory itself. But such theories are now themselves out of fashion. The motives of men are not determined by self-interest alone.

Not all the recent writers concerned with social history in the Revolutionary period are necessarily Beardian. There is by this time an impressive collection of social studies, some of them products of the work and stimulus of the Institute of Early American History and Culture at Williamsburg, which has helped to publish the *William and Mary Quarterly,* whose third series (since 1944) has made it the leading journal in the field and whose own publications are of outstanding quality. Among works of value published by the Institute or on its behalf are A. E. Smith, *Colonists in Bondage: White Servitude and Convict Labor in America, 1607-1776* (1947), Charles S. Sydnor, *Gentlemen Freeholders: Political Practices in Washington's Virginia* (1952), and Frederick B. Tolles, *Meeting House and Counting House: The Quaker Merchants of Colonial Philadelphia 1682-1763* (1948).

Particularly valuable are the social studies produced by Carl Bridenbaugh, one-time director of the Institute, especially his *Cities in the Wilderness: The First Century of Urban Life in America, 1625-1742* (1938), *Cities in Revolt: Urban Life in America, 1743-1776* (1955), *The Colonial Craftsman* (1950), and *Myths and Realities: Societies of the Colonial South* (1952). He has made the study of the urban environment, its traders and its artisans, his own specialty. "Commercial as well as agrarian interests dictated political if not also social revolution; most of the intellectual activity and much of the social and political advance of the eighteenth century depended upon an urban rather than a rural environment; certainly a large part of our radical thought came neither from farm nor forest but from the seaboard towns." [27] And as Bridenbaugh has emphasized, one of the most important aspects of this study is the role played by the town in "the transit of civilization from Europe to America." Not everyone agrees with some of Bridenbaugh's judgments—his view of some Southern aristocrats as "sports" in the biological sense was not everywhere received with pious acceptance south of the Mason-Dixon line—but he has done great service to the objective study of colonial social and political history.

In recent years attention has been paid also to the role of propaganda. In *Sam Adams: Pioneer in Propaganda* (1936), John C. Miller

26. Cf. Jackson Turner Main, "Charles Beard and the Constitution," a critical review of Forrest McDonald's *We the People, William and Mary Quarterly,* XVII (1960), 86-110.

27. Preface to *Cities in the Wilderness* (New York, 1938).

showed how one man led Massachusetts through the events that pre-cipitated revolt. In *Propaganda and the American Revolution, 1763-1783* (1941), Philip Davidson showed how other agitators and groups of agitators played on popular passions in all the colonies. Bruce Ingham Granger, produced a workmanlike study, *Political Satire in the American Revolution, 1763-1783* (1960), and in his *Prelude to Independence: The Newspaper War on Britain 1764-1776* (1958), Arthur Schlesinger estimates the contribution of the press to the Revolution. Although he admits that "a multitude of factors from the Sugar Act onward pushed the colonists along the road to independence, the movement could hardly have succeeded without an ever alert and dedicated press." The propaganda peaks coincided, of course, with the crises: 1765, 1767, 1773; but between were fallow years, without issues. The press was—refreshingly or disgustingly—non-neutral. The comment was free and no facts were ever sacred. The Whig papers, in general, worked hand-in-glove with the assemblies, the Merchants' Committees, the Committees of Safety, and the Sons of Liberty; the Tory papers worked equally closely with the royal governors, the pro-British Councils, the customs collectors, and the Tory Anglican preachers. It was a time of violence, violence of word and of deed; a violence the Whig papers encouraged. Toward the end they made it their business to justify violence on the ground "that rebellion was both right and practicable"; further, from proposing economic boycott of the mother country the newspapers became its enforcers, using for that purpose the publication of the names and misdeeds of those they judged culpable. The study of the Revolution has been greatly enriched by this vivid portrayal of the context in which it developed.

The Neo-Whigs

Charles Andrews died in 1943, Beard in 1948. A new generation of historians appeared.

In today's sophisticated academic climate, with the high professional standards demanded of its graduate students, and ample facilities for the publication of monographic studies, there is great precision in research and much excellent work appears that does not fall into a "school" at all. Indeed, most contemporary writers would, one hopes, deny that they write to any pre-determined pattern, or even to prove any case. Yet since 1948 a number of themes pointing in a conservative direction have been noticeable in American historical writing. The Puritans, the first Founding Fathers, have been seen not as narrow bigots but as enlightened, learned, and humane. "Puritan New England was a noble experiment in applied theology," says Daniel Boorstin—whereas H. L. Mencken saw it as a place for the "sour gatherings of hell-crazy deacons." The leaders of popular causes, like Roger Williams or Nathaniel Bacon, are no longer seen as precursors of democracy. The Populists have come in for criticism as progenitors of jingoism; even

Jackson has not been immune from criticism. Determinist and democratic patterns have become unfashionable. The emphasis has been on the detailed examination of the actions of men and women in particular situations, rather than on the hypotheses arrived at "without fear and without research," of which Beard has been so often found guilty. There is less interest in the contrasts of ideas and of men which Progressive writing dramatized; the emphasis is on the consensus within which such clashes and debates were—and are—usually worked out. The themes of social justice, of reformist crusades, and of revolution are less engrossing. In the post-1948 world, in our more affluent and more cynical age, it is harder to be a Utopian.

In the study of the Revolution this attitude has been especially striking. A group of writers has emerged which Jack Greene has described with accuracy and felicity as neo-Whig.

> The nature and direction of their inquiries differ markedly from those of earlier writers. Their emphasis has been upon immediate issues and individual actions rather than upon long-range determinants or underlying conditions. Although they have been cautious in using formal psychology, they have been interested mainly in psychological questions involving constitutional principles, political power, liberty, security of property, and legal rights. Moreover, they have taken a broader approach to the problem of human motivation, proceeding upon the assumption that man is not moved by economic considerations alone. Their primary focus has been upon American grievances against Britain, the central question in their studies being why Americans were angry in the fateful years after 1763. To answer this question they have explored the sources intensively and rigorously, concerning themselves with problems at once more limited and more ambitious. The scope of their works has been narrow. They have sought not to write an epic of the American Revolution but to define issues, fix responsibilities, and measure the impact of events and policies. The result has been a remarkable reinterpretation of the Revolution and the virtual elimination of hitherto widely accepted views. It is their contention that the Revolution was essentially a conservative movement, a defense of American rights and liberties against provocations by the mother country.[28]

At the hands of the neo-Whigs, the concern of the Progressives with the domestic achievement of the Revolution has gradually widened. Social conflicts are now given less emphasis, and the building of a new and distinct society is seen as the major feature. This is perhaps best evidenced in the writings of Daniel Boorstin—*The Lost World of Thomas Jefferson* (1948), *The Genius of American Politics* (1953), and *The Americans: the Colonial Experience* (1958), the first of a

28. "The Flight from Determinism: A Review of Recent Literature on the Coming of the American Revolution," *South Atlantic Quarterly*, LXI (1962), 237.

planned three-volume study; in Edmund Morgan, *The Stamp Act Crisis* (1953) and *The Birth of the Republic, 1763-1789* (1956); in Max Savelle, *Seeds of Liberty* (1948); in Clinton Rossiter, *Seedtime of the Republic* (1953) and a number of essays on conservatism; and in Bernhard Knollenberg, *Origin of the American Revolution, 1759-1766* (1960). It is impossible in reading these historians not to be struck by the note of national pride in the Revolution, its achievements, and its significance. Boorstin's emphasis is on its "given-ness" in an American environment. The liberalism that grew in the New World was no mere transplanted flower, growing in richer soil; much of the force that fed and nourished it was, he argues, indigenous. Universities and the professions, speech and accent, language and newspapers developed along distinct lines; even if the Virginians were, in Boorstin's word, "transplanters," the squirearchy that grew up was Virginian, not English. It was necessary to apply not only the laws of England but the still greater laws of common sense and practicability. Those who did not adapt to the pioneer land perished or were pushed aside, like the Quakers in Pennsylvania.

> "We hold these truths to be self-evident," the second sentence of the Declaration of Independence proclaims. In deriving the essential social truths from their "self-evidence"—rather than from their being "sacred & undeniable" as the original draft had read—the Declaration was building on distinctly American ground. The matured statement of this point of view is found in Franklin and Jefferson, the most eloquent spokesmen of an American and anti-aristocratic way of thinking about thinking.

In their study of the Stamp Act, Edmund and Helen Morgan contend that Grenville had decided upon it as early as 1764, despite his invitation to the colonies to consider plans for taxing themselves. The year's delay was simply a matter of administrative convenience to allow plans to be worked out in London. Accordingly, Grenville and not the colonists was responsible for the consequences. Equally, although it was a widely held belief in Britain that the colonists distinguished between internal and external taxes, the Morgans find no warrant for this. Delany did make this distinction but few followed him, and he became a Tory anyway. There was, from the first, strong opposition to any form of taxation designed to raise a revenue. The Stamp Act was really burdensome, but the opposition to it was first and last a matter of constitutional principle. 1765 was a decisive date less because it saw the emergence of leaders and organization than because the colonial standpoint did not basically change from this point until 1776.

But 1765 is for Bernhard Knollenberg already too late. Why, he asks, did the colonists react so violently to the Stamp Act? Because, he holds, between 1759 and 1766 a series of clashes developed between colonies and mother country that made reconciliation all but impossible. British warships patrolled the American coast and enforced the new or reinvigorated measures against smuggling that interfered with colonial trade with the West Indies. British officials enforced the laws against the cutting of white pine. Fears of prelacy grew as the plans of Archbishop Secker for an Anglican bishopric in the colonies became clear. There was discontent in Virginia because of the disallowance of the Twopenny Act in 1759, in New York and New Jersey with the issuance of the general instruction of 1761 stipulating that judicial tenure should be at the Crown's pleasure rather than during good behavior, and in South Carolina because of the disallowance of an election law in 1761 which was in part responsible for the bitter Gadsden election controversy. Expansion to the West was limited. An Indian War took place largely through the errors of Lord Amherst, the British commander-in-chief. And, above all, it was proposed to tax the colonists in order to maintain "a large, unrequested and ineffective force of British troops stationed in North America." Until 1759 there was no such wide divergence of views, no automatic trend toward independence in the colonies—indeed, the reverse. Had "the relationship not been disturbed by the many new and vexing British measures . . . it might, I think, have endured . . . for many generations, perhaps even to this day."

This thesis is novel. It is developed with great clarity and force; it is documented at length, and convincingly—almost half of Knollenberg's book consists of notes and appendices that prove him to be as familiar with these miserable seven years as with the eight years of the Revolutionary War; the first two-thirds of the book are a superb summary of these years from the Revolutionary point of view. On one point, particularly, Knollenberg is especially significant. He rejects Beer's thesis that troops were stationed in America to provide for colonial defense and to suppress Pontiac's rebellion. He points out that the rebellion began after the decision about the army had been made, and that troops organized during the war for frontier fighting were disbanded. The prime consideration, Knollenberg argues, was the general defense of the Empire as a whole. Troops for that purpose could be stationed as well in America as elsewhere and with less opposition from Parliament, and by stationing the troops in America, imperial officials could tax the colonies to provide for their support. This is, in any reckoning, a major piece of research and argument.

Knollenberg's study is, of course, partisan, a catalog of British errors. There is little attention in his pages to the positive merits of the plans being devised in London, or to the reasons for them. There was a case for asking the colonists to contribute to their defense. They had by no means been the ready defenders of their own liberty in the years 1754-1760. They paid fewer taxes than the British; they broke the laws against smuggling with impunity; they drew substantial advantages from the mercantile system. The blunt fact was that in British eyes the colonists' rights were derivative, as the colonies were derivative. There were then, as always, two views of colonial rights; and the British view, the view of Francis Bernard, was that the colonies were in law but the equivalent of municipal corporations. This view is now unpalatable, but it cannot be ignored in a study of the reasons for a revolution— for a revolution is always the struggle of conflicting rights. In Knollenberg's pages it tends to be a world of American rights and of British wrongs.

At whatever point they date the beginning of the Revolution, these writings are decisively American-centered. Democracy was widespread in Massachusetts and probably elsewhere, says Robert E. Brown in his *Middle-Class Democracy and the Revolution in Massachusetts, 1691-1780* (1955); there was no sharp class conflict, at least in Massachusetts, he argues; independence was in the main inevitable sooner or later, since British imperial policy threatened an existing middle class democratic society, and was both a democratic and a national "good." Much of the controversy aroused by recent revisionism is in fact a controversy over terminology; and a twentieth-century preoccupation with words as weapons—not least words like *class, democracy,* and *conservatism*—has crept into the argument. But at least the pendulum is swinging back; and if the pride is now in the extent of American democracy, in its "middle class" character, and in the smoothness of the changes between 1776 and 1787—pride, one feels, less in having a revolution than in having it on conservative lines—the emphasis on distinction, on uniqueness, on concern for "principles," on being a peculiar if not a chosen people, is closer to Bancroft than to Andrews. Bancroft, says Edmund Morgan, at least addressed himself to the central question, "How did the United States come into being as a nation dedicated to principles of liberty and equality?"

Apart from its emphasis, criticism can be made of the inherent contradictions of this school. Boorstin's writing denies that American civilization was built around a corpus of principles; rather it was the result of compromise, flexibility, and adaptation to a new environment. To play by ear was to survive, to adhere to ideology was to disintegrate. This is hardly Morgan's view. And Knollenberg discovers that there is, after all, evidence in Massachusetts and Connecticut of a colonial distinction between internal and external taxes. It is, however, improper to charge these writers with making their history a form of special pleading. For one thing, all these works are splendid pieces of research, richly detailed and convincingly argued. The quality of research in scholarly periodicals and books today has rarely been matched and certainly never excelled. Today's scholars have nothing to fear by comparison even with Andrews or with Osgood. And for another, alongside them and supporting them, there are monographic studies of individual states and topics that prove all too abundantly the errors and limitations of British policy, the maturity of American society, and in the latter the fairly widespread distribution both of suffrage and of property.

In his study of the Navigation Acts, O. M. Dickerson demonstrates that the colonists did not object to the Acts as such, but to the "customs racketeering" of the new commissioners set up by the Townshend Acts;

the merchants victimized included John Hancock and Henry Laurens. The riots that accompanied the seizure of Hancock's sloop *Liberty* and the burning of the revenue cutter *Gaspée* were provoked by what seemed the rapacity of the customs men. And, inevitably perhaps, the American distaste for this new "efficiency" was seen in Britain as a dislike—which at first it certainly had not been—for the Navigation Acts as such. Unimaginative administration of the Acts after 1767 transformed regulations designed for growth into regulations designed to thwart. The movement for independence was strongest where taxation was most burdensome and seizures most frequent.

Another monograph, Carl Ubbelohde's *The Vice-Admiralty Courts and the American Revolution* (1960) also shows how mischievous—in some situations—minor grievances can be. The court at Halifax was inconvenient but never seriously threatened colonial interests. It did not get its first case until 1766. The four new courts set up by Townshend were designed to offset the inconveniences of Halifax. But they were used to enforce unpopular acts. They were juryless. The extension of admiralty jurisdiction beyond what was normally exercised in Britain came increasingly to seem a threat to that most valuable and vulnerable of all property, the rights of the colonists as Englishmen. The courts, in themselves acceptable, were unacceptable as reminders of parliamentary interference in their rights. Ubbelohde stresses that, minor though this matter might appear, men fight "as much for images as realities." And David Lovejoy has reminded us that rights imply equality.[29]

The American Revolutionary cause had thus many constituents: merchants and artisans,[30] planters and patroons, frontiersmen and editors. The clergy were "disaffected." [31] So were the lawyers. In General Gage's opinion, the Stamp Act troubles in New York were due to the lawyers. They were indeed the source from "whence the clamors have flowed in every Province." The Reverend Samuel Johnson, the first president of King's College, and Cadwallader Colden, the pillar of the New York establishment, "one of the most permanent of all permanent officials in North America," [32] echoed his views:

> . . . a Domination of Lawyers was formed in this Province. . . .
> A Domination founded on the same Principles and carried on by
> the same wicked artifices that Domination of Priests formerly

29. David S. Lovejoy, "Rights Imply Equality: The Case Against Admiralty Jurisdiction in America, 1764-1776," *William and Mary Quarterly*, XVI (1959), 459-484.

30. Cf. Richard Walsh, *Charleston's Sons of Liberty: A Study of the Artisans, 1763-1789* (Columbia, S.C., 1959).

31. Cf. the shrewd observations of Louis Hartz: "The American liberals . . . did not need to make a religion out of the Revolution because religion was already revolutionary." "American Political Thought and the American Revolution," *American Political Science Review*, XLVI (1952), 325. Cf. also Carl Bridenbaugh, *Mitre and Sceptre: Transatlantic Faiths, Ideas, Personalities, and Politics, 1689-1775* (New York, 1962).

32. Wilbur Abbott, *New York in the American Revolution* (New York and London, 1929), p. 15.

was . . . Every Man's character who dares to discover his Sentiments in opposition to theirs is loaded with infamy by every
falsehood which malice can invent, and thereby exposed to the
brutal Rage of the Mob. Nothing is too wicked for them to
attempt which serves their purposes—the Press is to them what
the Pulpit was in times of Popery . . .

As Milton Klein has said, "No single group was better able to articulate
the Colonial position within the political, legal, and constitutional framework of the Anglo-American debate than the men of the legal profession. The right to jury trial as well as to internal taxation was part
of the privilege of being English." [33]

The constitutional case has been made equally convincingly in a number
of monographs on state politics: [34] the Revolution was, in essence and
in expression, a political and constitutional conflict between the mother
country and the colonies. And the work of the neo-Whigs has been
further buttressed by the series of biographies that have appeared since
1948, and the various collections of papers of the great men of the
Revolution. In the day-by-day accounts of so many of the major par-
ticipants, the day-by-day character of the decision-making becomes very
clear. We now know from John Adams' diary kept at the First Continental Congress that not until then, September, 1774, was any
"national" unity emerging. We know from Washington's letters that
as late as the summer of 1775 he was, although commander-in-chief of
an anti-parliamentary army, still no rebel against his King. Equally,
we know from these same sources that if the steps toward revolution
were empirically taken, they were product of a deep conviction, that
"rights" and "justice" were repeatedly being invoked.

The "Conservative" View of the Revolution

In Britain the rewriting of the history of the early years of George III
by Sir Lewis Namier and his followers has brought strong reinforcement
to the American conservative school. Namier broke completely with the
view of George III as a tyrant, dominated by his mother and Bute,
seeking to overthrow the constitution. Mediocre in abilities, yes; obstinate
and unimaginative, certainly; but no wielder of unconstitutional power.
After meticulous research on the five hundred volumes of the Newcastle papers in the British Museum, Namier produced an analysis of
Parliament not in terms of Whig and Tory parties but in terms of
"interest," "connection," and patronage. In 1930 he published *England
in the Age of the American Revolution*. In 1951 he revived a cooperative
enterprise, *The History of Parliament*, which had had an abortive start

33. Milton Klein, "Prelude to Revolution in New York: Jury Trials and
Judicial Tenure," *William and Mary Quarterly*, XVII (1960), 439-462. Cf.
C. H. Levermore, "The Whigs of Colonial New York," *American Historical
Review*, I (1896).
34. See the Bibliography which follows this Introduction.

in the thirties, a vast biographical project on which a number of editors and researchers in the University of London and elsewhere are now engaged.[35] And as by-product of this, new volumes are appearing from a group of historians who are Namier's disciples and who have been working on the large quantities of manuscript material in the British Museum or that have come into the hands of local record offices in recent years, mainly as an indirect result of the social changes since 1945.

England in the Age of the American Revolution is now a project, not a single volume, and three studies under that general title have now appeared: John Brooke, Namier's chief lieutenant, published *The Chatham Administration, 1766-1768* in 1956, Ian Christie followed with *The End of North's Ministry, 1780-1782* in 1958, and in 1965 Bernard Donoughue published *British Politics and the American Revolution: The Path to War, 1773-1775.* In 1957 John B. Owen published *The Rise of the Pelhams.* Other volumes are scheduled to fill the gaps from 1754 to 1784. Those published so far confirm the master's findings; all are admirably written; all are "historians' history," detailed and heavily biographical, but in general eschewing analysis. There have been, from A. J. P. Taylor and Herbert Butterfield, some criticisms of the Namier thesis, especially in the latter's article in *Encounter* (April, 1957), elaborated in his *George III and the Historians* (1957) and in his article in *History* (February, 1958). The work of the late Richard Pares, in his studies of colonial conflicts and business enterprise, *War and Trade in the West Indies, 1739-1763* (1936), *Colonial Blockade and Neutral Rights, 1739-1763* (1938), *Yankees and Creoles* (1956), and still more in his Ford Lectures, *King George III and the Politicians* (1953), broadly confirms, however, the theses of the Namier school. So do George H. Guttridge, *English Whiggism and the American Revolution* (1942), and Sir Keith Feiling, *The Second Tory Party, 1714-1832* (1938).[36] These writings have transformed the nationalist view of George III and his activities. The King's Friends were small in number and far from biddable in temper. The country gentlemen were far more significant: they were the largest group in number and the most erratic in attendance; in most cases they were very selfish over their main concern, the land tax, but in almost all crises they remained loyal to their country's interest as they saw it. Around them circulated a group of self-elected professionals, leaders of cliques and factions which formed and re-

35. Lewis B. Namier and John Brooke, *The House of Commons, 1754-1790,* (New York and London, 3 vols., 1964).

36. Cf. Jacob M. Price, "Party, Purpose and Pattern: Sir Lewis Namier and His Critics," *Journal of British Studies,* I (1961), 71-93; Harvey C. Mansfield, Jr., "Sir Lewis Namier Considered," *Journal of British Studies,* II (1962), 28-55; Henry R. Winkler, "Sir Lewis Namier," *Journal of Modern History,* XXXV (1963), 1-19; W. R. Fryer, "Namier and the King's Position in English Politics, 1744-1784," *Burke Newsletter,* V (1963), 246-258; Robert Walcott, " 'Sir Lewis Namier Considered' Considered," *Journal of British Studies,* III (1963), 85-108; and Harvey C. Mansfield, Jr., "Sir Lewis Namier Again Considered," *Journal of British Studies,* III (1963), 109-119.

formed governments in a constantly changing political kaleidoscope.

Two criticisms, however, of this new and now dominant historiography can be advanced. The first is that although it was the study of the imperial problem during the American Revolution that first suggested the enterprise to Namier, the colonies play a very small part in his analysis. He was himself preoccupied with the "political nation" at home in the years 1760-1765, and even his followers. in emphasizing connection and place (and perhaps minimizing "issues"?), make small and only incidental reference to the American problem. This is true even where, as in Christie's volume, the "political nation" can only be studied against the background of events in South Carolina and Virginia. Thus far America has been treated as only one section in Namier's *England in the Age of the American Revolution,* a section that he confessed needed much more attention than he could then give it.[37] In this sense the Namier volumes are not studies of the American Revolution, and their general title is misleading.

The second criticism that might be offered is this: it is impossible to study the reign of George III without concluding that there was a sense in which Burke was speaking not for posterity but for his own times. While no doubt not a party in the modern sense, the Rockinghams did have leaders who held fairly regular meetings; they had in the end a policy for the colonies in 1765-1766; they had a following so much larger than the other groups as to constitute almost a different animal; after some uncertainty in 1766 they acted as an opposition to the Chatham-Grafton ministry; they attached importance to consistency; and they survived long enough to take office in the final bankruptcy of the policy they had always opposed. It is true that they did not go into opposition in 1766 to resist the allegedly unconstitutional power of the King, or to secure more liberal treatment for the American colonists. But the American war, as Brooke admits, gave the Rockinghams "a policy and a cause, which brought them posthumous renown in the nineteenth century." By 1782, if not before, there were issues in politics that were strong enough to break factions if not yet to make parties: American independence, the Yorkshire movement, radicalism, the character of Indian government, electoral reform itself. Namier, by confining himself to the political nation, omits important elements wielding no little influence. Where America was concerned, the omissions are crucially important: dissenters, manufacturers, and shopkeepers were highly sympathetic to the colonies. There is little in his pages of the politics of the City of London or of Westminster or of the Yorkshire freeholders; there is even less of that half-world of politics in which Wilkes and Lord George Gordon moved, of the emotions in politics that led Fox and the Duchess of Devonshire to sport the buff and blue of Fairfax County. If men are not moved by

37. See also Namier's essay on "Charles Garth and His Connexions," *English Historical Review,* LIV (1939), 443-470, 632-652.

self-interest alone, this is especially so when they face the fact of revolution. It is one of the most curious of current historical paradoxes that the emphasis on "connection" and empiricism and the distaste for principle that mark British study of the eighteenth century should be paralleled by the emphasis in the United States that their own Revolution was the result of principles, issues, and an emerging sense of national unity.

The work of the Namier school has, however, revised all previous estimates of British politicians and of the King. George III is now seen as an obstinate man but not a tyrant, "the first among the borough-mongering, electioneering gentlemen of England," an industrious, constitutional, but unpliant King. He can perhaps be seen most vividly in his *Letters to Lord Bute, 1756-1766* (edited by Romney Sedgwick, 1939) and in his *Correspondence, 1760-1783* (edited by Sir John Fortescue, 6 vols., 1927-1928); to which should be added Sir Lewis Namier's *Additions and Corrections* (1937).

The researches of the Namier school have been particularly hard on Burke, seen by them as little more than a great and gifted rhetorician whose defense of the Old Whigs and use of the word *party* are held responsible for much of the false doctrine of George III's tyranny. There is a further paradox here: the hero of American conservatism is seen by some British writers as the *bête noire* of British politics. A recent biography by Sir Philip Magnus emphasizes that Burke was suspect in his own time for other reasons, and that he never held major office. Older studies of him all need revision, however, in the light of the *Burke Correspondence,* a major enterprise of the University of Chicago, of which Professor T. W. Copeland is general editor. A complete edition of all Burke's writings is now appearing under a team of editors, based largely on the Wentworth-Woodhouse manuscripts now housed in the Sheffield Public Library. Until this is completed and a rounded picture of the great Irishman emerges, some of the more extreme views of him that are now current should be treated with reserve. One of the best recent studies of Burke, and the first scholarly assessment of his role in American politics, is by Ross Hoffman, *Edmund Burke, New York Agent* (1956), which makes clear how circumscribed that role was. He did not see his post as colonial agent for New York as that of an ambassador to the British government, as Franklin did. He put his task as a member of Parliament well to the forefront. Associated with the most conservative colony, he remained blind to the growing radicalism in America and convinced until the war actually began that conciliation was possible. This view—of the moderation of American demands—harmonized with the aristocratic views of the Rockingham group. As in France, so in America, Burke's sources were tainted and partisan; in both he sought to prevent revolution.

But it still remains true that the conclusions of the Namier biographic emphasis have not yet been drawn. Indeed they give rise to a fundamental question, posed by Edmund Morgan:

How, for example, can we stress the imperial vision of a government dominated by local interests? Until the new views are reconciled in a new synthesis, we can only speculate on what relative importance to assign them. One thing, however, is clear: they all demand that we re-examine the question as to why there should have been a revolution at all. If the Navigation Acts were fair, if Americans were not initially attached to any particular view of Parliament's authority, if George III was no tyrant, why should the colonists have sought independence? What, again, *was* the Revolution? If Bancroft's answer was wrong, what should we put in its place?

* * *

All these writers agree, then, that between 1759 and 1776 Britain and America had become two distinct societies. One, the American, had become sensitive to injuries or usurpations of authority, real or imagined; the other, Britain, insensitive because physically and psychologically remote and, it thought, militarily superior. In an otherwise free and non-feudal British colonial society, in which a high percentage of the adult free male population was qualified to vote, a succession of bureaucratic irritations between 1759 and 1776 bred relatively small crises which, in turn, bred mounting criticism and mounting intercolonial solidarity; and in the process basic principles were expressed which in the beginning were held to be those of free-born Englishmen. To some, like James Otis or Sam Adams—though they numbered perhaps no more than a handful —the principles were anterior and superior to the crises in which they found expression. The rule of law which the seventeenth century set above both King and Parliament, which the Puritans had exalted in civil as well as in ecclesiastical affairs, and which the eighteenth-century philosophers saw as the governing principle of the universe, could be invoked to question the absolutism of Parliament.[38] To many more the crises gave such views substance. The transformation of the rights of Englishmen living in America into those of Americans was a smooth one and was decisively confined to the years from 1774 to 1776, or even, perhaps, from April, 1775 to July 4, 1776. Only in 1775—though Franklin begins to suggest it two years earlier—did the argument shift its ground from the follies of Parliament to those of the King. And the argument, only at the very end becoming an argument for separation, included no suggestions for basic social or economic change. There was no Thermidor in 1787 because there were no Jacobins in 1776. If the franchise was widely held it was in general used to elect an élite. If the

---

38. Caroline Robbins, *The Eighteenth-Century Commonwealthman* (Cambridge, 1959); R. A. Humphreys, "The Rule of Law and the American Revolution," *Law Quarterly Review*, LIII (1937), 80-98. Bernard Bailyn, "The Transforming Radicalism of the American Revolution," introduction to *Pamphlets of the American Revolution, 1750-1776*, I (Cambridge, 1965).

Establishment from being foreign became native, and if it was far easier to get into than in England, it remained, after 1787 as before, an élite and never a demos that ruled. There being no feudal system, there was no need for the establishment of a centralized power rooted in popular emotion to overthrow or to transform it. This was, after all, a reluctant, a pragmatic, and, as its course and results were to confirm, an unmessianic revolution. The richest irony of it is that, once independent, the new society introduced the bishops and vice-admiralty courts that it had so much feared, and then proceeded with equal reluctance to levy taxes on itself.

A GUIDE TO
THE BIBLIOGRAPHY
OF THE REVOLUTION

I. The Revolutionary Generation

Jonathan Boucher, *A View of the Causes and Consequences of the American Revolution* (London, 1797).

George Chalmers, *An Introduction to the History of the Revolt of the American Colonies* (Boston, 2 vols., 1845). Vol. I appeared in 1782 and was suppressed.

William Gordon, *The History of the Rise, Progress, and Establishment, of the Independence of the United States of America* (London, 4 vols., 1788).

Thomas Hutchinson, *The History of the Colony and Province of Massachusetts-Bay*, ed. by Lawrence S. Mayo (Cambridge, 3 vols., 1936).

———, ed., *A Collection of Original Papers relative to the History of the Colony of Massachusetts-Bay* (Boston, 1769).

John Marshall, *The Life of George Washington* (Philadelphia, 5 vols., 1804-1807).

Peter Oliver, *Origin and Progress of the American Revolution*, ed. by Douglass Adair and John Schutz (San Marino, Calif., 1961).

David Ramsay, *The History of the Revolution of South Carolina, from a British Province to an Independent State* (Trenton, N.J., 2 vols., 1785).

———, *The History of the American Revolution* (Philadelphia, 2 vols., 1789; London, 1793).

Charles Stedman, *The History of the Origin, Progress, and Termination of the American War* (London, 1794).

Mercy Otis Warren, *History of the Rise, Progress and Termination of the American Revolution, interspersed with Biographical, Political and Moral Observations* (Boston, 3 vols., 1805).

Mason Weems, *The Life of George Washington, with curious anecdotes, equally honourable to himself and exemplary to his young countrymen* (Philadelphia, 1810).

II. The Nationalists

George Bancroft, *History of the United States* (Boston, 10 vols., 1834-1874).

Jonathan Elliot, *The Debates in the Several State Conventions on the Adoption of the Federal Constitution* (Washington, 5 vols., 1836-1845).

John Fiske, *The Critical Period of American History, 1783-1789* (New York, 1888).

———, *The American Revolution* (New York, 1891).

Peter Force, *American Archives* (Washington, 9 vols., 1837-1853).

James Grahame, *The History of the United States of North America from the Plantation of the British Colonies till their Revolt and Declaration of Independence* (London, 4 vols., 1827-1836).

George Washington Greene, *Historical View of the American Revolution* (Boston, 1865).

Hezekiah Niles, *Principles and Acts of the Revolution in America* (Baltimore, 1822).

Jared Sparks, *The Diplomatic Correspondence of the American Revolution* (New York, 12 vols., 1829-1830).

———, *The Life and Writings of George Washington* (Boston, 12 vols., 1833-1839).

———, *The Works of Benjamin Franklin* (Boston, 10 vols., 1836-1840).

———, ed., *The Library of American Biography* (New York and London, 10 vols., 1834-1848).

———, *Correspondence of the American Revolution, being letters of eminent men to George Washington* (Boston, 4 vols., 1853).

George Otto Trevelyan, *The Early History of Charles James Fox* (London, 1880).

———, *The American Revolution* (London and New York, 6 vols., 1899-1914).

III. The Imperialists

BOOKS:

Randolph G. Adams, *The Political Ideas of the American Revolution* (Durham, N.C., 1922).

Clarence W. Alvord, *The Mississippi Valley in British Politics* (Cleveland, 2 vols., 1917).

Charles M. Andrews, *The Colonial Background of the American Revolution* (New Haven, 1924; revised ed., 1931).

———, *The Colonial Period of American History* (New Haven, 4 vols., 1934-1938).

George Louis Beer, *British Colonial Policy, 1754-1765* (New York, 1907).

———, *The Origins of the British Colonial System, 1578-1660* (New York, 1908).

———, *The Old Colonial System, 1660-1754* (New York, 1912).

Sydney G. Fisher, *The Struggle for American Independence* (Philadelphia and London, 1908).

Lawrence H. Gipson, *The British Empire Before the American Revolution* (Caldwell, Idaho, and New York, 12 vols. to date, 1936-   ).

———, *The Coming of the Revolution, 1763-1775* (New York, 1954).

Richard Hildreth, *The History of the United States of America* (New York, 3 vols., 1849).

Leonard W. Labaree, *Royal Government in America: A Study of the British Colonial System Before 1783* (New Haven, 1930).

———, *Royal Instructions to British Colonial Governors, 1670-1776* (New York and London, 2 vols., 1935).

———, *Conservatism in Early American History* (New York, 1948).

Charles H. McIlwain, *The American Revolution: A Constitutional Interpretation* (New York, 1923).

Herbert L. Osgood, *The American Colonies in the Seventeenth Century* (New York and London, 3 vols., 1904-1907).

———, *The American Colonies in the Eighteenth Century* (New York, 4 vols., 1924).

Jack M. Sosin, *Whitehall and the Wilderness: The Middle West in British Colonial Policy, 1760-1775* (Lincoln, Nebr., 1961).

Richard W. Van Alstyne, *The Rising American Empire* (New York, 1960).

Claude H. Van Tyne, *The Loyalists in the American Revolution* (New York and London, 1902).

——, *The Causes of the War of Independence* (New York, 1922).

——, *The War of Independence: American Phase* (New York, 1929).

ARTICLES:

Charles M. Andrews, "The Boston Merchants and the Non-Importation Movement," Colonial Society of Massachusetts *Publications,* XIX (1917).

——, "The American Revolution: An Interpretation," *American Historical Review,* XXXI (1926).

C. T. Atkinson, "British Forces in North America, 1774-1781: Their Distribution and Strength," Society for Army Historical Research *Journal,* XVI (1937).

Herbert C. Bell, "The West India Trade Before the American Revolution," *American Historical Review,* XXII (1917).

C. E. Carter, "The Significance of the Military Office in America, 1763-1775," *American Historical Review,* XXVIII (1923).

——, "The Office of Commander in Chief: A Phase of Imperial Unity on the Eve of the Revolution," in Richard B. Morris, ed., *The Era of the American Revolution* (New York, 1939).

Dora M. Clark, "The British Treasury and the Administration of Military Affairs in America, 1754-1774," *Pennsylvania History,* II (1935).

——, "The American Board of Customs, 1767-1783," *American Historical Review,* XLV (1940).

Max Farrand, "The Taxation of Tea, 1767-1773," *American Historical Review,* III (1898).

Lawrence H. Gipson, "Connecticut Taxation and Parliamentary Aid Preceding the Revolutionary War," *American Historical Review,* XXXVI (1931).

——, "Some Reflections upon the American Revolution," *Pennsylvania History,* IX (1942).

——, "The Art of Preserving an Empire," *William and Mary Quarterly,* II (1945).

——, "The American Revolution as an Aftermath of the Great War for the Empire, 1754-1763" *Political Science Quarterly,* LXV (1950).

Hubert Hall, "Chatham's Colonial Policy," *American Historical Review,* V (1900).

Emily Hickman, "Colonial Writs of Assistance," *New England Quarterly,* V (1932).

R. A. Humphreys, "Lord Shelburne and a Projected Recall of Colonial Governors in 1767," *American Historical Review,* XXXVII (1932).

——, "British Colonial Policy and the American Revolution, 1763-1776," *History,* XIX (1934).

——, "Lord Shelburne and the Proclamation of 1763," *English Historical Review,* XLIX (1934).

Theodore D. Jervey, "Barlow Trecothick," *South Carolina Historical Magazine* XXXII (1931).

Charles H. Levermore, "The Whigs of Colonial New York," *American Historical Review,* I (1896).

Charles F. Mullett, "Tory Imperialism on the Eve of the Declaration of Independence," *Canadian Historical Review,* XII (1931).

Herbert L. Osgood, "The American Revolution," *Political Science Quarterly,* XIII (1898).

Lillian M. Penson, "The London West India Interest in the Eighteenth Century," *English Historical Review,* XXXVI (1921).

Edwin P. Tanner, "Colonial Agencies in England During the Eighteenth Century," *Political Science Quarterly*, XVI (1901).

Claude H. Van Tyne, "Sovereignty in the American Revolution," *American Historical Review*, XII (1907).

———, "The Influence of the Clergy, and of Religious and Sectarian Forces on the American Revolution," *American Historical Review*, XIX (1913).

———, "French Aid Before the Alliance of 1778," *American Historical Review*, XXXI (1925).

Agnes M. Whitson, "The Outlook of the Continental American Colonies on the British West Indies, 1760-1775," *Political Science Quarterly*, XLV (1930).

IV. The Loyalists

BOOKS:

Jonathan Boucher, *Reminiscences of an American Loyalist, 1738-1789* (New York, 1925).

Arthur G. Bradley, *Colonial Americans in Exile* (New York, 1932).

North Callahan, *Royal Raiders: The Tories of the American Revolution* (Indianapolis, 1963).

Daniel P. Coke, *The Royal Commission on the Losses and Services of American Loyalists, 1783-1785*, ed. by Hugh E. Egerton (Oxford, 1915).

Robert O. DeMond, *The Loyalists in North Carolina During the Revolution* (Durham, N.C., 1940).

Lewis D. Einstein, *Divided Loyalties: Americans in England During the War of Independence* (New York and London, 1933).

Alexander C. Flick, *Loyalism in New York During the American Revolution* (New York, 1901).

Lawrence H. Gipson, *Jared Ingersoll: A Study of American Loyalism in Relation to British Colonial Government* (New Haven, 1920).

Otis G. Hammond, *Tories of New Hampshire in the War of the Revolution* (Concord, N.H., 1917).

Harold B. Hancock, *The Delaware Loyalists* (Wilmington, Del., 1940).

Isaac S. Harrell, *Loyalism in Virginia: Chapters in the Economic History of the Revolution* (Durham, N.C., 1926).

Janet B. Johnson, *Robert Alexander: Maryland Loyalist* (New York, 1942).

E. Alfred Jones, *The Loyalists of New Jersey: Their Memorials, Petitions, Claims, etc. from English Records* (Newark, N.J., 1927).

———, *The Loyalists of Massachusetts: Their Memorials, Petitions and Claims* (London, 1930).

Leonard W. Labaree, *Conservatism in Early American History* (New York, 1948).

Duane G. Meyer, *The Highland Scots of North Carolina, 1732-1776* (Chapel Hill, 1961).

William H. Nelson, *The American Tory* (New York and London, 1961).

Epaphroditus Peck, *The Loyalists of Connecticut* (New Haven, 1934).

Lorenzo Sabine, *Biographical Sketches of Loyalists of the American Revolution, with an Historical Essay* (Boston, 2 vols., 1864).

Wilbur H. Siebert, *The Flight of American Loyalists to the British Isles* (Columbus, Ohio, 1911).

———, *Loyalists in East Florida, 1774-1785* (De Land, Fla., 2 vols., 1929).

Paul H. Smith, *Loyalists and Redcoats: A Study in British Revolutionary Policy* (Chapel Hill, 1965).

James H. Stark, *The Loyalists of Massachusetts and the Other Side of the American Revolution* (Boston, 1910).

Howard Swiggett, *War Out of Niagara: Walter Butler and the Tory Rangers* (New York, 1933).

Moses Coit Tyler, *The Literary History of the American Revolution, 1763-1783* (New York and London, 2 vols., 1897).

Claude H. Van Tyne, *The Loyalists in the American Revolution* (New York and London, 1902).

William S. Wallace, *The United Empire Loyalists: A Chronicle of the Great Migration* (Toronto, 1914).

Esther C. Wright, *The Loyalists of New Brunswick* (Frederickton, N.B., 1955).

Harry B. Yoshpe, *The Disposition of Loyalist Estates in the Southern District of the State of New York* (New York and London, 1939).

ARTICLES:

John E. Alden, "John Mein: Scourge of Patriots," Colonial Society of Massachusetts *Publications,* XXXIV (1942).

Ernest H. Baldwin, "Joseph Galloway," *Pennsylvania Magazine of History,* XXVI (1902).

Viola F. Barnes, "Frances Legge, Governor of Loyalist Nova Scotia, 1773-1776," *New England Quarterly,* IV (1931).

Robert W. Barnwell, "The Migration of Loyalists from South Carolina," South Carolina Historical Association *Proceedings,* VII (1937).

R. R. Beirne, "Governor Robert Eden," *Maryland Historical Magazine,* XLV (1950).

Richard D. Brown, "The Confiscation and Disposition of Loyalists' Estates in Suffolk County, Massachusetts," *William and Mary Quarterly,* XXI (1964).

Ernest A. Cruikshank, "King's Royal Regiment," Ontario Historical Society *Papers,* XXVII (1931).

Catherine Fennelly, "Governor William Franklin of New Jersey," *William and Mary Quarterly,* VI (1949).

G. A. Gilbert, "Connecticut Loyalists," *American Historical Review,* IV (1899).

Isaac S. Harrell, "North Carolina Loyalists," *North Carolina Historical Review,* III (1926).

George W. Kyte, "Some Plans for a Loyalist Stronghold in the Middle Colonies," *Pennsylvania History,* XVI (1949).

Leonard W. Labaree, "Nature of American Loyalism," American Antiquarian Society *Proceedings,* LIV (1944).

Robert S. Lambert, "The Confiscation of Loyalist Property in Georgia, 1782-1786," *William and Mary Quarterly,* XX (1963).

Howard W. Preston, "Rhode Island and the Loyalist," Rhode Island Historical Society *Collections,* XXI (1928) and XXII (1929).

Wilbur H. Siebert and F. E. Gilliam, "Loyalists in Prince Edward's Island," Royal Society of Canada *Transactions,* IV (1910).

Wilbur H. Siebert, "American Loyalists in Eastern Quebec," Royal Society of Canada *Transactions,* VII (1913).

———, "The Legacy of the American Revolution to the British West Indies," Ohio State University *Bulletin,* XVII (1913).

———, "Loyalist Settlements on Gaspé," Royal Society of Canada *Transactions,* VIII (1914).

———, "The Exodus of Loyalists from Penobscot," Ohio State University *Bulletin,* XVIII (1914).

————, "The Dispersion of American Tories," *Mississippi Valley Historical Review*, I (1914).

————, "Loyalists in the Niagara Peninsula," Royal Society of Canada *Transactions*, IX (1915).

————, "Loyalist Refugees of New Hampshire," Ohio State University *Bulletin*, XXI (1916).

————, "Refugee Loyalists in Connecticut," Royal Society of Canada *Transactions*, X (1916).

————, "Loyalists in West Florida," *Mississippi Valley Historical Review*, II (1916).

————, "Loyalists of Pennsylvania," Ohio State University *Bulletin*, XXIV (1920).

————, "Kentucky's Struggle," *Mississippi Valley Historical Review*, VII (1920).

————, "Loyalist Troops of New England," *New England Quarterly*, IV (1931).

Jonathan Smith, "Toryism in Worcester County," Massachusetts Historical Society *Proceedings*, XLVIII (1915).

Moses Coit Tyler, "The Party of the Loyalists in the American Revolution," *American Historical Review*, I (1895).

Mabel G. Walker, "Sir John Johnson, Loyalist," *Mississippi Valley Historical Review*, III (1916).

Oscar Zeichner, "Rehabilitation of Loyalists in Connecticut," *New England Quarterly*, XI (1938).

————, "Loyalists Problem in New York After the Revolution," *New York History*, XXI (1940).

V. The Progressives

BOOKS:

Charles A. Beard, *An Economic Interpretation of the Constitution of the United States* (New York, 1913).

Charles A. and Mary Beard, *The Rise of American Civilization* (New York, 1927).

Carl Becker, *The History of Political Parties in the Province of New York, 1760-1776* (Madison, Wisc., 1909).

————, *The Declaration of Independence: A Study in the History of Political Ideas* (New York, 1922).

Carl and Jessica Bridenbaugh, *Rebels and Gentlemen: Philadelphia in the Age of Franklin* (New York, 1942).

Carl Bridenbaugh, *Cities in Revolt: Urban Life in America, 1743-1776* (New York, 1955).

Philip G. Davidson, *Propaganda and the American Revolution, 1763-1783* (Chapel Hill, 1941).

Elisha P. Douglass, *Rebels and Democrats: The Struggle for Equal Political Rights and Majority Rule During the American Revolution* (Chapel Hill, 1955).

E. James Ferguson, *The Power of the Purse: A History of American Public Finance, 1776-1790* (Chapel Hill, 1961).

Louis Hacker, *The Triumph of American Capitalism* (New York, 1940).

John Franklin Jameson, *The American Revolution Considered as a Social Movement* (Princeton, 1926).

Merrill Jensen, *The Articles of Confederation: An Interpretation of the Social-Constitutional History of the American Revolution, 1774-1781* (Madison, Wisc., 1940).

————, *The New Nation: A History of the United States During the Confederation, 1781-1789* (New York, 1950).

Jackson Turner Main, *The Antifederalists: Critics of the Constitution, 1781-1788* (Chapel Hill, 1961).

Irving Mark, *Agrarian Conflicts in Colonial New York, 1711-1775* (New York and London, 1940).

John C. Miller, *Origins of the American Revolution* (Boston, 1943).

————, *Triumph of Freedom, 1775-1783* (Boston, 1948).

Vernon L. Parrington, *Main Currents in American Thought* (New York, 3 vols., 1927-1931).

Arthur M. Schlesinger, *The Colonial Merchants and the American Revolution, 1763-1776* (New York, 1918).

————, *New Viewpoints in American History* (New York, 1922).

————, *Prelude to Independence: The Newspaper War on Britain, 1764-1776* (New York, 1958).

ARTICLES:

Carl Becker, "The Growth of Revolutionary Parties and Methods in New York Province, 1765-1774," *American Historical Review*, VII (1901).

Bruce M. Bigelow, "Aaron Lopez, Merchant of Newport," *New England Quarterly*, IV (1931).

B. W. Bond, Jr., "The Colonial Agent as a Popular Representative," *Political Science Quarterly*, XXXV (1920).

R. L. Brunhouse, "The Effect of the Townshend Acts in Pennsylvania," *Pennsylvania Magazine of History*, LIV (1930).

Philip G. Davidson, "Sons of Liberty and Stamp Act Men," *North Carolina Historical Review*, IX (1932).

F. J. Ericson, "The Contemporary British Opposition to the Stamp Act, 1764-1765," Michigan Academy of Science, Arts, and Letters, *Papers*, XXIX (1944).

Worthington C. Ford, "Colonial Commerce in 1774-1776," Massachusetts Historical Society *Proceedings*, LIX (1926).

Louis M. Hacker, "The First American Revolution," *Columbia University Quarterly*, XXVII (1935).

John Franklin Jameson, "St. Eustatius in the American Revolution," *American Historical Review*, VIII (1903).

R. S. Longley, "Mob Activities in Revolutionary Massachusetts," *New England Quarterly*, VI (1933).

H. M. Morais, "The Sons of Liberty in New York," in Richard B. Morris, ed., *The Era of the American Revolution* (New York, 1939).

Edgar L. Pennington, "The Anglican Clergy of Pennsylvania in the American Revolution," *Pennyslvania Magazine of History*, LXIII (1939).

A. S. Salley, Jr., "The Mecklenberg Declaration," *American Historical Review*, XIII (1907).

Arthur M. Schlesinger, "The American Revolution Reconsidered," *Political Science Quarterly*, XXXIV (1919).

————, "The Colonial Newspapers and the Stamp Act," *New England Quarterly*, VIII (1935).

————, "Politics, Propaganda and the Philadelphia Press, 1767-1770," *Pennsylvania Magazine of History*, LX (1936).

————, "Propaganda and the Boston Newspaper Press, 1767-1770," Colonial Society of Massachusetts *Publications*, XXXII (1937).

————, "Liberty Tree: A Genealogy," *New England Quarterly*, XXV (1952).

Arthur P. Scott, "The Parson's Cause," *Political Science Quarterly*, XXXI (1916).
George C. Wolkins, "The Seizure of John Hancock's Sloop 'Liberty'," Massachusetts
Historical Society *Proceedings*, LV (1922).

VI. The Neo-Whigs

BOOKS:

Daniel J. Boorstin, *The Lost World of Thomas Jefferson* (New York, 1948).
——, *The Genius of American Politics* (Chicago, 1953).
——, *The Americans: The Colonial Experience* (New York, 1958).
Robert E. Brown, *Charles Beard and the Constitution* (Princeton, 1956).
Robert E. and B. Katherine Brown, *Virginia, 1705-1786: Democracy or Aristocracy?*
(East Lansing, Mich., 1964).
O. M. Dickerson, *The Navigation Acts and the American Revolution* (Philadelphia,
1951).
Bernhard Knollenberg, *Origin of the American Revolution, 1759-1766* (New York,
1960).
Forrest McDonald, *We the People: The Economic Origins of the Constitution*
(Chicago, 1958).
——, *E Pluribus Unum: The Formation of the American Republic, 1776-1790*
(New York, 1965).
Edmund S. Morgan, *The Birth of the Republic, 1763-1789* (Chicago, 1956).
Edmund S. and Helen M. Morgan, *The Stamp Act Crisis: Prologue to Revolution*
(Chapel Hill, 1953).
Curtis P. Nettels, *George Washington and American Independence* (Boston, 1951).
Clinton Rossiter, *Seedtime of the Republic: The Origin of the American Tradition
of Political Liberty* (New York, 1953).
Carl Ubbelohde, *The Vice-Admiralty Courts and the American Revolution* (Phila-
delphia, 1951).

ARTICLES:

Bernard Bailyn, "The Transforming Radicalism of the American Revolution," intro-
duction to *Pamphlets of the American Revolution, 1750-1776*, I (Cambridge,
1965).
Philip G. Davidson, "Whig Propagandists of the American Revolution," *American
Historical Review*, XXXIX (1933-1934).
O. M. Dickerson, "John Hancock: Notorious Smuggler or Near Victim of British
Revenue Racketeers?", *Mississippi Valley Historical Review*, XXXII (1946).
——, "England's Most Fateful Decision," *New England Quarterly*, XXII (1949).
——, "British Control of American Newspapers on the Eve of the American
Revolution," *New England Quarterly*, XXIV (1951).
——, "The Commissioners of Customs and the Boston Massacre," *New England
Quarterly*, XXVII (1954).
Jack P. Greene, "The Gadsden Election Controversy and the Revolutionary Move-
ment in South Carolina," *Mississippi Valley Historical Review*, XLVI (1959).
Lawrence A. Harper, "The Effects of the Navigation Acts on the Thirteen Colonies,"
in Richard B. Morris, ed., *The Era of the American Revolution* (New York,
1939).
——, "Mercantilism and the American Revolution," *Canadian Historical Review*,
XXIII (1942).
R. M. Jellison and Jack P. Greene, "The Currency Act of 1764 in Imperial-
Colonial Relations, 1764-1776," *William and Mary Quarterly*, XVIII (1961).

D. L. Kemmerer, "Judges' Good Behavior Tenure in Colonial New Jersey," New Jersey Historical Society *Proceedings*, LVI (1938).

Cecilia Kenyon, "Republicanism and Radicalism in the American Revolution: An Old-Fashioned Interpretation," *William and Mary Quarterly*, XIX (1962).

Milton M. Klein, "Democracy and Politics in Colonial New York," *New York History*, XL (1959).

———, "Prelude to Revolution in New York: Jury Trials and Judicial Tenure," *William and Mary Quarterly*, XVII (1960).

David S. Lovejoy, "Rights Imply Equality: The Case Against Admiralty Jurisdiction in America, 1764-1776," *William and Mary Quarterly*, XVI (1959).

Edmund S. Morgan, "The Postponement of the Stamp Act," *William and Mary Quarterly*, V (1948).

———, "Colonial Ideas of Parliamentary Power," *William and Mary Quarterly*, VII (1950).

———, "The American Revolution: Revisions in Need of Revising," *William and Mary Quarterly*, XIV (1957).

———, "The American Revolution Considered as an Intellectual Movement," in Arthur Schlesinger, Jr., and Morton White, eds., *Paths of American Thought* (Boston, 1963).

Curtis P. Nettels, "British Mercantilism and the Economic Development of the Thirteen Colonies," *Journal of Economic History*, XII (1952).

Page Smith, "David Ramsay and the Causes of the American Revolution," *William and Mary Quarterly*, XVII (1960).

Thad W. Tate, "The Coming of the Revolution in Virginia: Britain's Challenge to Virginia's Ruling Class, 1763-1776," *William and Mary Quarterly*, XIX (1962).

VII. The Conservatives

John Brooke, *The Chatham Administration, 1776-1768* (New York and London, 1956).

Carl B. Cone, *Burke and the Nature of Politics* (Lexington, Ky., 1957).

Bernard Donoughue, *British Politics and the American Revolution: The Path to War, 1773-1775* (New York and London, 1965).

Keith G. Feiling, *The Second Tory Party, 1714-1832* (London, 1938).

John W. Fortescue, ed., *The Correspondence of King George III from 1760 to December 1783* (London, 6 vols., 1927-1928).

George H. Guttridge, *English Whiggism and the American Revolution* (Berkeley, 1942).

———, *The Early Career of Lord Rockingham, 1730-1765* (Berkeley, 1952).

Lewis B. Namier, *The Structure of Politics at the Accession of George III* (London, 2 vols., 1929).

———, *Additions and Corrections to Sir John Fortescue's Edition of the Correspondence of King George III* (Manchester, 1937).

———, *England in the Age of the American Revolution* (London, 1930).

Lewis B. Namier and John Brooke, *The House of Commons, 1754-1790* (New York and London, 3 vols., 1964).

———, *Charles Townshend* (New York and London, 1964).

Richard Pares, *King George III and the Politicians* (London, 1953).

Charles R. Ritcheson, *British Politics and the American Revolution* (Norman, Okla., 1954).

Eric Robson, *The American Revolution in Its Political and Military Aspects, 1763-1783* (New York and London, 1955).

Romney Sedgwick, *Letters from George III to Lord Bute, 1756-1766* (London, 1939).

Esmond Wright, *Fabric of Freedom, 1763-1800* (New York, 1961).

ARTICLES:

Lewis B. Namier, "King George III: A Study of Personality," Academy of Arts Lecture, 1953.

Jacob Price, "Party, Purpose and Pattern: Sir Lewis Namier and His Critics," *Journal of British Studies,* I (1961).

Richard W. Van Alstyne, "Parliamentary Supremacy versus Independence," *Huntington Library Quarterly,* XXVI (1963).

VIII. State Studies

BOOKS:

William W. Abbot, *The Royal Governors of Georgia, 1754-1775* (Chapel Hill, 1959).

Charles A. Barker, *The Background of the Revolution in Maryland* (New Haven, 1940).

Robert E. Brown, *Middle-Class Democracy and the Revolution in Massachusetts, 1691-1780* (Ithaca, 1955).

Robert L. Brunhouse, *The Counter-Revolution in Pennsylvania, 1776-1790* (Harrisburg, Pa., 1942).

Kenneth Coleman, *The American Revolution in Georgia, 1763-1789* (Athens, 1958).

Philip A. Crowl, *Maryland During and After the Revolution* (Baltimore, 1943).

Hamilton J. Eckenrode, *The Revolution in Virginia* (New York, 1916).

Dixon Ryan Fox, *Yankees and Yorkers* (New York and London, 1940).

Oscar and Mary Handlin, *Commonwealth: A Study of the Role of Government in the American Economy, Massachusetts, 1774-1861* (New York, 1947).

Donald L. Kemmerer, *Path to Freedom: The Struggle for Self-Government in Colonial New Jersey, 1703-1776* (Princeton and London, 1940).

Charles H. Lincoln, *The Revolutionary Movement in Pennsylvania, 1760-1776* (Philadelphia, 1901).

David S. Lovejoy, *Rhode Island Politics and the American Revolution, 1760-1776* (Providence, 1958).

Richard P. McCormick, *Experiment in Independence: New Jersey in the Critical Period, 1781-1789* (New Brunswick, N. J., 1950).

Ernest W. Spaulding, *New York in the Critical Period, 1783-1789* (New York, 1932).

Theodore G. Thayer, *Pennsylvania Politics and the Growth of Democracy, 1740-1776* (Harrsisburg, Pa., 1953).

Oscar Zeichner, *Connecticut's Years of Controversy, 1750-1776* (Chapel Hill, 1949).

ARTICLES:

George P. Anderson, "A Note on Ebenezer Mackintosh," Colonial Society of Massachusetts *Publications,* XXVI (1927).

Charles A. Barker, "Property Rights in Provincial Maryland," *Journal of Southern History,* II (1936).

———, "Maryland Before the Revolution," *American Historical Review,* XLVI (1940).

Elizabeth Donnan, "The Slave Trade in South Carolina Before the Revolution," *American Historical Review,* XXXIII (1928).

P. S. Flippin, "The Royal Government in Georgia, 1752-1776," *Georgia Historical Quarterly,* VIII (1924), IX (1925), X (1926), XII (1928), XIII (1929).

Joseph G. de R. Hamilton, "Southern Members of the Inns of Court," *North Carolina Historical Review,* X (1933).

Isaac S. Harrell, "Some Neglected Phases of the Revolution in Virginia," *William and Mary Quarterly,* V (1925).

Archibald Henderson, "The Origin of the Regulation in North Carolina," *American Historical Review,* XXI (1916).

W. R. Smith, "Sectionalism in Pennsylvania During the Revolution," *Political Science Quarterly,* XXIV (1909).

II

Causes

THE IMPERIALIST
INTERPRETATION

HERBERT L. OSGOOD
The American Revolution

🔲 Herbert Levi Osgood (1855-1918) * was a leading figure in the imperial school. His writing is descriptive and persuasive, but sober and unexciting. Though he has a distinct point of view, his articles are not in form nearly as argumentative or as tightly supported by evidence as scholarly writing is today.

The Revolution, he contended, was not the work of heroes and demons, of selfless patriots and ruthless autocrats; it must be viewed "not alone from the Colonial but as well from the imperial standpoint." The article that follows is in form a review of Moses Coit Tyler's *The Literary History of the American Revolution, 1763-1783* (1897). This book is not, he says, distinctively a history of the political ideas of the Revolution, since it excludes the correspondence and state papers of the period. It is, however, commendable because of its treatment of the Loyalists. "Nothing approximating in excellence to Professor Tyler's treatment has hitherto appeared in American historical literature." But it is to Tyler's treatment of the Declaration of Independence that Osgood devotes most of his review, and he uses it to give voice to a new view of the Revolution: an attempt to see it not in nationalist terms but in an Anglo-American setting. 🔲

FOR TEN YEARS prior to the outbreak of the war of the American Revolution a battle of words—a conflict of ideas—went on, both in England and in America, between the supporters and the opponents of the colonial cause. The controversy was maintained over the question what in reality

---

* Cf. Dixon Ryan Fox, *Herbert Levi Osgood: An American Scholar* (New York, 1924); E. C. O. Beatty, "Herbert Levi Osgood," in William T. Hutchinson, ed., *The Marcus W. Jernegan Essays in American Historiography* (Chicago, 1937). Cf. Osgood's many other reviews in the *Political Science Quarterly*, especially Vol. II (1887), "England and the Colonies," in which he argues that the supremacy of King and Parliament over the colonies was complete. "On the other hand we shall find reasons for the growth of a different doctrine here, and that it was put forth very early in the history of the Colonies. It will also appear that the whole struggle was but an episode in the development of the English Colonial System and of the law which governs it." (p. 441)

Reprinted from the *Political Science Quarterly*, XIII (1898), 41-59.

were the constitutional relations existing between Great Britain and her American dependencies, and what, in view of those relations, was the policy proper to be followed at the crisis. After the opening of the war and the Declaration of Independence the debate over constitutional questions closed, and the literature which proceeded from the Americans assumed mainly the forms of satire, of exhortations in prose and verse to energy and steadfastness in the conflict, of narratives of experience in field, camp and prison, of efforts at a reflective or historical reproduction of the events of the struggle. But the subject-matter of the literature, both before and after 1776, was mainly political and historical: it embodied the contemporary record of a great conflict, and contained the only permanent and abiding expression of the emotions to which that conflict gave rise. What was true of the American Revolution must be true in the case of any other similar movement. The subject-matter, then, of Professor Tyler's work takes it out of the category of mere histories of literature, and gives to it a peculiar value as a contribution to the political history of the period of which it treats. The criticism of style, the exposition of the æsthetic side of the literary product of those times, has occupied a secondary place in the mind and purpose of the author. His attention has been chiefly directed to the burden of thought which the writers of the time were seeking to express, and to the ascertainment of their position amid the stirring events of the period. . . .

To his treatment of the Declaration of Independence, however, some exception may perhaps be taken, and that on the ground of its inconsistency with the trend of opinion revealed elsewhere in his work. He admits in volume one, page 307, the validity of the doctrine of virtual representation. He says that "the historic meaning of the word representation . . . seemed fairly to justify the loyalist contention that the several organized British communities in America, as an integral part of the British Empire, were to all intents and purposes represented in the British Parliament. . . ." When speaking of the taxation of the colonies by Parliament (I, 310), he draws from the doctrine of virtual representation the logical conclusion. "It was then a question," says he, "of British constitutional law. Upon that question, which of the two parties was in the right? Is it now possible to doubt that it was the Tories?" Further, when treating of the third volume of Hutchinson's *History of Massachusetts,* he says (II, 407): "It is much to his praise to say that, throughout this third volume, the prevailing tone is calm, moderate, just, with only occasional efforts at pleading his own cause, with only occasional flickerings of personal or political animosity." It is believed that these quotations fairly represent Professor Tyler's views concerning the points upon which they touch.

But when he comes to discuss the Declaration of Independence, he pursues a line of thought which it is difficult to harmonize with the statements just quoted. Though he uses language which is measured and cautious, though he qualifies and softens the meaning of terms, yet he clearly holds that the two central charges urged against the British government in the Declaration were true (I, 510, *et seq.*). The first of these charges was that the various acts of Parliament of which the colonists complained were in design tyrannical, because they revealed a somewhat systematic plan to take away a part of the property of the American people without their consent. But, if the doctrine of virtual representation was true, how can it be said that any part of their property was to be taken without their consent? According to that view, their consent was presupposed, and that was the end of it. As there is no proof that Parliament intended to take oppressively large amounts, its policy could not, on the basis of that theory, be regarded as tyrannical. Had Professor Tyler insisted that, when applied to the colonies, the theory of virtual representation broke down, Jefferson's conclusion might have been approved with a greater appearance of consistency. But the two positions which he has chosen it seems impossible for him to maintain.

The second charge contained in the Declaration was that George III, because he was mainly responsible for the policy of taxing the colonies, was a tyrant. This seems to win more hearty approval from the author than does the previous count in the indictment. But, instead of adducing positive evidence on the subject, he contents himself with quoting the opinions of three English historians, two of whom were of well-known Liberal sympathies. With all due respect for authority, it must be said that the judgments of these historians on the American question cannot be accepted as conclusive, for a reason which will be stated later in this paper. Moreover, if Parliament intended only a moderate exercise of its constitutional powers in taxing the colonies and regulating their trade, the same thing must have been true of the king. Parliament and king were acting together and, at the outset at least, kept properly within their constitutional powers.

When the controversy with the colonials began, George III in British politics was asserting the latent power of the prerogative against certain groups of Whig politicians who had controlled affairs for nearly half a century. It was the last effort of the kingship to recover its ancient place in the constitution, and its patronage was used unscrupulously and to the fullest extent to break down a long-established majority in Parliament. But for twenty years Walpole, as premier, had controlled king and Parliament, and had maintained a system of personal rule. The king imitated this policy, as he had to do in order to attain the end at which he aimed, and as he might do consistently with law and established custom. The end which the king sought was to control ministry and Parliament. That, owing to the hereditary nature of the kingly office, this tended to unsettle relations and to destroy the balance of power within the constitution, is undoubted. It was a step backward rather than forward. But, because the policy of procuring a revenue by Parliamentary taxation of the colonies was adopted while the king was engaged in his efforts to secure control of Parliament, it is argued that the policy was the result of those efforts and of their success—that the two lines of action were related as cause and effect. This view underlies to an extent the indictments of the king in the Declaration of Independence. Otherwise it would have been impossible to regard the king as in this matter especially tyrannical. But it is certain that such causal connection between the two lines of policy as has been affirmed has never been demonstrated. To be sure, in its later stages, when the colonial policy had occasioned resistance and that had developed into war, the king proved to be more stubborn than some of the ministers in his adherence to the course which had been adopted. It is true that the war finally became the king's war, but from that it does not follow that the inception of the policy, or its development till the beginning of hostilities, was due more to the king than to responsible leaders in Parliament. Grenville, Townshend, Bedford, Halifax were Whigs, or had received their official training under Whig ministries. They were the men who initiated the colonial policy of this reign. The Sugar Act and the Stamp Act were to their minds the necessary means of procuring a revenue with which to provide salaries for the imperial officials in the colonies and to establish a military force there. The creation within the colonies of executives which, so far as possible, should be independent of the dictation of the assemblies; the development of machinery there which should be adequate to the enforcement of the acts of trade; the improvement of the system of defense by the establishment within the colonies of some 20,000 regular troops—these were the objects which they sought to attain, and that by means of taxation. It was a policy with which in outline they must have been familiar long before the accession of George III.

The two important acts which it was thought would furnish the necessary revenue were passed entirely without opposition. Whigs and Tories alike supported them. They were not even party measures. The king certainly acted in harmony with the will of the nation when he approved these acts and attempted to execute them. The nation had not been cajoled or coerced into the adoption of this policy. It then seemed natural and proper to all, save here and there an individual. In pursuance of the same object, though resistance in the colonies had revealed the difficulty of attaining it, the Townshend Acts were passed. In the Commons a numerous minority voted against these, but they were passed without difficulty and without the exertion of special influence on the part of the king. The decisive step was now taken. All the subsequent acts of both Parliament and executive were provoked by resistance, and must be judged with immediate reference to that fact. It is certain that, during the years of coercion preceding the war, decisive, if not overwhelming, majorities in Parliament supported the policy of the government, and that the politically active part of the nation, as then constituted, was in harmony with Parliament. The aristocracy, gentry and merchants—and these were the politically active nation—would probably have supported a more vigorous policy than was adopted. The explanation of its failure is to be found in the incapacity of the leaders, rather than in the temper of the classes named. If this view of the case be true, it is difficult to see why the king, during the early and middle periods of the American controversy, was not acting within his constitutional sphere as a constituent part of the British legislature and the imperial executive. In this matter he was not contending against Parliament or seeking to coerce its action. On this question he and Parliament were in agreement, and there was no occasion for special exertion of royal influence. If the policy was tyrannical, Parliament must bear at least an equal share of the blame: the king should not be singled out and made the special object of attack. The colonies were, in fact, resisting a united king, lords and commons.

But what bearing does this have upon the argument which the colonists at the time drew from Magna Carta, the Petition of Right and the Bill of Rights—an argument of which Professor Tyler, like many other modern writers, makes use? It is said that the colonists might properly appropriate to themselves and use for their special purpose the guaranties contained in those documents. Again and again this claim was made while the controversy was in progress: the changes were rung upon it in every possible form. But the fact was overlooked or obscured that these documents contained guaranties on behalf of the nation against the executive, and not against Parliament. Against the king, when acting as a component of Parliament or when taking proper steps for the execution of its will, they were inoperative. They were the outgrowth of a struggle between the nation and the crown, not of one between the nation and Parliament. They were guaranties of the independence of Parliament as against the crown; and thus they might have been utilized, had George III, in his efforts to reinvigorate the prerogative, come distinctly into conflict with Parliament and the nation. But for the purposes of the colonists—except to arouse popular prejudice—they were useless, because inapplicable. If one accepts the doctrine of virtual representation, this conclusion would seem to be unavoidable. But it also follows directly from the fact that, in the English system since 1689, there is no higher guaranty of rights or expression of power than an act of Parliament. Beyond that or out of reach of it one cannot go. No charter or other expression of the will of the executive can stand against it. Therefore, the fact of the case is that, except in the domain of private rights—and that only as the result of ancient and well-established precedents—the colonists had no effective legal guaranties against Parliament.

Parliament, then, and not the king, was to them the real source of danger. It was only when the two were actively cooperating that the colonists had serious reason for fearing the executive authority. For a hundred years they had been living under the government of the British executive, with only occasional, and never genuinely oppressive, interference of Parliament. After 1760 they began to feel the power which was latent in Parliament as the seat of sovereignty within the British Empire, and they sought in various directions for protection against it. They tried to find such security in the charters, of which a few still existed, but these were speedily proved to be insufficient. Very many affirmed that the authority of Parliament was limited—that within certain spheres it could not legislate concerning affairs outside the realm; but there was no agreement as to where to draw the line, and most of those who adopted this course of argument ended by denying *in toto* the legislative authority of Parliament over the colonies. Many, also, sought refuge in the theory of natural rights. But all these pleas, when viewed from the legal and historical standpoint, are seen to have been unavailing. The colonists stood face to face with a power, possessed of authority over them that was without legal limit, which had now resolved, if possible, to procure from them a revenue. Situated as they were, on a remote continent, under new social and political conditions which were very imperfectly understood, even by the best informed in England, it is clear that there was an element of peril for the colonists in the existing constitutional relations. The danger was inherent in the system itself, whatever might be the character of the personalities who were controlling and directing it. So long as Parliament had not by solemn act limited its power over the colonies, their inhabitants could not feel sure of the permanence of their institutions. Their only sufficient refuge, then, short of successfully achieved independence, was in the action of Parliament itself. Viewed in this light, the American controversy is seen to have resulted from an effort to find a tolerable solution for a difficult problem in government.

It has been intimated by some that the adoption of the policy by which the full extent of Parliament's authority over the colonies was revealed was an innovation. But in reality all the elements of that policy will be found to have been latent in the system, at least since 1689. It had always been held that the colonies were bound by any act of Parliament in which they were named or which might properly apply to them. Hence the passage of a group of acts like the laws of trade, carried with it the implication that similar laws might be passed binding the colonies in other departments of social or political activity. The existence of the laws of trade also meant that all the resources of the government might be used for their enforcement, and that, if it were thought necessary, Parliament might be resorted to for additional legislation. As a matter of fact, in 1694, on motion of the committee of trade, an order in council was sent to the governors of Maryland and Virginia to cause one or more small armed vessels to cruise along the middle Atlantic coast with power to examine all ships and their clearances on the collectors' books, so as to discover forged certificates. The measure was executed, but it did not stop the direct trade with Scotland and Ireland against which it was directed. To some extent before the revolution of 1689, and regularly thereafter till the colonial revolt, armed vessels were stationed at important points along the American coast for the purpose of capturing pirates, privateers and illegal traders. The law of 1696, by a natural extension of the functions of the admiralty courts in the colonies, provided that violations of the acts of trade should be tried by them; and special judges and other officers were appointed for the purpose. The language of the early charters implied the right of the home government to tax the colonists. The act of trade of 1672 provided for the levy **of** export duties in the colonies in a certain contingency. The Molasses Act of 1733 provided for the collection of import duties in the northern colonies on sugar, molasses and spirits brought from foreign plantations; and some revenue was collected under the law, notwithstanding the high rates of duty. The measures thus referred to furnished adequate precedents for the Sugar Act of 1764 and for the order that the vessels of the navy should aid in the work of suppressing contraband trade. The Sugar Act did not mean the adoption of a new policy or the assertion of new claims: it meant, rather, an extension of the old policy, while Parliament had certainly never abandoned its right to secure a revenue from the colonies. Viewed from the standpoint of sovereignty, of what consequence was it whether an act provided for protection with incidental revenue or revenue with incidental protection?

But, it is argued, when the scope of the imperial revenue system was extended so as to include a stamp duty, and the admiralty courts were given jurisdiction over violations of that law, a radical departure from earlier practice was made. So far as resort to the admiralty courts is concerned, it should be said that they were the only courts in the colonies before which such cases could be brought with the slightest assurance that the cause of the government would be fairly considered. The choice, then, was between the trial of the cases before these courts or their removal to England for trial. Moreover, the laws for the collection of stamp duties in Great Britain provided that violations of the acts should be tried before two justices without a jury. But a larger question here confronts us. What is the historical explanation of the resort to the stamp duty? Was it, as is usually represented, an act of wanton and arbitrary encroachment; or was it the result of existing conditions, and hence susceptible of a rational explanation? Upon the answer made to this question will depend, in the last analysis, the attitude which the historian shall hold toward the charge that the British government was at the time guilty of intentional tyranny toward the colonies.

It is true that the responsible heads of the government which passed the Stamp Act emphatically disclaimed any tyrannical purpose, and gave the colonists ample notice of their intention to pass the measure and opportunity to suggest other forms of taxation. But undue weight need not be given to these immediate preliminaries. Was there anything in the past history of the relations between Great Britain and her colonies which had convinced those immediately connected with colonial administration that a revenue which should be independent of grant by the assemblies in America was necessary? There was much of that nature, and it will be revealed if the history of the efforts of Great Britain to administer colonial affairs during the period from 1690 to 1760 is ever written. To a large extent the materials for such a history still exist only in manuscript. Some of them, though in fragmentary form, have been printed in the volumes of *Records* issued by a few of the American commonwealths; but these afford only a partial view of the subject. The historian of the American colonies usually treats with considerable fulness the period of settlement; but when he reaches 1690 the current of his narrative is deflected to Canadian affairs, and he devotes himself almost exclusively to the external history of the intercolonial wars. The drudgery which is involved in the reading of manuscript and the study of printed colonial records he avoids, and thus leaves the internal development of the colonies and their relations with England for seventy years almost a total blank. He therefore approaches the consideration of the Stamp Act and of later legislation without preparation, as if nothing had occurred since Andros was driven from Boston.

In reality very much had occurred in the interval, and that of a nature to aid materially in the explanation of the policy adopted by the British government about 1760. In their efforts to administer colonial affairs, imperial officials, whether resident in England or in America, had been contending against many obstacles. These they had encountered when attempting to enforce the acts of trade, to procure money and men with reasonable promptness for defense, to secure permanent and adequate salaries, and in other lines of effort. The struggle which they carried on was incessant; and its history may be read in the dispatches which they sent home and in the reports and correspondence of the administrative boards which were concerned with colonial affairs. The complaints came not simply from customs officials, like Randolph and Quary, but from practically all the governors, the best as well as the worst. The obstacles against which they contended were partly physical, partly social and political. The remoteness of the colonies from England, the lack of any easy means of communication within and between the colonies, the sparseness and poverty of their population, created a condition of isolation and inertia which it was very difficult in any degree to overcome. That was accompanied by a spirit of independence—individual, local and colonial—which naturally repelled restraint. Even among the first generation of settlers, there were very few who had had any training in English law or administration or who sympathized to any extent with its spirit; colonists of later generations knew little of it except as an irksome restraint, and were already developing traditions of their own. In New England the spirit of Puritan independence survived in almost its original strength. That feeling was shared by dissenters of the Puritan type wherever they appeared in the colonies. The corporate colony, which in its organization and policy was practically an independent commonwealth, survived in Connecticut and Rhode Island, and formed the substratum of the governmental system of Massachusetts under the second charter. Maryland and Pennsylvania continued as proprietary provinces throughout the entire period. In the corporate colonies and proprietary provinces, as a rule, the only officials appointed by the crown and directly responsible for the maintenance of imperial interests were those connected with the admiralty courts and with the customs administration. All the rest were officials of the special jurisdiction, and, as such, pledged to uphold its interests, often to the ignoring of those of the empire. This was emphatically true of the officials in the corporate colonies, and even

Pennsylvania is not free from the charge. The home government had good reason to regard the special jurisdictions, or "proprieties," as they were called, as obstacles in the way of the imperial policy, and to desire their abolition. In the growth of large states feudal dependencies have usually been so regarded, and in the progress toward national or imperial unity they have disappeared. The advantage which in this case would come to the imperial cause by the substitution of the royal province for the special jurisdiction would consist in the addition of a royal governor, a council, a surveyor general, a receiver general and an attorney general, to the customs and admiralty officials who, under the king's patents, were already serving in the colony. In each province a complete royal executive system would thus be created, upon which the king could immediately depend for the execution of his will. It is easy, then, to see why, under the pressure of colonial administration, the special jurisdictions tended steadily to disappear and their places to be taken by royal provinces. In the early years of the eighteenth century the plan of recalling all charters by act of Parliament was seriously considered, and that policy had the uninterrupted support of the Board of Trade and of many other officials throughout the century.

There was, however, one obstacle in the way of smooth and unhindered administration which the substitution of royal provinces for special jurisdictions could not remove, and that was the assemblies—the representative element in the provincial legislatures. Through the power which they early obtained over the purse, they were able either to fix the amount of appropriation or to prevent any whatever from being made. Through them the genuine economic weakness of the colonies, their special and real interests, as well as their prejudices, found expression. The existence of assemblies, however necessary they were to the preservation of colonial interests and independence, however naturally and inevitably they found a place in the English system, greatly complicated the problem of imperial administration. The assemblies opposed, hindered, harassed the executives in very many ways and on occasions almost unnumbered. While they were, no doubt, often justified in this attitude, on many occasions their opposition was factious and unreasonable in the extreme. They often prevented, or hindered till they were useless, measures which were undoubtedly wise and advantageous; sometimes, also, they checked corruption and extravagance. Perhaps as often as otherwise the views of the assemblies were narrow, prejudiced and unstatesmanlike. They found it very difficult to think or to act continentally, and the class of men who first sought to awaken broader sympathies among them were the imperial officials. But, in spite of continuous efforts of this kind, the assemblies, even within the royal provinces, continued slowly to encroach upon the executive, till it became clear that they were the strongest element in the system.

Especially serious, under the circumstances, were the obstacles in the way of successful military administration. This involved questions of greater importance, both to the colonists and to Great Britain, than did the commercial system; for, above all things, it was desirable that the colonies should not become subject to the great rival of England. If one would grasp the significance of the colonial wars in this connection, he should study them from the point of view of imperial administration. In the first place, the mother country had been compelled to depend for the aid which she received from the colonies, whether in men or in money, on requisitions. This was, as it always must be, a slow and unsatisfactory method of procuring help: it often failed wholly or in part of its object. When the safety of a colony was not immediately imperiled or its interests involved, vexatious delays usually ensued. Though the resources of many of the colonies were at times heavily taxed for purposes of defense, and though Great Britain sometimes failed to perform the part which she had promised, the system of requisitions was too faulty to be tolerated longer than was necessary. Viewing the matter from the imperial standpoint, the proposal to secure a partial relief from it through the exercise of the power of Parliament would seem to be worthy of fair consideration, if not of approval. The experience we had of the system under the Articles of Confederation would seem at least to make that much clear.

Furthermore, the troops of the colonies, after making proper allowance for their energy and bravery, for their endurance and their skill as woodsmen, were only militia—levied for short periods, imperfectly trained, officered, armed and provisioned, not fitted for long and distant campaigns or to cope with a regular and veteran soldiery. From the very nature of the case they could never fully emerge from the condition of raw recruits and become obedient by habit. From the correspondence of Washington we obtain abundant information concerning the nature of the Virginia levies, of their discipline and of the commissary department, during the last intercolonial war. From the same source we learn still more in detail the character of the militia during the Revolution and of the provision made for their support. The competent British governors and commanders during the colonial wars held the same opinion concerning these troops, though none of them expressed himself at such length or so forcibly as did the American leader. As Washington during the war for independence desired continental levies, enlistment for long terms of service and a commissary department properly organized and supported, so British officials saw the necessity for the same thing, if they were to cope longer with the French; and they also saw that the colonies could not be depended on to provide these. This was a fair inference from past experience, and it furnished one of the strongest possible arguments for the establishment of a standing force in the colonies. In order fully to appreciate the motives which could induce the British government to resort to imperial taxation, one should study the subject of defense as a problem in administration, and thus bring the history of the intercolonial wars into its proper connection with that of colonial government. He will not proceed far before he will begin to see the immense difficulties with which Great Britain had to cope in its prolonged struggle with France. The weight of the administrative reasons for the maintenance of regular troops in the colonies will become apparent. It will be seen that this was a measure which, under the circumstances, might naturally recommend itself to any well-ordered government. As the probability was very strong that France, as soon as she was able, would attempt to recover all or a part of what she had lost, it was necessary that careful attention should still be devoted to the subject of defense, and that the years of peace following 1763 should be utilized for inaugurating reform.

Believing that the facts and arguments which we have now hastily reviewed are of such a nature as to have justified, in the minds of men who were acquainted with them, an attempt so to reform the system of colonial administration as to make it more effective for imperial purposes, we now observe that about 1760 the conditions were ripe for such an effort. During the Walpole era the officials in the colonies and many of those at home had from time to time poured their complaints into the ears of the government; but they had met with little response. Walpole was a "Little England" man, and allowed affairs in the dependencies, so far as possible, to take their own course. But during the last intercolonial war there came a reaction. The successes of that conflict caused and were accompanied by a rapid growth of imperialist sentiment in Great Britain. Naturally this was felt first and most strongly in the offices where the work of colonial administration was carried on. The officials at last saw an opportunity for the realization of their ideal—the establishment of a more perfect control over the colonies, in order that imperial interests, particularly in war, trade and finance, might be better guarded, and that the administration might be systematized. Opposition to this had never been expressed by the nation, and now the responsible leaders of the ministries were men who had been trained in the administrative offices and who were therefore committed to the policy. By the triumphs of the last war the foundations of a maritime empire seemed to have been permanently laid; and a corresponding awakening of interest in the navy, the colonies, commerce and defense was felt throughout the nation. During the war there had been greater activity in colonial administration than at any time since the reign of William III. The enthusiasm aroused by the victories of Wolfe and Clive was at its height when George III came to the throne, and he could hardly fail to sympathize with the imperialist tendencies of the time. With king, ministry and nation under the influence of this sentiment, it would have been strange if some effort had not been made to strengthen the bonds which united the dependencies to the mother country. As there was no thought of changing the nature of the colonial system, and as the official mind never contemplated the possibility of serious opposition, the procuring of a revenue by Parliamentary taxation was necessarily regarded as the first step to be taken, after which the other reforms could be carried into execution without serious hindrance from the assemblies. Professor Tyler himself admits (I, 313) that clear-headed and honest-minded

Americans might at the time have held the opinion, as they did, that the British king and Parliament could be trusted to carry through this policy without imperiling the essential political privileges of the colonists.

If now we return to the Declaration of Independence, we find that it wholly ignores the imperialist point of view, and that in it no attempt is made to account rationally or historically for the conduct of the British government. By this I mean that the events and causes which probably led to the course which the government adopted are not referred to at all. Instead, a certain number of the acts of that government are taken out of their historic setting, are charged with being usurpations and are explained on the hypothesis of a design to place the colonists under an absolute despotism. The history of the reign since its beginning is said to reveal a settled purpose to establish "an absolute tyranny over these states." The articles in this indictment are taken largely from the history ⌐ of Massachusetts since 1767. It is not stated that the most offensive acts of the British government, thus referred to, formed no part of its original intent or policy, but were occasioned by the resistance and disorder which had developed in that and other colonies. Many of the acts referred to would have been perfectly constitutional in peaceful times, and some of them the imperial government was constantly performing. But in the Declaration they are all classed together as tyrannical and despotic. Hutchinson's third volume, however, shows that in the main they are capable of a different explanation; and if the account which it contains of the controversy in Massachusetts approximates the truth—as Professor Tyler intimates, and as the original authorities prove—it will be difficult to substantiate the charges made in the Declaration. The account given of those events by Hutchinson, and the view concerning them which one must form from a dispassionate study of the contemporary documents, cannot be harmonized with the theory of their origin which is given in the Declaration. If the one be true, the other must be essentially false. But the evidence of the tyranny of the British government must be found, if found at all, in its treatment of Massachusetts between 1767 and the beginning of the war. Moreover, he who seeks for it must do so with a full knowledge of the rights of Parliament, of the objects which the British government had been seeking in and through the colonies for generations and of the rights of the executive in the royal province. The problem in Massachusetts, as elsewhere, must be viewed not alone from the colonial, but as well from the imperial standpoint, and especially with an understanding of what the old British colonial system really was. That will not be possible until the early eighteenth century shall be studied much more thoroughly than it ever has been. Equal attention and care should be bestowed on the internal development of the colonies, on their institutions and their political conflicts, particularly on the social and political tendencies within them toward independence. It will then be seen that our early history had an imperial or British side, as well as a colonial or American side—that for two centuries the course we took was the resultant of forces coming from both these directions. But by far the strongest forces to which our ancestors were subjected were those of the New World. The consideration of these will lead the student to give due weight to colonial interests and demands; but, if he is loyal to truth, it must be in a spirit very different from the fervid radicalism of Jefferson.

CHARLES M. ANDREWS
The American Revolution: An Interpretation

🔲 Charles Andrews, the doyen of the imperial school, author of the classic four-volume study of *The Colonial Period of American History,* wrote with a superb if, perhaps, by our standards an overrounded style. Drawing on a wider acquaintance with British history and with a finer command of language than Osgood, his articles remain testaments to a point of view, rather than shop windows to show the processes whereby he reached it. He could indeed occasionally be petulant, as when he discussed the Beardian school in Volume IV of his *Colonial Period:*

> Writers of the economic determinist school, who of late years have been reviving a faith in the economic interpretation of history and seeking a place in the historical sunshine, believe that the Revolution was either an attempt of "the American merchant and planter-capitalism" to obtain "release from the fetters of the English Mercantile System" (Hacker, *The First American Revolution* and *A Graphic History*) or a movement "to free [America] from the colonial ban upon her industries" (Beard, *A History of the Business Man*).
>
> These and other similar theses can be maintained only by a system of clever, ingenious, and seemingly plausible but really superficial manipulations of fact and logic in the interest of a preconceived theory; by generalizations based on the grouping of occasional and widely scattered data; and by dependence on the statements of secondary authorities— statements frequently unfortified by proof and sometimes demonstrably untrue. . . .
>
> One may not doubt that behind the effort to obtain self-government and freedom from the restraints of British control there lay factors that were commercial, financial, legal, social, and industrial. But no one of these by itself would have brought on the Revolution. It is too great a simplification of history to regard the events of the past as nothing

but a struggle of classes, a clash of economic interests, for such an oversimplification of the problem leads inevitably to an oversimplified solution. No amount of study of the social side of colonial life—much vaunted today as if it were something new—will explain the events of 1775 and 1776. . . .

Modern industrialism would seem to be responsible for these latter-day attempts to interpret the past in the light of the present and to apply the Marxian doctrine that social progress is the outcome of class conflict and of nothing else.

But Andrews has left an imperishable record of scholarly writing behind him, and he wielded great influence. His presidential address to the American Historical Association in 1925, printed in *The American Historical Review* in 1926, has become the classic summary of the viewpoint of his "school." It has the quality of mature professionalism and all the grace of the best New England writing.

Andrews accepts Schlesinger's view that the Revolution arose from a conflict of interests, not a debate over rights. Colonial rights were a "subject of more or less legal and metaphysical speculation. . . . There is nothing to show that the somewhat precise and finely sprung reasoning of these intellectual leaders had any marked influence on the popular mind." * Equally, he admits that though there never was, *pace* Bancroft, a firm and binding mercantile system in operation, yet certainly until 1763 and perhaps until 1767 it was beneficial both to colony and mother country. The first colonial protests were designed simply to secure a redress of grievances, and no more. By and after 1770, however, it is the constitutional claim that comes to dominate the scene; freedom from outside control becomes the real objective. "Primarily, the American Revolution was a political and constitutional movement and only secondarily one that was either financial, commercial, or social. At bottom the fundamental issue was the political independence of the Colonies, and in the last analysis the conflict lay between the British Parliament and the Colonial assemblies, each of which was probably more sensitive, self-conscious, and self-important than was the voting population that it represented." The colonial assemblies were in process of becoming miniature parliaments. It was primarily a political revolution.

THAT THE IMPACT of convictions is one of the most frequent causes of revolution we must acknowledge; and I believe that we have not considered sufficiently the importance of this fact in determining the relations of England with colonial America. If I may, by way of illus-

---

* *The Colonial Background of the American Revolution* (New Haven, 1924), p. 135.

Reprinted by permission from the *American Historical Review*, XXXI (1926), 219-232.

trating my point, I should like to show that certain differences existing between England and her colonies in mental attitudes and convictions proved in the end more difficult to overcome than the diverging historical tendencies or the bridging the three thousand miles of the Atlantic itself. . . .

The middle period of the eighteenth century in England, resembling in some respects the mid-Victorian era of the next century, was intellectually, socially, and institutionally in a state of stable equilibrium. The impulses of the Revolution of 1689 had spent their force. English thought and life was tending to become formal, conventional, and artificial, and the English mind was acquiring the fatal habit of closing against novelty and change. The most enlightened men of the day regarded the existing order as the best that could be conceived, and in the main were content to let well enough alone. Those who held the reins of power were comfortable and irresponsible, steeped in their "old vulgar prejudices," and addicted to habits and modes of living that were approved by age and precedent. . . . Vested interests and the rights of property were deemed of greater importance than the rights of humanity, and society clung tenaciously to the old safeguards and defenses that checked the inrush of new ideas. There was a great absence of interest in technical invention and improvement. Because the landed classes were in the ascendant, agriculture was the only national interest receiving attention—drainage, rotation of crops, and the treatment of the soil being the only practical activities that attracted capital. The concerns and welfare of those without the right to vote were largely ignored; and it is no mere coincidence that the waste of human life, which was at its worst in London between 1720 and 1750, with the population of England declining during that period, should not have been checked until after 1780. The age was not one of progress in government, social organization, or humanitarianism; and it is important to note that the reconstruction of English manners and ways of living, and the movement leading to the diminution of crime, to sanitation, the greater abundance of food, and amelioration of living conditions—particularly in the towns and among the poorer classes—came after, and not before, the American Revolution.

The state of mind, to which were due the conditions thus described, permeated all phases of British life and government, and determined the attitude of the ruling classes toward the political, as well as the social, order. These classes were composed in a preponderant degree of landed proprietors, whose feeling of feudal superiority and tenacious adherence to the ideas and traditions of their class were determining factors in political life both in Parliament and the country. They believed that their institutions provided a sufficient panacea for all constitutional ills and could not imagine wherein these institutions needed serious revision. They were convinced that the existing system preserved men's liberties better than any that had gone before, and they wanted no experiments or dangerous leaps in the dark. They not only held as a tenet of faith that those who owned the land should wield political power, but they were certain that such an arrangement had the sanction of God. They revered the British system of government, its principles and philosophy, as the embodiment of human wisdom, grounded in righteousness and destined by nature to serve the purpose of man. . . .

Nor were they any less rigid in their attitude toward the colonies in America. Colonial policy had developed very slowly and did not take on systematic form until well on in the eighteenth century; but when once it became defined, the ruling classes regarded it in certain fundamental aspects—at least in official utterance—as fixed as was the constitution itself. At first England did not take her colonies seriously as assets of commercial importance, but when after 1704 naval stores were added to the tobacco and sugar of Virginia and the West Indies, and it was seen that these commodities enabled England to obtain a favorable balance of trade with European countries, the value of the plantations in British eyes increased enormously. However, it was not until after 1750, when a favorable balance of trade was reached with the colonies themselves, that the mercantilist deemed the situation entirely satisfactory; and from that time on for twenty years—epochal years in the history of England's relations with America—the mercantilist idea of the place that a colony should occupy in the British scheme of things became fixed and unalterable. Though the colonies were growing by leaps and bounds, the authorities in Great Britain retained unchanged the policy which had been adopted more than half a century before. They did not essentially alter the instructions to the Board of Trade in all the eighty-six years of its existence. They created no true colonial secretary, even in 1768, and no department of any kind at any time for the exclusive oversight of American affairs. They saw no necessity for adopting new methods of managing colonial trade, even though the colonial situation was constantly presenting new problems for solution. Manufacturing was undoubtedly more discouraged in 1770 than it had been in 1699, when the first restrictive act was passed; and the idea that the colonies by their very nature were ordained to occupy a position of commercial dependence to the advantage and profit of the mother country was never more firmly fixed in the British mind than just before our Revolution. In fact, that event altered in no essential particular the British conception of the status of a colony, for as late as 1823, Sir Charles Ellis, undoubtedly voicing the opinion of his day, could say in Parliament that the colonial system of England had not been established for the sake of the colonies, but for the encouragement of British trade and manufactures. Thus for more than a century England's idea of what a colony should be underwent no important alteration whatever.

Equally unchangeable was the British idea of how a colony should be governed. In the long list of commissions and instructions drawn up in England for the guidance of the royal governors in America, there is to be found, with one exception only, nothing that indicates any progressive advance in the spirit and method of administration from 1696 to

1782. Year after year, the same arrangements and phraseology appear, conforming to a common type, admitting, it is true, important modifications in matters of detail, but in principle undergoing at no time in eighty-six years serious revision or reconstruction. These documents were drawn up in Whitehall according to a fixed pattern; the governors and councils were allowed no discretion; the popular assemblies were confined within the narrow bounds of inelastic formulae, which repeated, time after time, the same injunctions and the same commands; while the crown reserved to itself the full right of interference in all matters that were construed as coming under its prerogative. These instructions represented the rigid eighteenth-century idea of how a colony should be retained in dependence on the mother country. And what was true of the instructions was true of other documents also that had to do with America. For instance, the lists of queries to the governors, the questionnaires to the commodore-governors of the Newfoundland fishery, and the whole routine business of the fishery itself had become a matter of form and precedent, as conventional and stereotyped as were the polite phrases of eighteenth-century social intercourse. Rarely was any attempt made to adapt these instructions to the needs of growing communities such as the colonies were showing themselves to be; and only with the Quebec instructions of 1775, issued after the passage of the Quebec Act and under the guidance of a colonial governor of unusual common-sense, was there any recognition of a new colonial situation. In this document, which appeared at the very end of our colonial period, we do find something of a break from the stiff and legalistic forms that were customary in the earlier royal instructions, some appreciation of the fact that the time was approaching when a colony should be treated with greater liberality and be allowed to have some part in saying how it should be administered.

Without going further with our analysis we can say that during the half-century preceding our Revolution English habits of thought and methods of administration and government, both at home and in the colonies, had reached a state of immobility. To all appearances the current of the national life had settled into a backwater, and as far as home affairs were concerned was seemingly becoming stagnant. At a time when Pitt was breaking France by land and sea, and men on waking were asking what new territories had been added during the night to the British dominions, occurrences at home were barren of adventure, either in society or politics. Ministers were not true statesmen; they had no policies, no future hopes, no spirit of advance, no gifts of foresight or prophecy. In all that concerned domestic interests, they were impervious to suggestions, even when phrased in the eloquence of Pitt and Burke. They wanted no change in existing conditions; their eyes were fixed on traditions and precedents rather than on the obligations and opportunities of the future. Their tenure of office was characterized by inactivity, a casual handling of situations they did not understand and could not control, and a willingness to let the ship of state drift for itself. As a modern critic has said, they were always turning in an unending circle, one out, one in, one in, one out, marking time and never going forward.

To a considerable extent the narrow point of view and rigidity of attitude exhibited by the men who held office at Whitehall or sat in Parliament at Westminster can be explained by the fact that at this time officials and members of Parliament were also territorial magnates, lords of manors, and country squires, who were influenced in their political life by ideas that governed their relations with their tenantry and the management of their landed estates. It is not necessary to think of them as bought by king or ministers and so bound and gagged against freedom of parliamentary action. In fact, they were bound and gagged already by devotion to their feudal privileges, their family prerogatives, and their pride of landed proprietorship. They viewed the colonies somewhat in the light of tenancies of the crown, and as they themselves lived on the rents from their estates, so they believed that the king and the kingdom should profit from the revenues and returns from America. The point of view was somewhat that of a later Duke of Newcastle, who when reproached for compelling his tenants to vote as he pleased said that he had a right to do as he liked with his own. This landed aristocracy reflected the eighteenth-century spirit. It was sonorous, conventional, and self-satisfied, and shameless of sparkle or humor. It clung to the laws of inheritance and property, fearful of anything that might in any way offend the shades of past generations. In its criticism of the manners of others it was insular and arrogant, and was mentally so impenetrable as never to understand why any one, even in the colonies, should wish things to be other than they were or refuse to accept the station of life to which by Providence he had been called.

A government, representative of a privileged social and political order that took existing conditions as a matter of course, setting nature at defiance and depending wholly on art, was bound sooner or later to come into conflict with a people, whose life in America was in closest touch with nature and characterized by growth and change and constant readjustments. In that country were groups of men, women, and children, the greater portion of whom were of English ancestry, numbering at first a few hundreds and eventually more than two millions, who were scattered over many miles of continent and island and were living under various forms of government. These people, more or less unconsciously, under the influence of new surroundings and imperative needs, were establishing a new order of society and laying the foundations of a new political system. The story of how this was done—how that which was English slowly and imperceptibly merged into that which was American—has never been adequately told; but it is a fascinating phase of history, more interesting and enlightening when studied against the English background than when construed as an American problem only. It is the story of the gradual elimination of those elements, feudal and pro-prietary, that were foreign to the normal life of a frontier land, and of the gradual adjustment of the colonists to the restraints and restrictions that were imposed upon them by the commercial policy of the mother country. It is the story also of the growth of the colonial assemblies and of the education and experience that the colonists were receiving in the art of political self-government. It is above all—and no phase of colonial history is of greater significance—the story of the gradual transformation of these assemblies from the provincial councils that the home government intended them to be into miniature parliaments. At the end of a long struggle with the prerogative and other forms of outside interference, they emerged powerful legislative bodies, as self-conscious in their way as the House of Commons in England was becoming during the same eventful years.

Here was an *impasse,* for the British view that a colonial assembly partook of the character of a provincial or municipal council was never actually true of any assembly in British America at any time in its history. From the beginning, each of these colonial bodies, in varying ways and under varying circumstances, assumed a position of leadership in its colony, and exercised, in a manner often as bewildering to the student of to-day as to an eighteenth-century royal governor, a great variety of executive, legislative, and judicial functions. Except in Connecticut and Rhode Island, requests for parliamentary privileges were made very early and were granted year after year by the governors—privileges that were essentially those of the English and Irish Houses of Commons and were consciously modeled after them. At times, the assemblies went beyond Parliament and made claims additional to the usual speaker's requests, claims first asked for as matters of favor but soon demanded as matters of right, as belonging to representative bodies and not acquired by royal gift or favor. One gets the impression that though the assemblies rarely failed to make the formal request, they did so with the intention of taking in any case what they asked for and anything more that they could secure. Gradually, with respect to privileges, they advanced to a position of amazing independence, freeing themselves step by step from the interfering power of the executive, that is, of the royal prerogative. They began to talk of these rights as ancient and inherent and necessary to the orderly existence of any representative body, and they became increasingly self-assertive and determined as the years passed.

Nor was this the only change affecting the assemblies to which the eighteenth-century Englishman was asked to adapt himself. The attitude of the assemblies in America found expression in the exercise of powers that had their origin in other sources than that of parliamentary privilege. They adopted rules of their own, that were sometimes even more severe than those of Parliament itself. They regulated membership, conduct, and procedure; ruled against drinking, smoking, and profanity, against unseemly, unnecessary, and tedious debate, against absence, tardiness, and other forms of evasion. They punished with great severity all infringement of rules and acts of contempt, and defended their right to do so against the governor and council on one side and the courts of the colony on the other. Nor did they even pretend to be consistent in their opposition to the royal prerogative, as expressed in the instructions to the royal governors, and in their maneuvers they did not follow any uniform policy or plan. They conformed to these instructions willingly enough, whenever it was agreeable for them to do so; but if at any time they considered an instruction contrary to the best interest of a particular colony, they did not hesitate to oppose it directly or to nullify it by avoidance. In general, it may be said that they evaded or warded off or deliberately disobeyed such instructions as they did not like. Thus both consciously and unconsciously they were carving out a *lex parliamenti* of their own, which, evolving naturally from the necessity of meeting the demands of self-governing communities, carried them beyond the bounds of their own membership and made them responsible for the welfare of the colony at large.

The important point to remember is that the plan of governmental control as laid down in England was never in accord with the actual situation in America; that the Privy Council, the Secretary of State, and the Board of Trade seem not to have realized that their system of colonial administration was breaking down at every point. Their minds ran in a fixed groove and they could construe the instance of colonial disobedience and aggression, which they often noted, in no other terms than those of persistent dereliction of duty. Either they did not see or else refused to see the wide divergence that was taking place between colonial administration as they planned it and colonial administration as the colonists were working it out. Englishmen saw in the American claims an attack upon an old, established, and approved system. They interpreted the attitude of the colonists as something radical and revolutionary, menacing British prosperity, British political integrity, and the British scheme of colonial government. Opposed by tradition and conviction to new experiments, even at home, they were unable to sympathize with, or even to understand, the great experiment, one of the greatest in the world's history, on trial across the sea. There in America was evolving a new idea of sovereignty, inherent not in crown and Parliament but in the people of a state, based on the principle— self-evident it may be to us today but not to the Englishman of the eighteenth century—that governments derive their just powers from the consent of the governed. There was emerging a new idea of the franchise, as a natural right, under certain conditions, of every adult citizen, an idea which theoretically is not even yet accepted in Great Britain. There was being established a new order of society, without caste or privilege, free from economic restrictions and social demarcations between class and class. There was taking shape a new idea of a colony, a self-governing dominion, the members of which were competent to develop along their own lines, while working together with the mother country as part of a common state.

For us to-day with our perspective it is easy to see the conflict approaching and some of us may think perhaps that the British ministers and members of Parliament ought to have realized that their own ideas

and systems were fast outgrowing their usefulness even for Great
Britain herself; and that their inflexible views of the colonial relationship
were fast leading to disaster. Yet we must keep in mind that it is always
extraordinarily difficult for a generation reared in the environment of
modern democracy to deal sympathetically with the Englishman's point
of view in the eighteenth century, or to understand why the ruling
classes of that day so strenuously opposed the advance of liberalism both
in England and America. The fact remains, however, that the privileged
and governing classes in England saw none of these things. They were
too close to events and too much a part of them to judge them dispas-
sionately or to appreciate their real significance. These classes, within
which we may well include the Loyalists in America, were possessed of
inherited instincts, sentiments, and prejudices which they could no more
change than they could have changed the color of their eyes or the
texture of their skins. That which existed in government and society
was to them a part of the fixed scheme of nature, and no more called
for reconsideration than did the rising of the sun or the budding of
the trees in spring. If Lord North had granted the claims of the colonists
he probably would have been looked on by Parliament as having betrayed
the constitution and impaired its stability, just as Peel was pilloried by
a similar landowning Parliament in 1845, when he advocated the repeal
of the corn laws. One has only to read the later debates on the subject
of enclosures and the corn laws to understand the attitude of the British
landowners toward the colonies from 1763 to 1776. To them in each
instance it seemed as if the foundations of the universe were breaking
up and the world in which they lived was sinking beneath their feet.

Primarily, the American Revolution was a political and constitutional
movement and only secondarily one that was either financial, commercial,
or social. At bottom the fundamental issue was the political independence
of the colonies, and in the last analysis the conflict lay between the
British Parliament and the colonial assemblies, each of which was probably more sensitive, self-conscious, and self-important than was the voting
population that it represented. For many years these assemblies had
fought the prerogative successfully and would have continued to do so,
eventually reducing it to a minimum, as the later self-governing dominions have done; but in the end it was Parliament, whose powers they
disputed, that became the great antagonist. Canning saw the situation
clearly when, half a century later, he spoke of the Revolution as having
been a test of the equality of strength "between the legislature of this
mighty kingdom . . . and the colonial assemblies," adding further that
he had no intention of repeating in the case of Jamaica, the colony then
under debate, the mistakes that had been made in 1776. Of the mistakes
to which he referred the greatest was the employment of the deadly
expedient of coercion, and he showed his greater wisdom when he
determined, as he said, to keep back "within the penetralia of the
constitution the transcendental powers of Parliament over a dependency
of the British crown" and not "to produce it upon trifling occasions or

in cases of petty refractoriness and temporary misconduct." How he would have met the revolution in America, based as it was on "the fundamental principles of political liberty," we cannot say; but we know that he had no sympathy with any attempt to force opinion back into paths that were outworn. That he would have foreseen the solution of a later date and have granted the colonies absolute and responsible self-government, recognizing the equality of the assemblies in domestic matters and giving them the same control over their home affairs as the people of Great Britain had over theirs, can be conjectured only by inference from his liberal attitude toward the South American republics. He stood half-way between the ministers of the Revolutionary period—blind, sensitive, and mentally unprogressive—and the statesmen of the middle of the nineteenth century, who were willing to follow the lead of those courageous and far-sighted Englishmen who saved the empire from a second catastrophe after 1830 and were the founders of the British colonial policy of today.

The revolt of the colonies from Great Britain began long before the battles of Moore's Creek Bridge and Lexington; before the time of James Otis and the writs of assistance; before the dispute over the appointment of judges in North Carolina and New York; before the eloquence of Patrick Henry was first heard in the land; and even before the quarrel in Virginia over the Dinwiddie pistole fee. These were but the outward and visible signs of an inward and factual divergence. The separation from the mother country began just as soon as the mercantile system of commercial control, the governmental system of colonial administration, and the whole doctrine of the inferior status of a colonial assembly began to give way before the pressure exerted and the disruptive power exercised by these young and growing colonial communities. New soil had produced new wants, new desires, new points of view, and the colonists were demanding the right to live their own lives in their own way. As we see it to-day the situation was a dramatic one. On one side was the immutable, stereotyped system of the mother country, based on precedent and tradition and designed to keep things comfortably as they were; on the other, a vital, dynamic organism, containing the seed of a great nation, its forces untried, still to be proved. It is inconceivable that a connection should have continued long between two such yoke-fellows, one static, the other dynamic, separated by an ocean and bound only by the ties of a legal relationship.

If my diagnosis is correct of the British state of mind in the eighteenth century, and the evidence in its favor seems overwhelming, then the colonists were as justified in their movement of revolt as were the Englishmen themselves in their movement for reform in the next century. Yet in reality no great progressive movement needs justification at our hands, for great causes justify themselves and time renders the decision. The revolt in America and the later reforms in Great Britain herself were directed against the same dominant ruling class that in their colonial relations as well as in their social and political arrangements at home preferred that the world in which they lived should remain as it was. Reform or revolt is bound to follow attempts of a privileged class to conduct affairs according to unchanging rules and formula. The colonies had developed a constitutional organization equally complete with Britain's own and one that in principle was far in advance of the British system, and they were qualified to co-operate with the mother country on terms similar to those of a brotherhood of free nations such as the British world is becoming today. But England was unable to see this fact or unwilling to recognize it, and consequently America became the scene of a political unrest, which might have been controlled by compromise, but was turned to revolt by coercion. The situation is a very interesting one, for England is famous for her ability to compromise at critical moments in her history. For once at least she failed. In 1832 and later years, when she faced other great constitutional crises at home and in her colonies, she saved herself from revolution by understanding the situation and adjusting herself to it. Progress may be stemmed for a time, but it cannot be permanently stopped by force. A novelist has expressed the idea in saying: "You cannot fight and beat revolutions as you can fight and beat nations. You can kill a man, but you simply can't kill a rebel. For the proper rebel has an ideal of living, while your ideal is to kill him so that you may preserve yourself. And the reason why no revolution or religion has ever been beaten is that rebels die for something worth dying for, the future, but their enemies die only to preserve the past, and makers of history are always stronger than makers of empire." The American revolutionists had an ideal of living; it can hardly be said that in 1776 the Englishmen of the ruling classes were governed in their colonial relations by any ideals that were destined to be of service to the future of the human race.

LAWRENCE HENRY GIPSON
The American Revolution as an Aftermath of the Great War for the Empire, 1754-1763

The *ne plus ultra* of the imperialist view was reached in the magnificently cast project of Lawrence H. Gipson, *The British Empire Before the American Revolution* (1936-   ). In his range and quality and attitude, Gipson has something of the spirit of Parkman, though without his Churchillian majesty of language. Superficially put and oversimplified, Gipson's view is that Wolfe's victory in 1759 and the cession of Canada by France to Britain in 1763 brought into sharp contrast two distinct societies—the British (including her colonies in and beyond the North American continent) and the French. Faced with new problems of defense and administration, the British government sought new devices to raise money, including a Sugar Act and a Stamp Act. Defense was primary and the colonists should make some contribution to it. With this a frontier-line concept was also introduced. But with the removal of the French threat—even if it was replaced by the perhaps less imperial, but, to the colonists, equally menacing threats of the Indians—a new situation arose in the mainland colonies. Here—though not elsewhere—came a sense of distinctness, a sharp response to irritations, a capacity for political action out of which a new nation was born. Professor Gipson's viewpoint ranges over the seven seas, and the twelve volumes of his saga thus far written are splendid history, written not from a colonial, and not even from a London, but from a global point of view.   回

GREAT WARS in modern times have too frequently been the breeders of revolution. The exhausting armed struggles in which France became engaged in the latter half of the eighteenth century led as directly to the French Revolution as did the First World War to the Russian Revolution; it may be said as truly that the American Revolution was an aftermath of the Anglo-French conflict in the New World carried on between 1754 and 1763. This is by no means to deny that other factors were involved in the launching of these revolutionary movements. Before proceeding with an analysis of the theme of this paper, however, it would be well to consider the wording of the title given to it.

Words may be used to disguise or to distort facts as well as to clarify them, but the chief task of the historian is to illuminate the past. He is faced, therefore, with the responsibility of using only such words as will achieve this broad objective of his calling and to reject those that obscure or defeat it. For this reason "the French and Indian War," as a term descriptive of the conflict to which we have just referred, has been avoided in this essay as well as in the writer's series on the *British Empire before the American Revolution*. This has been done in spite of the fact that the term has been employed by most Americans ever since the early days of our Republic and that it therefore has the sanction of long usage—not to mention the sanction of American national tradition, which assigns to the revolt of the thirteen colonies a position of such commanding importance that all other events in American history, both preceding and following it, have been quite subordinated to the War for Independence. In contrast to this traditional interpretation of our history one may affirm that the Anglo-French conflict settled nothing less than the incomparably vital question as to what civilization—what complex cultural patterns, what political institutions—would arise in the

Reprinted by permission from the *Political Science Quarterly*, LXV (1950), 86-104, with minor revisions by the author.

great Mississippi basin and the valleys of the rivers draining it, a civilization, whatever it might be, surely destined to expand to the Pacific seaboard and finally to dominate the North American continent. The
determination of this crucial issue is perhaps the most momentous event
in the life of the English-speaking people in the New World and quite
overshadows in importance both the Revolutionary War and the later
Civil War, events which, it is quite clear, were each contingent upon
the outcome of the earlier crisis.

A struggle of such proportions, involving tremendous stakes, deserves
a name accurately descriptive of its place in the history of the English-
speaking people, and the title "the French and Indian War," as suggested,
in no way fulfills this need. For the war was not, as the name would
seem to imply, a conflict largely between English and French New
World colonials and their respective Indian allies, nor was it localized
in North America to the extent that the name would appear to indicate.
On the contrary, the conflict which extended both before and after an
open declaration of war, was waged by the British and French nations
with all their resources for nine years on three oceans, and much of
the land washed by their waters; it ultimately brought in both Spain,
allied to France, and Portugal, allied to Great Britain. While it involved,
it is true, as the name would connote, wilderness fighting, yet of equal,
if not greater, importance in assessing the final outcome was the pouring
forth of Britain's financial resources in a vast program of shipbuilding,
in the equipping and support of the British and colonial armies and
the royal navy, and in the subsidization of allies on the European continent and of the colonies in America. If it also involved the reduction
of the fortress of Louisbourg, Fort Niagara, Fort Duquesne, Quebec and
Montreal in North America—each in turn to fall to British regulars
aided by American provincial troops—these highly significant successes
were, in fact, really contingent upon the resounding British naval victories
in the Mediterranean, off the Strait of Gibraltar, in the Bay of Biscay,
and elsewhere. For it was these successes of the British navy that brought
about the virtual extinction of the French navy and merchant marine and
thereby presented to France—seeking to supply her forces in Canada and
elsewhere with adequate reinforcements and matériel—a logistical problem so insoluble as to spell the doom of her North American empire
and of her possessions in India and elsewhere.

If the term "the French and Indian War" meets none of the requirements of accurate historical nomenclature, neither does the term "the
Seven Years' War"—a name appropriately enough employed by historians
to designate the mighty conflict that raged for seven years in Germany
before its conclusion in the Treaty of Hubertusburg in 1763. The prin-
cipals in this war were Prussia, allied with Great Britain, Hanover,
Brunswick and Hesse, facing Austria, most of the Holy Roman Empire,
Russia and Sweden, all allied with France and receiving subsidies from
her. Although George II, as King of Great Britain and Elector of
Hanover, in the treaty of 1758 with Frederick of Prussia, promised not

to conclude peace without mutual agreement with the latter, and although large subsidies were annually paid to Prussia as well as to the other continental allies out of the British treasury and troops were also sent to Germany, it must be emphasized that these aids were designed primarily for the protection of the King's German Electorate. In other words, the British alliance in no way supported the objectives of the Prussian King, when he suddenly began the German war in 1756 by invading Saxony—two years after the beginning of the Anglo-French war. In this connection it should be borne in mind that throughout the Seven Years' War in Germany Great Britain remained at peace with both Russia and Sweden and refused therefore to send a fleet into the Baltic in spite of the demands of Frederick that this be done; nor were British land troops permitted to assist him against Austria, but only to help form a protective shield for Hanover against the thrusts of the French armies. For the latter were determined not only to overrun the Electorate—something that they succeeded in doing—but to hold it as a bargaining point to be used at the conclusion of hostilities with Great Britain, a feat, however, beyond their power of accomplishment. Closely related and intertwined as were the two wars, they were, nevertheless, distinct in their beginning and distinct in their termination.

Indeed, while British historians at length were led to adopt the nomenclature applied by German and other continental historians to all hostilities that took place between 1754 and 1763 in both the Old and New Worlds, American historians, by and large in the past, have rejected, and rightly so, it seems, the name "the Seven Years' War" to designate specifically the struggle during these years in North America with the fate of that continent at stake; so likewise many of them have rejected, as equally inadmissible, the name "the French and Indian War." Instead, the late Professor Osgood employed the title "the Fourth Intercolonial War," surely not a good one; George Bancroft called the war "the American Revolution: First Phase," still more inaccurate in some respects than the names he sought to avoid; Francis Parkman, with the flair of a romanticist, was at first inclined to call it "the Old French War" but finally, under the influence of the great-man-in-history thesis, gave to his two remarkable volumes concerned with it the totally misleading name, *Montcalm and Wolfe;* finally, John Fiske, the philosopher-historian, as luminous in his views as he was apt to be careless in the details of historical scholarship, happily fastened upon the name "the Great War." In the series on the *British Empire before the American Revolution* the writer has built upon Fiske's title and has called it "the Great War for the Empire" in order to emphasize not only the fact that the war was a very great conflict both in its scope and in its lasting effects, as Fiske saw with clearness, but also that, as a war entered into specifically for the defense of the British Empire, it was by far the most important ever waged by Great Britain to this end.

It may be pointed out that later charges, especially by American writers, that the war was begun by Great Britain with less **worthy** motives in mind, are not supported by the great mass of state papers and the private correspondence of British statesmen responsible for making the weighty decisions at the time. The writer has attempted to analyze in detail these materials, now available to the student, in the two volumes of his series that appeared under the title of *Zones of International Friction, 1748-1754*. In other words, the idea that the war was started as the result of European balance-of-power politics or by British mercantilists for the purpose of destroying a commercial rival and for conquering Canada and the French West Indies, and for expelling the French from India, rather than for the much more limited and legitimate objective of affording the colonies—and particularly the new province of Nova Scotia and the Old Dominion of Virginia—protection against the aggressive aims of France, must be dismissed by students brought face to face with impressive evidence to the contrary.

The development of the war into one for the military mastery of the North American continent came with the growing conviction on the part of the British ministers that nothing short of this drastic step would realize the primary aims of the government, once it had reached the determination to respond to the appeals from the colonies for assistance and to challenge the right of French troops to be planted well within the borders of the Nova Scotia peninsula and at the forks of the Ohio. One may go as far as to state that the acquisition of Canada—as an objective sought by mercantilists to contribute to the wealth of Great Britain—would have seemed fantastic to any contemporary who had the slightest knowledge of the tremendous financial drain that that great possession had been on the treasury of the French King for over a century before 1754. Moreover, the motives that ultimately led, after much searching of heart, to its retention after its conquest by Great Britain were not commercial but strategic and had primarily in view the general security and welfare of the older American colonies.

In view of these facts, not to be confused with surmises, the name "the Great War for the Empire" seems to the writer not only appropriate but, among all the names heretofore applied to the war in question, by far the most suitable that can be used by anyone concerned with the history of the old British Empire, who seeks earnestly to maintain that standard of exactness in terminology and scholarship in general which the public has a right to demand of him.

The description just given of the motives that led to the Great War for the Empire, nevertheless, runs counter, as suggested, to American national tradition and most history that has been written in harmony with it by American historians. This tradition had a curious beginning. It arose partly out of Pitt's zealous efforts to energize the colonies to prosecute the war most actively; but there also was another potent factor involved in its creation. Before the conclusion of hostilities in 1763 certain powerful commercial interests—centered particularly at Newport, Rhode Island, Boston, New York City, and to a less extent in Philadelphia—in a desire to continue an enormously lucrative trade with the

French West Indies, and therefore with the enemy, all in the face of Pitt's determination to keep supplies from the French armed forces operating in the New World, began to express themselves in terms that implied that the war was peculiarly Great Britain's war and only incidentally one that concerned her colonies and that the French, really friendly to the aspirations of British colonials, were opposed only to the mercantilistic ambitions of the mother country. By 1766—just twelve years after the beginning of the war and three years after its termination —this extraordinary tradition had become so well established that Benjamin Franklin, astonishingly enough, could actually assert in his examination before a committee of the House of Commons:

> I know the last war is commonly spoke of here as entered into for the defence, or for the sake of the people of America; I think it is quite misunderstood. It began about the limits between Canada and Nova Scotia, about territories to which the crown indeed laid claim, but were not claimed by any British colony. . . . We had therefore no particular concern or interest in that dispute. As to the Ohio, the contest there began about your right of trading in the Indian country, a right you had by the Treaty of Utrecht, which the French infringed . . . they took a fort which a company of your merchants, and their factors and correspondents, had erected there to secure that trade. Braddock was sent with an army to retake that fort . . . and to protect your trade. It was not until after his defeat that the colonies were attacked. They were before in perfect peace with both French and Indians. . . .

By the beginning of 1768 the tradition had been so extended that John Dickinson—voicing the popular American view in his highly important *Letters from a Farmer in Pennsylvania.* No. VIII—felt that he not only could affirm, as did Franklin, that the war was strictly Britain's war and fought for selfish purposes, but could even insist that the acquisition of territory in North America as the result of it "is greatly injurious to these colonies" and that they therefore were not under the slightest obligation to the mother country.

But to return to the last phases of the Great War for the Empire. The British customs officials—spurred into unusual activity in the face of Pitt's demand for the strict enforcement of the Trade and Navigation Acts in order to break up the pernicious practice of bringing aid and comfort to the enemy—were led to employ writs of assistance for the purpose of laying their hands upon goods landed in American ports and secured in exchange for American provisions sent for the most part either directly or indirectly to the French ·West Indies. Although the British Empire was in the midst of hostilities, most of the merchants in Boston showed bitter opposition to the writs and gave ardent support to James Otis' declaration made in open court in 1761 that Parliament was powerless to extend the use of these writs to America, whatever its constitutional authority might be in Great Britain. The importance of this declaration lies not so much in its immediate effect but rather in the fact that it was indicative of the line of attack that would be followed during the developing crisis not only by Otis but also by the Adamses, Hawley, Hancock, and other popular leaders in the Bay colony as they laid down constitutional restrictions upon the power of Parliament to legislate for America. Further, it is clear that, even before the Great War for the Empire had been terminated, there were those in the province who had begun to view Great Britain as the real enemy rather than France.

Just as clearly related to the war under consideration as was the issue over writs of assistance was that growing out of the twopenny acts of the Virginia Assembly. In search of funds for maintaining the frontier defensive forces under the command of Colonel George Washington, the Assembly was led to pass in 1755 and 1758 those highly questionable laws as favorable to the tobacco planters as they were indefensibly unjust to the clergy. Even assuming the fact that these laws were war measures, and therefore in a sense emergency measures, it was inconceivable that the Privy Council would permit so palpable a violation of contractual relations as they involved. The royal disallowance of the laws in question opened the way for Patrick Henry, the year that hostilities were terminated by the Peace of Paris, to challenge in the Louisa County courthouse the right of the King in Council to refuse approval to a law passed by a colonial assembly—a good law in the judgment of the colony—and to affirm that such refusal was nothing less than an act of tyranny on the part of the King. It was thus resentment at the overturning of Virginia war legislation that led to this attack upon the judicial authority of review by the Crown—an authority exercised previously without serious protest for over a century. It should also be noted that the Henry thesis helped to lay the foundation for the theory of the equality of colonial laws with those passed by Parliament, a theory of the constitution of the empire that most American leaders in 1774 had come to accept in arguing that if the King could no longer exercise a veto over the acts of the legislature of Great Britain, it was unjust that he should do so over those of the colonial assemblies.

But the most fateful aftermath of the Great War for the Empire, with respect to the maintenance of the historic connection between the mother country and the colonies, grew out of the problem of the control and support of the vast trans-Appalachian interior, the right to which was now confirmed by treaty to Great Britain, as well as of the new acquisitions in North America secured from France and Spain. Under the terms of the royal Proclamation of 1763, French Canada to the east of the Great Lakes was organized as the Province of Quebec; most of old Spanish Florida became the Province of East Florida; and those areas, previously held by Spain as well as by France to the west of the Apalachicola and to the east of New Orleans and its immediate environs, became the Province of West Florida. The Proclamation indicated that proper inducement would be offered British and other Protestants to establish themselves in the new provinces. With respect to the trans-Appalachian region, however, it created there a temporary but vast Indian reserve by laying down as a barrier the crest of the mountains beyond which there should be no white settlement except by specific permission of the Crown.

The Proclamation has been represented not only as a blunder, the result largely of carelessness and ignorance on the part of those responsible for it, but also as a cynical attempt by the British ministry to embody mercantilistic principles in an American land policy that in itself ran counter to the charter limits of many of the colonies and the interests in general of the colonials. Nevertheless, this view of the Proclamation fails to take into account the fact that it was the offspring of the war and that the trans-Appalachian aspects of it were an almost inevitable result of promises made during the progress of hostilities. For both in the Treaty of Easton in 1758 with the Ohio Valley Indians, a treaty ratified by the Crown, and in the asseverations of such military leaders as Colonel Bouquet, these Indians were assured that they would be secure in their trans-Appalachian lands as a reward for deserting their allies, the French. As a sign of good faith, the lands lying within the bounds of Pennsylvania to the west of the mountains, purchased by the Proprietors from the Six Nations in 1754, were solemnly released. Thus committed in honor in the course of the war, at its termination what other step could the Cabinet Council have taken? But the Proclamation of 1763 was in opposition to the interests of such groups of land speculators as, for example, the Patrick Henry group in Virginia and the Richard Henderson group in North Carolina, both of whom boldly ignored the Proclamation in negotiating with the Cherokee Indians for land grants. It also led to open defiance by frontiersmen who, moving beyond the mountains by the thousands, proceeded to settle within the Indian reserve—some on lands previously occupied before the beginning of the late war or before the great Indian revolt in 1763, and others on new lands.

The Proclamation Line of 1763 might have become an issue, indeed a most formidable one, between the government of Great Britain and the colonials, had not the former acquiesced in the inevitable and confirmed certain Indian treaties that provided for the transfer of much of the land which had been the particular object of quest on the part of speculators and of those moving westward from the settled areas to establish new homes. Such were the treaties of Hard Labor, Fort Stanwix, Lochaber, and the modification of the last-named by the Donelson agreement with the Cherokees in 1771. Nor did the regulation of the trans-Appalachian Indian trade create serious colonial irritation, especially in view of the failure of the government to implement the elaborate Board of Trade plan drawn up in 1764. The same, however, cannot be said of the program put forward by the ministry and accepted by Parliament for securing the means to maintain order and provide protection for this vast area and the new acquisitions to the north and south of it.

Theoretically, it would have been possible for the government of Great Britain to have dropped onto the lap of the old continental colonies the entire responsibility for maintaining garrisons at various strategic points in North America—in Canada, about the Great Lakes, in the Ohio and Mississippi valleys, and in East and West Florida. In spite, however, of assertions made in 1765 and 1766 by some prominent colonials, such as Franklin, that the colonies would be able and were willing to take up the burden of providing for the defense of America, this, under the circumstances, was utterly chimerical. For it would have involved not only a vast expenditure of funds but also highly complicated inter-colonial arrangements, especially in the face of serious inter-colonial rivalries, such as the one between Pennsylvania and Virginia respecting the control of the upper Ohio Valley. The very proportions of the task were an insuperable obstacle to leaving it to the colonies; and the colonies, moreover, would have been faced by another impediment almost as difficult to surmount—the utter aversion of eighteenth century Americans, by and large, to the dull routine of garrison duty. This was emphasized by the Massachusetts Bay Assembly in 1755 in its appeal to the government of Great Britain, after Braddock's defeat, to send regulars to man the frontier forts of that province; the dispatches of Colonel George Washington in 1756 and in 1757 respecting the shameful desertion of militiamen, ordered to hold the chain of posts on the western frontier of Virginia in order to check the frightful French and Indian raids, support this position, as does the testimony in 1757 of Governor Lyttelton of South Carolina, who made clear that the inhabitants of that colony were not at all adapted to this type of work. The post-war task of garrison duty was clearly one to be assumed by regulars held to their duty under firm discipline and capable of being shifted from one strategic point to another as circumstances might require. Further, to be effective, any plan for the defense of the new possessions and the trans-Appalachian region demanded unity of command, something the colonies could not provide. Manifestly this could be done only through the instrumentalities of the mother country.

Thus confronted with the problem of guaranteeing the necessary security for the extended empire in North America, which it was estimated would involve an annual expenditure of from three to four hundred thousand pounds for the maintenance of ten thousand troops—according to various estimates made by General Amherst and others in 1764 (to be found among the Shelburne Papers)—the British ministry was impelled to raise the question: Should not the colonials be expected to assume some definite part of the cost? Since the government felt that they were in a position to do so and that the stability of these outlying possessions was a matter of greater concern and importance generally to them, by reason of their proximity, than to the people of the mother country three thousand miles away, the answer was in the affirmative. The reason for this is not hard to fathom. The nine years of war had involved Britons in tremendous expenditures. In spite of very heavy taxation during these years, the people were left saddled at the termination of hostilities with a national debt of unprecedented proportions for that day and age of over one hundred and forty million pounds. It was necessary not only to service and to retire this debt, in so far as was possible, but also to meet the ordinary demands of the civil government and to maintain the navy at a point of strength that would offer some assurance that France and Spain would have no desire in the future to plan a war to recover their territorial losses. In addition to all this, there was now the problem of meeting the charges necessary for keeping the new possessions in North America under firm military control for their internal good order and for protection from outside interference.

It may be noted that before the war the British budget had called for average annual expenditures of six and a half million pounds; between the years 1756 and 1766 these expenditures mounted to fourteen and a half million pounds a year on the average and from the latter date to 1775 ranged close to ten million pounds. As a result, the annual per capita tax in Great Britain, from 1763 to 1775, without considering local rates, was many times the average annual per capita tax in even those American colonies that made the greatest contribution to the Great War for the Empire, such as Massachusetts Bay and Connecticut—without reference to those colonies that had done little or nothing in this conflict, and therefore had accumulated little in the way of a war debt, such as Maryland and Georgia. The student of the history of the old British Empire, in fact, should accept with great reserve statements to the contrary—some of them quite irresponsible in nature—made by Americans during the heat of the controversy, with respect to the nature of the public burdens they were obliged to carry in the years preceding the outbreak of the Revolutionary War. In this connection a study of parliamentary reimbursement of colonial war expenses from 1756 to 1763 in its relation to public debts in America between the years 1763 and 1775 is most revealing.* As to American public finance, all that space will here permit is to state that there is abundant evidence to indicate that, during the five-year period preceding the outbreak of the Revolutionary War, had the inhabitants of any of the thirteen colonies been taxed in one of these years at the average high per capita rate that the British people were taxed from 1760 to 1775, the proceeds of that one year's tax not only would have taken care of the ordinary expenditures of the colony in question for that year but also would have quite liquidated

* See in the writer's series on *The British Empire before the American Revolution*, Volume X, Chapter 2.

its war debt, so little of which remained in any of the colonies by 1770.* Well may John Adams have admitted in 1780 what was equally true in 1770: "America is not used to great taxes, and the people there are not yet disciplined to such enormous taxation as in England."

Assuming, as did the Grenville ministry in 1764, the justice of expecting the Americans to share in the cost of policing the new possessions in North America, the simplest and most obvious way, it might appear, to secure this contribution to a common end so important to Americans and Britons was to request the colonial governments to make definite grants of funds. This was the requisition or quota system that had been employed in the course of the recent war. But the most obvious objections to it were voiced that same year by Benjamin Franklin, who, incidentally, was to reverse himself the following year in conferring with Grenville as the Pennsylvania London agent. In expressing confidentially his personal, rather than any official, views to his friend Richard Jackson on June 25, 1764 he declared: "Quota's would be difficult to settle at first with Equality and would, if they could be made equal at first, soon become unequal, and never would be satisfactory." Indeed, experience with this system in practice, as a settled method of guaranteeing even the minimum essential resources for the purpose in view, had shown its weakness and utter unfairness. If it could not work equitably even in war time, could it be expected to work in time of peace? It is, therefore, not surprising that this method of securing even a portion of the funds required for North American security should have been rejected in favor of some plan that presented better prospects of a definite American revenue.

The plan of last resort to the ministry was therefore to ask Parliament to act. That Grenville, however, was aware that serious objections might be raised against any direct taxation of the colonials by the government of Great Britain is indicated by the caution with which he approached the solution of the problem of securing from America about a third of the total cost of its defense. The so-called Sugar Act first of all was passed at his request. This provided for import duties on certain West Indian and other products. Colonial import duties imposed by Parliament, at least since 1733, were no innovation. But the anticipated yield of these new duties would fall far short of the desired one hundred thousand pounds. He therefore, in introducing the bill for the Sugar Act, raised the question of a stamp duty but requested postponement of parliamentary action until the colonial governments had been consulted. The latter were thereupon requested to make any suggestions for ways of raising an American fund that might seem more proper to the people than such a tax. Further, it would appear—at least, according to various London advices published in Franklin and Hall's *Pennsylvania Gazette*— that proposals were seriously considered by the Cabinet Council during

* *Ibid.*, X, Chaps. 3 and 4.

the fall of 1764 for extending to the colonies representation in Parliament through the election of members to the House of Commons by various colonial assemblies. However, it is quite clear that by the beginning of 1765 any such proposals as may have been under deliberation by the ministry, had been put aside when Grenville at length had become convinced that representation in Parliament was neither actively sought nor even desired by Americans. For the South Carolina Commons House of Assembly went as strongly on record against this idea in September 1764 as did the Virginia House of Burgesses in December. In fact, when in the presence of the London colonial agents the minister had outlined the objections raised by Americans to the idea of such representation, no one of them, including Franklin, was prepared to deny the validity of these objections. That he was not mistaken in the opposition of Americans at large to sending members to Parliament, in spite of the advocacy of this by James Otis, is clear in the resolutions passed both by colonial assemblies other than the ones to which reference has been made and by the Stamp Act Congress in 1765. Indeed, in 1768 the House of Representatives of Massachusetts Bay went so far in its famous Circular Letter framed in opposition to the Townshend duties as to make clear that the people of that colony actually preferred taxation by Parliament without representation to such taxation with representation.

When—in view of the failure of the colonial governments to suggest any practicable, alternate plan for making some contribution to the post-war defensive program in North America—Grenville finally urged in Parliament the passage of an American stamp bill, he acted on an unwarranted assumption. This assumption was—to paraphrase the minister's remarks to the colonial agents in 1765—that opposition to stamp taxes, for the specific purpose in mind, would disappear in America both in light of the benefits such provision would bring to colonials in general and by reason of the plain justice of the measure itself; and that, in place of opposition, an atmosphere of mutual good-will would be generated by a growing recognition on the part of Americans that they could trust the benevolence of the mother country to act with fairness to all within the empire. Instead, with the news of the passage of the Stamp Act, cries of British tyranny and impending slavery soon resounded throughout the entire eastern Atlantic American seaboard. What would have been the fate of the empire had Grenville remained in office to attempt to enforce the act, no one can say. But as members of the opposition to the Rockingham ministry, he and his brother, Earl Temple, raised their voices—one as a commoner, the other as a peer— in warning that the American colonies would inevitably be lost to the empire should Parliament be led to repeal the act in the face of colonial resistance and the pressure of British merchants. Had Parliament determined, in spite of violence and threats of violence, to enforce the act, it might have meant open rebellion and civil war ten years before it actually occurred. Instead, this body decided to yield and, in spite of the passing of the so-called Declaratory Act setting forth its fundamental powers to legislate on all matters relating to the empire, suffered a loss of prestige in the New World that was never to be regained.

But the Stamp Act was not the sole object of attack by colonials. To many of them not only the Sugar Act of 1764 but the whole English pre-war trade and navigation system was equally, if not actually more, obnoxious. Indeed, the unusual energy displayed by the navy and the customs officials, spurred into action by Pitt during the latter years of the war—bringing with it the condemnation in courts of vice-admiralty of many American vessels whose owners were guilty of serious trade violations or even greater crimes—generated a degree of antagonism against the whole body of late seventeenth- and early eighteenth-century restrictions on commercial intercourse such as never had previously existed. It is not without significance that the greatest acts of terrorism and destruction during the great riot of August 1765 in Boston were directed not against the Massachusetts Bay stamp distributor but against those officials responsible for encouraging and supporting the enforcement, during the late war, of the various trade acts passed long before 1754. The hatred also of the Rhode Island merchants, as a group, against the restrictions of the navigation system as well as against the Sugar Act of 1764, remained constant. Moreover, in December 1766 most of the New York merchants, over two hundred in number, showed their repugnance to the way that this system was functioning by a strongly worded petition to the House of Commons in which they enumerated an impressive list of grievances that they asked to be redressed. Even Chatham, the great friend of America, regarded their petition "highly improper: in point of time most absurd, in the extent of their pretensions, most excessive; and in the reasoning, most grossly fallacious and offensive." In fact, all the leading men in Great Britain supported the system of trade restrictions.

Nevertheless, the government was now determined—in view especially of the great financial burdens that the late war had placed upon the mother country—to enforce the trade laws now much more effectively than had been done before 1754. To that end in 1767 it passed appropriate legislation in order to secure funds from the colonies by way of import duties so that public officials in America might be held to greater accountability when paid their salaries by the Crown. This attempt to enforce the regulation of trade and the Townshend Revenue Act could have only one result: the combined resistance of those, on the one hand, opposed to any type of taxation that Parliament might apply to America and of those, on the other, desiring to free the colonies of hampering trade restrictions.

The suggestion on the part of the Continental Congress in 1774 that Americans would uphold the British navigation system, if exempted from parliamentary taxation, while a shrewd gesture to win support in England, had really, it would seem, no other significance. For it is utterly inconceivable that the Congress itself, or the individual colonial governments, could have set up machinery capable of preventing wilful violations of the system by those whose financial interests were adversely affected by its operation. Moreover, it is obvious that, by the time the news had reached America that Lord North's ministry had secured the passage of the coercive acts—for the most part directed against Massachusetts Bay for the defiant destruction of the East India Company's tea— leading colonials, among them Franklin, had arrived at the conclusion that Parliament possessed powers so very limited with respect to the empire that without the consent of the local assemblies it could pass neither constitutional nor fiscal legislation affecting Americans and the framework of their governments. It is equally obvious that this represented a most revolutionary position when contrasted with that held by Franklin and the other delegates to the Albany Congress twenty years earlier. For it was in 1754 that the famous Plan of Union was drawn up and approved by the Congress—a plan based upon the view that Parliament, and not the Crown, had supreme authority within the empire, an authority that alone was adequate in view of framers of the Plan to bring about fundamental changes in the constitutions of the colonies in order legally to clothe the proposed union government with adequate fiscal as well as other powers.

In accounting for the radical change in attitude of many leading colonials between the years 1754 and 1774 respecting the nature of the constitution of the empire, surely among the factors that must be weighed was the truly overwhelming victory achieved in the Great War for the Empire. This victory not only freed colonials for the first time in the history of the English-speaking people in the New World from dread of the French, their Indian allies, and the Spaniards, but, what is of equal significance, opened up to them the prospect, if given freedom of action, of a vast growth of power and wealth with an amazing westward expansion. Indeed, it is abundantly clear that a continued subordination of the colonies to the government of Great Britain was no longer considered the asset in the eyes of many Americans by 1774 it had been judged by them to be in 1754, but rather an onerous liability. What had the debt-ridden mother country to offer in 1774 to the now geographically secure, politically mature, prosperous, dynamic, and self-reliant offspring along the Atlantic seaboard, except the dubious opportunity of accepting new burdens in addition to retaining the old ones? And these burdens would have to be borne in order to lighten somewhat the great financial load that the taxpayers of Great Britain were forced to carry because of obligations the nation had assumed both in the course of the late war and at its termination. If many Americans thought they had a perfect right to profit personally by trading with the enemy in time of war, how much more deeply must they have resented in time of peace the serious efforts made by the home government to enforce the elaborate restrictions on commercial intercourse? Again, if, even after the defeat of Colonel Washington at Great Meadows in 1754, colonials such as Franklin were opposed to paying any tax levied by

Parliament for establishing a fund for the defense of North America, how much more must they have been inclined to oppose such taxation with the passing in 1763 of the great international crisis?

At this point the question must be frankly faced: If France had won the war decisively and thereby consolidated her position and perfected her claims in Nova Scotia, as well as to the southward of the St. Lawrence, in the Great Lakes region, and in the Ohio and Mississippi valleys, is it at all likely that colonials would have made so fundamental a constitutional issue of the extension to them of the principle of the British stamp tax? Would they have resisted such a tax had Parliament imposed it in order to provide on an equitable basis the maximum resources for guaranteeing their safety, at a time when they were faced on their highly restricted borders by a militant, victorious enemy having at its command thousands of ferocious redskins? Again, accepting the fact of Britain's victory, is it not reasonable to believe that, had Great Britain at the close of the triumphant war left Canada to France and carefully limited her territorial demands in North America to those comparatively modest objectives that she had in mind at its beginning, there would have been no very powerful movement within the foreseeable future toward complete colonial autonomy—not to mention American independence? Would not Americans have continued to feel the need as in the past to rely for their safety and welfare upon British sea power and British land power, as well as upon British resources generally? In other words, was Governor Thomas Hutchinson of Massachusetts Bay far mistaken in his analysis of the American situation late in 1773, when he wrote to the Earl of Dartmouth:

> Before the peace [of 1763] I thought nothing so much to be desired as the cession of Canada. I am now convinced that if it had remained to the French none of the spirit of opposition to the Mother Country would have yet appeared & I think the effects of it [that is, the cession of Canada] worse than all we had to fear from the French or Indians.

In conclusion, it may be said that it would be idle to deny that most colonials in the eighteenth century at one time or another felt strongly the desire for freedom of action in a wider variety of ways than was legally permitted before 1754. Indeed, one can readily uncover these strong impulses even in the early part of the seventeenth century. Yet Americans were, by and large, realists, as were the British, and under the functioning of the imperial system from, let us say, 1650 to 1750 great mutual advantages were enjoyed, with a fair division, taking everything into consideration, of the financial burdens necessary to support the system. However, the mounting Anglo-French rivalry in North America from 1750 onward, the outbreak of hostilities in 1754, and the subsequent nine years of fighting destroyed the old equilibrium, leaving the colonials after 1760 in a highly favored position in comparison with the taxpayers of Great Britain. Attempts on the part of the Crown and Parliament to restore by statute the old balance led directly to the constitutional crisis, out of which came the War for American Independence. Such, ironically, was the aftermath of the Great War for the Empire, a war that Britons believed, as the Earl of Shelburne affirmed in 1762 in Parliament, was begun for the "security of the British colonies in N. America. . . ."

THE PROGRESSIVE
INTERPRETATION

ARTHUR M. SCHLESINGER
The American Revolution Reconsidered

▣ Arthur M. Schlesinger has greatly aided research on the Revolution with his studies *The Colonial Merchants and the American Revolution* (1918) and *Prelude to Independence: The Newspaper War on Britain, 1764-1776* (1958). He is widely read and highly professional, and his study of the role of the merchants pioneered in the use of newspaper files, letter-books, diaries, and pamphlets. While emphasizing the importance of economic and sectional forces, and devoid of any false *pietas,* his viewpoint is balanced and shrewd.

His article "The American Revolution Reconsidered" notes the changing patterns of interpretation of the Revolution. While accepting, as far as Britain is concerned, the views of the imperial school of Osgood, Beer, and Andrews, he considers that the major emphasis should be placed on "the clashing of economic interests and the interplay of mutual prejudices, opposing ideals and personal antagonisms—whether in England or in America—which made inevitable in 1776 what was unthinkable in 1760." His view of George III is pre-Namierist: he was, he says, seeking to convert "the British government from an aristocracy of great Whig families into a personal autocracy." But this apart, he offers an excellent and balanced survey of developments from 1763 to 1776 against a background of colonial protest. There has been, in his view, too much attention to men and all too little to the forces they unleashed. The Revolution was the result not of a few heroic leaders only, nor of a great forensic controversy over abstract governmental rights. The major emphasis should be put firmly on the clash of economic interests. But this no longer meant, as it did to Bancroft, putting the responsibility squarely on the Navigation Acts. A variety of groups and sections and classes contributed. And only slowly did the idea of separation come to be held. Only with the Declaration of Independence did patriotism become for the first time "synonymous with disloyalty to England"; rather it was the result of the refusal of a self-reliant people to be "confined against their will, whether by an irresponsible imperial government or by the ruling minorities in their midst." 〽

. . . THE TERM "American Revolution" is itself not without difficulties and its use has led to misconception and confusion. In letter after letter John Adams tried to teach a headstrong generation some degree of exactness in the use of an expression whose meaning they had knowledge of only by report. "A history of the first war of the United States is a very different thing from a history of the American Revolution," he wrote in 1815. ". . . The revolution was in the minds of the people, and in the union of the colonies, both of which were accomplished before hostilities commenced. This revolution and union were gradually forming from the year 1760 to 1776." And to another correspondent he wrote: "But what do we mean by the American Revolution? Do we mean the American war? The Revolution was effected before the war commenced. The Revolution was in the minds and hearts of the people." [1]

This distinction is not only valid in point of fact but it offers a helpful avenue of approach for a consideration of the facts of the nation's birth. If the period from 1760 to 1776 is not viewed merely as the prelude to the American Revolution, the military struggle may frankly be regarded for what it actually was, namely a war for independence, an armed attempt to impose the views of the revolutionists upon the British government and a large section of the colonial population at whatever cost to freedom of opinion or the sanctity of life and property. The major emphasis is thus placed upon the clashing of economic interests and the interplay of mutual prejudices, opposing ideals and personal antagonisms—whether in England or America—which made inevitable in 1776 what was unthinkable in 1760.

Without considering here the remote and latent causes of the revolt, a discussion of the American Revolution may profitably begin with the effort of the British government to reorganize the British empire after the Peace of Paris of 1763. Of this empire the thirteen colonies along the Atlantic seaboard had, by virtue of the recent peace, become but a small part. British statesmen felt the imperative need of correcting the slothful and unsystematic methods of colonial management by which some of the older colonies had been granted more liberal government than that enjoyed by organized territories of the United States today, and under which all the continental American colonies had become neglectful or defiant of ordinary imperial obligations. There was a need that all the outlying British possessions should be more closely integrated for purposes of administration and that the far-flung empire should be defended against the ambitions of England's traditional enemies, France

Reprinted by permission from the *Political Science Quarterly*, **XXXIV** (1919), 61-78.

1. For these and other similar views, see Adams, J., Works (Boston, 1850-1856), vol. v, p. 492; vol. x, pp. 180, 182, 197, 282-283.

and Spain, as well as against the restlessness of the alien subject popula-
tions. The problem which confronted the British government was much
more difficult than the questions of colonial organization with which the
American government has wrestled since 1898; but the American adventure in imperialism, involving, as it did, the question of whether the
constitution followed the flag, should enable Americans of the present
generation to view with sympathy the British experiment of the eighteenth
century.

The king's ministers glimpsed too narrowly the task before them.
What they regarded as an exercise in the mechanics of legislation was
really an innovation in imperial relations that touched the dynamic currents of colonial opinion and colonial economic interest at many vital
points. Moreover their attempt was being made at a time when the
colonies were, for the first time in their history, relieved of their most
urgent need of British protection by the removal of the French menace
from their frontiers. Under the earlier imperial policy of "salutary
neglect" the colonies had grown in wealth and political capacity, so that
by the middle of the eighteenth century they had become accustomed to
conduct themselves toward England as substantially equal commonwealths
in a federation. For them the new imperial policy involved additional
tax burdens, loss of trading profits and limitations of self-government,
liberties that were none the less precious because derived from an unwritten and unsanctioned constitution. Fundamentally, the great problem
of the decade following the peace of 1763 was the problem of the
reconciliation of centralized imperial control with colonial home rule.
This, unfortunately, was never clearly perceived by the dominant element
on either side, the issue being obscured by a blind officialism on the
one hand and by an unillumined particularism on the other.

Perhaps the problem was incapable of solution; but we can see now
that the best opportunity for a satisfactory outcome lay in the application
to the situation of an enlightened statecraft on the part of Great Britain.
To this the posture of political affairs in the country was not well adapted.
George III, who had ascended the throne in 1760, was already devoting
every political and financial resource in his power to the task of converting the British government from an aristocracy of great Whig families
into a personal autocracy. His parliament and ministers did not seek to
reflect the aspirations of the British public and therefore lacked a potent
incentive for the formulation of a conciliatory program of colonial subordination. The minority in parliament represented by Pitt and Burke
readily identified the struggle of the colonists to preserve home rule
with their own struggle in England against autocratic rule. Pitt was
thinking primarily of Englishmen at home when he exclaimed on the
occasion of the Stamp Act commotions: "I rejoice that America has
resisted." If his counsels had been followed by the government, it is
entirely possible that the colonial revolt might have been forestalled by
some plan of imperial federation.

With this brief view of affairs in Great Britain it is now possible to consider the situation in America. Conditions there were both simpler and more complex than the traditional accounts represent. In place of thirteen units of population thinking alike on most public questions, there were in fact two or possibly three major groupings of population, differentiated by physiographical conditions, economic interests and political ideals. The communities on the coastal plain from New Hampshire to Pennsylvania constituted one of these divisions; the settlements of the tidewater regions from Maryland to Georgia formed another; and the third, less clearly outlined geographically, consisted of the western sections of many of the provinces. These three divisions represented modes of living and attitudes of mind much more fundamental than those indicated by arbitrary political boundaries.

The first area may conveniently be called the commercial section because the dominant economic interest of the people was the carrying trade and shipbuilding. Here great mercantile families had grown up, who had gained their wealth through smuggling with the West Indies or else through legitimate trading enterprises that embraced the entire world. The merchants were keenly alive to the golden benefits which membership in the British empire had always yielded; and like the business interests of any generation or clime, they might be expected to combat any effort to tamper with the source of their profits. For the merchants the unfolding of the new imperial program involved a very serious interference with their customary trading operations; and during the decade from 1764 to 1774 their constant aim was to effect a restoration of the commercial conditions of 1763. As a class they entertained neither earlier nor later the idea of independence, for withdrawal from the British empire meant for them the loss of vital business advantages without corresponding benefits in a world organized on a basis of imperial trading systems. They strove to obtain the most favorable terms possible within the empire but not to leave it. Indeed they viewed with no small concern the growth of republican feeling and leveling sentiment which the controversy occasioned.

The great ports of the north—Boston, New York, Philadelphia, Newport—bore eloquent testimony to the prosperity of the mercantile class; and on the continuance of this prosperity depended the livelihood of the mechanics and petty shopkeepers of the towns and, to a lesser degree, the well-being of the farmers whose cereals and meats were exported to the West Indies. This proletarian element was not inclined by temperament to that self-restraint in movements of popular protest which was ever the *arrière pensée* of the merchant class; and being for the most part unenfranchised, they expressed their sentiments most naturally through boisterous mass meetings and mob demonstrations.

In the southern coastal area colonial capital was invested almost exclusively in plantation production; and commerce was carried on chiefly by British mercantile houses and their American agents, the factors. The only town in the plantation provinces that could compare with the teeming ports of the north was Charleston; and political life was focused in the periodical meetings of the great landed proprietors in the assemblies. Under the wasteful system of marketing, which the apparent plenty of plantation life made possible, the planters found themselves treading a morass of indebtedness to British merchants from which it seemed that nothing less than virtual repudiation could extricate them. In the last twenty-five years of colonial dependence the assemblies passed a succession of lax bankruptcy acts and other legislation prejudicial to nonresident creditors; but these laws nearly always ran afoul the royal veto. This fact, together with the sturdy sense of self-determination which the peculiar social system fostered, made the plantation provinces ready to resent any new exercise of parliamentary authority over the colonies, such as the new imperial policy involved. Georgia, as the youngest colony, not yet self-sustaining, and dependent on the home government for protection against a serious Indian menace, was less a part of this picture than the other provinces of the group.

On the western fringe of the coastal communities lay an irregular belt of back-country settlements whose economy and modes of thought were almost as distinctive as those of the two tidewater regions. Certainly the western sections of many of the provinces had grievances in common and resembled each other more than they did the older sections with which they were associated by provincial boundaries. These pioneer settlements extended north and south, up and down the valleys between the fall line of the rivers and mountains, from New England to Georgia. Outside of New England the majority of the settlers were of non-English strains, mostly German and Scotch-Irish; but throughout the long frontier the people cultivated small isolated farms and entertained democratic ideas commensurate with the equalitarian conditions to which their manner of living accustomed them. In many of the provinces they had long been discriminated against by the older settlements in the matter of representation in the assemblies, the administration of justice and the incidence of taxation; and they were thus familiar, of their own experience, with all the arguments which the Revolution was to make popular against non-representative government and unjust taxation. Being self-sustaining communities economically, their zeal for popular rights was in no wise alloyed by the embarrassment of their pocketbooks. Although out of harmony with the popular leaders of the seaboard in both the commercial and plantation provinces on many matters of intracolonial policy, they could join forces with them against the new imperial policy; and they brought to the controversy a moral conviction and bold philosophy which gave great impetus to the agitation for independence.[2]

The history of the American Revolution is the story of the reaction of

2. In Georgia, however, the frontier settlers were pro-British in their sympathies because of their dependence on the home government for protection against the ever-present menace of the Creeks. Twenty-five years ago Professor J. S. Bassett, in a discriminating study, showed why the people of the interior counties of North Carolina became loyalists when the issue of independence was raised. Had the friction between the interior democracies and coastal minorities developed to the point of armed rebellion in other provinces prior to 1776, the back-country folk might everywhere have thrown their weight on the side of the British government and thus have defeated the Revolution.

these three sections to the successive acts of the British government and of their interaction upon each other. The merchants of the commercial colonies were the most seriously affected by the new imperial policy and at the outset assumed the leadership of the colonial movement of protest. They were closely seconded by the planters of the south as soon as enough time had elapsed to make clear to the latter the implications of the issue of home rule for which the merchants stood. The democratic farmers of the interior, more or less out of contact with the political currents of the seaboard, were slower to take part; and it is largely true that their measure of participation varied inversely according to the degree of their isolation. Patrick Henry and his fellow burgesses from the western counties of Virginia began to undermine the conservatism of the tidewater statesmen as early as 1765, but the Germans and Scotch-Irish of Pennsylvania did not make their influence fully felt until the critical days of 1774-1775.

The new British policy of imperial control assumed its first form under George Grenville (1764-1765). The numerous regulations of trade, which need not be analyzed here, injured fair traders and smuggling merchants alike and threatened bankruptcy to the great mercantile houses of Boston, New York and Philadelphia. The prohibition of colonial legal tender added to their woes and indeed made the hard-pressed planters of the south sharers in the general distress. The Stamp Act, with its far-reaching taxes burdensome alike to merchant and farmer, sealed the union of commercial and plantation provinces at the same time that it afforded an opportunity for placing the colonial argument on constitutional grounds; and because of the character of the taxation, it rallied to the colonial position the powerful support of the lawyers and newspaper proprietors. The plan of the British to garrison their new acquisitions in America and to station a few detachments of troops in the older colonies was, in the feverish state of the public mind, envisaged as a brazen attempt to intimidate the colonists into submission. The merchants of some of the ports, intent on restoring the conditions of their former prosperity, adopted resolutions of non-importation; and little recking the future, they aroused the populace to a sense of British injustice, even to the extent of countenancing and instigating mob excesses and the destruction of property.

In the end parliament resolved upon the passage of certain remedial laws (1766), an outcome which, from the standpoint of the more radical colonists, can be regarded as little more than a compromise. The Stamp Act was indeed repealed and important alterations were made in the trade regulations; but the Currency Act, the regulations against smuggling and the provisions for a standing army remained unchanged. In addition the Declaratory Act was passed; and the new molasses duty was an unvarnished application of the principle of "taxation without representation" announced in the Declaratory Act. The rejoicing of the colonists can be explained only on the ground that the merchants of the north dominated colonial opinion; and like practical men of affairs, they were contemptuous, if not fearful, of disputes upon questions of abstract right.

The passage of the Townshend Acts in 1767 was the second attempt of parliament to reconstruct the empire in the spirit of the Grenville experiment. Again the merchants of the commercial colonies perceived themselves as the class whose interests were chiefly imperiled; but sobered by the mob outrages of Stamp Act days, they resolved to guide the course of American opposition in orderly and peaceful channels. They, therefore, began an active agitation for corrective legislation through merchants' petitions and legislative memorials to parliament; and after much questioning of each others' sincerity they succeeded in developing an elaborate system of commercial boycott, which united the commercial colonies in an effort to secure the repeal of the objectionable laws. After a year or so this movement in a much modified form spread to the plantation provinces, where, under the leadership of Washington and other planters, it was employed as a means of preventing the landed aristocracy from falling more deeply into the toils of their British creditors.

Meantime the merchants began to see that in organizing their communities for peaceful resistance to Great Britain they were unavoidably releasing disruptive forces which, like Frankenstein, they were finding it impossible to control. The failure of non-importation to effect swift redress compelled the merchant bodies, as the months passed, to depend more and more upon the tumultuous methods of the proletariat in order to keep wavering merchants true to the cause. Increasing friction between smuggling merchants and customs officers also produced outbreaks of mob violence in many provinces, and led by a broad, smooth road to such distressing affairs as the Boston "Massacre" on the one hand and to the destruction of the revenue cutter *Gaspee* on the other. As the political agitators and turbulent elements gained the upper hand, the contest began to assume more clearly the form of a crusade for constitutional and natural rights; and when word arrived in May, 1770, that parliament had repealed all the Townshend duties except the trifling tax on tea, the merchants found it difficult to reassert their earlier control and to stop a movement that had lost all significance for hard-headed men of business. The merchants of New York, under the leadership of their newly formed Chamber of Commerce, were the first who were able to wrench loose from their enforced alliance with the radicals; and the cancellation of their boycott resolutions was soon followed by similar action in the ports of Philadelphia and Boston. The plantation provinces were coolly left in the lurch notwithstanding that parliament had not receded from its position of arbitrary taxation, and the movement there soon died of inanition.

The two or three years that followed the partial repeal of the Townshend duties were, for the most part, years of material prosperity and political calm. The merchants had grown to look askance at a doctrine of home rule which left it uncertain who was to rule at home. As a class they eagerly agreed with the merchant-politician Thomas Cushing that "high points about the supreme authority of Parliament" should best "fall asleep." [3] And so—John Hancock as well as Isaac Low—they deserted politics for business, even to the extent of importing dutied tea which people imbibed everywhere except at Philadelphia and New York, where local conditions made it possible for merchants to offer the cheaper Dutch tea to consumers. The sun of the radicals had suffered an eclipse; and quietly biding their time, they began to apply to their own following the lessons of organization that they had learned from the "mercantile dons." In the commercial colonies Sam Adams—"that Matchiavel of Chaos"—sought, through the establishment of town committees of correspondence, to unite the workingmen of the port towns and the farmers of the rural districts in political action;[4] and the burgesses of Virginia launched their plan of a provincial committee of correspondence that might give uncensored expression to the political grievances of the southern planters.

In May, 1773, a new tea act was passed by parliament, which stampeded the merchants into joining forces once more with the political radicals and irresponsible elements. This new law, if put into operation, would have enabled the great East India Company to monopolize the colonial tea market to the exclusion of both American smugglers and law-abiding tea traders.[5] Alarmed at this prospect and fearful lest further monopoly privileges in trade might follow from the success of the present experiment, the colonial merchant class joined in an active popular agitation for the purpose of preventing the landing of any of the tea importations of the East India Company. Though their efforts for a vigorous but restrained opposition met with substantial success elsewhere, they were overreached at Boston by the superior management of Sam Adams and the unintelligence of Governor Hutchinson; and the British trading company became the involuntary host at a tea party costing £15,000.

The Boston Tea Party marked a turning point in the course of events both in America and Britain. In both countries it was regarded by the merchants and moderates as a lawless destruction of private property and an act of wanton defiance which no self-respecting government could wisely ignore. Plainly the issue between the colonies and the mother country had ceased to be one of mere trading advantage. Outside of New England, colonial opinion, so far as it expressed itself, greeted the event with a general disapproval and apprehension. In the mother country parliament proceeded to the passage of the severe disciplinary measures of 1774.

3. 4 *Mass. Hist. Soc. Colls.,* vol. iv, p. 360.

4. This characterization of Adams is one of many with which Thomas Hutchinson sought to give vent to his feelings. British Museum, Additional MSS., no. 35912, f. 225 *(Library of Congress Transcripts).*

5. See article by the present writer entitled "The Uprising against the East India Company," *Political Science Quarterly,* vol. xxxii, pp. 60-79. For a detailed discussion of mercantile and proletarian influences throughout the period of revolutionary agitation, see *The Colonial Merchants and the American Revolution, 1763-1776* (New York, 1918), by the present writer.

The effect of this punitive legislation cannot be overestimated, for it convinced many colonists who had disapproved of the Boston vandalism that the greater guilt now lay on the side of parliament. "They look upon the chastisement of Boston to be purposely rigorous, and held up by way of intimidation to all America . . . ." wrote Governor Penn from Philadelphia. "Their delinquency in destroying the East India Company's tea is lost in the attention given to what is here called the too severe punishment of shutting up the port, altering the Constitution, and making an Act, as they term it, screening the officers and soldiers shedding American blood." 6 From this time on there occurred in the several provinces a contest for the control of public policy between the moderates on the one hand and the radicals or extremists on the other, the former receiving aid and comfort from the royal officials and their circle of friends. This line of cleavage is unmistakable in the case of practically every province.

The moderates as a group wanted to pay for the tea destroyed and to propose to parliament an act of union which should automatically dispose of all controversial questions for the future. The radicals were opposed to compromise and as a class desired a comprehensive and drastic boycott of Great Britain with which to exact from parliament recognition of the colonial claim to complete home rule. Both parties were willing to make a trial of strength in an intercolonial congress; and after bitter contests in each province to control the *personnel* of the irregularly elected delegations, the First Continental Congress assembled in Philadelphia in September, 1774. In this notable gathering the moderates discovered to their dismay that they were outnumbered; and, in the disconsolate phrase of a Maryland merchant, "Adams, with his crew, and the haughty Sultans of the South juggled the whole conclave of the Delegates." 7 Indeed this extralegal body, by adopting the Association, decreed that the merchants of America should sacrifice their trade for the benefit of a cause from which they had come to be alienated; and the radicals in congress provided for spreading a network of committees over the continent to insure obedience to their decree.

In the popular conventions called prior to the First Continental Congress and in the provincial meetings that were held to ratify its doings, the people from the back-country counties of many provinces were, for the first time, admitted to that full measure of representation which had long been denied them by the unjust system of apportionment in the colonial assemblies. Deeply stirred by the political slogans of the tidewater radicals, they ranged themselves by their side and lent momentum to an agitation that was hastening toward independence. In closely divided provinces like Pennsylvania and South Carolina their voice was undoubtedly the decisive factor.

The proceedings of the First Continental Congress were viewed with mixed feelings by the colonists. The moderates who had lingered in

6. 4 American Archives (Force, P., comp.), vol. i, 514.
7. *Ibid.*, vol. i, p. 1194.

the popular movement in order to control it began to withdraw, although it required the outbreak of hostilities at Lexington or even the Declaration of Independence to convince some that their efforts could be of no avail. The merchants perforce acquiesced in the regulations of the Association, which, in the early months, were not without profit to them. The radical committees of the coast towns, formerly controlled by the merchants, began to fall into the hands of the democratic mechanic class. In New York, Boston and Philadelphia alike, "nobodies" and "unimportant persons" succeeded to power; and even in Savannah, Governor Wright declared that "the Parochial Committee are a Parcel of the Lowest People, Chiefly Carpenters, Shoemakers, Blacksmiths, &c. . . ." [8] Flushed with success, the radical leaders busied themselves with consolidating their following in town and country through the creation of committees of observation and provincial committees and conventions. Little wonder was it that, in this changed aspect of public affairs, a worthy minister of Charleston, S. C., should be dismissed by his congregation "for his audacity in . . . saying that *mechanics* and country *clowns* had no right to dispute about politics, or what kings, lords and commons had done," or that the newspaper account should add: "All *such* divines should be taught to know that mechanics and country clowns (infamously so called) are the real and absolute masters of king, lords, commons and priests . . ." [9]

Events had reached a stage where the extremists in both countries were in control. What Chatham and Joseph Galloway might have adjusted to their mutual satisfaction could not be rationally discussed by North and Sam Adams. Under the circumstances it was inevitable that the policy of commercial coercion, adopted by the First Continental Congress, should soon be superseded by armed warfare as the weapon of the radicals, and that open rebellion should in turn give way to a struggle for independence. The thronging events of these later months are familiar enough in outline and need not be recounted here. The key to these times is to be found in the fact that the radical elements were a minority of the colonial population and that only through their effective organization and aggressive tactics could they hope to whip into line the great body of timid and indifferent people who lacked either organization or a definite program.

The successive steps leading to independence were not taken without great mental travail, without suspicion of each other's motives, without sordid consultation of economic advantage, or without doubt as to the rectitude of the course or fear of the consequences. Thousands of men of recognized social and business connections, who had been active in the earlier agitation for colonial home rule, opposed separation and left their native land rather than be witnesses to its undoing. One of these earnestly warned his countrymen in April, 1776, that "a set of men whom nobody knows . . . are attempting to hurry you into a scene of

8. *Ga. Hist. Soc. Colls.*, vol. iii, p. 228.
9. *Newport Mercury*, Sept. 26, 1774; also Pinkney's *Va. Gazette*, Oct. 13.

anarchy; their scheme of Independence is visionary; they know not themselves what they mean by it." [10] On the other hand, John Adams found food for sober reflection in the rejoicing of a horse-jockey friend of his: "Oh! Mr. Adams, what great things have you and your colleagues done for us! . . . There are no courts of justice now in this Province and I hope there never will be another." [11] Many a man of property, like the patriot, Henry Laurens, wept when he listened to the reading of the Declaration of Independence, or else, like John Ross of Philadelphia, "loved ease and Madeira much better than liberty and strife," and decided to be neutral in the struggle.[12]

The real significance of the American Revolution, however, is not to be measured in terms of the conflicting emotions and purposes of those who, wittingly or unwittingly, helped to bring it about. What great issue in history has not been scarred by sordid motives, personal antagonisms and unintelligent decisions? Fundamentally, the American Revolution represented the refusal of a self-reliant people to permit their natural and normal energies to be confined against their will, whether by an irresponsible imperial government or by the ruling minorities in their midst.

The popular view of the Revolution as a great forensic controversy over abstract governmental rights will not bear close scrutiny. How could a people, who for ten years were not in agreement among themselves as to their aims and aspirations, be said to possess a common political philosophy? Before assuming that Otis or Dickinson or Thomson Mason spoke the voice of the colonists, the historian must first ascertain what class or section of the population each represented and how widespread its influence was. At best, an exposition of the political theories of the anti-parliamentary party is an account of their retreat from one strategic position to another. Abandoning a view that based their liberties on charter grants, they appealed to their constitutional rights as Englishmen; and when that position became untenable, they invoked the doctrine of the rights of man. Likewise, their sincere devotion to the kingship was not open to question through ten years of controversy, when suddenly, a few months before the end, an English immigrant jerked the bandages from their eyes and revealed the goal of republicanism and independence at which they had already arrived in fact. Without discounting in any way the propagandist value attaching to popular shibboleths as such, it may as well be admitted that the colonists would have lost their case if the decision had turned upon an impartial consideration of the legal principles involved.

Some of the difficulties in arriving at the truth concerning the Tories may also be apparent. Prior to 1774, it would be a distortion of the facts to picture the country as divided into two major parties, one representing blind attachment to the doctrine of parliamentary supremacy and

10. 4 American Archives, vol. v, pp. 1141-1142.
11. *Works,* vol. ii, pp. 420-421.
12. Graydon, A., *Memoirs of His Own Time* (Littell, J. S., ed.), p. 118.

the other a narrow partisanship of the doctrine of colonial home rule. Rather, the American colonists, united in desiring a large degree of colonial autonomy, differed in opinion as to what limitations of home rule were admissible and as to what methods of opposition were best adapted to secure the relief they desired. In this period every true American was a loyalist in the sense that he favored the permanent integrity of the British empire. Indeed, to regard "Tory" and "loyalist" as equivalent terms would place the historian in the predicament of classing practically the entire colonial population as Tories until 1776.

Excepting always the royal official class and its social connections, the terms "Tory" and "patriot" became intelligible for the first time when the First Continental Congress defined the radical program in the Continental Association and stigmatized those who opposed the program as "enemies of American liberty." As the radical program advanced from commercial coercion to armed rebellion, the local committees applied a new test of patriotism, that of allegiance to the rebellion. It should be remembered, however, that the object of this armed uprising was not independence but, as often in English history, a change in ministerial policy. With the Declaration of Independence patriotism became for the first time synonymous with disloyalty to England. Many men, like Daniel Dulany and Joseph Galloway, who may rightly be considered broad-minded patriotic Americans in the earlier years of the revolutionary contest, became Tories by the new definitions; and John Dickinson is the example of a man who narrowly escaped the infamy of not making up his mind in favor of independence as quickly as the majority of the Second Continental Congress. The disorders of the Confederation period were a justification of the decision made by the Tories; but the reconstructive forces in American society which built a nationalistic republic under the Constitution have eloquently vindicated the choice made by the revolutionists.

LOUIS M. HACKER
The First American Revolution

🔲 The clearest statement of the Beardian point of view on the causes of the Revolution came from Louis Hacker. His viewpoint is not only vigorously expressed but his articles are richer in argument than his predecessors, and the quality of the debate is now infinitely higher than in Osgood's day. Passion is now conceded to be permissible in history and in historians, even in the pages of scholarly quarterlies. "The struggle," said Hacker, "was not over high-sounding political and constitutional concepts: over the power of taxation and, in the final analysis, over natural rights: but over colonial manufacturing, wild lands and furs, sugar, wine, tea and English merchant capitalism within the imperial-colonial frame-currency, all of which meant, simply, the survival or collapse of work of the mercantilist system." ▣

THAT AMERICA has had a revolutionary past is, by this time, common knowledge; but that the first American Revolution, the war of independence against England, in quite every significant particular conformed to the revolutionary outlines of those better-known uprisings, the French Revolution and the Russian Revolution, is not generally understood. It is difficult to find disinterested students who are willing to contend that the French Revolution and the Russian Revolution could have been averted; for it must be apparent, given the character of the existing productive forces and the economic and social relations growing out of them, the shaping class antagonisms, and the onset of crisis, that the revolutionary challenge to authority on the part of the French bourgeoisie in one instance and of the Russian proletariat in the other was as inevitable as the normal progression of human life from birth to death. In both France and Russia, continued existence within the restricting forms of a declining productive system had become impossible; in each case, matters had been brought to a head within a brief and crowded interval by desperate efforts on the part of the ruling classes to continue in control of the corporate agencies of privilege; in each, the revolt was undertaken by underprivileged classes who, forming themselves into extra-legal groups, swept aside the by then dead hand of prerogative authority and erected revolutionary governments.

Such, also, were the broad outlines of the revolutionary process in colonial America, beginning with the last third of the eighteenth century: the general characteristics of contradiction, repression, crisis and thrust for power all were present. All these things we know: there are any number of American scholars who can without difficulty tick off the titles of virtually hundreds of monographs and learned articles that in detail support such an interpretation. And yet, it is one of the curiosities of American scholarship that no effort has been made to unite all these generally accepted facts into a coherent pattern.

Many historians, today, in trying to plumb the mystery of the American Revolution, seem to be quite as ingenuous in their approach as Parson Weems, the redoubtable creator of the Washingtonian myth. To the good preacher the reason for American revolt was altogether simple: the colonies were being plundered to take care of the royal poor relations and to feed the insatiable appetites of the ministers surrounding the English throne. Such an explanation, by personalizing the oppressive forces, undoubtedly serves an important patriotic function when all the issues of the struggle have not yet been resolved, but obviously it will

Reprinted by permission from the *Columbia University Quarterly*, XXVII (1935), 259-295. Copyright 1935 by Columbia University Press.

not do long after passions have cooled. Incredible as it may seem, this explanation has not altogether disappeared from history books, although, of course, its present-day guise is surrounded perhaps with an air of greater thoughtfulness. Thus, Professor Channing, writing in 1909, could say that the issue was not forced by the patriots of 1763-1775: "That was the work of selfish placemen in England, whose horizon was bounded by the narrow seas of their own island, and of over-zealous and stubborn officials in America, whose thoughts were ever intent upon places and pensions—Townshend, Hillsborough, and Lord North in England; Hutchinson, Dudingston and Tryon in America."

Also, to see the Revolution simply as a struggle for democratic rights in the political sphere: to build the whole theory of the Revolution around the slogan "No Taxation Without Representation" and to consider it merely as a continuation of "the Englishman's long struggle for political liberty," in the face of the almost immediate repeal by Parliament of the Stamp Tax Act and the Townshend duties and despite the fact that in the colonies themselves (as in England) the great mass of the adult population was disfranchised anyway: this is to make confusion only worse confounded. Nor is it possible to regard the struggle as arising out of a change in English colonial policy: that, beginning with 1763, the doctrine of mercantilism, with its more or less casual relations between mother country and dependencies, was replaced by the more modern concept of imperialism, under which the colonies were to be closely integrated into the political life of the whole empire. We are to believe (at least upon the authority of Professor Van Tyne) that a race of stubborn imperial patriots, originating in the landed classes entirely, had suddenly come into control of affairs with the termination of the Seven Years' War and was bent upon consolidating the empire in the interests of the greater glory of England, the opposition of the home merchant classes to the contrary notwithstanding.

At the basis of these various beliefs is the supposition that if only wiser heads had been guiding the English ship of state, if a beneficent statesmanship and not embittered partisanship had prevailed—if only Burke, Barré and a well Chatham had been the directors of the empire's destinies!—then Americans today, like all good British subjects, would be celebrating the King's Jubilee along with Canadians, Jamaicans and Fiji Islanders. For had not the great Whig leaders continuously pleaded for conciliation: for an end to colonial coercion, for withdrawal of troops, for the abandonment of all those policies whose only effect was to convert contented colonials into disloyal and plotting subjects? In short, accommodation was possible. (This thought, like a minor theme, runs through the writings of all modern American scholars. So, Professor Andrews declares: "We are driven to believe that a little more yielding, a little more of the spirit of friendliness and compromise, and a little less of British ignorance, stubbornness and prejudice would have calmed the troubled waters and stilled the storm that was brewing.") Accommodation was possible: the dispute about trade was a minor matter, the heated controversy over taxation was quickly adjusted in America's favor, the troops were insignificant irritants and could quickly have been removed: for, in effect, the English Whigs were right in assuming that mercantilism could work forever—if there could be only a fair degree of give and take. We shall see—obviously the Revolution can have no meaning otherwise—that the break took place not because of the inauguration by England of a new policy but because the sharpening of the contradictions that lay at the heart of mercantilism had to tear asunder the imperial-colonial relations.

Finally, scholars find refuge in an obscurantism that is difficult to penetrate; and there is nothing more surprising than to see Professor Andrews, who has done so much to clarify the nature of the commercial relations existing between England and its colonies, adopting such a position. The following is Professor Andrews' argument. For one hundred and fifty years, from the very hour of settlement itself, mother country and colonies had been growing farther and farther apart psychologically and institutionally. England was "an old, well-settled, highly organized land"; its social and economic life had hardened into iron-bound molds; its ruling class, seated on its great estates and in firm possession of all the citadels of privilege, was guided by "rigid and sinister ideas of power and government." The colonies, on the other hand, were youthful, growing, and filled with "a frontier people instinct with individualism and possessed of but a rudimentary sense of obligation and duty." Thus, it really was the old, old struggle between aristocracy and democracy, between settled areas, with an ancient culture and a caste tradition, and the frontier with a fluid institutional life and a passionate belief in egalitarianism. The magical concept of the frontier, it seems, will explain everything to American historians. What if class divisions were as sharply drawn in the colonies as in England, that the colonial merchants and their legal spokesmen were as contemptuous of "mobsters" as were their English counterparts, that colonial planters settled on their broad acres in Virginia, Maryland and South Carolina lived as much in the aristocratic tradition as noble lords with estates in Surrey and Kent? All this, apparently, is irrelevant. The frontier made Americans free and out of this individualism was engendered a spirit of liberty.

In the face of these conflicting and implausible theories of learned scholars, bewilderment on the part of the uninformed is only natural. Unless we are prepared to start out with the premise that the economic and social relations flowing out of the prevailing system of the day, that is to say, mercantilism, no longer could be maintained, then the whole history of the critical period that preceded the American Revolution is simply unintelligible. And if the past does not make sense, then we must consign its study over to the pure and simple antiquarians. But because the past has a clear and inevitable logic, our study of this period in America's development is of the greatest contemporary significance because we, today, living as we do also in an era of productive decline, class oppressions and approaching crisis, have much to learn from the ways employed by American patriots of an earlier time in the resolution of their perplexities.

II

The economic program the rulers of England adopted following the successful termination of the Puritan Revolution of 1641-49 (all the gains of the Revolution were finally consolidated with the establishment of the constitutional monarchy in 1689) we have come to call mercantilism. What mercantilism was, simply, was a policy to assure the continued advance of the English merchant, or pre-industrial, capitalism, once the restrictive ties of the absolute and medieval state had been cast off. In this sense, therefore, mercantilism had two faces: at home it utilized the agency of the state to strengthen the position of commercial enterprisers in trade, manufacturing and agriculture; and abroad, particularly in the colonial relations, it from the beginning attached the oversea possessions in a subordinate capacity to the economy of the mother country. We shall not understand the character of the American crisis of 1763-1775 unless we are prepared to hold ever in mind the fact that every imperial administrative program, whether in the economic or political realms, was designed to further this end: to utilize the colonies as an economic appanage of the mother country. That the English from the very beginning were fully conscious of the nature of this relationship, there is ample evidence. Thus, as early as 1726, a member of the Board of Trade wrote:

> Every act of a dependent provincial government ought therefore to terminate in the advantage of the mother state unto whom it owes its being and protection in all its valuable privileges. Hence it follows that all advantageous projects or commercial gains in any colony which are truly prejudicial to and inconsistent with the interests of the mother state must be understood to be illegal and the practice of them unwarrantable, because they contradict the end for which the colony had a being and are incompatible with the terms on which the people claim both privileges and protection. . . . For such is the end of the colonies, and if this use cannot be made of them it will be much better for the state to be without them.

It is apparent, therefore, that mercantilism was more than a monetary policy, as is so commonly believed. It is true that mercantilism did place a high value on a favorable balance of trade and as a result sought to encourage a flow of the precious metals into the home country. But there was no confusion in the minds of merchant capitalists of the day as to the real nature of wealth, they did not see it, that is to say, as merely money stocks but also as ownership of the means of production. Money was not unprofitably employed in the foreign trade even if exports exceeded imports; for balances could be converted into means for the acquisition of the agencies of production, notably oversea lands, and in this way the stimulation of further raw materials encouraged. Under the system of imperial-colonial relations there took place a constant flow of English capital into the staple-producing colonies. Where mercantilism broke down, as we shall see, was in the fact that these investments were made only in land and not in manufacturing. Had the policy permitted the expansion of English capitalist enterprise into colonial large-scale manufacturing, the colonial tie would never have been sundered; at any rate, certainly not in 1776.

At home in England, the mercantilist policy was developed along the following lines: in the interests of commercial agriculture, the process of enclosure was renewed on the one hand and the Corn Laws were revived and strengthened on the other to assure the country of the continuance of an adequate fiber and food supply; in the interests of industry, the state bent every energy to assure a steady flow of raw materials, protect the domestic market, and prescribe standards of quality so that competition in oversea markets with foreign producers could be successfully overcome; in the interests of commerce, the carrying trade was made a national monopoly through the agency of the Navigation Acts. With the measures taken to support English agriculture, we have no immediate concern here; but English policy in the fields of industry and commerce merits some examination.

Throughout the whole period in which the mercantilist theory was the guide to state conduct, Parliament was constantly exercising itself on behalf of the manufacturing interest. It discouraged the importation of foreign finished goods, of course, through the imposition of high duties and embargoes; it removed duties on foreign raw materials; it forbade the exportation of wool; and it controlled standards of quality, so that as regards the woolen industry alone, by the end of the eighteenth century, there were on the statute books some three hundred pieces of legislation which laid down rules for the maintenance of fineness of cloth, dimensions, composition of raw materials entering into fabrics, and the like. But even more important, Parliament and its administrative agencies granted enterprisers fiscal immunities, paid bounties, prevented the emigration of skilled workers, placed embargoes on the exports of tools, by regulation compelled the compulsory wearing of home-produced textiles, and finally, seriously circumscribed the processes by which English capital might be exported out of the country into any fields other than the production of raw materials.

As regards encouragement of trade, the devices employed by the English government are well known. The Navigation System, reinaugurated in 1650, had as its initial purpose the wresting of sea power away from the Dutch; but its subsequent extensions were openly designed to shut down English ports to foreign ships. The intention behind the policy was the building up of the English merchant marine and the creation of a national monopoly of the carrying trade, still that chief source of profit of merchant capitalist enterprise.

III

In the interests of English merchant capitalism, control over the economic life of the colonies was even more closely supervised. It has only too frequently been assumed that English colonial policy underwent a marked transformation in the middle of the eighteenth century and that this change was responsible for the onset of the crisis of 1763-75. Whereas, up to about the middle of the eighteenth century, Englishmen looked upon the colonies merely as sources for the production of raw materials, after that period they regarded them chiefly as markets for finished goods; and the desire to extend the market led to the acquisition of Canada and the western lands, and therefore the creation of that whole imperial administrative machinery of taxation, the quartering of troops, and the like, which inevitably brought on the break. A moment's reflection must indicate the inadequacy of this theory. Commercial intercourse between home country and colonies was possible only on the basis of the steady flow of goods and services between the two; and if the colonies were to be encouraged to sell their raw materials in the home country it was imperative that they be created into open markets for the absorption of English finished goods and the services of English ship-owners, merchants and financiers. The balance of payments was largely to be maintained by the colonial export of sugar, tobacco, indigo, dye-woods, logwoods and naval stores to England and the colonial import from England of drygoods and hardware as visible items. Invisible items, to the credit of English merchant capitalism, were to be freights, brokerage, insurance, commissions, profits and interest on borrowings. But what if the flow of goods and services from the colonies did not equal the flow of goods and services to the colonies? What was to be the utilization of the surpluses to the credit of the mother country? For sooner or later, in all imperial-colonial relations, the tendency for colonial debits is to outstrip credits: this was particularly true under mercantilism where the mother country was virtually the only source of finished goods and the principal outlet for raw materials.

The only factor that distinguished mercantilist imperial-colonial relations from modern-day imperialist imperial-colonial relations was the utilization of the capital surpluses. Under mercantilism, the colonies were pressed to make returns on unfavorable balances in specie and when specie was not constantly available (as it usually was not), the creditor home country was compelled to invest its surpluses in the colonies in land and land operations. Under imperialism, the investment of surpluses is in all types of capital goods: in land of course, but with an accelerating tempo in factories, public utilities, means of transportation and the like. In other words, under mercantilism the colonies could never look forward to duplicating the advancing industrial economy of the mother country, for native capital accumulations or foreign capital surpluses could not be employed in manufacturing but always in agricultural and trading operations; under imperialism, industrial duplication sooner or later becomes the prime characteristic, so that we see today, for example, British Indians, utilizing English capital, engaged in the manufacture of cotton textiles to compete with English textiles in the Far Eastern market.

The American colonies, therefore, from the very beginning, were attached to the English leading string; and it was their economic function to produce raw materials that England needed and to consume (but not manufacture themselves) English finished goods. The development of forms of enterprise calculated to enter into competition with English capitalism was seriously frowned upon, efforts were made to check them, and when everything else failed rigorous measures aiming at suppression were adopted.

The whole purpose of the Acts of Trade and Navigation was this design to keep in balance the economic relations between mother country and colonies; and all the administrative devices utilized had the same function in the social and legal spheres. Outstanding among the methods employed to assure the flow of colonial raw materials into the English market was that known as the enumeration of articles, as a result of which certain commodities might be exported only to England. In the act of 1660, the first list of enumerated articles contained sugar, tobacco, ginger, cotton-wool and fustic and other dyewoods; in an act of 1706, rice, naval stores, hemp, masts and yards were added to the list; in 1722, copper ore and beaver and other furs were included; in 1733, molasses was listed; and in 1764, whale fins, hides, iron, lumber, raw silk and potash and pearl ashes were enumerated.

On a second front, control over the colonial economy was pressed through prohibitions against the establishment of local manufactures. This had two effects: it prevented English capital surpluses from being invested in the colonies in large-scale industry, diverting them largely into land speculation and commercial agriculture; and it similarly prevented colonial surpluses from finding outlets in industrial enterprise, diverting them into commercial, or trading, activities. The placing of insuperable obstacles in the way of the employment of capital in the expansive field of colonial manufactures was undoubtedly the outstanding reason for breakdown in the imperial-colonial relations and the bringing on of the revolutionary crisis that led to the War of Independence. By specific enactment, in 1699, Parliament sought to check the development of a colonial woolen industry by forbidding the entrance of colonial wool, woolen yarn and woolen manufactures into foreign or intercolonial commerce. In 1732, similar action was taken in the case of the growing colonial hat-making industry by preventing the exportation of hats out of the separate colonies and by restricting colonial hat makers to two apprentices. In 1750, colonials were denied the right to extend the manufacture of wrought iron, by being forbidden to erect new slitting and rolling mills, plating forges and steel furnaces. It has been generally stated that these prohibitions were uniformly disregarded and that the reasons why large-scale manufacturing did not flourish in the colonies were to be found elsewhere. There are plain evidences why we may assume that manufacturing was retarded in the colonies exactly because of the operations of the mercantilist prohibition. Thus, at the very time in England when domestic manufacturing was rapidly being converted into the factory system, and great advances were being made in the perfection of machinery exactly because the existence of a growing market was demanding more efficient methods of production, in the colonies methods of production remained at a hopelessly backward level because of the impossibility of setting up large workshops without running foul of the law. Again, the great expansion of the colonial crude iron industry and its outstripping of the English industry in less than half a century points to the advancing development of colonial merchant capitalism. Also, the heavy investments made by colonials in the carrying trade, and in commercial enterprise generally, during the greater part of the eighteenth century, indicates that there was no dearth of colonial capital accumulations.

Nor was there the absence of a colonial market. With the opening of the eighteenth century the population of America had begun to increase by leaps and bounds, doubling itself every generation. Coastal America presented all the aspects of a well-established and secure society. The British controlled the seaboard region in an unbroken stretch from Maine to Florida and in it improved areas were virtually continuous; the line of the wilderness was steadily being pushed back to the crest of the Appalachians; there were adequate facilities for communication and intelligence. The countryside, in every section of the domain, was dotted with pleasant farmhouses whose occupants had long ago learned to enjoy many of the amenities and conveniences of a settled civilization. Everything was ready for the coming of industrialism; everything, that is, but a fluid and free capital supply, and this waited on the release of American merchant capitalism from the constricting limitations of English mercantilist policy.

IV

The economy of the Southern continental colonies was based on the commercial production of a number of raw materials, or staples, vital to the continuance of merchant capitalism in England. These were tobacco, rice, furs, naval stores and indigo. The most important of these, of course, was tobacco and, as we have seen, the English monopolized the tobacco trade by requiring that the whole Southern crop be shipped only to English ports. Throughout the eighteenth century, as the Southern tobacco crop grew larger and larger, the unit price in London tended to drop periodically below the cost of production; in addition, capital costs of plantation operation mounted due to the high cost of labor (the price of indentured servants and more particularly that of slaves went up while their productivity remained constant), the exhaustion of the soil in the older regions, and the necessity on the part of the planters to buy new lands to which they could be ready to transfer their activities when the older areas no longer were economically cultivatable. There were other charges against operations that did not fall with the unit price of tobacco but tended to remain constant or indeed increased: freight costs, insurance, merchants' commissions and profits (for handling the crop and purchasing the planters' necessaries), and interest on borrowings: and all these items were paid in England in pounds sterling.

Thus, virtually from the beginning, the plantation system was conducted on a narrow margin of profit which, by the middle of the eighteenth century, probably had contracted almost to the vanishing point. What sustained the Southern plantation economy? It was nothing else than the presence of easily preempted lands in the wilderness areas west of the regions of cultivation which planters were able to buy up for speculative purposes. The ability of planters to make a profit (not on the cultivation of their staples but in their rôle as speculative landlords) furnished the incentive for the flow of short-term capital from England into the Southern colonies for the financing of the planting, cultivating, harvesting, and shipping of their crops, the purchase of their servants and slaves, and the satisfaction of their personal and household needs. And short-term borrowings were converted into long-term indebtedness by the placing of mortgages on plantations and slaves. When these profits from speculative land operations threatened to disappear the flow of English credit ceased: and Southern planters were confronted by wholesale bankruptcy.

Because the wild lands of the frontier areas were so important to the maintenance of the stability of the Southern planting economy, Southern merchant capitalism was constantly preoccupied with them. The west was not opened up by the hardy frontiersman; it was opened up by the land speculator who preceded even the Daniel Boones of the wilderness. When the young Washington surveyed the lands around the waters of the upper Potomac in 1748 he was doing so as the representative of a great colonial landlord and as the scion of a rich land-owning family; and when he bought up soldier bounty claims in the decade following he was only pursuing the same line of interest already marked out by the Fairfaxes, the Lees, and the Mercers.

But the English (and the Scotch, in this case) had also learned to regard with more than a curious interest these wild lands of the west: they saw in them opportunities for profits from the fur trade and from the speculative exploitation of the region by their own capitalist enterprise. It was at this point that English and American merchant capitalism came into conflict and when, as a result of the promulgation of the Proclamation Line of 1763 and the Quebec Act of 1774, the western lands were virtually closed to colonial enterprising, Southern merchant capitalism began to totter on its throne. Without the subsidiary activity of land speculation, the planting economy could not continue solvent; there is no cause for wonder therefore that Southern planters were among the first to swell the ranks of the colonial revolutionary host.

Nothing indicates more completely the debtor position of Southern commercial agriculture than the mounting burden of debt and the almost continuous attention devoted by Southern assemblies to cheap-money measures. At the outbreak of the Revolution it was not unlikely that the American colonies were indebted to English merchant capitalists to the extent of fully £5,000,000, of which at least five-sixths had been incurred by the Southern planters. These bore heavy interest charges, and funds for short-term operations and for the long-term renewals were becoming increasingly difficult to obtain as English creditors took alarm after 1763. I. S. Harrell, whose excellent monograph [1] plainly reveals the economic basis of revolutionary crisis and struggle in the most important Southern colony, Virginia, sums up the situation in these words: "With their plantations, slaves, and sometimes household furniture hypothecated, the planters were in an almost inextricable position in 1775."

V

The Northern economy in its capitalist relations was based chiefly not on agriculture, as in the case of the South, but on trade. The Northern colonies directly produced little of those staples that England required: the grains, provisions and work animals of New England and New York and Pennsylvania could not be permitted to enter England lest they disorganize the home commercial agricultural industry; and the fishing catches of the New England fishing fleets competed with the English fishery industry operating in the North Sea and off the Newfoundland coast. The Northern colonies, of course, were a source for lumber, naval stores, furs, whale products and iron, and these England sorely needed to maintain her independence of European supplies. By bounties, the relaxing of trade restrictions, and the granting of favored positions in the home market, England sought to encourage these industries, partly because it required these staples and partly to divert Northern capital from expanding further into shipbuilding, shipping and manufacturing. But the policy yielded no really successful results. The advance of population into frontier zones cut down the field of operations of the fur trade; the Northern merchants found more profitable outlets for their lumber in the West Indian sugar islands and in the Spanish and Portuguese wine islands off the African coast; although the production of crude iron received a great stimulus as a result of English encouragement, most of the pigs and bars came to be absorbed in the colonies themselves so that the export of iron to

1. *Loyalism in Virginia* (Durham, N.C., 1926).

England was disappointing; while the production of naval stores, despite a consistent program of bounties launched upon by England as early as 1706, never took hold in the Northern colonies and therefore the plan of the Board of Trade to keep Northern merchant capitalism entirely dependent upon England completely failed.

The Northern colonies, therefore, produced little for direct export to England to permit them to pay their balances; for balances there were to be paid despite the household manufacturing of textiles and the fabrication of iron goods. They were buying increasing quantities of English drygoods, hardware and house furnishings, and were thus heavy debtors on visible account (and even on invisible items, although they were using their own services of shipping, commercial exchanges and the like) in the direct trade. Also—and this is an economic factor of the utmost significance—the Northern colonies never, to any appreciable extent, presented important opportunities for English capital investment. As we have seen, the English capital stake was largely in the South: only to a very slight degree was any of it to be found in the North. The result was the imperative necessity for the Northern colonies to develop returns in order to obtain specie and bills of exchange with which to balance payments in England.

The most important of these was trade (and the subsidiary industries growing out of trade) with areas outside of England. Northern merchants and shipowners opened up regular markets in Newfoundland and Nova Scotia for their fishing tackle, salt, provisions and rum; they established a constant and ever-growing commercial intercourse with the wine islands of the Canaries and Madeira, from which they bought their light and fortified wines direct instead of by way of England and to which they sold barrel staves, foodstuffs and live animals; they sold fish to Spain, Portugal, and Italy; their ports to a measurable extent during the eighteenth century (and in this way they competed directly with the English shipping fleets plying between England and the Southern colonies) acted as entrepôts for the transshipment of Southern staples—tobacco, hardwoods and dyewoods, indigo—to England and of rice to Southern Europe.

The trade with the West Indian sugar islands—as well as the traffic in Negro slaves and the manufacture of rum, which grew out of it— became the cornerstone of the Northern colonial capitalist economy. Northern merchants, loading their small swift ships with all those necessaries the sugar planters of the West Indies were economically unable to produce—work animals for their mills; lumber for houses and outbuildings; staves, heads and hoops for barrels; flour and salted provisions for their tables; and low-grade fish for their slaves—made regular runs from Salem, Boston, Bristol, Newport, New York and Philadelphia originally to the British islands of Barbados, the Leeward Islands and Jamaica, and then increasingly to the French, Spanish, Dutch and Danish islands and settlements dotting the Caribbean. Here they acquired in return specie for the payment of their English balances, indigo, cotton, ginger, allspice and dyewoods for transshipment to England and, above all, sugar and molasses for conversion into rum in the distilleries of Massachusetts and Rhode Island. It was this wondrous alcoholic beverage that served as the basis of the intercourse between the Northern colonies and the African coast: and in return the Northern traders picked up ivory, gums and beeswax and, most important of all, Negro slaves which were again carried to the sugar islands on that famous Middle Passage to furnish the labor supply without which the sugar plantation economy could not survive.

The freights, commissions and profits earned as a result of the successful conduct of trading enterprise thus furnished important sources of return through which Northern merchant capitalists obtained specie and foreign bills of exchange with which to pay English balances. Shipbuilding, with New England and later Philadelphia as the leading centers, was another source. Northern ships were sold for use in the intercolonial trade and in the local trades of the West Indies and the wine islands; also ships were frequently sold in England and Southern Europe after the completion of voyages. Still another source of return was the colonial fisheries. Northern fishermen, operating in fishing craft and whalers owned by colonial merchant capitalists, fished and hunted the waters off the New England coast and increasingly penetrated northward into the Newfoundland Banks.

Apparently, however, despite the complexity of all this activity still other means of obtaining remittances had to be developed: and these Northern merchant capitalists soon found in three illegal forms of enterprise—piracy, smuggling generally, and particularly the illicit sugar and molasses trade with the foreign West Indian islands.

It is not generally appreciated to what extent piracy—at least up to the end of the seventeenth century—played a significant rôle in maintaining the merchant capitalism of the Northern colonies. English and colonial pirates, fitted out in the ports of Boston, Newport, New York and Philadelphia and backed financially by reputable merchants, preyed on the Spanish fleets of the Caribbean and even boldly fared out into the Red Sea and the Indian Ocean to terrorize ships engaged in the East Indies trade; and with their ships heavily laden with plate, drygoods and spices, they put back into colonial ports where they sold their loot and divided their profits with the merchants who had financed them. It is impossible, of course, to estimate the size of this traffic; that it was great every evidence indicates. Curtis P. Nettels cites reports that single pirate ships frequently brought in cargoes valued at between £50,000 and £200,000; that New York province alone obtained £100,000 in treasure yearly from the illicit traffic; and that the greater supply of specie in the colonies before 1700 than after (after that date England began its successful war of extermination against the seafaring marauders) undoubtedly was due to the open support of piratical expeditions and the gains obtained thereby by some of the wisest mercantile heads in the Northern towns.[2]

Smuggling also contributed its share to swell the remittances the Northern merchants so badly needed. Smuggling traffic could be carried on in a number of directions. In the first place, there was the illegal direct intercourse between the colonies and European countries in the expanding list of enumerated articles; and in the second place, ships on the home-bound voyages from Europe or from the West Indies brought large supplies of drygoods, silk, cocoa and brandies into the American colonies without having declared them at English ports and paid the duties. Most important of all, of course, was the trade with the foreign West Indian sugar islands which was rendered illegal, after 1733, as a result of the imposition by the Molasses Act of prohibitive duties on the importation into the colonies of foreign sugar, molasses and rum. It is imperative that something be said of the productive system and the social and economic relations prevailing in the sugar islands, for just as the western lands constituted the Achilles heel of the Southern planting economy so the trade with the sugar islands—and notably that with the foreign islands—was the highly vulnerable point in Northern commercial economy. When England, beginning with 1763, struck at these two vital and exposed centers, it immediately threatened the very existence of colonial merchant capitalism.

VI

By the opening of the second third of the eighteenth century, the English sugar planters of the West Indies were beginning to find themselves hard pressed, in the great colonial sugar market, by the steadily growing competition of the foreign sugar planters in the islands and settlements owned by the French, Spanish, Dutch and Danes. The British sugar planters occupied a unique position in the imperial-colonial sphere. Favored from the very beginning by the tender solicitude of English imperial officialdom, supported in all their extravagant demands for protection by the great English merchant capitalist interest allied with and dependent upon them, in time represented in Parliament itself by what today we would call a sugar bloc, the plantation lords of Barbados, the Leeward Islands and Jamaica exerted an influence on British colonial policy that, in the words of Professor Andrews, "was probably greater than even that of politics, war and religion." The reasons for this are not difficult to find. Sugar, more so even than tobacco, was the great oversea staple of the eighteenth-century world; it was a household neces-

2. See his *The Money Supply of the American Colonies Before 1720* (Madison, Wis., 1934), one of the truly outstanding monographs in American colonial history. The writer is deeply indebted to Professor Nettels, and much of his own analysis of the money relations existing between mother country and colonies follows this pioneer work.

sary, it had a constant and growing market everywhere in Western Europe, it was the basis for the flourishing of a ramified English commercial industry made up of carriers, commission men, factors, financiers, processors and distributors. Also, sugar was converted into molasses which in turn was distilled into rum; and it was rum that was the very heart of the unholy slave traffic and the unsavory Indian trade. Small wonder, therefore, that sugar cultivation attracted at once the concentrated attention of English merchant capitalism: and by the time Adam Smith was writing English capitalism had succeeded in building up in the islands plantations with a capital worth of fully £60,000,000—a gigantic sum even in our modern imperialist age. Of this amount, at least half continued to remain the stake of home English investors in long-term (land titles and mortgages) and short-term investments. When it is recalled that in the whole of the North American continental colonies the English capitalist stake at most was only one-sixth as great, the reason for the favoring of the sugar colonies as against the Northern commercial colonies, after 1763, is revealed in a single illuminating flash.

By the second third of the eighteenth century it was everywhere being admitted that the English sugar planting economy was being uneconomically operated.[3] Plantations were large and were worked by inefficient slave labor and primitive methods; affairs of business were in the hands of paid clerks; no attention was paid to the restoration of the soil's fertility; the single crop was planted year in and year out without thought to the state of the market and mounting operating costs; and the whole system was stripped of its productive capital to sustain in idleness and luxury an absentee owning class. It was the dream of every British West Indian to flee from his tropical estate and settle in England, where he could buy a country property and a seat in Parliament and play the English country gentleman. This was generally realized: and by the early 1770's more than seventy plantation lords sat for country boroughs in the English Parliament and were therefore in a position to fight savagely all efforts at survival on the part of Northern colonial merchant capitalism.

This was all very well as long as nothing appeared to endanger the sugar monopoly of the English planters. But with the third decade of the eighteenth century, following the establishment of peace, such rivals appeared in the shape of foreign planters, notably the French: and the British planting interest was being threatened. The foreign planters clearly were at an advantage: their lands were newer and therefore more productive, ownership-operation, on the basis of small holdings, was the rule, with therefore more efficient methods and lower operating and capital costs; and diversification was practiced, the coffee crop of some of the islands often exceeding the sugar crop. These factors, growing out of their superior economy, permitted the French

---

3. See L. J. Ragatz's *The Fall of the Planter Class in the British Caribbean, 1763-83* (New York, 1928); and F. W. Pitman's *Development of the British West Indies, 1700-63* (New Haven, 1917).

and other foreign sugar planters to undersell the British. There were other reasons, implicit in the English mercantilist scheme, which strengthened further their command of the market; British sugar was compelled to pay a heavy export tax ($4\frac{1}{2}$ per cent) at the island ports; also, it was an enumerated commodity and could be sold only to England or its colonies; on the other hand, foreign sugar was free of imposts and enjoyed lower marketing costs as a result of its ability to reach oversea markets directly.

All this Englishmen and colonials saw. Adam Smith referred to the "superiority" of the French planters; while John Dickinson spoke of the British in the following slurring terms: "By a very singular disposition of affairs, the colonies of an *absolute monarchy* [France] are settled on a *republican principle;* while those of a kingdom in many respects *resembling a commonwealth* [England] are cantoned out among a *few lords* vested with despotic power over *myriads of vassals* and supported in the pomp of *Baggas* by *their* slavery." [4]

In short, foreign sugar and molasses could be had cheaper by from 25 to 40 per cent: it is not hard to see, therefore, why Northern colonial ship captains should take increasingly to buying their sugar at the foreign islands. They found it possible also to develop new markets here for their flour, provisions, lumber, work animals and fish, thus obtaining another source from which specie and bills of exchange could be derived. So great had this traffic become by the 1720's that the British planter interest took alarm and began to appeal to Parliament for succor: in 1733, Parliament yielded to pressure and passed the Molasses Act, which sought to outlaw the colonial-foreign island trade by placing prohibitive import duties on sugar, molasses and rum. But the act did not have the desired effect because it could not be adequately enforced: the British customs machinery in the colonies was weak and venal and the naval patrols that could be allocated to this duty were inadequate because of England's engagements in foreign wars from 1740 almost continuously for twenty years. Within these twenty years the illicit intercourse with the foreign West Indies took on such great proportions that it virtually became the foundation of Northern colonial merchant capitalism. By the late 1750's, when the traffic was at its height, at least 11,500 hogsheads of molasses reached Rhode Island annually from the foreign islands, as against 2,500 from the British; in Massachusetts the ratio was 14,500 to 500. In Massachusetts alone there were some sixty-three distilleries in 1750 and perhaps half that number existed in Rhode Island: the manufacture of rum undoubtedly was the most important single industrial enterprise existing in New England in the second quarter of the eighteenth century. Rum was a magical as well as a heady distillation: its fluid stream reached far Guinea, distant Newfoundland, remote Indian trading posts: and it joined slaves, gold dust, the mackerel and cod, and peltries with the fortunes of the New England trading enterprisers.

4. Italics in original.

Peter Faneuil, regular church attendant, kindly, charitably disposed bachelor was one of the greatest of these. He traded all over the world, paying English duties on his cargoes when he had to, avoiding them when he could. He was interested, of course, in rum and slaves. The distinguished historian of New England, Weeden, speaks in the following bitter terms of one of Faneuil's ships, the *Jolly Bachelor:* "Did Peter slap his fair round belly and chuckle when he named the snow *Jolly Bachelor?*—or was it the sad irony of fate that the craft deliberately destined to be packed with human pains and to echo with human groans should in its very name bear the fantastic image of the luxury-loving chief owner? If these be the sources of profit and property, where is the liberty of Faneuil Hall, where the charity of good Peter's alms?"

It is not to be wondered, therefore, that British planters kept up a constant clamor for the enforcement of the laws and the total stoppage of the foreign island trade; in this they were joined by the merchants and manufacturers whose fortunes were linked with theirs, and the bankers and rentiers who saw their great capital investment in the British islands threatened with destruction unless the British West Indians once more obtained a monopoly of the production of sugar and molasses. The Northern colonial merchant capitalists were the foes of British prosperity. The very reasonable exposition of the situation coming from Rhode Island's governor attracted no sympathy; apparently, it was to be the British West Indies or the Northern colonies and the stake involved in the former, as far as England was concerned, was far, far greater.

Wrote Governor Stephen Hopkins to England:

> By the best computation I have seen, the quantity of flour made in these colonies yearly is such, that after all the English inhabitants, as well of the continent as of the islands, are fully supplied, with as much as they can consume with the year, there remains a surplusage of at least one hundred thousand barrels. The quantity of beef and pork remaining after the English are in like manner supplied is very large. The fish, not fit for the European market, and the lumber produced in the Northern colonies, so much exceed the market found for them in the English West Indies, that a vast surplusage remains that cannot be used. . . . From the money and goods produced by the sale of the surplusages, with many others of less consequence, sold by one means or other to the Spaniards, French and Dutch in America, the merchants of those Northern colonies are principally enabled to make their remittances to the mother country for the British manufactures consumed in them. . . .
>
> Supposing this intercourse of the colonies with the Spanish, French and Dutch entirely stopped, the persons concerned in pro-

ducing the surplusages will of course change the manner of their industry, and improvement and, compelled by necessity, must set about making those things they cannot live without, and now rendered unable to purchase from their mother country.

When, during the Seven Years' War, the colonial "Smuggling Interest" extended the bounds of its activities and openly set about supplying the French enemy of the mother country with provisions, lumber, drygoods and the like, British sugar planters in Parliament, confronted by bankruptcy, found ready allies in outraged patriotic statesmen. Then it was that Pitt, deeply angered by knowledge of the open sale by colonial officials of commissions for flags of truce and the winking at the whole illegal practice by vice-admiralty courts, bitterly wrote to America that it was "an illegal and most pernicious trade . . . by which the enemy is, to the greatest reproach and detriment of government, supplied with provisions and other necessaries, whereby they are principally, if not alone, enabled to sustain and protract this long and expensive war." The process of repression began in 1760 with the stricter enforcement of the Acts of Trade and Navigation; from thence on, particularly after the last imperial rival, France, had been disposed of and the country at last was at peace, the screws came to be applied tighter and tighter. Soon, Northern merchant capitalists, aware that every avenue of continued activity was being blocked to them, moved into the colonial revolutionary host.

VII

It has been said that the mercantilist policy of English merchant capitalism demanded that the economic life of the American colonies be kept subservient to that of the mother country. From the very beginning—certainly, at any rate, from the turn of the eighteenth century when merchant capitalism was fully installed in the economy of the empire and in possession of its prerogative power—this was so: and a governmental apparatus was set up whose purpose it was consciously and constantly to maintain the imperial-colonial connection in this relationship. The real significance of all those imperial administrative agencies—the Privy Council, the Board of Trade, the Secretary of State in charge of Colonial Affairs, the Commissioners of Customs, the Treasury, the Admiralty and the royal governors—lay in the fact not that they created political or constitutional ties to unite colonies to the mother country but that they forged the fetters that bound the colonial merchant capitalism to that of England.

An examination of the activities of the imperial administrative agencies will plainly indicate that such an economic policy was consistently pursued: the period after 1763 merely marked its intensification as a result of the sharpening of the contradictions that appeared in mercantilism itself. The Board of Trade had been established in 1696, as O. M. Dickerson [5] points out largely "to make the colonies commercially profitable to the mother country." And this it sought to do, over a period of more than three-quarters of a century, with a devotion and singleness of purpose that left small room for complaint. The commissioners, of course, made it their business to keep the Privy Council and Parliament informed as to the progress of the oversea possessions; but their powers were more than reportorial, for through four specific devices they were able to direct and supervise closely the economic development of the colonies. The Board of Trade was more or less in charge of preparing the colonial civil list, and it was also its function to supervise the activities of the colonial judiciary: by control over personnel its influence therefore was measurable. But more important were: first, its power to review colonial legislation and, if the purposes of provincial statutes ran counter to the welfare of the mother country, recommend their disallowance by the Privy Council; and second, its power to prepare specific instructions to the governors for their guidance in the exercise of the veto over colonial encroachments on the privileges and prerogatives of English citizens.

There were at least a dozen points at which the Board of Trade (representing English merchant capitalism) and the colonial legislatures (representing colonial merchant capitalism) constantly were in conflict, exactly because of the clash of economic interests. The outstanding of these were: colonial interference with the mother country's hold on foreign trade and shipping; attempts by the colonies to control the traffic in convicts and slaves; and colonial efforts to permit the payment of quit rents in paper money, to lower interest rates, to ease the judicial burdens imposed on debtors and to monopolize the Indian trade for colonials. Most important were the stern checks imposed by the Board of Trade on attempts by the colonial assemblies to encourage native manufacturing and to relieve the oppression of debts (because every section of colonial America, as we have seen, was in a debtor relationship toward England) through the increase of the money supply of the colonies.

In order to maintain the English control over trade and commerce, the Board of Trade recommended and obtained the disallowance by the Privy Council of legislation placing export duties on colonial raw materials needed by English enterprise; it was equally successful in outlawing acts whose purpose it was, through the grant of exemptions, to favor colonial shipowners in the carrying trade; and it ceaselessly moved against measures placing import duties on foreign wines and liquors and on English merchandise. Finally, when this last threatened to become a general practice, the Board issued blanket instructions to the governors ordering them to veto laws placing duties on European goods imported in English vessels (1724) and on the produce or manu-

5. See his important and pioneer monograph, *American Colonial Government, 1695-1765* (Cleveland, 1912).

factures of Great Britain (1732), and all those laws under which the natives of a province were given preferential treatment over those of Great Britain (1732).

The Privy Council repeatedly was called upon to disallow legislation laying high or prohibitive duties upon the importation of Negro slaves and interfering with the free transport of convicted felons overseas. The colonies for the most part were moving to protect themselves against the growth of undesirable elements in their population; although the motives of revenue and the protection of the quality of the slaves also were present. But the Board and the Privy Council were not unmindful of the great English slave-carrying trade that was bound to be affected by such legislation: its solicitude therefore was plain. Finally, in 1731, when the colonies persisted in their efforts to pass such bills, circular instructions were sent to the governors ordering them to veto legislation interfering with the free importation of Negroes and felons.

VIII

When colonies sought to foster local manufacturing enterprise, the Board of Trade could be expected to exercise an unceasing vigilance. Partly due to the abundance of raw materials and the constantly growing market but largely because of the accumulation of capital surpluses won in trade, colonial merchant capitalists always were pressing for the passage of laws to help the development of native industries. They obtained them: and colonial statute books, therefore, were filled with legislation that was, in effect, only modeled after those acts Parliament itself was passing: measures calling for the payment of bounties to private enterprisers and the extension of public credit to them, for exemptions from taxation, for easy access to raw materials, for the maintenance of standards of quality and for the encouragement of the location of new towns and of the settling of artisans in new and old urban communities.

Against such legislation the Board of Trade regularly moved; more than the colonial manufacturing of woolen goods, hats and wrought iron therefore was outlawed. Thus, in 1705, a Pennsylvania law for building up the shoemaking industry was disallowed on the ground that, as the Board said, "it cannot be expected that encouragement should be given by law to the making any manufactures made in England . . . , it being against the advantage of England." And in 1706, a New York law for developing the sailcloth industry was disallowed because, said the Board, it would be "more advantageous to England that all hemp and flax of the growth of the plantations should be imported hither, in order to manufacturing of it here." And in 1756, a Massachusetts law for encouraging the production of linen was disallowed on the general ground that "the passing of laws in the plantations for encouraging manufactures, which any ways interfere with the manufacture of this kingdom, has always been thought improper, and has ever been discouraged." Nothing was too minute to escape the Board's attention in its zeal to protect England merchant capitalism. So, in 1706, 1707 and 1708, it went so far as to call for the rejection of laws passed in Virginia and Maryland providing for the establishment of new towns, on the grounds that such new communities must invariably lead to a desire to found manufacturing industries and that their existence would draw off persons from the countryside where they were engaged in the production of tobacco. To cap it all, the governors were closely instructed to veto all legislation designed to assist the development of such manufactures as might compete with those of England; this had its effect, so that E. B. Russell,[6] the outstanding authority upon the subject, has been led to conclude: "Largely as a result of the government's determined attitude in the matter, comparatively few laws for this purpose were enacted in the plantations."

The Board of Trade, always supported by Parliament, was equally vigilant in safeguarding the interests of English merchant capitalism in the financial sphere. It has been pointed out how the colonies, under the mercantilist system, were kept almost constantly in a debtor status within the imperial-colonial relations: and how their plight was accentuated by the insistence upon the payment of colonial unfavorable balances in specie. It has also been indicated how illegal activities—piracy, smuggling, trade with the foreign sugar islands—were compulsory precisely because of these unrelaxing pressures. The heavy burden of debts, therefore, the paucity of specie, and the absence of easy credit facilities made all the colonies steadily preoccupy themselves with the money question: efforts to debase the currency, on the part of the colonies and, contrariwise, efforts to maintain it at a high value, on the part of England, were symptomatic of the disharmony that existed within the mercantilist framework. When, in 1764, all the devices at the service of the Board of Trade having failed, Parliament passed its act (the so-called Currency Act) outlawing the use of legal-tender paper money in all the colonies, it was apparent that the crisis had been reached: whether it meant universal breakdown for the colonial economic life or not, England was going to insist that debts be paid in pounds sterling in order to protect English merchant capitalism.

The colonies resorted to innumerable means to expand their available money supply. They employed commodity money, the assemblies fixing the value; but Parliament warned the colonists that they could not impair contracts by fixing rates for commodities contrary to those stipulated in agreements. They tried to mint their own money; but in 1684 colonial mints were forbidden. They sought to place embargoes on the exportation of coin; but beginning with 1697 the Privy Council regularly disallowed such laws. They tried, by statute, to raise the legal value of foreign coins in circulation, particularly the Spanish pieces of eight; such acts in Maryland and Virginia (and in Barbados and Jamaica) were dis-

6. See his monograph *The Review of American Colonial Legislation by the King in Council* (New York, 1915).

allowed, and when, as a result, the tobacco and sugar colonies were drained entirely of coin, in 1704 Parliament proceeded to fix a uniform value for pieces of eight in all the plantations and in 1708 prescribed prison sentences for those failing to observe the regulations.

Beginning as early as 1690, in Massachusetts, the colonies turned to the emission of paper money. This currency started out by being short-term bills of credit issued in anticipation of taxes (and therefore retirable at fixed dates after the taxes had been collected) and to be employed only for public purposes: the enactments specifically declared that the bills were not to be held as lawfully current money and could be submitted only in payment of public obligations. Within the first third of the eighteenth century, all of New England, as well as New York, New Jersey, the two Carolinas, Pennsylvania and Maryland had emitted such bills. It was an inevitable corollary that the bills of credit next be declared legal tender not only for public but for all private transactions: the intention was a sorely needed currency expansion, to be pursued by the road of a paper inflation. The steps by which the various colonies sought to attain this end may be briefly indicated: some tried to issue bills based not only on tax anticipations but on private land securities (utilizing the agency of public and private mortgage banks); some pushed the dates of collection of taxes on which the bills were based so far ahead that the issues virtually became permanent paper currency; some failed to provide adequate taxes from which the bills were to be redeemed; and some colonies openly embarked on a course of repudiation, merely reissuing bills when the dates set for cancellation had arrived. Also, steps were taken to compel the acceptance of these bills as legal tender by fixing penalties to be imposed on those individuals refusing to honor them in private transactions.

The establishment of so-called public banks, which really were agencies for the issuance of notes against the security of land mortgages, was particularly common. The first such provincial institution was set up in South Carolina and before 1750 every colony except Georgia had followed its example. Massachusetts went a step further when it permitted a group of private individuals to organize a "Land and Manufactures Bank" in 1740; this society, capitalized at £150,000, was to accept land as security for its stock and against this real estate it was to print notes to be used for lending purposes. Stockholders were to pay 3 per cent interest for the privilege of putting up their land as security, to be paid either in bills of the company or in non-perishable raw materials or rough manufactures (hence the use of the term "manufactures" in the title); also, every year 5 per cent of the principle of the subscription was to be amortized in the same way. Loans, too, could be paid off in bills or in the same commodities. The purpose here, obviously, was the expansion of credit through the utilization of non-perishable commodities as a base for currency issue; and within the single year of its operation the bank succeeded in lending out and therefore issuing notes to the extent of £40,000. But Parliament insisted upon regarding the bank as a dangerous speculative enterprise and descended on it at once; it extended to it the terms of the Bubble Act of 1720 and the bank was outlawed.

A notion of the mounting size of the paper currency in circulation may be gained from the experiences of Massachusetts. When this province emitted its first bills in 1690, it was ordered that the issues should not exceed £40,000; by 1750, however, some £4,630,000 in bills had been released, of which fully half still remained outstanding. Depreciation was inevitable. In Massachusetts, the value of sterling to paper money reached a maximum ratio of 11 to 1; in Connecticut it was 8 to 1; in New Hampshire it got to 24 to 1 and by 1771 sterling had vanished altogether; in Rhode Island it was 26 to 1; in North Carolina it was 10 to 1; in South Carolina it was 7 to 1. Only in New York and Pennsylvania was there some effort made to check the downward career of the bills, the depreciation here never reaching more than 25 per cent.

It was the steadfast English policy to maintain a sound (that is to say, a contracted) currency in the colonies; and provincial acts were closely scrutinized from this point of view. Acts were disallowed and instructions issued, as affecting bills of credit, therefore, on the basis of the following general principles: that the amount of bills to be issued was to be limited to the minimum requirements necessary for the legitimate needs of the colonies; that there be created adequate provisions for refunding; that the term of issues be fixed and no reissues be permitted; and that the bills could not be made legal tender for the payment of private debts. Finally, when these methods seemed to be without avail, Parliament was resorted to. It has already been pointed out with what swiftness Parliament acted in the case of the Massachusetts land bank. A decade later, in 1751, an act was passed forbidding the New England colonies to make any further issues of legal tender bills of credit or bank notes; the only exceptions permitted were in the case of issues to cover current expenses or to finance war costs. And in 1764, by the Currency Act, the prohibition was extended to include all the colonies, even the exception in the case of military financing being rescinded; further, provision was to be made for the retirement of all outstanding bills. The currency immediately began to contract; and by 1774 there was not much more than £2,400,000 in the colonies available for exchange and the financing of the credit operations of colonial enterprise. John Dickinson was scarcely exaggerating the plight of colonial merchant capitalism when in 1765 he wrote:

> Trade is decaying and all credit is expiring. Money is becoming so extremely scarce that reputable freeholders find it impossible to pay debts which are trifling in comparison to their estates. If creditors sue, and take out executions, the lands and personal estates, as the sale must be for ready money, are sold for a small part of what they were worth when the debts were contracted. The debtors are ruined. The creditors get back but part of their

debt and that ruins them. Thus the consumers break the shopkeepers; they break the merchants; and the shock must be felt as far as London.

IX

This is the pattern of imperial-colonial relations which makes the events of 1763-1775 intelligible. Not human stupidity, not dreams of new splendor for the empire, not a growing dissimilarity of psychological attitudes, but economic breakdown in the mercantilist system: the inability of both English merchant capitalism and colonial merchant capitalism to operate within a contracting sphere in which clashes of interest were becoming sharper and sharper: such was the basic reason for the onset of crisis and the outbreak of revolutionary struggle. The mother country had bound the colonies to itself in an economic vassalage: opportunities for colonial enterprise were possible only in commercial agriculture (supported by land speculation) and in trade. But when the expanding commercial activities of Northern merchant capitalists came into conflict with the great capitalist interest of British West Indian sugar and the related merchant and banking groups dependent upon it; when the Southern tobacco and rice planters, in their rôle of land speculators, collided with English land speculators and the mighty fur interest; and when colonial pressure to expand into manufacturing and to develop adequate credit facilities for its growing enterprises threatened the very existence of English merchant capitalism in all its ramifications: then repression, coercion, even the violence of economic extinction (as in the case of the Boston Port Bill) had to be resorted to. There could be no accommodation possible when English statesmen were compelled to choose between supporting English merchant capitalism and supporting colonial merchant capitalism.

As Professor Nettels has so justly insisted, American scholars for more than a generation have been led astray by George Louis Beer's erroneous interpretation of the motives that prompted Pitt in 1763 to demand Canada instead of the sugar islands Guadeloupe, Martinique and St. Lucia from vanquished France. Pitt had great visions of empire: and it was this dream and the imperial policies that stemmed from it that prepared the way for conflict between colonies and mother country. For a mighty western empire, based as yet on a wilderness, demanded the formulation of a wise program with regard to the Indian problem—hence the shutting off of the lands beyond the crest of the Alleghenies to further settlement and the checks placed on the exploitation of the Indians by colonial traders; it demanded a system of defence —hence the dispatching of a British army to the colonies and provisions for its quartering and maintenance; it demanded a revenue—hence all those methods resorted to by a hardpressed home government to develop new sources of financing. Thus the chain of circumstances was completed; it had to snap at its weakest link—the raising of funds through tax measures among a liberty-loving and individualistic colonial people which too long had been permitted to go its own way. So Mr. Beer, and after him virtually every American colonial scholar.

The events of 1763–1775 can have no meaning unless we understand that the character of English imperial policy was never changed: that Pitt and his successors at Whitehall were following exactly the same line that Cromwell had laid down more than a century before; that the purpose of the general program was to protect the English capitalist interests which now were being jeopardized as a result of the intensification of colonial capitalist competition; and that English statesmen yielded quickly when a fundamental principle was not at stake and only became more insistent when one was being threatened. If in the raising of a colonial revenue lay the heart of the difficulty, how are we to account for the quick repeal of the Stamp Tax and the Townshend Acts and the lowering of the molasses duty? And, on the other hand, how are we to account for the tightening of enforcement of the Acts of Trade and Navigation at a dozen and one different points, the passage of the Currency Act, the placing of iron on the enumerated list, English seizure of control of the wine trade, and the attempt to give the East India Company a monopoly over the colonial tea business? The struggle was not over high-sounding political and constitutional concepts: over the power of taxation and, in the final analysis, over natural rights: but over colonial manufacturing, wild lands and furs, sugar, wine, tea and currency, all of which meant, simply, the survival or collapse of English merchant capitalism within the imperial-colonial framework of the mercantilist system.

X

Even before Pitt gave up the French sugar islands in 1763 because of the insistence of the British sugar interest in Parliament, he had already moved to protect the same monopoly group through his orders to the navy to stamp out colonial smugglers operating in the illicit foreign West Indian trade. The colonial courts were directed to issue and recognize the doubtfully legal writs of assistance (general search warrants), as early as 1761. Two years later, the peace-time navy was converted into a patrol fleet with powers of search even on the high seas. In the same year, absentee officials in the customs service were ordered to their colonial posts. A vice-admiralty court was set up for all America in 1764 and the number of local admiralty courts (sitting without juries)) was increased. In 1768 a new board of five customs commissioners to be resident in America was created. By statutes, by orders, by instructions, every conceivable weapon was employed to break up a traffic and therefore to weaken a group so dangerous to English capitalist interests. Spying was encouraged by offers to share with informers the sequestered cargoes; customs officials were protected from damage suits for unwarranted seizures when they were declared non-liable personally and when the burden of proof was placed on the owners of vessels and goods; the stricter registration and inspection of vessels were ordered; to protect informers and make possible the easier obtaining of verdicts, it was provided that suits for the seizure of cargoes might be tried directly in the vice-admiralty court and that revenue cases might be heard in the admiralty instead of the local courts; and to further free the courts from local pressure, the payment of the salaries of judges was to be made out of customs revenues.

The revenue acts of 1764 and later were used as a screen behind which the work of compressing within even narrow limits the economy of colonial merchant capitalism and of fastening tighter on it a dependent status was to go on. The Act of 1764 and the Stamp Act of 1765 called for the payment of duties and taxes in specie, thus further draining the colonies of currency and contracting the credit base. To divert colonial capital into raw materials, the first measure increased the bounties paid for the colonial production of hemp and flax, placed high duties on the colonial importation of foreign indigo, and removed the English import duties on colonial whale fins. To cripple the trade with the foreign West Indies a high duty was placed on refined sugar. The importation of foreign rum was forbidden altogether, and lumber was placed on the enumerated list. To give English manufacturers a firmer grip on their raw materials, hides and skins (needed for the boot-and-shoe industry), pig and bar iron (needed in the wrought iron industry), and potash and pearl ashes (used for bleaching cloth and hence needed in the woolen industry), were placed on the enumerated list. To maintain the English monopoly of the colonial finished-goods market in 1764 the entrance into the colonies of certain kinds of French and Oriental drygoods was taxed for the first time; in 1765, the importation of foreign silk stockings, gloves and mitts was altogether forbidden; also the drawbacks of duties paid on foreign goods landed in England and re-exported to the colonies were rescinded. To extend the market of English merchants in Europe, in 1766 Parliament ordered that all remaining non-enumerated articles (largely flour, provisions and fish) bound for European ports north of Cape Finisterre be landed first in England. And to weaken further colonial commercial activity, in 1764 high duties were placed on wines from the wine islands and wine, fruits and oil from Spain and Portugal brought directly to America (in American ships, as a rule), while such articles brought over from England were to pay only nominal duties.

As has been said, the revenue features of these acts were quickly abandoned; the Stamp Act was repealed; and in 1770, three years after their passage, the Townshend duties on paper, paint and glass were lifted. Only the slight tax on tea remained and even this was lightened in 1773 when the new Tea Act provided for a full drawback of English import duties on British tea shipped to the American colonies.

But it was exactly this new Tea Act which clearly revealed the intention of London: that not only was the economic vassalage of the

American colonies to be continued but the interest of colonial enterprisers was to be subordinated to every British capitalist group that
could gain the ear of Parliament. For, to save the East India Company from collapse, that powerful financial organization was to be
permitted to ship in its own vessels and dispose of, through its own
merchandising agencies, a surplus stock of 17,000,000 pounds of tea in
America: and, in this way, drive out of business those Americans who
carried, imported and sold into retail channels British tea (and indeed,
foreign tea, for the British tea could be sold cheaper even than the
smuggled Holland article). The merchants all over America were not
slow to read the correct significance of this measure. Their spokesmen
sounded the alarm. As Arthur M. Schlesinger [7] has put it, pamphleteers
set out to show "that the present project of the East India Company
was the entering wedge for larger and more ambitious undertakings
calculated to undermine the colonial mercantile world. Their opinion
was based on the fact that, in addition to the article of tea, the East
India Company imported into England vast quantities of silks, calicos
and other fabrics, spices, drugs and chinaware, all commodities of
staple demand; and on their fear that the success of the present venture
would result in an extension of the same principle to the sale of the
other articles." The result would be, as a Philadelphia pamphleteer
signing himself "A Mechanic" warned:

> They will send their own factors and creatures, establish houses
> among us, ship us all other East India goods; and in order to full
> freight their ships, take in other kinds of goods at under freight,
> or (more probably) ship them on their own accounts to their
> own factors, and undersell our merchants, till they monopolize
> the whole trade. Thus our merchants are ruined, ship building
> ceases. They will then sell goods at any exorbitant price. Our
> artificers will be unemployed, and every tradesman will groan under
> dire oppression.

By 1773, therefore, it was plain that America was to be sacrificed:
colonial merchant capitalists were compelled to strike back through
the destruction of the tea and the writing and enforcement of the
Continental Association.

XI

The blows aimed at colonial merchant capitalism through the strength-
ening of the Acts of Trade and Navigation, the promulgation of the
Proclamation Line of 1763 and the passage of the Currency Act of
1764 precipitated the crisis in the imperial-colonial relations: and
merchant capitalists (whether land speculators or traders) were soon
converted from contented and loyal subjects into rebellious enemies of

7. See his distinguished monograph, *The Colonial Merchants and the American
Revolution, 1763-1776* (New York, 1917).

the crown. But, to be successful, the revolutionary host had to be swelled from the ranks of the lower middle-class small farmers and traders and the working-class artisans, mechanics, seamen, fishermen and lumbermen. This was not difficult: for the material well-being of the lower classes was tied to the successful enterprising of the upper, and contraction of economic opportunity in the higher sphere was bound to bring want and suffering in the lower.

The colonies had enjoyed a period of unprecedented prosperity during the Seven Years' War: the expanding market in the West Indies, the great expenditures of the British quartermasters, the illegal and contraband trade with the enemy forces, all had furnished steady employment for workers and lucrative outlets for the produce of small farmers. But with the end of the war and the passage of the restrictive legislation of 1763 and after, depression had set in. With stringency and bankruptcy everywhere confronting merchant capitalists, it was inevitable that mechanics, artisans, seamen and lumbermen should be thrown out of employment, small tradesmen should be compelled to close the doors of their shops, and that small farmers should be confronted with an expanded acreage, a diminished market and heavy fixed charges made even more onerous as a result of currency contraction. Into the bargain, escape into the frontier zones—always the last refuge of the dispossessed —was shut off. Openly abetted by merchants and land speculators, the lower classes moved into the revolutionary host.

It would be a mistake to assume, however, that the working class and lower middle-class groups surrendered up their identities completely and operated only at the behest and with the encouragement of the merchant capitalists. Under the direction of their own leaders in the Sons of Liberty and the Committees of Correspondence, they were able to articulate their own class demands: the result was, the period of revolutionary crisis saw the development of a radical program which merchants and planters regarded with misgivings and dread but with which they dared not interfere lest, in alienating the underprivileged farmers, tradesmen and workers, they lose that mass support upon which their own destiny so completely was dependent. The lower classes began to look upon the revolution as the instrument for attaining their freedom: from the civil disability of almost universal disfranchisement, from the inequalities of entail and primogeniture, from oppression at the hands of engrossing landlords and from the threatened dominance and exactions of an oversea ecclesiastical authority.

For these and similar class reasons, the lower middle classes and the workers of colonial America joined with the merchants and planters in demonstrations against the imperial program: and when peaceful agitation and pressure proved unavailing, they were ready to take up arms when England resorted to coercion and violence. In 1774 and 1775, through the agencies of the Coercive Acts and the Restraining Acts, England, by striking at the economic life of the colonies directly, virtually opened hostilities. The colonists replied with two declarations of freedom. The first, naturally representing the dominant interest of merchant capitalism, was embodied in a series of resolutions passed by the Second Continental Congress, 6 April, 1776; these nullified the Acts of Trade and Navigation and put an end to the colonial slave trade: and with this single blow colonial merchant capitalism smashed the hampering fetters of the imperial-colonial relations. The second, adopted by the Congress, 4 July, 1776, was the Declaration of Independence: written by the radicals, this was a political manifesto which called upon the masses to defend the revolution. The first American Revolution then moved fully into the stage of armed resistance.

THE NEO-WHIG
INTERPRETATION

PHILIP G. DAVIDSON
Whig Propagandists of
the American Revolution

🔁 The neo-Whigs not only bring the argument back to American issues and see them as richly varied in character, but, still more, they realize how revolutionary forces are made and manufactured. One of the first to study the operation of the Revolutionary press was Philip Davidson, and his article outlines some of the issues raised in his book *Propaganda and the American Revolution, 1763-1783* (1941). It is especially useful for its examination of the reaction of the Whig propagandists to the British peace overtures in 1778, the last major challenge to them. Davidson proves that the familiar *eminence grise* of Boston, Sam Adams,* had a considerable number of aids and abettors. Josiah Quincy the younger "could popularize a constitutional argument as well as anyone in the colonies and knew the central fact of crowd psychology—that emotion, not reason, determines action." Joseph Warren was another of the militant minority who stirred the laggard spirits of the colonists. "He used every position he held for the dissemination of propaganda, and not a committee he served on but became an agency for spreading the ideas of the radical party." It was Warren who cautioned the infants visiting the scene of their fathers' martyrdom after the Boston massacre to "take heed, lest . . . your feet slide on the stones bespattered with your fathers' brains." Another was James Otis, "whose wild harangues in Boston town meeting did more for the cause among the lower people than did his bitter pamphlets. . . . His speeches against British officials were so inflammatory that mob action was almost inevitable." Joseph Hawley, Stephen Hopkins, William Livingston, William Gordon, Francis Hopkinson, John Trumbull, James Wilson, and Thomas Mifflin should be added also. Samuel Chase of Maryland did not hesitate to lead a mob to demonstrate against the Stamp Act; Isaac Sears and Alexander McDougall of New York were mob masters with more courage and more integrity than most of their breed. Finally there was Tom Paine, certainly the greatest pamphleteer of them all. Davidson describes

* Cf. John C. Miller, *Sam Adams: Pioneer in Propaganda* (Boston, 1936).

also the mechanics of revolution: the familiar committees of correspondence, churches, clubs, schools and colleges, masonic lodges, workingmen's societies, and merchant organizations in nearly every colony and town. Other channels of communication and agitation included the Sons of Liberty, "the finest organization for the dissemination of propaganda among the working classes," the Mechanics party, the Mohawk River Indians, the Philadelphia Patriotic Society, and many others. Practically all the forty-two newspapers published in America in 1775 were under Whig control. "Not a single paper prior to 1774 was exclusively an organ of pro-Bitish propaganda, and even after 1774 there were only a few." His work has been developed by others, notably by Arthur M. Schlesinger in *Prelude to Independence: The Newspaper War on Britain, 1764-1776* (1958), and Bruce Ingham Granger in *Political Satire in the American Revolution, 1763-1783* (1960), and there are some useful articles, especially Davidson's own study of the Stamp Act riots in "Sons of Liberty and Stamp Act Men," *North Carolina Historical Review*, IX (1932).   🔲

"I TAKE IT THAT clamour is at present our best policy," wrote William Livingston in 1768; and just a few months later Samuel Adams said to James Otis, who objected to publishing the letter of the Massachusetts Assembly to Lord Hillsborough before he could possibly receive it, "What signifies that? You know it was designed for the people, and not for the minister." [1] Here we have clearly expressed the purpose of that bewildering mass of articles, essays, pamphlets, speeches, and sermons of the Revolutionary period; their varied appeal was to make coherent and articulate the growing opposition to Great Britain. We understand to-day that sufficient unity of opinion to result in concerted action is achieved only after an intensive propaganda campaign. Inflamed patriotism alone could conceive of the American Revolution as the spontaneous uprising of an outraged and indignant people; clearly the propagandists had been at work long before the nineteenth of April in '75.

If we define propaganda in the broad sense as a systematic effort through mass suggestion to gain public support for a particular idea or course of action,[2] our Revolutionary propagandist is then a man who systematically prepared the people for opposition to Great Britain and her colonial program. A quick survey of some leading Revolutionary

Reprinted by permission from the *American Historical Review*, XXXIX (1933-1934), 442-453.

1. Theodore Sedgwick, Jr., *Memoir of the Life of William Livingston* (New York, 1833), p. 136; William V. Wells, *Life and Public Services of Samuel Adams* (Boston, 1866), I, 196.

2. Definitions abound. An excellent list may be found in Frederick E. Lumley, *The Propaganda Menace*, ch. II. There is a general feeling that propaganda is not really propaganda unless it is evil and insidious. As Edward L. Bernays puts it (*Crystallizing Public Opinion*, p. 212), "The advocacy of what we believe in is education. The advocacy of what we don't believe in is propaganda." Professor

figures, without any attempt to be inclusive, will show what a surprising number fitted this description, and how generally they appreciated the prior necessity of opinion to action.

Two—Samuel Adams and Thomas Paine—may almost be called professionals, save that their interest alone employed them. Emerson's explanation of great men illuminates our knowledge of these two: "Every master has found his materials collected, and his power lay in his sympathy with his people and in his love of the materials he wrought in." At hand for their use were the accumulated discontent of a hundred and fifty years' restive development under English control, the turbulent forces creating the inchoate Americanism they perceived, and the eighteenth century compact philosophy that was to make them free. To unite all America in one pulsating hope, to vitalize that hope with the new philosophy, this was their task. They could succeed, for they had a secret knowledge of what the people thought, wished, feared, and hated, and the power to interpret for the public "its own conscience and its own consciousness"—therein lay their strength.[3]

Many others, though not exclusively propagandists, engaged in such activities. There were John Adams, worried about his vacant law office, helping the Sons of Liberty with their transparencies, and writing steadily though heavily for the press; [4] and James Otis, whose wild inflammatory harangues in Boston town meetings did more for the cause than his bitter pamphlets.[5] Then there was Joseph Warren, whose work on the Boston committee of correspondence was made easier by his preparatory essays and speeches, none more notable than the famous Fifth of March

3. Moses Coit Tyler, *Literary History of the American Revolution*, II, 42.

4. "I have not drawn a writ since the first of November," Diary, Dec. 18, 1765, *The Works of John Adams*, Charles Francis Adams, ed., II, 155, 178 ff., 183-184.

5. "This gentleman . . . has, I believe, contributed more than any *one* man to bring us into the state of *out-lawry* and confusion we are now in," Boston *Gazette*, Dec. 28, 1767, quoting a statement made in 1765. At one meeting he "inveighed against the Lieut. Governor in terms most suitable to have raised another Mob against him," British Museum Transcripts in the Library of Congress, C. O. 5, vol. 43, f. 121, p. 136.

Lumley's own definition is a precise description of evil propaganda. Such definitions, though justified by current usage, are entirely too narrow for the student, who is not concerned with whether propaganda is good or bad, but simply with propaganda. Professor Friedrich Schönemann, in his *Die Kunst der Massenbeeinflussung in den Vereinigten Staaten von Amerika* (Berlin, 1924), calls it, as his title indicates, "the art of mass suggestion." Reynell J. R. G. Wreford neatly describes it as "the dissemination of interested information and opinion," Propaganda, Evil and Good, *Nineteenth Cetnury and After*, XCIII, 514. Professor Harold D. Lasswell in a more academic definition sees it as "the management of collective attitudes by the manipulation of significant symbols," The Theory of Political Propaganda, *American Political Science Review*, XXI, 627. Whatever definition is accepted there must be understood the twofold task of the propagandist: to present his own suggestions as favorably as may be, and to neutralize if he cannot actually censor inconvenient suggestions. The public must hear only one side of the case, for there is no room in the art of the propagandist for tolerance. Mr. Walter Lippmann even questions whether there can be true propaganda without some form of censorship, *Public Opinion*, p. 43.

Oration, commemorating the Boston Massacre, which contains such incredible passages as this: [6]

> Approach we then the melancholy walk of death. Hither let me call the gay companion, here let him drop a farewell tear upon that body which so late he saw vigorous and warm with social mirth—hither let me lead the tender mother to weep over her beloved son—come widowed mourner, here satiate thy grief; behold thy murdered husband gasping on the ground, and to complete the pompous show of wretchedness, bring in each hand thy infant children to bewail their father's fate—take heed, ye infant babes, lest, whilst your streaming eyes are fixed upon the ghastly corpse, *your feet slide on the stones bespattered with your father's brains.*

Even young Alexander Hamilton, whose pamphlet attacks and scattered handbills, as he said, gave the "necessary alarm" against the Tories, inspired the Whigs during the war by accounts of battles done up with the usual newspaper embellishments.[7] John Dickinson began early with a pamphlet on the Stamp Act, wrote the *Farmer's Letters,* composed the American Liberty Song, and answered Sam Adams's request in 1773 for further efforts with a broadside opposing the Tea Act, not because of the legal principles involved but because the British East India Company now "cast their Eyes on *America,* as a new Theatre, whereon to exercise their Talents of Rapine, Oppression and Cruelty." [8]

Thomas Jefferson, now learning the arts of party leadership which were to secure him the presidency, knew how to inspirit the people with wonderful words of delusive hope. The Declaration of Independence, surpassed by few if any propaganda efforts, placed within seeming grasp the unattainable aspirations of men. It recorded no accomplished fact; it evidenced no new social order. Only as men fought for it did they give meaning to it. Each effort should *now* be made to keep up the spirits of the people, said Jefferson on July 1, 1776; [9] he knew the Declaration was inadequate in itself.

The more obscure Colonel Landon Carter, whose essays in the press were brought home to the people on county court days, tried knowingly but vaguely, as all good propagandists should do, to convince them "that the case of the Bostonians was the case of all America & if they submitted to this arbitrary taxation begun by the Parliament, all America must, and then farewell to all our Liberties." [10] James Iredell, future

6. H. Niles, *Principles and Acts of the Revolution* (Baltimore, 1822), p. 20; reprinted in the *Pennsylvania Journal, Supplement,* Mar. 29, 1775.

7. *The Correspondence and Public Papers of John Jay,* Henry P. Johnston, ed., I. 41; *The Works of Alexander Hamilton,* John C. Hamilton, ed., I, 85.

8. "Rusticus," conveniently found in *The Writings of John Dickinson,* Paul Leicester Ford, ed., I, 460. He first refused, saying that he took up his pen only from a sense of duty, but later changed his mind. Charles J. Stillé, *Life and Times of John Dickinson,* pp. 103 ff.

9. *The Writings of Thomas Jefferson,* Paul Leicester Ford, ed., II, 41.

10. Diary of Col. Landon Carter, *William and Mary College Quarterly,* XIV, 246. See also *The Letters of Richard Henry Lee,* James Curtis Ballagh, ed., I, 8 f., 12, and Lee Transcripts (Virginia Historical Society), pp. 66 f.

dignitary of the Supreme Bench, passed from hand to hand a manuscript he had written on the advantages of independence and in the charges to his grand juries declared that British depravity and cruelty were almost solely responsible for the war. And William Henry Drayton, effective essayist until his death in 1779, though first set against the rising Americanism, finally reached the astounding position that [11]

> The Almighty created America to be independent of Britain: let us beware of the impiety of being backward to act as instruments in the Almighty Hand, now extended to accomplish his purpose. . . .

Other political figures depended largely upon oratory to win a following. Mob leaders—Isaac Sears, Ebenezer Mackintosh—raised the pitch of emotional tensity in words now lost save as we know what crowd leaders have always said to their followers. Although their mad and devilish speeches made sober citizens tremble behind barred doors and windows, they guided the stirrings of social discontent into the comparatively peaceful paths of imperial revolution. In the epitaph of a New York leveler, shot on the thirteenth of March, 1775, we hear faint echoes of mob appeals which aided in subtly changing social revolution into political revolution: [12]

> HERE WILLIAM FRENCH his Body lies,
> For Murder his Blood for Vengeance cries.
> King Georg the third his Tory crew
> tha with a bawl his head Shot threw.
> For Liberty and his Country's Good,
> he Lost his Life his Dearest Blood.

Still others, themselves doing no speaking or writing, knew the necessity for first converting the people, and hoped with William Hooper that "nothing will be omitted that they may work upon their Reason, or affect their passions." [13] Washington himself realized that no plans could be successful unless the leaders would "be at some pains to explain matters to the people, and stimulate them to cordial agreements." As commander in chief of his little army he saw the dampening effect of flagging spirits and constantly urged his more literary friends to act upon the "hopes and fears of the people at large . . . in such a manner, as to make them approve and second your views." [14]

11. John Drayton, *Memoirs of the American Revolution* (Charleston, 1821), II, 274.

12. Frank Moore, *Diary of the American Revolution* (New York, 1860), I, 51. This is simply to say that the Revolution was not primarily or exclusively a class movement.

13. William Hooper to Joseph Hewes and John Penn, 1776, Hayes Collection, North Carolina Historical Commission.

14. Kate Mason Rowland, *Life of George Mason*, I, 139; *The Writings of George Washington*, Jared Sparks, ed., VII, 62.

Preachers and writers, too, were propagandists. Most of them no doubt caught their tone from the spirit of the times, as must all whose livelihood depends upon intimate emotional contacts with their followers. Some, however, worked clearly and definitely to formulate public opinion. Dr. Samuel Cooper, to select only one, wrote constantly for the press, took political affairs into his pulpit, wrote Hancock's Oration on the Fifth of March, and kept in close touch with the Sons of Liberty. Francis Hopkinson, writer, called his own political squibs "ammunition," and spread through the papers his attacks on the British administration.[15]

One man, William Livingston, so perfectly exemplifies the typical propagandist of the Revolution that a more detailed treatment of him may well stand for them all. Above rather than of the people, he knew them shrewdly, and was one of the few who during the war not only realized the urgency of reanimating their enthusiasm, but set about it. The family, politically influential in New York, dour Presbyterians, found their most determined opposition in the wealthier, Anglican De Lanceys. Young Will, studying away in the 1740's at the parentally imposed law books (for he had wanted to paint), saw Anglicans taking over the newly founded King's College, Anglicans arrogantly demanding an American bishop, and Anglican De Lanceys about to wreck the political power of the family. His Presbyterian dislike of establishments fully confirmed by this doleful outlook, Livingston began a long fight on the Anglicans, writing persistently against the plans for an American episcopate until his essays had, as he said, "an universal alarm. . . . For I take it that clamour is at present our best policy, and that if the country can be animated against it, our superiors at home will not be easily induced to grant so arrogant a claim, at the expense of the public tranquility."[16] With such ideas and with his background, William Livingston could not conceivably have been a Tory, but he was in some apparent doubt himself, and it was not until independence was safely declared and he was irrevocably bound to the cause as governor of New Jersey that he again called upon his abilities as a propagandist, aware that the campaign of mind was as hard as the campaign of arms. He established the first New Jersey newspaper during the Revolution and used its columns extensively. His essays, broadsides, and speeches all show a real knowledge of crowd psychology. The most important motive in war psychosis is not reason or justice, or even self-interest, but hate, and he knew it. Compare this paragraph from one of his addresses to the New Jersey legislature with the anti-German propaganda of the last war:[17]

15. Alice M. Baldwin, *New England Clergy and the American Revolution,* pp. 93, 156; *The Writings of Benjamin Franklin,* Albert Henry Smyth, ed., VII, 351, n. To his wife Hopkinson wrote an account of the destruction of his home by the British and said: "I will send some of the enclosed Papers to camp and take care it shall be in every News Paper." Charles Hildeburn, Loyalist Ladies of the Revolution, p. 64, MS. in the Historical Society of Pennsylvania.

16. Sedgwick, pp. 136 f.

17. *Archives of the State of New Jersey,* ser. 2, vol. I, pp. 301-305.

They have warred upon decripid age; warred upon defenceless youth. They have committed hostilities against the possessors of literature; and the ministers of religion: Against public records; and private monuments; and books of improvement; and papers of curiosity; and against the Arts and Sciences. They have butchered the wounded, asking for quarter; mangled the dying, weltering in their blood; refused to the dead the rights of sepulture; suffered prisoners to perish for want of sustenance; violated the chastity of women; disfigured private dwellings of taste and elegance; and in the rage of impiety and barbarism, profaned edifices dedicated to Almighty God . . . who will not always suffer *the sceptre of the wicked to rest on the lot of the righteous. . . .*

That might have been written in 1918.

This rapid sketch of Revolutionary propagandists has shown how generally it was understood that prepared opinion was requisite to concerted action; it has shown presidents, governers, judges, preachers, writers, and mob leaders uniting to excite the people against England. Without this background of propaganda there would have been no war in 1775 and no Declaration of Independence in 1776.

A concrete example of how the propagandists handled a specific problem—the defeatist movement of 1778—will give substantive proof of what has been said.

The year 1778 marks that period in the American Revolution which comes in every war, when the opposing forces, tired out, draw apart to gauge each other's determination, sparring cautiously as they gather strength. In America the army was weary, starved, and almost naked; desertions increased dangerously and sixteen thousand militiamen went home. Money depreciated and prices soared; supplies could hardly be bought. The Tories, taking hope from the distressing state of affairs, became unusually active. In ·Boston doubtful Whig and reviving Tory were almost indistinguishable and town meetings "got to be just as the affair of the witches at Salem,—everyone naming his neighbor." Tory propagandists filled the few papers open to them with ridicule of the American leaders, criticism of Washington, and well-founded satires upon the fruits of independence. Even the new French treaty, the aggrieved patriots found, did not bring the immediate relief they had anticipated, for it cut off supplies from France, who needed them herself, it brought no French army or navy to America, and Tories charged that it simply meant the establishment of popery, the rebuilding of the French empire in the Western Hemisphere, and the destruction of American commerce, absorbed by France. Everywhere men were puzzled and uncertain. America was tired and discouraged.

At this moment Lord North introduced two bills providing for reconciliation with the colonies. They meant in effect a return to the status of 1763, with certain modifications in favor of the colonies. Commissioners—Lord Carlisle, Sir George Johnstone, and William Eden—were chosen to present the terms to anyone authorized to treat. The bills together with Lord North's speech to Parliament were distributed from Sir William Howe's headquarters at Philadelphia on April 18.

Here was a real test of the Whig propagandists, and they prepared to meet it. Washington obtained copies immediately and forwarded them to Congress with the hurried advice that they be published, "and persons of leisure and ability set to work to counteract the impressions they may make on the minds of the people." [18] Before night on the twentieth, congressional leaders were spreading the alarm. Copies were sent to state governors and other people of authority. Henry Laurens, President of Congress, forwarded a copy to Governor Trumbull of Connecticut urging that "its wicked designs ought to be repelled [writing "compelled" in his haste] everywhere, with the utmost energy"; and to James Duane he wrote, "your Morris and our Drayton have it in hand I make no doubt but that we shall return it decently tarred and feathered." [19] The Maryland delegates, John Henry, Jr., Samuel Chase, and Charles Carroll, warned Governor Johnson to publish the proposal only when proper strictures had been made upon it, the first writing, "it will prove more dangerous to our cause than ten thousand of their best Troops," the second, "The Hour to try the Firmness and prudence of Man is near at Hand," and the third, "try, for God sake and the sake of human Nature, to rouse our countrymen from their lethargy." [20] On April 22 Congress itself published an address warning the people against what it still thought were spurious terms of peace; and while riders were posting from York to carry the news, Washington was calling upon William Livingston for his support: [21]

> You will see that their aim is, under offers .of peace, to divide and disunite us; and, unless their views are early investigated and exposed in a striking manner and in various shapes by able pens, I fear they will be but too successful, and that they will give a very unhappy if not a ruinous cast to our affairs. . . . If your leisure will possibly permit, I should be happy that the whole should be discussed by your pen.

Livingston replied immediately: [22]

18. *Writings of Washington*, V, 328.

19. Laurens Letter Book, Mar. 6-Sept. 23, 1778, pp. 53 f., South Carolina Historical Society; *Letters of Members of the Continental Congress*, Edmund C. Burnett, ed., III, 171.

20. Burnett, III, 178, n., 180, 181.

21. *Writings of Washington*, V, 331-332.

22. Sedgwick, p. 282. Collins was the editor of the *New Jersey Gazette*. The same day Livingston wrote Laurens: "I hope we shall not be such Blockheads as to accede to ridiculous Terms when we have so fair a Prospect of obtaining Peace, upon almost any Terms—Tho' my good friends in New-York have faithfully promised to cut my throat for writing, which they seem to resent more than fighting, I have already begun to sound the Alarm in our Gazette in a variety of Letters, as tho' every body execrated the proposals of Britain." Henry Laurens Papers, South Carolina Historical Society.

I have sent Collins a number of letters, as if by different hands, not even excluding the tribe of petticoats,[23] all calculated to caution America against the insidious arts of enemies. This mode of rendering a measure unpopular, I have frequently experienced in my political days to be of surprising efficacy, as the common people collect from it that everybody is against it, and for that reason those who are really for it grow discouraged, from magnifying in their own imagination the strength of their adversaries beyond its true amount.

Samuel Adams, with his rare ability to find out things before anyone else, had already written Richard Henry Lee from Boston the day the bills were distributed from Philadelphia: [24]

As there [are] every where awful Tories enough to distract the Minds of the People, would it not be wise for Congress by a Publication of their own to set this important Intelligence in a clear Light before them, and fix in their Minds the first Impressions in favor of Truth?

His letter, of course, arrived too late to influence the decision of Congress.

Confirmation of the French alliance and the retreat of the British from Philadelphia buoyed the hopes of Congress, and when the commissioners arrived in June they were met with a flat refusal to treat on any other terms than the removal of all British forces and the recognition of American independence. This did not end the matter, however, for the commissioners continued to demand a hearing and appealed to the people through proclamations and private letters, while Tories aided them with pleas for a return to the "most wise and gracious of governments," saying that Americans had been duped into continuing the unnatural war simply "To pursue a PHANTOM OF INDEPENDENCY; or, in other Words, to support at the Expence of her own Blood and Treasure; *the* POWER *and consequence of a Set of Men, who oppose Peace merely because such an Event would sink them into Obscurity."* [25]

To hold the allegiance of the people, to defeat the peace movement, the propagandists exercised their every ability. William Livingston began

23. On May 6 there appeared in the *New Jersey Gazette* a contribution signed BELINDA, calling upon all women to enter a solemn protest against the proposals, and reported that "the fair ones in our neighbourhood have already entered into a resolve for every mother to disown her son, and refuse the caresses of her husband, and for every maiden to reject the addresses of her gallant, where such husband, son or gallant, shows the least symptoms of being imposed upon by this flimsy subterfuge, which I call the dying speech, and last groans of Great-Britain." Belinda was, of course, Governor Livingston, but the editor of the *New Jersey Archives* in a note declares that this was "probably the first political communication ever written by a New Jersey woman and addressed to the editor of a newspaper." Ser. 2, vol. II, pp. 195 f.

24. *The Writings of Samuel Adams*, Harry Alonzo Cushing, ed., IV, 22 f.

25. *Royal Gazette*, June 3, 1778. Tory propaganda was unusually adroit during this controversy.

the essays of "Hortentius" early in May and continued them until the commissioners were safely aboard ship for England, supplementing them by such conceits as his rather heavy satire would permit; William Henry Drayton performed one of his last services to America in the series of articles initialed W. H. D.; Gouverneur Morris wrote under the pen name "An American"; and Tom Paine devoted two numbers of the *Crisis* to the peace proposals. Important newspapers reprinted these essays and they were read everywhere.[26]

The general course of the argument against reconciliation was that England made the proposals only because she was convinced of the impossibility of winning the war, that it would ruin America to come to terms at this time, that the French alliance assured American independence, and that instead of listening to compromises, the people should redouble their efforts. The commissioners' proclamations were parodied, their characters impugned, their authority questioned, and their good faith denied.[27] Every statement they made was contradicted. Their charge that France would prolong the war in her own interests brought an immediate repudiation from the treaty itself and a challenge from the intense Marquis de Lafayette. When they threatened America with the extremes of war, from which so far the "benevolence" of England had saved her, propagandists asked with apparent horror, are you men or devils? "You have already equalled, and in many cases excelled, the savages of either Indies; and if you have yet a cruelty in store, you must have imported it, unmixed with every human material, from the original warehouse of hell." [28] On every hand the people were warned not to be led astray by false offers: [29]

> Be not deceived by any specious pretences of friendship that may be offered you by Britain; justly may you suspect the root from whence they spring, hypocrisy and inability conjoined. Were they able to subdue you, they would delight to trample you to mortar, and the crackling of your bones under their horses hoofs, would be to them an agreeable sound. . . .

26. *E.g.*, New York *Journal*, July-Aug., 1778; *Pennsylvania Packet*, July, 1778, Feb., 1779; *Pennsylvania Evening Post*, July, 1778; *New Jersey Gazette*, July, 1778; Mar., 1779; *North Carolina Gazette*, July, 1778; *Connecticut Journal*, July-Aug., 1778; *Massachusetts Spy*, Oct., 1778; *South Carolina and American General Gazette*, Apr., 1779. Similar in character was "Bob Centinel," which appeared in the *Massachusetts Spy*, July 23, 1778; New York *Journal*, Sept. 14, 1778; *Pennsylvania Packet*, Sept. 26, 1778; and the Boston *Independent Ledger*, clipped in the *Connecticut Courant*, Nov. 3, 1778.

27. Sir George Johnstone issued a statement by the Whigs as an attempt to bribe congressional leaders. Laurens sent this and other papers of the commissioners to William Livingston, saying, "Mr. Johnstone's Declaration in particular cannot escape in New Jeresy the correction it deserves, when the proper time shall come, of which due notice shall be given, it ought to be bated everywhere." September, 1778, Laurens Letter Book, Mar. 6–Sept. 23, 1778.

28. *The Crisis*, No. VI, *The Complete Works of Thomas Paine* (New York, 1922), II, 171.

29. Fitzhugh McKay, *American Liberty Asserted* (Lancaster, 1778), p. 14. A printed sermon in the Library of Congress.

The peace proposals received the same treatment. Parliament, it was said, offered to absorb sufficient Continental currency to pay off colonial debts; the propagandists said England could not discharge her own. Parliament offered representation; propagandists said America wanted no representation in a British Parliament. Parliament offered to give up taxation of the colonies except that necessary to regulate trade, and to use any money so collected in the colony which paid it; propagandists denied the right of any nation or group to control American commerce. As William Livingston put it: [30]

> And what can be more provoking than for Great Britain, after acknowledging the superiority of our arms, to propound such a controul over our commerce as we remonstrated against before the commencement of the war; and which would infallibly render us and our remotest posterity the slaves and tributaries of a nation venal, corrupt, abandoned, and rushing headlong into inextricable perdition? But to palliate this ruinous measure, it is sugar'd over with "that the net-proceeds of such duties shall be always paid and applied to and for the use of the colony, &c. in which the same shall be respectively levied;" that is, in plain English, to maintain legions of hungry ministerial dependents, who are to be sent amongst us to accumulate fortunes, and then re-cross the Atlantic to dissipate in luxury what they amassed by iniquity, and thus make room for another set equally penurious and rapacious. For my own part I would rather pay the tax immediately into the English exchequer, as I think it infinitely more eligible to support a number of rogues in London than in America.

In short, said the propagandists: [31]

> Away with your fleets and armies, acknowledge the independence of America, and as Ambassadors, not Commissioners, solicit a treaty of peace, amity, commerce and alliance with the rising Stars of this western world. Your nation totters on the brink of a stupendous precipice, and even delay will ruin her.

Other forms of suggestion popularized and supported straight argument. The celebrations on the Fourth of July were more impressive than usual, for it was such demonstrations, as John Adams had said several years before, that cultivated the sensations of freedom, tinged the minds of the people, impregnated them with the sentiments of liberty, and rendered them fond of the leaders in the cause, and averse and bitter against all opposers.[32] Orations attacked the compromise measures and held out the glorious benefits of independence. David Ramsay closed a long discourse in Charleston with words full of hope, hope vague and unreal, but the more significant in its unreality: [33]

30. *New Jersey Gazette*, May 6, 1778.
31. New York *Journal*, July 6, 1778.
32. *Works*, II, 218.
33. Niles, *Principles*, pp. 64–72.

Our sun of political happiness is already risen, and hath lifted its head over the mountains, illuminating our hemisphere with liberty, light, and polished life. Our independence will redeem one quarter of the globe from tyranny and oppression, and consecrate it the chosen seat of truth, justice, freedom, learning and religion.

Facts were distorted and rumors propagated. It was said that fifteen hundred Hessians had deserted from the army in New York, and that the British were so discouraged they were planning to give up the contest in America and look to their interests in the West Indies. Arthur Lee gave color to this rumor by reporting that a broadside had been distributed in London on the authority of Lord North himself containing the words: "All hope of conquest is . . . over. *America stands on high ground; France and England must now court her.* We have no possible chance of making peace with her, but by an immediate act of parliament, giving her perfect independence." [34] Every instance of American bravery or success was magnified, for as Tom Paine said, "It is always dangerous to spread an alarm . . . unless the prospect of success be held out with it, and that not only as probable but naturally essential." [35] American resources, American manpower, American generals could never be overcome, and with God's manifest intention to preserve his chosen people in the Western World, independence was inevitable. "If God be for us," said triumphant Whigs, "who can be against us?" And Tom Paine taunted the commissioners with not possessing, after three years of war, a single foot of land on the *continent* of America: "Staten Island, York Island, a small part of Long Island, and Rhode Island, circumscribe your power." [36] By such arts the commissioners were completely routed, and on October 17 they sailed for England, beaten men.

We know now that America could not stop. The propagandists, recognizing this, knew that before the finishing blow to British power in America could be given, courage must rise with danger and hope with fear, and that they alone could so inspire the people: they had possessed for themselves the words of St. Paul, "For if the trumpet give an uncertain sound, who shall prepare himself to the battle?"

34. New York *Journal,* Sept. 7, 1778.
35. Moncure D. Conway, *Life of Thomas Paine,* I, 159.
36. *The Crisis,* No. VI.

LAWRENCE A. HARPER
Mercantilism and the
American Revolution
WITH SOME COMMENTS BY O. M. DICKERSON

In many respects the symposium on the American Revolution held at the annual meeting of the American Historical Association in Chicago in December, 1941, marked a turning point in Revolutionary studies. Lawrence A. Harper's paper on the operation of the Navigation Acts is lucid and balanced. It was not fair, he concluded, "to blame British mercantilism for prescribing regulations which were demanded by the circumstances of the time." The system did not discriminate against the colonists. In his own comments Professor Dickerson went further and outlined a thesis to which he addressed himself in a most impressive series of articles: that the Navigation Acts, far from causing the Revolution, brought precise benefits to "large sections of American business," but that after 1764 a new policy was introduced "in direct violation of the established principles" of the mercantile system.

THE CYNIC who declared that history is the process whereby a complex truth becomes a simplified falsehood may have had in mind interpretations of the American Revolution. Even before the Revolution occurred, Vergennes prophesied that France's loss of Canada would eventually bring it about.[1] The very document which made the severance final attributed the blame to George III, a fashion which has been generally followed, and some years ago was ardently expounded by a former mayor of this city, Big Bill Thompson. These points, however, are called to attention merely to remind us of what Professor Root will expound more fully—that there are many interpretations. Our immediate task is to concentrate upon one—the relation of English mercantilism to the American Revolution.

The term "mercantilism" is one of those words which have different meanings for different people. On the one hand, George Louis Beer claimed that English mercantilism was a well-balanced system designed for the benefit of the colonies as well as the mother country, and on the other, Sir William Ashley declared that the regulations of English mer-

Reprinted by permission from the *Canadian Historical Review*, XXIII (1942), 1-15, 29-34.

1. George Bancroft, *History of the United States of America from the Discovery of the Continent to the Establishment of the Constitution in 1789* (1885 ed., 6 vols), II, 564.

cantilism were either pious formulas nullified in the actual world of commerce by fraud and evasion, or merely a codification of commercial habits which would have been followed in any case. For reasons which have been explained more fully elsewhere [2] we shall reject Beer's claim that there was no exploitation and accept the statements of the mercantilists themselves that they planned to exploit the colonies for the benefit of the mother country. We shall deny the Ashley view that there was no actual regulation and conclude from more recent studies of the evidence that the English laws did regulate trade and commerce.

These two conclusions provide us with a working definition of English mercantilism in its colonial aspects. It had as its purpose, exploitation, and as its means, regulation. Both phases of the problem, exploitation *and* regulation, are important. To understand the relationship of mercantilism and the Revolution we must not only analyse the extent to which the colonists were exploited but also consider the skill with which they were regulated.

An analysis of how the colonists were exploited is no easy task, as any one knows who has struggled with the many statutory ambiguities involved. The calculations involved in estimating the burdens placed upon the colonial economy are complicated. They call for arithmetical computations involving duties, preferences, or drawbacks of such odd amounts as 1s. 10d. and 15 16/75 of a twentieth of a penny per pound of tobacco. They run afoul of complicated analyses of costs and close decisions about the incidence of taxation. The answer required some thousands of hours of WPA and NYA labour in tabulating the necessary data and hundreds more in analysing and correlating them, the details of which have been compressed in thirty-eight rather dull pages.[3] All that can be attempted here is to state the conclusions and indicate the grounds upon which they are based. We can, however, simplify our analysis of the mercantilist code which exploited the colonies by dividing it into four parts: first, the basic provisions concerning the trans-Atlantic trade; second, the supplementary measures restricting manufactures; third, the subsidiary rules with reference to the American trade; and fourth, the much discussed measures enacted after the French and Indian War.

In examining the first part, we find that the basic provisions concerning the trans-Atlantic trade placed a heavy burden upon the colonies. By means of the Navigation Acts England attempted both to keep foreign vessels out of the colonies and to enable English merchants to share in the more profitable parts of the trans-Atlantic trade. The enumeration of key colonial exports in various Acts from 1660 to 1766 and the Staple Act of 1663 hit at colonial trade both coming and going. The Acts required the colonies to allow English middlemen to distribute such crops as tobacco and rice and stipulated that if the colonies would not buy English manufactures, at least they should purchase their European

2. L. A. Harper, *The English Navigation Laws* (New York, 1939), chap. xix.
3. L. A. Harper, "The Effect of the Navigation Acts on the Thirteen Colonies" (in *The Era of the American Revolution,* ed. by Richard B. Morris, New York, 1939).

goods in England. The greatest element in the burden laid upon the colonies was not the taxes assessed. It consisted in the increased costs of shipment, trans-shipment, and middleman's profits arising out of the requirement that England be used as an *entrepôt*.

The burdens were somewhat lightened by legislation favouring the colonies, but not as much as usually alleged. The suppression of tobacco production in England, for example, was comparatively unimportant to the colonies since the great quantities of colonial tobacco re-exported caused its price to be determined by a world rather than an English market. Moreover, the motive was not goodwill for the colonists but fiscal, since the heavy revenues derived from tobacco could be collected more easily at the waterfront than upon the farm. Likewise, although colonial shipbuilders and shipowners approved the clauses of the Navigation Acts which eliminated Dutch rivals, they did not need such protection. They had managed to carry cargoes and to build ships which could be sold in the world market before the laws were enacted and they continued to do so after the Revolution. The fact is that colonial shipowners suffered, directly, and colonial shipbuilders, indirectly, under the Navigation Acts since other clauses enabled English shipowners (as contrasted with American) to carry eighty per cent of the trade between the British Isles and the Thirteen Colonies whereas they carried only twenty per cent after the Revolution.[4]

Similarly the drawbacks, bounties, and tariff preferences, of which

4. *Ibid.,* 8-10, 37. Richard Champion, *Considerations on the Present Situation of Great Britain and the United States* (London, 1784) declares at pages 27-8 that the ships in the trade between Europe and the Thirteen Colonies totalling 195,000 tons "were generally the property of British merchants, navigated by British seamen" and that they formed "no less than a sixth of our whole shipping," which had previously (p. 13) been stated to be about 1,300,000 tons. Obviously the trans-Atlantic trade of Boston, New York, and Philadelphia included a substantial percentage of colonial-owned ships, but the *trans-Atlantic* trade of those ports was less than that of Virginia, Maryland, and South Carolina, which was overwhelmingly in the hands of British vessels. Thus it seemed wisest to modify Champion's statement somewhat and the estimate of eighty per cent was taken as being a fairly reasonable approximation. Subsequent analyses of the Naval Office lists show that the percentages differ radically from port to port and even within the same port during different years:

OWNERSHIP OF TONNAGE IN TRADE WITH BRITISH ISLES

Ports	Exports for	By British	By British and colonial jointly	By colonial	By others	Total
New York	1754	340	550	2,585	20	3,495
" "	1764	1,362	740	2,010	100	4,212
Port York	1768	2,376		350		2,726
Port Hampton	1758	2,627		465	80	3,172
" "	1766	3,436		1,385	35	4,856
South Carolina	1758	8,649		1,825	670	11,144
" "	1766	13,982	1,691	1,205	605	17,483

we are so often reminded, did not materially offset the burdens placed upon the trans-Atlantic trade. The drawbacks paid by English customs authorities on foreign products re-exported to the colonies should not be listed as a benefit to the colonies. There would have been no duties to be drawn back except for the requirement that the colonists purchase their European goods in England. The portion of the duties which England retained, while less than it might have been, was obviously greater than nothing at all.[5] Likewise, *bounties paid upon English manufactures* exported to the colonies, were of advantage to the English producer, who received them whether his goods were exported to the colonies or anywhere else, rather than of benefit to the colonial consumer who otherwise would, and often did, buy competitive European goods.[6]

On the other hand, however, the bounties paid upon colonial products were of real advantage to the colonies. They sustained the growth of

5. It is, of course, true that, if one wishes to consider the fairness of the burdens laid upon the colonists, it is relevant to remember that the allowance of drawbacks enabled them to pay lower taxes upon the same goods than the English were assessed. An analysis of the economic burdens upon the colonies, however, is concerned primarily with ascertaining how much the colonists had to pay, not with determining how fair the assessment was. If one lists the drawbacks as a colonial advantage in such an analysis, the entire tax should be calculated as a colonial burden, in which case one will attain exactly the same result reached in the calculations which follow, since the drawback has already been deducted from the gross tax and the only burden considered has been the net tax retained in Britain.

6. The grant of the bounty did not depend upon exportation *to the colonies* in the case of any of the bounty-paid products (cordage, corn, certain fish, beef, pork, gunpowder, linen, sailcloth, silk manufactures, and refined sugar), nor in the case of the candles, glass, hides, lace, thread and fringes, leather manufactures, paper, calicoes, silks, salt, soap, and starch, the "exciseable goods" which received specified drawbacks or bounties upon exportation (Samuel Baldwin, *A Survey of the British Customs*, London, 1770, Part II, 19-22). In the case of linens the bounty was paid only for exportations to Africa, America, Spain, Portugal, Gibraltar, Minorca, and the East Indies, but those were the only regions in

An attempt was made to calculate the average for all the colonies on the assumption that the average of the New York percentages would be typical of that of the colonies north of the Mason and Dixon line, while an average of the Virginia and Charleston figures would represent that of the Southern colonies. The averages thus derived were then weighted in accordance with the ratio of Northern (30) and Southern (70) tonnages engaged in the Anglo-American trade in 1769 (Public Record Office, London, Customs 16, vol. 1), with the result that the percentage of British-owned ships was found to be 74.5 per cent and that of colonial-owned ships 16.9 per cent. The procedure, however, involved other complications. Vessels listed as colonial-owned in Virginia and Charleston were listed as colonial but they were probably owned in most cases by Scottish factors who might well be classed as British. Vessels carrying rice to southern Europe were considered to be engaged in trade with the British Isles because they virtually all engaged in a triangular voyage which started and ended there. Owners listed as residing in Madeira, Rotterdam, and elsewhere (3.4 per cent) probably should have been listed as British since only ships of British subjects were allowed to trade in the colonies. Finally, there is the question of how great was the British and how great was the colonial interest in the vessels owned jointly (5.2 per cent). Thus the best estimate now possible would seem to be that the British controlled about 80 per cent of the tonnage in the Anglo-American trade under mercantilism.

indigo in South Carolina, did much to foster the development of naval stores in North Carolina, encouraged the lumber industry in New England, and at the end of the colonial period averaged more than £65,000 a year for the Thirteen Colonies alone. Similarly the preferences granted colonial products were beneficial in so far as they operated. Although they had no effect upon such commodities as tobacco and rice and their effect upon other commodities is somewhat uncertain, colonial raw silk, naval stores, and lumber definitely benefited. Yet the total sum represented by such preferences was never great and it is doubtful whether the benefit the Thirteen Colonies thus derived amounted to even one-twentieth of that obtained by the British West Indian planters who in the year 1773 alone, pocketed £446,000, thanks to a preferential rate which enabled their sugar to hold the English market despite a five-shilling-per-hundred-weight differential in price.[7]

The uncertainties underlying many of our calculations do not permit an exact statement, but judging from calculations for the year 1773, it would seem that after all proper allowances have been made for bounties and other preferences, the net burden imposed upon the Thirteen Colonies by the restraints upon the trans-Atlantic trade was between two million and seven million dollars a year. In these days of astronomical budgets such figures do not seem especially impressive, but the annual per capita burden represented by the lower estimate would come close to meeting all the expenses of operating the national government during Washington's administration, and an annual per capita tax based upon the higher estimate would, in addition to paying the current expenses of government, have raised in twelve years (from 1790-1801) a sum sufficient to pay both the domestic and foreign debt incurred by the United States government during the Revolutionary War.[8]

7. Harper, "Effect of the Navigation Acts," *passim.* As Professor Gipson points out, the British West Indies had their own burdens, such as the $4\frac{1}{2}$ per cent tax in Barbados, but their increasing inability to meet world competition as shown by the decrease in re-exports of sugar from England (Frank W. Pitman, *The Development of the British West Indies,* New Haven, 1915, 156 ff.) indicates that retention of England's market was very important to them. Also one must remember that the British fleet, as well as economic interests, helped to prevent their joining the Thirteen Colonies in revolt, just as the Canadians were kept loyal to the mother country partly by their distrust of the Thirteen Colonies and partly by the profits to be derived in the fur trade from an uninterrupted supply of British manufactures.

8. The estimate of the net burden given here has been modified slightly from that given in Harper, "The Effect of the Navigation Laws," in order to make greater allowances for the possibly beneficial effects of preferential rates on colonial products and for possible errors in estimating the ratio between the pound and the dollar.

which British linen had an opportunity to compete successfully. It is also important to note that in the year 1773 the exports to the American colonies of bounty-paid linen totaled £348,464 (of which £168,314 went to the continental colonies), while less than £68,000 worth of bounty-paid linen was exported to the rest of the world. During the same year the continental colonies imported almost the same amount of duty-burdened linens, valued at £137,248, and similar exports to the British Carribbean amounted to £102,754 (Customs 3, vol. 73).

When we turn to the second part of our discussion, the supplementary measures restricting manufacture, we find a difference of opinion concerning the effect of English restrictions upon manufacturing wool, hats, and iron. The earlier tendency was to dismiss the regulations as immaterial, but recently some have swung the pendulum to the other extreme and argue that the restraints were very important.[9] Neither extreme appears to accord with the facts. In the case of hats, proximity to the source of supply of furs and the comparatively simple process of manufacturing had led to the development of an industry which appears to have been injured by the legislation,[10] but the hat industry played only a minor part in the total economy. Woollen manufactures were, of course, much more important, but there is much evidence to indicate that the English prohibitions had little material effect. The colonies found that they were handicapped by an inadequate supply of good wool when they tried to develop homespun goods at the time of the Revolution—and even as late as 1791 Hamilton found that an adequate supply of labour was one of the chief stumbling blocks to his programme for encouraging industry. It required an embargo, a war, and a protective tariff before large-scale woollen manufacturing began to develop, and it did not pass beyond the household stage until many years after being freed of English mercantilism—which, incidentally, had never forbidden the manufacture of homespun for domestic use or local distribution.[11]

In the case of iron manufactures the British legislation encouraged the development of pig and bar iron and tried to discourage the manufacture of more advanced forms, but in both respects the influence of the legislation is doubtful. Because of the proximity of iron ore to forests America had a great advantage in producing crude iron, before coke replaced charcoal, and probably did not need legislative encouragement. With such an advantage in producing crude iron it was only natural that some more advanced iron articles would be produced in the colonies, whatever thorough-going mercantilists might dream about having the crude iron sent over to England and having it returned in the form of pots, pans, and other manufactures.[12]

The various disallowances of colonial laws which were intended to foster colonial manufacturing further illustrate the English intention of discouraging it but, despite that intent, English mercantilism as a whole

9. Cf. Victor S. Clark, *History of Manufactures in the United States, 1607-1860* (2 vols., Washington, 1916-28) with Miriam Beard, *A History of the Business Man* (New York, 1938); L. M. Hacker, *The Triumph of American Capitalism* (New York, 1940) and "The First American Revolution" (*Columbia University Quarterly,* XXVII, Sept., 1935).

10. Harper, "The Effect of the Navigation Acts," 6-7.

11. *Report on Manufactures,* Dec. 5, 1791, in American State Papers, Finance I, 123-44; Arthur H. Cole, *The American Wool Manufacture* (2 vols., Cambridge, Mass., 1926), *passim.*

12. A. C. Bining, *British Regulation of the Colonial Iron Industry* (Philadelphia, 1933); *Pennsylvania Iron Manufacture in the Eighteenth Century* (Harrisburg, 1938).

probably had a greater tendency to promote than to hinder colonial industry. The colonies' most dangerous industrial competitors were in many respects, not the English, but the Dutch, the Germans, and other Europeans—to say nothing of the natives of India—against whose competition the provisoes of the Staple Act of 1663 provided a very useful tariff barrier. Moreover, the large sums which mercantilism withheld from the colonies reduced their available cash, and probably forced many colonists to use homespun or other American products instead of buying British.[13]

The third point of our inquiry into colonial exploitation by England should not detain us long. Until the Molasses Act of 1733 the inter-American trade had been left virtually alone except for the requirement that the English colonies trade in English or colonial ships. Even after 1733, the prohibitive duties on foreign sugar, molasses, and rum were usually evaded. Such evasion required bribery, fraud, or concealment which probably served as a mildly protective tariff in favour of the British sugar islands, but the prices quoted in the Thirteen Colonies for sugar, molasses, and rum do not indicate that the legislation had any radical effect upon the trade.[14]

The fourth part of our inquiry—that relating to the period after 1763 —is a different matter. The researches of Schlesinger and others have demonstrated how the British measures of that period aroused the resentment of the merchants who unleashed an avalanche of agitation which soon went beyond their control. The agitation was not directed toward revolution at first, but agitation by its very nature promotes conditions favourable for revolution—and revolution followed as a natural sequence. Yet, conceding all the irritation thus aroused, we must still face the questions: Were the measures unduly exploitive? Did they fundamentally upset the economic equilibrium? Were they fatal ills which would inevitably lead to the death of the Empire, or merely minor upsets from which the Empire might have recovered—granted otherwise favourable conditions and good luck?

In reviewing the period it does not seem fair to blame British mercantilism for prescribing regulations which were demanded by the circumstances of the time. The British currency and land policies seem to fall under this category. The restrictions upon paper money undoubtedly distressed those who lacked funds, but they merely affirmed a truth which Americans had to learn from sad experience—that in the eighteenth century at least, no political alchemy could transmute paper into gold. Similarly the Proclamation of 1763 and the Quebec Act of 1774 essentially concerned imperial problems and American imitation of the

13. Cf. *Calendar of State Papers, Colonial*, XXVIII, 225, July 7, 1715; XXXII, 413-14, Sept. 8, 1721; XXXVIII, 326-7, Nov. 5, 1731.

14. See Anne Bezanson, Robert D. Gray, and Miriam Hussey, *Prices in Colonial Pennsylvania* (Philadelphia, 1935); Arthur H. Cole, *Wholesale Commodity Prices in the United States, 1700-1861*, and *Statistical Supplement* (Cambridge, Mass., 1939).

policy after independence was not mere flattery but a tribute to its inherent soundness. The measures disappointed those who had hoped to acquire fortunes from land speculation, but what else could the British have done? Neither they nor the United States government after them could allow private individuals to stir up trouble by moving into Indian territory before the way had been prepared for settlement by negotiations which extinguished the Indians' claims to the area. In view of the British debt it was merely good fiscal policy to charge for the land, and the prices and terms of sale proposed by the British mercantilists seem very reasonable when compared with the prices and terms adopted by the federal government after 1787.[15] And what solution did the Thirteen States themselves find for the conflicting claims to the territory west of the Alleghanies except to create a new governmental unit?

To one who frankly does not profess to be an expert on the point, it is difficult to understand how British mercantilism discriminated materially against the colonists. It is true that in the manœuvering for land grants, British interests sometimes clashed with colonial interests, but we hear fully as much about clashes between different colonial groups. Both the small frontiersmen and the big speculators were charged more for land than they were accustomed to pay, but it was not as much as they were to be charged by the United States government thereafter. In the readjustments which accompanied the establishment of the new policies the fur traders of the Thirteen Colonies suffered somewhat because of the machinations of British opponents but their loss was not great, and in any event by the Revolutionary period trade in furs formed only a negligible fraction of the colonial economy.[16]

15. The conditions of sale established by the British in 1774, stipulated sale by public auction and a minimum price of 6d. per acre (which however bore an annual quit-rent of 1/2d. per acre) and terms, cash (New York Colonial Documents, VIII, 410-13). The Ordinance of 1785 stipulated a 640 acre unit of purchase and a minimum price of one dollar an acre, terms, cash. The Land Act of 1796 retained the 640 acre unit of purchase but raised the minimum price to two dollars an acre and stipulated a down payment of one-half, half of the remainder within thirty days, and the balance within one year. The Harrison Land Act of 1800 reduced the unit of purchase to 320 acres but retained the minimum price of two dollars an acre and stipulated a down payment of one quarter, and the balance in four equal yearly payments. The Land Act of 1820 reduced the unit of purchase to 80 acres and the minimum price to $1.25 an acre but abolished the credit system and re-instituted cash terms (Benjamin H. Hibbard, A History of the Public Land Policies, New York, 1924).

16. According to tables compiled by Murray G. Lawson from the Inspector General's accounts (Customs 3), the imports of colonial furs decreased from 1.0 per cent of the total exports from the Thirteen Colonies to England in 1750 to 0.87 per cent in 1755, to 0.51 per cent in 1760, 0.94 per cent in 1765, 0.6 per cent in 1770, and 0.45 per cent in 1775. These percentages, however, should be further reduced because exports of the Thirteen Colonies to Scotland amounted to about one-half of the exports to England in 1769 (Customs 14, vol. 1B) and the value of exports elsewhere than Great Britain almost equalled the value of exports to Great Britain (T. Pitkin, A Statistical View of the Commerce of the United States of America: Its Connection with Agriculture and Manufactures . . . , Hartford, Conn., 1816, 21-3). Thus at the outbreak of the Revolution

The pre-Revolutionary taxation measures, however, are a different matter, and one for which British mercantilism must bear full responsibility.[17] Yet in analyzing the figures we find that the average annual revenue raised by the Sugar Acts, the Townshend Acts, and all the other taxes collected in the Thirteen Colonies by the British government amounted to only £31,000. This sum barely exceeded the indirect taxes which were collected on colonial merchandise passing through England. Moreover, both the taxes collected indirectly in England and directly in the colonies failed to equal the bounties which the British government was paying to the colonies—to say nothing of the advantages which they were deriving from preferential duties on their shipments to England. More interesting still, calculated on an annual per capita basis, the taxes collected during the Revolutionary period directly in the colonies and indirectly in England, totalled less than one-seventh of the taxes assessed at the beginning of the century.[18]

Yet even though the amount of taxation was not great, we must consider the possibility that the form of its assessment detrimentally affected colonial interests. The Tea Act, for one, definitely injured the illicit trade in tea by so reducing the price of the legal article that it lessened, if it did not eliminate, the profit from smuggling.[19] However unfair smugglers may have thought such tactics, they can hardly be said to have injured the economy of the country—especially since tea was not a pivotal commodity.

Molasses, the rum which was made from it, and the provision trade which accompanied it, however, were vital factors in colonial economy, and historians have often called attention to their importance in such books as *Rum, Romance, and Rebellion.*[20] The Sugar Act of 1764 served

17. These taxes, of course, differed in many ways from earlier measures but they had very definite economic effects, however political some of their aims may have been. Consequently, it seemed necessary to include them if our discussion of mercantilism was to be complete.

18. Harper, "Effect of the Navigation Acts," 27-9.

19. V. D. Harrington, *The New York Merchant on the Eve of the Revolution* (New York, 1935), 249, 344; A. M. Schlesinger, *The Colonial Merchants and the American Revolution, 1763-1776* (New York, 1918), 262-7.

20. By Charles W. Taussig, New York, 1928.

---

the fur trade constituted less than one-fifth of one per cent of the total exports of the Thirteen Colonies and probably had never greatly exceeded one-third of one per cent in the second half of the century. An examination of the figures in Pitkin (*ibid.*) discloses (when the £91,486 there given for the value of furs is reduced to almost one-seventh to allow for the inclusion of furs from Canada, Hudson Bay, and similar regions) that the fur trade was less important in 1770 to the Thirteen Colonies than that in spermaceti candles or in horses, to say nothing of the more important staple commodities like indigo, rice, tobacco, or provisions. The decline in importance of the fur trade dates back far before 1763. In New York, the colony most interested in the trade, furs had constituted 32 per cent of the exports to England in 1720 and had declined to 30 per cent in 1730, 23 per cent in 1740, 16 per cent in 1750, 13.8 per cent in 1755, 4.8 per cent in 1760, 10.1 per cent in 1765, 3.3 per cent in 1770, and 2.1 per cent in 1775.

notice that the British government intended to make its regulations effective when it lowered the duty on foreign sugar and molasses and prohibited the importation of foreign rum entirely. The provisions concerning sugar and rum were comparatively immaterial since no great quantities were imported, but the duty of 3d. per gallon on molasses was another matter, since literally millions of gallons came from the foreign West Indies.[21] Many feared that the trade could not bear a tax of 3d. per gallon, and in response to their pleas the duty was reduced in 1766 to 1d. per gallon and the tax was assessed on both British and foreign molasses. The excitement aroused by these taxes leads one to look for evidence of the havoc which they wrought in trade, but an examination of the wholesale prices of molasses does not disclose any noticeable change attributable to the legislation.[22] And if we carry our investigations further we find that the tax which the federal government placed and kept upon imports of molasses after 1790 almost equaled the 3d. per gallon placed upon foreign molasses in 1764 and materially exceeded the 1d. duty retained after 1766.[23] In brief, whatever the connection between rum and romance, the statistics of colonial trade disclose no correlation between rum and rebellion.

In so far as the statistics can be followed, the correlation between wine and rebellion is much closer. The Sugar Act of 1764 had also placed a duty upon wines which gave those imported by way of Britain a preferential rate of £3 per ton. The preference was not sufficient to enable the English to capture the trade in Madeira wine, but it enabled them to gain a flourishing trade in port which previously had been negligible.[24]

21. Customs 16, vol. 1 gives the following figures concerning the imports of molasses:

	FROM FOREIGN WEST INDIES	FROM BRITISH WEST INDIES
	Gallons	Gallons
1768	2,803,275	326,675
1769	3,413,367	299,678
1770	3,408,784	226,876

Figures for the importation of rum are not so satisfactory as we could desire, but according to Pitman (*British West Indies*, 208, n. 36) importations of foreign molasses exceeded those of foreign rum 27 to 1 in 1714, 39 to 1 in 1715, 34 to 1 in 1716, and 64 to 1 in 1717. According to the Naval Office Lists for 1764, approximately 38,000 gallons of rum were imported to Boston from the British West Indies as compared with 200 gallons from the foreign West Indies (Public Record Office, London, C.O. 58, vol. 850); at Salem and Marblehead the corresponding figures (for a half year only) were 22,000 and 1,000 (C.O. 5, vol. 850); at New Hampshire 63,000 and none (C.O. 5, vol. 969); at New York 87,000 and 5,000 (C.O. 5, vol. 1228).

22. *Supra*, note 14.

23. Adam Seybert, *Statistic Annals . . . of the United States* (Philadelphia, 1818), 398-9, 455-6, 469-70.

24. In 1750 (before the new tax was placed on Madeira wine) England exported to the Thirteen Colonies 15 tons, 1 hogshead and 13 gallons of Madeira; in 1765 and 1773 (after the imposition of the new tax), the exports were only 22 tons, 1 hogshead, 62 gallons, and 23 tons, 1 hogshead, 48 gallons, respectively. In the case of port, however, England's exportations rose from only 15 tons, 2 hogsheads, and 3 gallons in 1750 to 385 tons, 53 gallons in 1765, and 860 tons, 2 hogsheads, 60 gallons in 1773 (Customs 3, vols. 50, 65, 73).

Yet such an infringement of colonial taste hardly seems to justify a revolt—especially when we note that the quantity involved was not large, and that by the post-Revolutionary period Americans preferred port and other wines to Madeira.[25]

Thus, an analysis of the economic effects of British mercantilism fails to establish its exploitive aspects as the proximate cause of the Revolution. The only measures which afforded a sufficient economic grievance were the *entrepôt* provisions of the Navigation Acts, which governed the trans-Atlantic trade. They helped to create a fundamental economic unbalance, but cannot be connected directly with the Revolution. The colonists had lived under them for more than a century without desiring independence and even in the Revolutionary period with few exceptions the *entrepôt* provisions were accepted as the mother country's due for the protection which she afforded.[26] In fact, the official representatives of the colonies were willing to guarantee the British commercial system provided that the measures of political taxation were withdrawn.[27] If there were any inexorable economic forces which were inevitably drawing the colonies toward revolution, they are hard to detect and the colonists were unaware of them.

Anyone who maintains that the Revolution resulted from the inevitable clash of competing capitalisms must reckon with several points: That burdens upon the trans-Atlantic trade were proportionately greater at the beginning of the eighteenth century than in 1776; that the restraints of the land and currency policies were basically the same as those prescribed by the federal government; and that after 1766 the taxes laid on molasses by Britain were less than those imposed by the United States after 1790. He should also explain why the surplus colonial capital

25. Seybert, *Statistical Annals,* 164-9, 260.

26. The necessity of taking considerable space to calculate the burdens laid upon the colonies by mercantilism should not be regarded as a denial that Britain had real contributions to make. The benefits of military and naval protection were very important. British merchants also probably helped the colonists to find markets for their products but it is easy to overemphasize such assistance. During the greater part of the time the *entrepôt* requirements were operative the Dutch were much better qualified to serve efficiently as middlemen in colonial products than the English. Similarly the flattening of the curve of the American tobacco exports after the Revolution is not as significant as it seems at first glance. The destruction wrought by the Revolution, and the interruption to the trade, first by the Revolution, and then by the wars in Europe, would appear to have done much more to discourage tobacco production than the elimination of the laws making Britain an *entrepôt.*

27. Resolve no. 4 of the "Declaration and Resolves of the First Continental Congress, October 14, 1774" (as quoted in *Documents Illustrative of the Formation of the Union of the American States,* selected, arranged, and indexed by Charles C. Tansill, Washington, 1927, 3) contains the following statement: "But, from the necessity of the case, and a regard to the mutual interest of both countries, we cheerfully consent to the operation of such acts of the British parliament as are bona fide, restrained to the regulation of our external commerce, for the purpose of securing the commercial advantages of the whole empire to the mother country, and the commercial benefits of its respective members, excluding every idea of taxation internal or external, for raising a revenue on the subjects in America without their consent."

alleged to be bursting its confines did not venture into the manufacturing enterprises which the law did not prohibit; why the colonists did not finance their own middlemen in England; and, finally, why they did not pay their debts. If by a clash of expanding capitalism is meant that colonists with money were irritated because their freedom of action was restrained by outside regulation, one must immediately concede that the charge is justified; but such colonial resentment seems more properly classified as a political rather than an economic factor. It is merely an old point dressed in new garb and was better expressed by John Adams when he declared that the American Revolution began when the first plantation was settled.[28]

When we turn, however, from the economic effects of mercantilism to its regulatory aspects, we are faced with a different story. We can establish a direct correlation between mercantilism and the Revolution. Although earlier English regulations had been reasonably satisfactory the regulatory technique of the British government under George III was pitifully defective. As a mother country, Britain had much to learn. Any modern parents' magazine could have told George III's ministers that the one mistake not to make is to take a stand and then to yield to howls of anguish. It was a mistake which the British government made repeatedly. It placed a duty of 3d. per gallon on molasses, and when it encountered opposition, reduced it to 1d. It provided for a Stamp Act and withdrew it in the face of temper tantrums. It provided for external taxes to meet the colonial objections and then yielded again by removing all except one. When finally it attempted to enforce discipline it was too late. Under the circumstances, no self-respecting child—or colonist— would be willing to yield.

Moreover, British reforming zeal came at a very bad time. The colonists were in a particularly sensitive state due to the post-war deflation and the economic distress which accompanied it. The British also attempted to exert unusual control at a time when the removal of the French from Canada had minimized the colonists' dependence upon Britain. Most important of all, the reforms followed one another too rapidly.

In social reform, irritation often is to be measured not so much by what a regulation attempts to achieve as by the extent to which it changes established habits. The early history of English mercantilism itself offers a good illustration of the point. Bitter complaints came from Virginia and Barbados when tobacco and sugar were first enumerated because those colonies had become accustomed to conditions of comparatively free trade, whereas few or no complaints were heard from Jamaica which had developed under the restrictive system.[29] The mercantilist

28. *Works of John Adams,* ed. by Charles F. Adams (10 vols., Boston, 1856), X, 313.

29. George L. Beer, *The Old Colonial System, 1660-1754* (2 vols., New York, 1912), I, 162-3 (Virginia); I, 164-5 (Barbados); II, 83 (Jamaica); Harper, *The English Navigation Laws,* 246, n. 37.

system was geared for leisurely operation and before George III's reign succeeded by virtue of that fact. Its early restraints led to Bacon's rebellion in Virginia but fortunately for the mother country the pressure against New England was deferred until the next decade when it, too, led to an explosion in the form of revolt against Andros.[30] These uprisings were separated both geographically and chronologically so that neither attained dangerous proportions, and both were followed by a reasonably satisfactory settlement of at least some of the colonial grievances.

During the Revolutionary era, however, the tempo of reform was not leisurely. Doubtless all the colonists were not irritated by any one British reform, but each individual had his own feeling of grievance which enabled him to agree fervently with the complaints of others against British policy and thus add to the heated tempers of the time. The politician who objected to the political implications in taxation reforms found an audience in the land speculators and frontiersmen who complained that the colonists were being deprived of the reward of their blood and suffering by the Proclamation of 1763 and the Quebec Act of 1774. Debtors and inflationists chimed in to tell of the iniquities of the Currency Act; lawyers and printers could not forget the threat to their interests in the Stamp Act. On Sundays the preachers thundered against the dangers of popery in Quebec and voiced their fear that Britain planned to establish an Anglican Church in the colonies. The merchant was always ready to explain not merely how harmful British taxes were to colonial economy, but how irksome were the new administrative rules and regulations. Such chronological and geographical barriers as existed were overcome and a community of antagonisms was maintained by the Committees of Correspondence and other agitators, but such revolutionary forces could not have succeeded if the different elements of the colonies had not recently experienced a mutual sense of grievance.

In short, many of the misunderstandings which have arisen in connection with mercantilism and the American Revolution have grown out of the failure to distinguish between the two phases of mercantilism: exploitation and regulation. The fact that the colonists were exploited by English mercantilism does not necessarily mean that mercantilism caused the American Revolution. Economic forces are not magnets which inexorably move men in predetermined patterns. For better or for worse, men try to regulate their economic as well as their political destiny. A large part of governmental activity consists in attempting to mould economic conduct and to minimize the friction which results from clashes or constraints. English mercantilism was such an attempt. It succeeded rather well in minimizing friction until 1764. For the next decade it bungled badly, and the penalty was the loss of the Thirteen Colonies.

---

30. Beer, *Old Colonial System*, II, 148 ff.; Thomas J. Wertenbaker, *Torchbearer of the Revolution: The Story of Bacon's Rebellion and its Leader* (Princeton, 1940).

Comments by O. M. Dickerson

For some years I have been studying contemporary opinion on the eve of the Revolution. Consequently I shall confine my discussion mainly to Professor Harper's paper. His study of the Navigation Acts is a rare piece of objective scholarship. It is the first attempt of any scholar to determine just what the many complicated measures were and how they worked. His conclusion that the commercial system as a whole did not place upon the colonies oppressive ecomonic burdens, and could not have done so to the extent of inciting active opposition, is what was to be expected. My own studies of contemporary opinion confirm his conclusions. The Americans did not oppose the commercial system under which they lived. In no case could I find that any responsible individual assailed the Navigation Acts, and very few indeed assailed any of the genuine trade acts during the years of agitation, 1765-1775. Every individual who participated actively in the Revolution was dead before a historian advanced the theory that the Navigation Acts were a cause of the Revolution. The original author of the theory seems to have been George Bancroft, who based it upon economic theology and cites no contemporary evidence that Americans actually opposed the Navigation Acts. The myth has continued to grow as later writers expanded it without seeking actual evidence.

Mr. Harper has referred to his essay on the "Effect of the Navigation Acts," [1] and I assume it is a part of his presentation. In that he concludes that the net cost of the mercantile system to the Americans was not less than $2,560,000 and not more than $7,038,000. In arriving at that figure he omitted one very important item of colonial advantage— that of export bounties paid in Britain on articles of British manufacture exported to the colonies. This amounted to £37,395 for 1773, and an average annual payment for the five years 1770-1774, inclusive, of £49,950 or about $250,000. In addition he omits the drawbacks on goods exported to the colonies from England. These drawbacks ran into large sums. They have been estimated by taking the total drawbacks, determining the percentage they were of total exports, and then applying this to the known exports of America. The result is £497,092 for 1773 and an annual average for the five years, 1770-1774, of £593,291. (The figures in all cases are directly from the Treasury Papers.) If these figures are included, and certainly the first should be, the estimate of the economic burden of the navigation system should be modified. It was costing even less than Mr. Harper has estimated.

I am not suggesting that there was no net cost to American trade as a whole. I am merely pointing out that large sections of American business benefited very largely from the actual operation of the system. Americans

---

1. L. A. Harper, "The Effect of the Navigation Acts on the Thirteen Colonies" (*The Era of the American Revolution: Studies Inscribed to Evarts Boutell Greene*, ed. by Richard B. Morris, New York, 1939, 1-39).

freely admitted that the routing of a considerable part of the trade through England carried a hidden tax. They said that was their fair share of the costs of the Imperial Government. They never claimed that they should be favoured parasites enjoying the benefits of a central government, without contributing to its support. To the advantages the colonies received should also be added the benefits of protection, surveys of the Indian country, keeping the Indians in order, use of a diplomatic and consular system, protection of ships from pirates in the Mediterranean, a common postal system, the benefits of a sound currency, and free access to the markets of the greatest self-sufficient empire in the world. It was many years before they could establish similar benefits for themselves.

Mr. Harper is on sound ground when he excludes the Indians and the western land policies from a discussion of the mercantile system. He should have excluded the Stamp Act and the other taxation measures on the same ground. They were political and not economic measures. I could find no political writer of the time that did not admit that these Acts were basically different from the trade regulations. Sound trade policies encouraged trade, and certainly did not burden the trade of the home country nor burden a colonial trade to encourage one from a foreign country. The Sugar Act of 1764 in lowering the duties on molasses by fifty per cent was designed to raise a revenue by opening the colonial market to a competing foreign product. In 1766 when duties were lowered to one cent a gallon and imposed equally upon British and foreign molasses there was no possible resemblance to a trade act. The Stamp Act was also purely a revenue measure adopted for political purposes and laid its heaviest burdens upon the instruments of trade, whether these were used by Americans or by residents of England doing business in America. Consequently, it was anti-trade in character and a direct departure from the most cherished principles of the mercantilist system. Even the King's Friends could not defend the Act when it was attacked on this ground by the mercantile interests of England.

The Townshend Revenue Act was a most flagrant violation of sound trade policies. Taxing British products on their export to the colonies was directly contrary to any sound theory of trade legislation. The articles could all be made in America. A colonial import duty operated directly as a protective tariff to encourage production of goods here to displace similar products from England. The law was anti-trade and commercial interests on both sides of the Atlantic attacked it as dangerous to British trade. It was the opposition in England and not merely in America that forced the repeal of the tax upon articles of English production. Professor Root's general statement that the Americans nullified the Townshend Acts is not descriptive of what is in the contemporary evidence. They were never nullified, nor were they repealed before the outbreak of hostilities. Every effort along that line failed, and the more than £300,000 collected by the Customs Commissioners, with the friction set up in the process, were the most important causes of the Revolution.

Instead of the Revolution being the inevitable result of the century-old trade and navigation policies called the British mercantile system, it was in fact the result of adopting a new programme in direct violation of the established principles of that system. American resolutions, pamphlets, and signed articles emphasized this over and over again. The First Continental Congress, in its Resolutions of October 14, 1774, begins its list of infamous measures with the Sugar Act of 1764, pointing to it as the first that departed from the old programme, and does not cite a single measure as objectionable that was a *bona fide* trade or navigation act.

There is one phase of the pre-Revolution mercantile system that has been omitted from consideration by Mr. Harper. Probably it is incapable of statistical evaluation. Any distributing system is expensive to create, but when once created it works to the mutual advantage of producers and consumers and at the same time yields profits to those who operate it and taxes to the government that protects it. Routing goods through the English distribution system was certainly not a burden in all cases. Let us take tobacco for example. It was the Thirteen Colonies' most important enumerated product. There were three centres to the distribution system, one in Scotland, and the other two in England. Together these received, processed, and distributed 105,000,000 pounds of American tobacco in 1771 and more than 101,000,000 pounds during 1775. A foreign market for this tobacco was found and systematically developed. The peculiarities of each group of customers were determined and the tobacco prepared, processed, and packaged to satisfy varying tastes. Vast capital became involved in this business, including warehouses, factories, ships, salesmen, credits, banking facilities, advertising, etc. From these centres came the capital to develop the growing industry in America, to establish new plantations, buy slaves to stock them, grow the crops, and provide adequate fleets of ships to carry the crop to market.

To assume that freeing the American tobacco grower of enumeration would at once open to him the vast market thus built up for his product is fundamentally unsound. The Revolution freed him of enumeration, but did not open for him the assumed markets, and his export trade steadily declined for more than thirty years after the Revolution. It would be easy to present plausible proof that freeing the tobacco growers from the pre-Revolutionary trade system was a serious injury to that industry and not a benefit. The export market for rice and indigo, next to tobacco the two most important enumerated products, suffered even a worse fate. Clearly these industries lost something when they escaped from the navigation system and undertook to re-route their products directly to world markets. We need detailed studies as to just how enumeration worked. Surely the Americans were not just dumb when they failed to protest against the enumeration policy.

American and British producers and merchants were aware of the benefits to themselves that were arising from the vast organized protected markets within the Empire and the even greater markets that had been built up outside. There is a reason why leading American merchants in the important trading centres remained loyalists as did many of the great land owners. In my opinion this also helps to account for the overwhelming support given to the Americans in the earlier stages of the controversy by the mercantile interests in Great Britain.

Although the Navigation Acts were not a cause of active revolutionary agitation in America, there is a sense in which they become a cause of the Revolution. The system had been in operation more than a century. The colonies had grown rich and prosperous. Pamphleteers drafted tables of future American and English population growth which showed an American population of 130,000,000 when England would have less than 30,000,000. The American market for British goods had expanded until exports to the colonies exceeded those to the entire continent of Europe. Industry of all kinds on both sides of the Atlantic had settled into well-established grooves of trade. This trade had grown with the mercantile system and had become associated in men's minds as a result of that system. Obviously the overwhelming majority believed that any disturbance of that system would mean economic ruin to thousands. They thought of it as we do of our American capitalist economy and would fight to preserve it.

George III's personal political organization sought to shift a part of the old costs of defending America to the colonies, and at the same time to find a new source to provide for its swarms of political workers. America was to be "exploited" in the bad sense of that word, not by trade laws, but by direct political plunder, using the taxing power to supply jobs and salaries, the enforcement machinery to seize the property and fortunes of wealthy Americans, and the vast western public lands to reward the faithful. Self-government in England and America was at stake, and American personal fortunes endangered. American opposition was in part stirred up by the political opponents of the King's Friends in England. The American opposition in turn sought aid from the mercantile interests and political opposition in the home country.

The strength of the American opposition lay in its support by the manufacturing and port cities of England and the vast English population dependent upon American trade. To undermine this support unscrupulous partisans in the King's party started the report that the American opposition was really aiming at escape from the trade and navigation system. Mostly it was a whispering programme, but it did great damage. Franklin, Burke, and others devoted their major energies from 1773 on to meeting this charge. Resolutions of American Assemblies and Congresses were directed along the same line, but the lie still made headway enough to enable Lord North and Germaine to stay in power till hostilities finally broke out. So the Navigation Acts were a cause of the Revolution, but in an entirely different sense from that current in our text-books. In his final efforts to prevent a civil war, Benjamin Franklin offered to have all of the fundamental trade and navigation laws separately re-enacted by every colonial Assembly in America, provided the king and his followers would abandon the taxation programme. Appeasement then was as futile as in 1939. The war party had its way and refused to abandon taxation and coercion.

The war was never popular in England. The great commercial interests opposed it and it was they that finally forced a peace policy favourable to the Americans. The people who profited from the American mercantile relations in England were not the enemies of America but our staunchest friends.

EDMUND S. MORGAN
The American Revolution Considered as an Intellectual Movement

🔲 Edmund Morgan can with some truth be seen as the leading Neo-Whig historian; in the quality of his scholarship as in his capacity to look with new insight at hitherto familiar topics, he is a true successor to Charles Andrews. In *The Stamp Act Crisis: Prologue to Revolution* (1953), written in collaboration with his wife; in his valuable accompanying volume of documents, *Prologue to Revolution* (1959); in his *Birth of the Republic, 1763-1789* (1956); in his more recent study of Ezra Stiles (*The Gentle Puritan*); and in a number of articles he has produced major revisionist studies. And, as in his article "The American Revolution: Revisions in Need of Revising," he continues to ask fundamental questions of himself and others. Of these studies *The Stamp Act Crisis* is especially important. That crisis was fundamental, the Morgans contend, partly because it produced the leaders who were to carry the Revolution through to its conclusion; partly because the opposition to the Act arose promptly and spontaneously and was more completely united on this issue than on anything that followed; and most of all because from the first the issue was "no taxation without representation," no more and no less. The colonial leaders, the Morgans claim, were from the first fully aware where the logic of their position could lead them but kept their peace. The growing conflict, they write, "was not irretrievable, but that to retrieve it would have required an understanding on each side of the exact limits of the other's claims." While "the English thought that they saw the Americans inching their way toward independence, the Americans thought that they saw a sinister party in England seeking by gradual degrees to enslave them." Trade regulations by Parliament, yes; taxation by Parliament, no.

The American Revolution must also be seen in the context of the history of political ideas. Never before in modern times had a colony revolted against the mother country and survived; never before had it, after physical survival, embarked on a republican experiment in government; and never before had it dared to risk such an experiment on so vast and scattered a territory as did the United States. In doing so its leaders discussed the political issues all too openly and frankly: the literature of the American Revolution is first and last a political, and largely a pamphlet, literature. They drew heavily, of course, on the study of the Roman republic and on the republican ideas of seventeenth-century England, ideas associated with the Commonwealth and with the levelers. See on this subject Caroline Robbins, *The Eighteenth-Century Commonwealthman* (1959) and Bernard Bailyn's searching introductory essay, "The Transforming Radicalism of the American Revolution," to the first volume of *Pamphlets of the American Revolution, 1750-1776* (1965). Bailyn argues that the Revolution was "above all else an ideological-constitutional struggle and not primarily a controversy between social groups undertaken to force changes in the organization of society" (p. viii), and that "the fear of a comprehensive conspiracy against liberty throughout the English-speaking world . . . lay at the heart of the Revolutionary movement" (p. x).

In the article that follows, Edmund Morgan distinguishes the main intellectual elements in the Revolution: the notion of self-government and the colonists' demand for equality of treatment, along with British-born, as subjects of the King; the notion of the social compact, of the belief that the government was designed to serve the people, and that popular control was best expressed through a written constitution drawn up by a specially chosen convention; and not least the notion of federalism itself. In the debate on these issues between 1776 and 1787 the Americans emerged as one people; in the *Federalist Papers* their leaders provided in classic form a discussion of the basic issues in government; and the Constitution that emerged was to prove in all its compromises not only "the most stable popular government ever invented" but one that was well suited to the next century and a half of explosive economic and human growth. 回

IN 1740 AMERICA'S leading intellectuals were clergymen and thought about theology; in 1790 they were statesmen and thought about politics.

Reprinted by permission of Houghton Mifflin Co. from Arthur M. Schlesinger, Jr., and Morton White, *Paths of American Thought* (Boston, 1963), pp. 11-33.

A variety of forces, some of them reaching deep into the colonial past, helped to bring about the transformation, but it was so closely associated with the revolt from England that one may properly consider the American Revolution, as an intellectual movement, to mean the substitution of political for clerical leadership and of politics for religion as the most challenging area of human thought and endeavor.

The American colonies had been founded during the seventeenth century, when Englishmen were still animated by the great vision of John Calvin, the vision of human depravity and divine perfection. Every human being from Adam onward must be counted, Calvin insisted, in the ranks of "those whose feet are swift to shed blood, whose hands are polluted with rapine and murder, whose throats are like open sepulchres, whose tongues are deceitful, whose lips are envenomed, whose works are useless, iniquitous, corrupt, and deadly, whose souls are estranged from God, the inmost recesses of whose hearts are full of pravity, whose eyes are insidiously employed, whose minds are elated with insolence—in a word, all whose powers are prepared for the commission of atrocious and innumerable crimes." If a man did not actually commit such crimes, it was not for want of a desire to do so. God might furnish restraints of one sort or another to prevent "the perverseness of our nature fom breaking out into external acts, but does not purify it within." [1]

The official church of England, born of a licentious monarch's divorce, had never fully shared in Calvin's vision. Though it absorbed much of his theology during the reign of Queen Elizabeth I, it retained a more flattering view than his of human capacities and priestly powers. The more thoroughgoing English Calvinists, the Puritans, were hopeful of effecting further reforms, but during the late 1620's and 1630's the Church and the king who headed it drew ever closer to old Roman Catholic doctrines. In the 1640's the Puritans resorted to arms, killed the king, purged the Church, and turned England into a republic. But in 1660 the monarchy was restored. Puritans, now called dissenters, were dismissed from office in both church and state; and the Church of England resumed its old ways, unimpeded by Calvinism.

It is no coincidence that England's American colonies were settled before 1640 or after 1660. Emigration offered a substitute for revolution to thousands of men and women who were discontented with the Church of England and with the government that fostered it. Puritans settled all the New England colonies, overran the Catholic refuge of the Calvert family in Maryland, and later furnished substantial numbers of settlers to New York, New Jersey, and the Carolinas. They came even to Virginia, where the majority of settlers, though remaining within the Church of England, did not share in its high-church movement. After the Resto-

1. John Calvin, *Institutes of the Christian Religion,* trans. John Allen (sixth American edition, Philadelphia, 1932), I, 263.

ration, the colonies attracted large numbers of English Quakers and Scotch-Irish Presbyterians, not to mention French Huguenots and German Protestants of various denominations. Anglicans came too, and the Anglican Church was supported by law in several colonies, but the flavor of American colonial life was overwhelmingly that of the Reformation.[2]

The intellectual center of the colonies was New England, and the intellectual leaders of New England were the clergy, who preached and wrote indefatigably of human depravity and divine perfection. These two axioms, for the Puritans as for Calvin himself, required the eternal damnation of most mankind. And since God knew all and decreed all from eternity, it followed that He had determined in advance who should be damned and who should be saved. One of the principal tasks of the ministry was to explain to men how bad they were, so bad that they all deserved damnation. That God had chosen to save any was simply through mercy, another attribute of His perfection. No man deserved salvation, no one was less guilty than another, so that God's choice rested only in Himself.

To explain these doctrines was the easiest part of the preacher's task, for most of his audience was already persuaded of them. A more difficult assignment was to assist men in discerning where they stood in the divine scheme. No man could be certain whether he was saved until the day of judgment, but there were stages in the process of redemption that took place in this life; and ministers devoted much of their preaching and writing to descriptions of them. One of the first stages was conviction, a full recognition of man's helpless and hopeless condition. A man destined for damnation could reach this stage, but not the next one, conversion. Conversion was an act of God, infusing a man's soul with the Holy Spirit, "justifying" him through the attribution of Christ's merits. Conversion, for the Puritan, was so clear and precise an experience that a man who had undergone it could often specify the time and place. After conversion came sanctification, a gradual improvement in conduct, approximating, though only outwardly, the obedience which God had demanded of Adam. Sanctification could never be complete in this world, but it might be sufficiently marked to be discernible. Guided by the clergy, Puritans and other Calvinist Protestants became familiar with the morphology of redemption and expert in searching their own souls for signs of metamorphosis.

Just as the Puritans' theology revolved around human depravity and divine perfection, so did their political theory. And Puritan ministers instructed their congregations in politics as well as religion. They taught that society originates in a contract between God on the one hand and the people on the other, whereby if the people agreed to abide by His commands (though again, only outwardly, for true, inner obedience was

---

2. Cf. Frederick B. Tolles, *Quakers and the Atlantic Culture* (New York, 1960), p. 11; Babette M. Levy, "Early Puritanism in the Southern and Island Colonies," American Antiquarian Society, *Proceedings*, LXX (1960), 69-348.

beyond them) He would assure them outward prosperity. Having made such an agreement, the people, in another compact, voluntarily subjected themselves to a king or to other civil rulers. This was the origin of government; and the purpose of government was to restrain the sinfulness of man, to prevent and punish offenses against God. As long as a king enforced God's commands, embodying them in human laws, the people owed him obedience and assistance. If, however, moved by his own depravity he violated God's commands or failed to enforce them, he broke the compact on which his political authority rested, and it was the people's duty to remove him lest God visit the whole community with death and destruction.[3]

These ideas had developed in England at a time when reigning monarchs exhibited (by Puritan standards) far too much depravity. Three generations of Puritans nervously scolded their kings and queens and momentarily expected God's wrath to descend on England. Finally, in 1649, they did away with both king and kingship. But even after monarchy ended, human depravity remained, and Englishmen faced the problem of controlling it in the new context of a republic. Ideas about the maintenance of purity, probity, and stability in a republic were offered by a number of men, the most influential of whom was James Harrington. In his *Oceana* (1656) Harrington associated republican government with widespread distribution—approaching equality—of property. He also advocated religious toleration, rotation in public office, and separation of governmental powers. With the restoration of the monarchy, Harrington's work continued for several generations to excite the admiration of a small group of British political thinkers, who probed the nature of government and speculated about methods of keeping it responsible to the people.[4] The best known of them, John Locke, re-emphasized the idea of a compact between rulers and people in order to justify the exclusion of James II from the throne.[5]

The English republican writers were read in the colonies, and Locke's political doctrines were assimilated by American clergymen and dispensed in their sermons along with the older ideas. Every generation learned of its duty to pull down bad rulers and to uphold good ones. The colonists did not, however, develop a separate school of republican political theory. The clergy, who continued to be the principal exponents of political ideas and the most influential members of the community, devoted their creative intellectual efforts to theology, and their congregations continued to search souls. Every Sunday they

3. Perry Miller, *The New England Mind: The Seventeenth Century* (New York, 1939), pp. 398-431; E. S. Morgan, *The Puritan Dilemma* (Boston, 1958), pp. 18-100.

4. In *The Eighteenth-Century Commonwealthman* (Cambridge, Mass., 1959), Caroline Robbins has identified and discussed this political tradition.

5. Peter Laslett, "The English Revolution and Locke's Two Treatises," *Cambridge Historical Journal*, XII (1956), 40-55.

attended at the meetinghouse morning and afternoon to hear the theological expositions that were always the principal ingredient in a Puritan church service. Then they went home to write in their diaries and measure their lives against what they had learned in the sermons. Daily they read their Bibles and prayed, in private and with their families. Theology was as much a part of their lives as meat and drink.

By the middle of the eighteenth century, however, a change had begun. A series of developments, culminating in the Revolution, combined to effect a weakening of popular interest in theology and a decline in clerical leadership.

The first development, and the most difficult to assess, was the growth in England and Europe, transmitted gradually to America, of a new confidence in human reason. The achievements of Sir Isaac Newton and of other seventeenth-century astronomers and mathematicians belied the low estimate hitherto entertained of man's capacity to understand, without the assistance of divine revelation, God's government of the universe. The Enlightenment, as the new attitude came to be called, promised to reveal the mysteries of creation simply through the application of human intelligence.

New England ministers at first perceived no threat to religion from the Enlightenment. Although they thought poorly of human reason, they were themselves assiduous in making the most of it. They had applied it primarily to the Bible, but they now welcomed every new piece of observational knowledge in the assurance that it would help to fill out the data derived from the Bible. With the success of Newton to spur them, they began to pay more attention to the physical world and made observations of plants and animals, of comets and stars; and they sent these observations to England to assist the progress of knowledge about God's wonderful universe.

It became apparent only gradually—first in England, then in America —that reason, instead of assisting revelation, might replace it. Though Newton himself retained a firm belief in the Scriptures and spent his later years unraveling Biblical prophecies, many of his admirers became deists, who believed that God reveals Himself only through the operation of His universe and not through prophets, priests, or holy scriptures. In America deism claimed few adherents before the last quarter of the eighteenth century; and it seems probable that the Enlightenment appreciably lowered the prestige of the clergy only after they had already lost much of their influence through the paradoxical operation of a religious revival.

The Great Awakening of the 1740's began when a young English minister, George Whitefield, showed American preachers how to convey the full meaning of human depravity. Traveling throughout the colonies, he preached wherever he could find an audience, whether inside a church or under a tree, and everywhere his message was the same: men deserve hell. Whitefield's talent lay in depicting the torments of hell dramatically and vividly. He could weep at will, over the fate of the men and women before him; he could impersonate God delivering the awful sentence against them. When he wept they did too, and when he pronounced the sentence against them, they fell to the ground in agony.[6]

Whitefield had already earned some notoriety by these methods before crossing the ocean. In the colonies his success was overwhelming. People flocked to him as to a new messiah. Though Anglicans remained largely unmoved, most Americans had been brought up on the doctrine of the depravity of man, and they could not find any expression of it too strong. Whitefield merely brought them a new and more emotional appreciation of truths they had known all along. Other preachers quickly imitated his methods and outdid him in the extravagance of their gestures. Gilbert Tennent of Pennsylvania made a specialty of roaring with holy laughter at sinners whom he had awakened to their helpless condition. James Davenport of Long Island liked to preach at night, when smoking candles and torches gave verisimilitude to his fiery denunciations.[7] These self-appointed apostles and dozens more like them imitated Whitefield not only in their manner of preaching but in wandering from place to place to deliver their fearful message.

Terror was the object; and terror was right. If a man faces eternal, unbearable pain, deserves it, and can do nothing to avoid it he ought to be terrified. The preachers had another word for it, familiar to all Calvinists: they called it conviction, the awareness, denied to the complacent, of one's hopeless condition. The great thing about the new preaching was that it destroyed complacency and brought conviction to thousands. And the great thing about conviction was that conversion could be expected in many cases to follow it. Calvinist ministers for two centuries had described the divine process and in the Great Awakening the course of conviction and conversion ran true to form. Not everyone who trembled in terror rose to the joy of conversion, but hundreds did.

As the churches filled with them, it seemed apparent that God approved the new method of preaching and the men who practiced it. Whether He also approved the old methods was questionable. Men and women who had worshiped for years without result under the guidance of an erudite but undramatic minister, found grace after a few hours at the feet of some wandering apostle. The itinerant was often a layman who had never been to college and knew no Greek, Latin, or Hebrew, but had a way with an audience. If God selected him to do

6. On Whitefield, see Luke Tyerman, *The Life of the Rev. George Whitefield* (New York, 1877) and John Gillies, *Memoirs of Rev. George Whitefield* (New Haven, 1834). Originally published in 1772, Gillies's work was considerably expanded in later editions. On Whitefield in New England, see Edwin L. Gaustad, *The Great Awakening in New England* (New York, 1957).

7. Charles Chauncy, *Seasonable Thoughts on the State of Religion in New England* (Boston, 1743), pp. 127, 151-168; *Boston Weekly News-Letter,* June 24–July 1, 1742; "Diary of Joshua Hempstead," New London Historical Society, *Proceedings,* I (1901), 379 ff.

so much without learning, was learning perhaps more a hindrance than a help to true religion? The thought occurred to many converts and was encouraged by the increasingly confident, not to say arrogant, posture of the itinerants. Whitefield had warned broadly against ministers who preached an unknown and unfelt Christ. His followers did not hesitate to name individual ministers as dead of heart, blind leaders of the blind.

After such a pronouncement, a congregation, or a substantial portion of it, might desert their old minister. If they were a majority, they could dismiss him; if a minority they might secede to form a church of their own, with some newly discovered prophet to lead them. Congregations had left their ministers before, especially in New England, but never before had the desertions been so many or so bitter.

At first the deserted clergymen merely looked upon the Awakening with skepticism. But as its exponents (known to the time as New Lights) became more and more extravagant, skepticism spread and grew to hostility. Ministers who had spent their lives in the study of theology and who had perhaps been touched by the Enlightenment, were appalled at the ignorance of New Light preachers and dismissed their convictions and conversions as hysteria. Many of these opposers (Old Lights), though reluctant to recognize the fact, were already several steps down the road that led to Arminianism, Universalism, Unitarianism, and deism. The most outspoken of them, Charles Chauncy, eventually became a Universalist. But most of them pulled up short of these extremes, and those who went the whole way found few followers. The majority, clinging to the old doctrines of Calvinism, mitigated in some measure by the Enlightenment, were a humane and pious group, perhaps the most likeable of New England clergymen. Some of them retained or rewon the loyalty of large congregations. But they never regained the broad influence they had enjoyed over the colonial community before the Great Awakening.

The failure of the Old Light clergy to retain intellectual leadership was due partly to the fact that they failed to win the minds of the next generation of ministers. The New Lights, in spite of their ignorance, enjoyed the blessing of Jonathan Edwards, America's foremost intellectual. It was inevitable that bright young divinity students should follow his lead. Edwards, the most brilliant theologian the country ever produced, had already generated a minor awakening of his own at Northampton, Massachusetts, six years before the Great Awakening. By comparison with Whitefield his technique was muted: he talked almost in a monotone, and never resorted to dramatic gestures, but when he spoke of eternal torments in as matter-of-fact a manner as he spoke of the weather, the effect on a New England audience could be devastating. Observing the beneficial effects of terror, Edwards applauded when Whitefield and Tennent brought the fires of hell to New England.

In ensuing years Edwards wrote a series of treatises to demonstrate the importance of the emotions or "affections" in religion and to affirm, more rigorously than ever before in New England, the dogmas of divine perfection and human depravity. By the time he died in 1758, he had gathered a tight band of followers, who continued his doctrines and developed them into a theological system known as the New Divinity.[8] The high priest of the movement was Samuel Hopkins, who preached at Great Barrington, Massachusetts, and later at Newport, Rhode Island. Other leading figures were Edwards's son, Jonathan Jr., of New Haven, and Joseph Bellamy, who from the small village of Bethlehem, Connecticut, earned the title of pope of Litchfield County.

New Divinity men were often rough and domineering with their congregations, exploding in angry denunciations; and their doctrines matched their manners. It was wrong, they said, for the unregenerate to pray, since an unregenerate man, lacking real love for God, could not pray without hypocrisy and would anger God further by his futile efforts. The only way in which the unregenerate could contribute to the glory of God was to rejoice in their own damnation—an attitude which their very unregeneracy made improbable. The New Divinity also called for a restoration of the standards of church membership that had prevailed in New England before the Half-Way Covenant of 1662: a man could join the church only if he demonstrated to the satisfaction of the other members that God had predestined him to eternal salvation. Only such persons were entitled to take communion or to have their children baptized. The remainder of the community could only listen to the minister's preaching, in hopes that God would use this means to achieve a salvation already determined though as yet undisclosed.

The New Divinity had a consistency and rigor that young intellectuals found challenging. It was the fashionable, avant-garde movement of the seventeen-fifties, sixties, seventies, and to some extent the eighties. During these years many young men had already begun to find politics or the law more satisfying intellectually than religion, but insofar as religion continued to draw young minds, they gravitated to men like Bellamy and Hopkins for guidance. As a result, by 1792 the New Divinity claimed half the pulpits in Connecticut (and an increasing number in the rest of New England), together with virtually all the candidates for the ministry—this on the testimony of Ezra Stiles, president of Yale from 1778 to 1795, who despised the New Divinity and lamented its attraction for the young men he had educated.[9]

But the success of the New Divinity among the rising generation of clergy was not matched among the people at large. Its harsh doctrines

8. On Edwards, see Ola Winslow, *Jonathan Edwards* (New York, 1940); Perry Miller, *Jonathan Edwards* (New York, 1949). On the New Divinity, see F. H. Foster, *A Genetic History of the New England Theology* (Chicago, 1907); Joseph Haroutunian, *Piety versus Moralism* (New York, 1932).

9. *The Literary Diary of Ezra Stiles,* ed. F. B. Dexter (New York, 1901), III, 464. Cf. Conrad Wright, *The Beginnings of Unitarianism in America* (Boston, 1955), pp. 252-259.

could be sustained only by intellectual or religious fervor, and the religious fervor of Americans was already waning before the complexities of the system had been completely worked out. Even as Jonathan Edwards turned out his massive justifications of the Great Awakening, that movement subsided in the manner of later religious revivals. By the time Edwards had devised an intellectual foundation for emotionalism in religion, he had begun to lose his popular audience. When he announced that he would apply new standards of church membership, excluding all but the demonstrably regenerate from the sacraments, his church at Northampton dismissed him. America's greatest intellectual of his time spent most of his later years preaching, for want of a wider audience, to the Indians, who perhaps least of any group in America could understand him.

The careers of Edwards's disciples were somewhat more fortunate but not dissimilar. Samuel Hopkins, ministering to a large congregation at Great Barrington, saw it dwindle away until he was obliged to leave. At Newport, Rhode Island, he found another large congregation and again watched it decline. The history of New Haven's Second Church, formed during the Great Awakening by a seceding New Light minority from New Haven's First Church, reveals the same development. The new church prospered under the ministry of the Reverend Samuel Bird. But after Jonathan Edwards, Jr., took charge in 1769 and the relative simplicity of New Light gave way to the complexities of New Divinity, the congregation diminished until by 1795 there were not enough left or willing to support him.[10]

Hopkins and Jonathan Edwards, Jr., enjoyed the admiration of their ministerial colleagues, as did many other fearlessly consistent theologians of the New Divinity, but few of them could retain a popular following. Even while they justified emotionalism in religion, their sermons became complex, abstruse, metaphysical, devoted to details of theology that the layman found incomprehensible. During a revival of religion, their arid doctrines might still send shudders of horror through a receptive audience, but most of the time their congregations found them simply dull.

Their fault lay in addressing themselves more to each other than to their people. Engrossed in the details of their system, they delighted in exploring new elements of consistency in it and neglected the central problems of Christianity, until they scarcely knew how to deal with the elementary questions of salvation that their people put to them. Nowhere is the paradox of the New Divinity's intellectual success and popular failure more graphically demonstrated than in a letter from a young minister to his mentor. Medad Rogers, after graduating from Yale in 1777, had studied theology with Benjamin Trumbull, the New Divinity minister of North Haven. When Rogers began to preach, he discovered

10. Stiles, *Diary*, III, 344, 438, 562.

for the first time that he did not know the answers to the questions that Christians have always had to wrestle with.

"Sir," he wrote to Trumbull,

> if you do not think I desire more reproof than direction, some of your kind instructions, would be most timely to me—as also some directions how we should begin, spend, and end the day—What to say to those under concern for a future existence, when they enquire how they shall come to the foot of a sovereign God. They try to, but cannot. They would bow to Christ's sceptre but are not able. How are we to blame, say they? We would be saved but can't be saved. How are such to be dealt with? As also, if God hath decreed all things, why is he not the Author of sin? How can any man do otherwise than he does? If God hath elected a particular number, what is there for the others to do? Why had we not Just as good lie still and do nothing? Where is the criminality of their conduct in not embracing the Gospel offers, when they were not elected? What Justice, say they, in punishing those who miss of Salvation, for not accepting the offer, when they were not elected to it? Is not God partial? If we are to be saved we shall, if not we shall be cast away. Then, what good do our works do? Will persons who lived morally honest lives, have any respect shown them upon that account, in the day of Judgment, if they appear on the left hand of the Judge? Sir, if you could find yourself willing and at leasure Just to touch upon some, or all of these, you would do me a very great favour, and perhaps be a greater monument of glory to you, Kind sir, at last, than if you had written an hundred thousand volumes of Phylosophy, Rhetorick, Logick, and History.[11]

Trumbull's answer to Rogers is not preserved. But the very fact that a young minister should ask such questions speaks volumes about the state of religion in New England. The clergy for the first time in their history had contact with the people. In the seventeenth century when Roger Williams debated fine points of theology with John Cotton, or Increase Mather with Solomon Stoddard, people had not been bored. But the New Divinity ministers were unable to carry their congregations with them.

In earlier decades when a people became disgruntled with their minister, they had replaced him. But the American population had increased so rapidly that there were not enough ministers to go around; and since the New Divinity claimed such a large percentage of ministerial candidates, congregations were regularly faced with the necessity of taking a New Divinity man or leaving their pulpit vacant. The resultant discontent contributed in the last quarter of the eighteenth

11. Rogers to Trumbull, March 17, 1783, Benjamin Trumbull Correspondence, Yale University Library.

century to the rapid growth of Anglicanism, Methodism, deism, and what people at the time called "nothingarianism," a total indifference to religion. The clergy, once the most respected members of the community, became the objects of ridicule and contempt, especially in Connecticut, the stronghold of the New Divinity. In 1788, when the ministers of the state published a rebuke to the people for their neglect of public worship, the newspapers carried some rude answers. "We have heard your animadversions," said one, "upon our absence from Sabbath meetings, and humbly conceive if you wish our attendance there, you would make it worth our while to give it. To miss a sermon of the present growth, what is it but to miss of an opiate? And can the loss of a nap expose our souls to eternal perdition?" [12]

Such indifference to religion, edged with hostility to the clergy, was the end product of the developments we have been tracing from the 1740's. But though the clergy could blame themselves for much of their loss of prestige and for much of the decline of popular interest in religion, it was Parliament's attempt to tax the colonists in the 1760's that caused Americans to transfer to politics the intellectual interest and energy that were once reserved for religion. This reorientation was directed partly by the clergy themselves. They had never stopped giving instruction in political thought; and (except for the Anglicans) throughout the 1760's and 1770's they publicly and passionately scored the actions of George III and his Parliament against the standards by which their English Puritan predecessors had judged and condemned Charles I.

Presbyterian and Congregational ministers also raised the alarm when a movement was set afoot for the establishment in the colonies of state-supported bishops. The American clergymen developed no new general ideas about government—there was no New Light in political thought, no New Politics to match the New Divinity—but the old ideas and those imported from English political theorists served well enough to impress upon their congregations the tyrannical nature of taxation without representation, and of bishops who might establish ecclesiastical courts with jurisdiction extending beyond their own denomination.

Although the clergy were a powerful influence in molding American political opinion during the Revolutionary period, they did not recover through politics the intellectual leadership they had already begun to lose. Their own principles barred them from an active role in politics. While they had always given political advice freely and exercised their influence in elections, most of them would have considered it wrong to sit in a representative assembly, on a governor's council, or on the bench. To them as to their Puritan ancestors the clerical exercise of temporal powers spelled Rome. A minister's business was, after all, the saving of souls. By the same token, however outraged he might be by the actions of the English government, however excited by the achievement of American independence, a minister could not devote his prin-

12. *New Haven Gazette and Connecticut Magazine*, July 31, October 9, 1788.

cipal intellectual effort to the expounding of political ideas and political principles. As the quarrel with England developed and turned into a struggle for independence and nationhood, though the ministers continued to speak up on the American side, other voices commanding greater attention were raised by men who were free to make a career of politics and prepared to act as well as talk.

There had always, of course, been political leaders in the colonies, but hitherto politics had been a local affair, requiring at most the kind of talents needed for collecting votes or pulling wires. A colonial legislative assembly might occasionally engage in debates about paper money, defense, or modes of taxation; but the issues did not reach beyond the borders of the colony involved and were seldom of a kind to challenge a superior mind. No American debated imperial policy in the British Parliament, the Privy Council, or the Board of Trade. The highest political post to which a man could aspire in the colonies was that of governor, and everywhere except in Connecticut and Rhode Island, this was obtained not through political success but through having friends in England. Few native Americans ever achieved it or even tried to.

But the advent of Parliamentary taxation inaugurated a quarter-century of political discussion in America that has never since been matched in intensity. With the passage of the Stamp Act in 1765, every colonial legislature took up the task of defining the structure of the British empire; and as colonial definitions met with resistance from England, as the colonies banded together for defense and declared their independence, politics posed continental, even global, problems that called forth the best efforts of the best American minds. In no other period of our history would it be possible to find in politics five men of such intellectual stature as Benjamin Franklin, John Adams, Alexander Hamilton, James Madison, and Thomas Jefferson; and there were others only slightly less distinguished.

Whether they hailed from Pennsylvania or Virginia, New England or New York, the men who steered Americans through the Revolution, the establishment of a new nation, and the framing of the Constitution did not for the most part repudiate the political ideas inherited from the period of clerical dominance. Like the clergy, they started from a conviction of human depravity; like the clergy, they saw government originating in compact, and measured governmental performance against an absolute standard ordained by God. Like the clergy too, they found inspiration in the example of seventeenth-century Englishmen. Sometimes they signed their own attacks on George III or his ministers with the names of John Hampden, William Pym, or other Parliamentary heroes in the struggle against Charles I. They read the works of Harrington and of Harrington's later admirers; and after the Declaration of Independence, when they found themselves in a position similar to that of England in the 1650's, they drew heavily on the arsenal of political ideas furnished by these latter-day republicans.

Indeed, most of the ideas about government which American intellectuals employed first in their resistance to Parliament, and then in constructing their own governments, had been articulated earlier in England and were still in limited circulation there. The social compact, fundamental law, the separation of powers, human equality, religious freedom, and the superiority of republican government were continuing ideals for a small but ardent group of Englishmen who, like the Americans, believed that the British constitution was basically republican and drew inspiration from it while attacking the ministers and monarch who seemed to be betraying it.[13] It is perhaps no accident that the work in which Americans first repudiated monarchy, *Common Sense,* was written by an Englishman, Thomas Paine, who had come to America only two years before.

But if Englishmen supplied the intellectual foundations both for the overthrow of English rule and for the construction of republican government, Americans put the ideas into practice and drew on American experience and tradition to devise refinements and applications of the greatest importance. That republican ideas, which existed in a state of obscurity in England, should be congenial in the colonies, was due in the first place to the strong continuing Calvinist tradition which had been nourished over the years by the American clergy. But fully as important was the fact that during a hundred and fifty years of living in the freedom of a relatively isolated and empty continent, the colonists had developed a way of life in which republican ideas played a visible part. When Parliamentary taxation set Americans to analyzing their relationship to the mother country, they could not escape seeing that the social, economic, and political configuration of America had diverged from that of England in ways that made Americans better off than Englishmen. And the things that made them better off could be labeled republican.

England's practical experience with republicanism had lasted only eleven years. With the return of Charles II in 1660, Englishmen repudiated their republic and the Puritans who had sponsored it. Though a small minority continued to write and talk about republicanism and responsible government, they wielded no authority. The House of Commons grew more powerful but less common, and the main current of English national life flowed in the channels of monarchy, aristocracy, and special privilege. Americans, by contrast, though formally subjects of the king, had lived long under conditions that approximated the ideals of the English republican theorists. Harrington thought he had found in the England of his day the widespread ownership of property that seemed to him a necessary condition for republican government; but throughout the colonies ownership of property had always been more widespread than in England. Furthermore no member of the nobility had settled in America, so that people were accustomed to a greater

13. See again Robbins, *Eighteenth-Century Commonwealthman.*

degree of social as well as economic equality than existed anywhere in England.

During the 1640's and 1650's England had seen a rapid multiplication of religious sects, which produced a wide belief in religious freedom, but after the Anglican Church had reimposed its controls in the 1660's, the most that other denominations could hope for was toleration. In America, religious diversity had steadily increased, and with it came a religious freedom which, if still imperfect, surpassed anything England had ever known.

Though the English people had twice removed an unsatisfactory king, in 1649 and in 1688, the English government remained far less responsible and far less responsive to the people than any colonial government. While the members of Parliament disclaimed any obligation to their immediate constituents, the members of American representative assemblies knew that they were expected to look after the interests of the people who elected them. Nor were the voters in America only a small minority of the population as in England. In most colonies probably the great majority of adult males owned enough property to meet the qualification (which varied from colony to colony) for voting. In England, the government paid hundreds of office-holders whose offices, carrying no duties, existed solely for the enrichment of those who held them. In the colonies such sinecures were few. Americans thought that government existed to do a job, and they created no offices except for useful purposes.

Thus when the quarrel with Parliament began, the colonists already had what English reformers wanted. And the colonists were inclined to credit their good fortune not to the accident of geography but to their own superior virtue and political sophistication. The interpretation was not without foundation: since Calvinist traditions were still strong among them and since they had often learned of British republican ideas through the sermons of Calvinist clergymen, Americans retained what the Enlightenment had dimmed in England and Europe, a keen sense of human depravity and of the dangers it posed for government. Although their own governments had hitherto given little evidence of depravity, by comparison with those of Europe, they were expert at detecting it in any degree. They had always been horrified by the open corruption of British politics and feared it would lead to tyranny. When Parliament attempted to tax them and sent swarms of customs collectors, sailors, and soldiers to support the attempt, their fears were confirmed. In resisting the British and in forming their own governments, they saw the central problem as one of devising means to check the inevitable operation of depravity in men who wielded power. English statesmen had succumbed to it. How could Americans avoid their mistakes?

In the era of the American Revolution, from 1764 to 1789, this was the great intellectual challenge. Although human depravity continued to pose as difficult theological problems as ever, the best minds of the period addressed themselves to the rescue, not of souls, but of governments, from the perils of corruption. Of course the problem was not new, nor any more susceptible of final solution than it had been in an earlier time, but Americans in the Revolutionary period contributed three notable principles to men's efforts to deal with it.

The first principle, which evolved from the struggle with Parliament, was that the people of one region ought not to exercise dominion over those of another, even though the two may be joined together. It was an idea that overlapped and greatly facilitated the slower but parallel development of the more general belief in human equality. In objecting to British taxation in 1764 the colonists had begun by asserting their right to equal treatment with the king's subjects in Great Britain: Englishmen could not be taxed except by their representatives; neither therefore could Americans. Within a year or two the idea was extended to a denial that Parliament, representing the electors of Great Britain, could exercise any authority over the colonies. The empire, according to one American writer, was "a confederacy of states, independent of each other, yet united under one head," namely the king. "I cannot find," said another, "that the inhabitants of the colonies are dependent on the people of Britain, or the people of Britain on them, any more than Kent is on Sussex, or Sussex on Kent." [14]

It took varying lengths of time for other Americans to reach the position thus anonymously expressed in the press in 1765 and 1766. Franklin stated it later in 1766; [15] Jefferson, James Wilson, and John Adams had all expressed it by the beginning of 1775.[16] It was frequently buttressed by the citation of precedents from English constitutional history, but it rested on a principle capable of universal application, the principle stated in the preamble of the Declaration of Independence, that every people is entitled, by the laws of nature and of nature's God, to a separate and equal station.

Before Independence this principle offered a means of reorganizing the British empire so as to defeat the tyranny which Americans thought English statesmen were developing in the extension of taxation. If a British legislature, in which the colonists were not represented, could govern them, then neither British nor colonial freedom could be safe. Americans without a voice in the government could not defend their rights against corrupt rulers. Englishmen, relieved of expenses by American taxation, might rejoice for the moment, but their rulers, no longer dependent on them financially, would be able to govern as they pleased and would eventually escape popular control altogether. The

14. E. S. Morgan, *Prologue to Revolution: Sources and Documents on the Stamp Act Crisis* (Chapel Hill, 1959), pp. 73, 91.

15. Verner Crane, *Benjamin Franklin's Letters to the Press, 1758-1775* (Chapel Hill, 1950), p. xlii.

16. Thomas Jefferson, *A Summary View of the Rights of British America* (Williamsburg, 1774); James Wilson, *Considerations on the Nature and the Extent of the Legislative Authority of the British Parliament* (Philadelphia, 1774); John Adams, *Works,* ed. C. F. Adams (Boston, 1850-56), IV, 3-177.

only solution was to give each legislature power only over the people who chose it.

In the 1770's England was unwilling to listen to the colonial arguments, but ultimately adopted the American principle in forming the Commonwealth of Nations. The independent United States applied the principle not only in the confederation of states but in the annexation of other areas. When Virginia in 1781 offered the United States Congress her superior claim to the old Northwest, it was with the stipulation that the region be divided into separate republican states, each of which was to be admitted to the Union on equal terms with the old ones. The stipulation, though not accepted by Congress at the time, was carried out in Jefferson's land ordinance of 1784 and in the Northwest Ordinance of 1787 which superseded it. The United States never wavered from the principle until after the Spanish-American War, when it temporarily accepted government of areas which it had no intention of admitting to the union on equal terms.

The second contribution of the American Revolutionists was an application of the assumption, implicit in the whole idea of a compact between rulers and people, that a people can exist as a people before they have a government and that they can act as a people independently of government. The Puritans had distinguished between the compact of a group of individuals with God, by which they became a people, and the subsequent compact between this people and their rulers, by which government was created. John Locke had similarly distinguished between the dissolution of society and of government, and so, at least tacitly, had the Revolutionists. They would have been more daring, not to say foolhardy, if they had undertaken to destroy the bonds of society as well as of government. But in their haste to form new governments after the royal government in each colony dissolved, the Revolutionists followed a procedure that did not clearly distinguish the people from the government. Provincial congresses, exercising a *de facto* power, drafted and adopted permanent constitutions, which in most cases then went into effect without submission to a popular vote.

When the Massachusetts provincial congress proposed to follow this procedure in 1776, the citizens of the town of Concord pointed out the dangerous opening which it offered to human depravity. A *de facto* government that legitimized itself could also alter itself. Whatever safeguards it adopted against corruption could easily be discarded by later legislators: "a Constitution alterable by the Supreme Legislative is no Security at all to the Subject against any Encroachment of the Governing part on any or on all of their Rights and privileges." The town therefore suggested that a special popularly elected convention be called for the sole purpose of drafting a constitution, which should then be submitted to the people for approval.[17]

17. Robert J. Taylor, ed., *Massachusetts, Colony to Commonwealth: Documents on the Formation of its Constitution, 1775-1780* (Chapel Hill, 1961), p. 45.

It is impossible to determine who was responsible for Concord's action, but the protest displays a refinement in the application of republican ideas that does not appear to have been expressed before. Concord's suggestion was eventually followed in the drafting and adoption of the Massachusetts constitution of 1780 and of every subsequent constitution established in the United States. By it the subservience of government to the people was secured through a constitution clearly superior to the government it created, a constitution against which the people could measure governmental performance and against which each branch of government could measure the actions of the other branches. The separation of governmental powers into a bicameral legislature, an executive, and a judiciary, which was an older and more familiar way of checking depravity, was rendered far more effective by the existence of a written constitution resting directly on popular approval. The written constitution also proved its effectiveness in later years by perpetuating in America the operation of judicial review, of executive veto, and of a powerful upper house of the legislature, all of which had been or would be lost in England, where the constitution was unwritten and consisted of customary procedures that could be altered at will by Parliament.

Thus by the time the Revolution ended, Americans had devised a way to establish the superiority of the people to their government and so to control man's tyranny over man. For the same purpose Americans had formulated the principle that no people should exercise dominion over another people. But the way in which they first employed the latter principle in running the new nation did not prove satisfactory. As thirteen separate colonies the people of America had joined to combat Parliamentary taxation, and the result had been thirteen independent republics. It had been an exhilarating experience, and it had led them almost from the beginning to think of themselves in some degree as one people. But the thought was not completed: they did not coalesce into one republic with one government. Instead, as thirteen separate and equal peoples, they set up a "perpetual union" in which they were joined only through a Congress in which each state had one vote. They gave the Congress responsibility for their common concerns. But they did not give it the ordinary powers of a government to tax or legislate.

Because of the straightforward equality of the member states and because the Congress did not possess the means by which governments generally ran to tyranny, the confederation seemed a safe shape in which to cast the new nation. Actually danger lurked in the fact that the Congress had insufficient power to carry out the responsibilities which the states assigned to it. After the British troops were defeated and the need for united action became less obvious, state support of the Congress steadily declined. Without coercive powers, the Congress could not act effectively either at home or abroad, and the nation was increasingly exposed to the danger of foreign depredations. At the same time, the state governments were proving vulnerable to manipulation by corrupt or ambitious politicians and were growing powerful at the expense not only of the Congress but of the people. Some undertook irresponsible inflationary measures that threatened property rights. Unless the state governments were brought under more effective control, local demagogues might destroy the union and replace the tyranny of Parliament with a new domestic brand.

Although a few men foresaw the drawbacks of a weak Congress from the beginning, most people needed time to show them. The Massachusetts legislature, perceiving that the experience of the state could be applied to the whole United States, in 1785 suggested a national constitutional convention to create a central authority capable of acting effectively in the interests of the whole American people. But in 1785, Americans were not yet convinced that what they had was inadequate. The Massachusetts delegates to the Congress replied to their state's suggestion with the same arguments that had in the first place prompted Americans to base their union on a weak coordinative Congress rather than a real national government: it would be impossible, they said, to prevent such a government from escaping popular control. With headquarters remote from most of its constituents, with only a select few from each state engaged in it, a national government would offer too many opportunities for corruption.[18] The fear was supported by the views of respected European political thinkers. Montesquieu, who had been widely read in America, maintained that republican government was suited only to small areas. A confederation of republics might extend far, but a single republican government of large extent would either fall a prey to the ambitions of a few corrupt individuals, or else it would break up into a number of smaller states.[19]

These sentiments were so widely held that they prevented any effort to establish a national government until 1787. And when a convention was finally called in that year it was charged, not to create a new government, but simply to revise the Articles of Confederation. The members of the Convention, without authorization, assumed the larger task and turned themselves into a national Constitutional Convention. They did so because they became convinced that, contrary to popular belief, a large republic would not necessarily succumb to corruption. The man who persuaded the Convention, insofar as any one man did it, was James Madison, one of the delegates from Virginia.

In the month before the Convention assembled, Madison had drawn up some observations on the "Vices of the Political System of the United States." Following a hint thrown out by David Hume, he reached the conclusion that "the inconveniences of popular States con-

18. Edmund C. Burnett, ed., *Letters of Members of the Continental Congress* (Washington, 1921-36), VIII, 206-210.

19. Montesquieu, *Spirit of the Laws* (New York, 1949), p. 120 (Book VIII, c. 16).

trary to the prevailing Theory, are in proportion not to the extent, but to the narrowness of their limits." In the state governments that had operated since 1776, the great defect was a tendency of the majority to tyrannize over the minority. Madison took it as axiomatic that "in republican Government the majority however composed, ultimately gave the law." Unless a way could be found to control them, the majority would inevitably oppress the minority, because the individuals who made up the majority were as susceptible as any king or lord to the operation of human depravity. The most effective curb, Madison suggested, was to make the territory of the republic so large that a majority would have difficulty forming. Men being hopelessly selfish would inevitably seek to capture the government for selfish purposes, and in a small republic they might easily form combinations to secure the necessary majority. But in a large republic, "the Society becomes broken into a greater variety of interests, of pursuits of passions, which check each other, whilst those who may feel a common sentiment have less opportunity of communication and concert." [20]

The insight, later given classic expression in the tenth *Federalist* paper, was the most fruitful intellectual achievement of the Revolutionary period, the third of the three principles mentioned earlier. It gave Madison and his colleagues at Philadelphia the courage to attempt a republican government for the whole nation. The constitution which they drew up would provide the American peoples with a government that would effectively make them one people. The government would incorporate all the protections to liberty that they still cherished from their British heritage; it would preserve both imported and home-grown republican traditions; and it would employ the political principles developed during the Revolution. It would be a government inferior to the people and one in which no people should have dominion over another, a government in which almost every detail was prompted by the framers' determination to control the operation of human depravity. Many Americans, doubting that the safeguards would work, opposed the adoption of the Constitution. But the character of American politics from 1789 to the present day has borne out Madison's observation: majorities in the United States have been composed of such a variety of interests that they have seldom proved oppressive, and the national government has been a stronger bulwark of freedom than the state governments.

The establishment of a national republic renewed the challenge which the contest with Great Britain had presented to the best minds of America. In the Constitutional Convention and in the conduct of the new national government, Americans found scope for talents that the Revolution had uncovered. Jefferson, Hamilton, Madison, and John Adams received from national politics the stimulus that made them

20. James Madison, *Writings,* ed. Gaillard Hunt (New York, 1900-1910), II, 361-369.

great. The writings in which they embodied their best thoughts were state papers.

In the course of the nineteenth century the stimulus was somehow lost, in hard cider, log cabins, and civil war. Intellect moved away from politics; and intellectual leadership, having passed from clergy to statesmen, moved on to philosophers, scientists, and novelists. But during the brief period when America's intellectual leaders were her political leaders, they created for their country the most stable popular government ever invented and presented to the world three political principles which men have since used repeatedly and successfully to advance human freedom and responsible government.

THE CONSERVATIVE
INTERPRETATION

LEWIS B. NAMIER
King George III: A Study of Personality

📖 The Progressive school, although it shifted the main center of debate to the New World and brought economic, social, and sectional forces into sharp focus, did not question Bancroft's two basic assumptions: that the wicked Navigation Acts had driven the Americans into revolt, and that George III was an autocrat who had threatened the liberties both of freeborn Englishmen and equally freeborn Americans. Charles Andrews destroyed the myth of the uniform malevolence of the mercantile system; Sir Lewis Namier destroyed the myth of the malevolence of the British King. Namier proved beyond further question that the Burkeian view of party was in essence contemporary propaganda, and that the idea of party as a body united on doctrine did not, whatever Burke's prescience, hold in the mid-eighteenth century. The reality of politics was the quest for office of various factions or alliances of factions, and office depended on the royal choice; all groups sought royal favor, and the King alone conferred it; with the control of patronage and the right to choose his ministers he played a necessary and constitutionally proper role in politics. And the man himself, in all his rigidity of mind and in the end his insanity, was at once a warmer, more sympathetic, and more real figure in Namier's hands. 📖

. . . FATE HAD MADE George III ruler when kings were still expected to govern; and his active reign covered half a century during which the American conflict posed the problem of Imperial relations, while at home political practice constantly ran up against the contradiction inherent in the then much belauded 'mixed form of government': personal monarchy served by Ministers whose tenure of office was contested in Parliament. Neither the Imperial nor the constitutional problem could have been solved in the terms in which the overwhelming majority of the politically minded public in this country considered them at the time; but George III has been blamed ever since for not having thought

Reprinted by permission of The Macmillan Co. from *Crossroads of Power* (New York, 1963), pp. 124-140.

of Dominion status and parliamentary government when constitutional theory and the facts of the situation as yet admitted of neither.

In the catalogue, *Kings and Queens,* on sale at the exhibition, the introduction dealing with the reign of George III gave the traditional view of his reign:

> Conscientious and ambitious, he tried to restore the political influence of the Crown, but his intervention ended with the humiliating American War of Independence.

Conscientious he certainly was, painstakingly, almost painfully, conscientious. But was he ambitious? Did he try to exercise powers which his predecessors had relinquished, or claim an influence which was not universally conceded to him? And was it the assertion of Royal, and not of Parliamentary, authority over America which brought on the conflict and disrupted the First British Empire?

Let us place ourselves in March 1782. Dismal, humiliating failure has turned public opinion, and the House of Commons is resolved to cut losses and abandon the struggle; it is all over; Lord North's government has fallen; and the King is contemplating abdication. He has drafted a message to Parliament (which was never sent); here are its first two paragraphs:

> His Majesty during the twenty-one years he has sate on the throne of Great Britain, has had no object so much at heart as the maintenance of the British Constitution, of which the difficulties he has at times met with from his scrupulous attachment to the rights of Parliament are sufficient proofs.
>
> His Majesty is convinced that the sudden change of sentiments of one branch of the legislature has totally incapacitated him from either conducting the war with effect, or from obtaining any peace but on conditions which would prove destructive to the commerce as well as essential rights of the British nation.[1]

In the first paragraph the King declares his unswerving devotion to the British Constitution, and shows himself conscious of his difficulties in America having arisen through 'his scrupulous attachment to the rights of Parliament'; the second paragraph pointedly refers to the Commons as 'one branch of the legislature,' and gives the King's view of the American war: he is defending there the vital interests and essential rights of the British nation.

A year later, in March 1783, when faced by the necessity of accepting a Government formed by the Fox-North coalition, George III once more contemplated abdication; and in a letter (which again was never sent) he wrote to the Prince of Wales:

> The situation of the times are such that I must, if I attempt to carry on the business of the nation, give up every political prin-

1. Fortescue, *Correspondence of King George III,* vol. v, no. 3061.

ciple on which I have acted, which I should think very unjustifiable, as I have always attempted to act agreable to my duty; and must form a Ministry from among men who know I cannot trust them and therefore who will not accept office without making me a kind of slave; this undoubtedly is a cruel dilemma, and leaves me but one step to take without the destruction of my principles and honour; the resigning my Crown, my dear Son to you, quitting this my native country for ever and returning to the dominions of my forefathers.

Your difficulties will not be the same. You have never been in a situation to form any political system, therefore, are open to addopt what the times may make necessary; and no set of men can ever have offended you or made it impossible for you to employ them.[2]

Alongside this consider the following passage from a letter which George III wrote on 26 December 1783, after having dismissed the Coalition and while he was trying to rally support for the newly formed Administration of the younger Pitt:

The times are of the most serious nature, the political struggle is not as formerly between two factions for power; but it is no less than whether a desperate faction shall not reduce the Sovereign to a mere tool in its hands: though I have too much principle ever to infringe the rights of others, yet that must ever equaly prevent my submitting to the Executive power being in any other hands, than where the Constitution has placed it. I therefore must call on the assistance of every honest man . . . to support Government on the present most critical occasion.[3]

Note in these two passages the King's honest conviction that he has always attempted to do his duty; that he has been mindful not to infringe the rights of others; but that it would be equally wrong in him to submit 'to the Executive power being in any other hands, than where the Constitution has placed it.' And while I do not for a moment suggest that these things could not have been done in a happier manner, I contend that the King's statements quoted above are substantially correct.

In the eighteenth century, a proper balance between King, Lords, and Commons, that is, the monarchical, aristocratic, and representative elements of the Constitution acting as checks on each other, was supposed to safeguard the property and privileges, the lives and liberty of the subjects. Single-Chamber government would have been no less abhorrent to the century than Royal autocracy. The Executive was the King's as truly as it is now of the President in the United States; he, too, had to choose his Ministers: but from among Parliamentary leaders. And

2. Windsor MSS.
3. Windsor MS. 5709.

while aspirants to office swore by the 'independency' of the Crown and disclaimed all wish to force themselves on the King, if left out they did their level best to embarrass and upset their successful rivals. The technique of Parliamentary opposition was fully established long before its most essential aim, which is to force a change of government, was recognized as legitimate; and because that aim could not be avowed in its innocent purity, deadly dangers threatening the Constitution, nay the life of the country, had to be alleged for justification. Robert Walpole as 'sole Minister' was accused of arrogating to himself the powers of both King and Parliament; the very tame Pelhams, of keeping George II 'in fetters'; Bute, who bore the name of Stuart, of 'raising the standard of Royal prerogative'; and George III of ruling not through the Ministers of his own choice whom he avowed in public, but through a hidden gang of obscure and sinister 'King's friends.' It is obviously impossible here to trace the origin and growth of that story, or to disprove it by establishing the true facts of the transactions to which it has become attached—it was a figment so beautifully elaborated by Burke's fertile imagination that the Rockinghams themselves finished by believing it, and it grew into an obsession with them. In reality the constitutional practice of George III differed little from that of George I and George II. William Wyndham was proscribed by the first two Georges as a dangerous Jacobite, and C. J. Fox by the third as a dangerous Jacobin; while the elder Pitt was long kept out by both George II and George III on personal grounds. But for some the Royal veto and Royal influence in politics lose their sting if exercised in favour of successful monopolists in Whiggery.

I go one step further: in the eighteenth century the King had to intervene in politics and was bound to exercise his political influence, for the party system, which is the basis of Parliamentary government, did not exist.[4] Of the House of Commons itself probably less than half thought and acted in party terms. About one-third of the House consisted of Members who looked to the King for guidance and for permanency of employment: epigoni of earlier Courts or forerunners of the modern Civil Service; and if they thus pursued their own interest, there is no reason to treat them as more corrupt than if they had done so by attaching themselves to a group of politicians. Another one-fifth of the House consisted of independent country gentlemen, ready to support the King's Goverment so long as this was compatible with their conscience, but averse to tying themselves up with political groups: they did not desire office, honours, or profits, but prided themselves on the disinterested and independent line they were pursuing; and they rightly claimed to be the authentic voice of the nation. In the centre of the arena stood the politicians, their orators and leaders fighting for the highest prizes of Parliamentary life. They alone could supply the façade of governments: the front benches in Parliament. But to

4. For more on this point see my essay, "Monarchy and the Party System."

achieve stability a Government required the active support of the Crown and the good opinion of the country. On matters about which public opinion felt strongly, its will would prevail; but with the House constituted as it was, with the electoral structure of the unreformed Parliament, and an electorate which neither thought nor voted on party lines, it is idle to assume that modern Parliamentary government was possible.

I pass to the next point: was George III correct in saying that it was 'his scrupulous attachment to the rights of Parliament' which caused him the difficulties in America? Undoubtedly yes. It was not Royal claims that the Americans objected to, but the claims of 'subjects in one part of the king's dominions to be sovereigns over their fellow-subjects in another part of his dominions.' [5] 'The sovereignty of the Crown I understand,' wrote Benjamin Franklin; 'the sovereignty of Britain I do not understand. . . . We have the same King, but not the same legislature.' Had George III aspired to independent Royal Power nothing could have suited him better than to be Sovereign in America, the West Indies, and possibly in Ireland, independent of the British Parliament; and the foremost champions of the rights of Parliament, recalling the way in which the Stuarts had played off Ireland and Scotland against England, would have been the first to protest. But in fact it would be difficult to imagine a King simultaneously exercising in several independent countries executive powers in conjunction with Parliamentary leaders. It will suffice to remember the difficulties and jealousies which Hanover caused although itself politically inert. The two problems which George III is unjustly accused of having mismanaged, those of Imperial and constitutional relations, were interconnected: only after responsible government had arisen did Dominion status within the Commonwealth become possible. Lastly, of the measures which brought on the American conflict none was of the King's making: neither George Grenville's Stamp Act, nor the Declaratory Act of the Rockinghams, nor the Townshend Duties. All that can be said against him is that once the struggle had started, he, completely identifying himself with this country, obstinately persevered in it. He wrote on 14 November 1778:

> If Lord North can see with the same degree of enthusiasm I do, the beauty, excellence, and perfection of the British Constitution as by law established, and consider that if any one branch of the Empire is alowed to cast off its dependency, that the others will infalably follow the example . . . he . . . will resolve with vigour to meet every obstacle . . . or the State will be ruined.[6]

And again on 11 June 1779, expecting that the West Indies and Ireland would follow:

5. Benjamin Franklin to the Rev. Samuel Cooper of Boston, 8 June 1770.
6. Fortescue IV, no. 2451.

> Then this island would be reduced to itself, and soon would be a poor island indeed.[7]

On March 1780:

> I can never suppose this country so far lost to all ideas of self importance as to be willing to grant America independence, if that could ever be universally adopted, I shall despair of this country being ever preserved from a state of inferiority and consequently falling into a very low class among the European States . . .[8]

And on 26 September 1780:

> . . . giving up the game would be total ruin, a small State may certainly subsist, but a great one mouldering cannot get into an inferior situation but must be annihilated.[9]

When all was over, Lord North wrote to the King on 18 March 1782:

> Your Majesty is well apprized that, in this country, the Prince on the Throne, cannot, with prudence, oppose the deliberate resolution of the House of Commons . . . Your Majesty has graciously and steadily supported the servants you approve, as long as they could be supported: Your Majesty has firmly and resolutely maintained what appeared to you essential to the welfare and dignity of this country, as long as this country itself thought proper to maintain it. The Parliament have altered their sentiments, and as their sentiments whether just or erroneous, must ultimately prevail, Your Majesty . . . can lose no honour if you yield at length . . .
>
> Your Majesty's goodness encourages me . . . to submit whether it will not be for Your Majesty's welfare, and even glory, to sacrifice, at this moment, former opinions, displeasures and apprehensions (though never so well-founded) to . . . the public safety.[10]

The King replied:

> I could not but be hurt at your letter of last night. Every man must be the sole judge of his feelings, therefore whatever you or any man can say on that subject has no avail with me.[11]

What George III had never learnt was to give in with grace: but this was at the most a defect of character.

---

7. *Ibid.*, no. 2649.
8. Fortescue V, no. 2963.
9. *Ibid.*, no. 3155.
10. Fortescue V, no. 3566.
11. *Ibid.*, no. 3567.

2

Lord Waldegrave, who had been Governor to the Prince of Wales 1752–6, wrote in 1758 a character sketch of him so penetrating and just that it deserves quoting almost in full.[12]

> The Prince of Wales is entering into his 21st year, and it would be unfair to decide upon his character in the early stages of life, when there is so much time for improvement.

A wise preamble: yet a long and eventful life was to change him very little. Every feature singled out by Waldegrave finds copious illustration in the fifty years that followed (in one case in a superficially inverted form).

> His parts, though not excellent, will be found very tolerable, if ever they are properly exercised.
>
> He is strictly honest, but wants that frank and open behaviour which makes honesty appear amiable. . . .
>
> His religion is free from all hypocrisy, but is not of the most charitable sort; he has rather too much attention to the sins of his neighbour.
>
> He has spirit, but not of the active kind; and does not want resolution, but it is mixed with too much obstinacy.
>
> He has great command of his passions, and will seldom do wrong, except when he mistakes wrong for right; but as often as this shall happen, it will be difficult to undeceive him, because he is uncommonly indolent, and has strong prejudices.
>
> His want of application and aversion to business would be far less dangerous, was he eager in the pursuit of pleasure; for the transition from pleasure to business is both shorter and easier than from a state of total inaction.
>
> He has a kind of unhappiness in his temper, which, if it be not conquered before it has taken too deep a root, will be a source of frequent anxiety. Whenever he is displeased, his anger does not break out with heat and violence; but he becomes sullen and silent, and retires to his closet; not to compose his mind by study or contemplation, but merely to indulge the melancholy enjoyment of his own ill humour. Even when the fit is ended, unfavourable symptoms very frequently return, which indicate that on certain occasions his Royal Highness has too correct a memory.

Waldegrave's own endeavour was to give the Prince 'true notions of common things.'[13] But these he never acquired: which is perhaps the deepest cause of his tragedy.

12. James, 2nd Earl Waldegrave, *Memoirs* (1821), pp. 8-10.
13. *Ibid.*, p. 64.

The defect Waldegrave dwells upon most is the Prince's 'uncommon indolence,' his 'want of application and aversion to business.' This is borne out by other evidence, best of all by the Prince's own letters to Bute: [14]

> *July 1st*, 1756: I will throw off that indolence which if I don't soon get the better of will be my ruin.
> *March 25th*, 1757: I am conscious of my own indolence . . . I do here in the most solemn manner declare, that I will throw aside this my greatest enemy . . .
> *September 25th*, 1758: . . . that incomprehensible indolence, in-attention and heedlessness that reigns within me . . .

And he says of his good resolutions: 'as many as I have made I have regularly broke'; but adds a new one: 'I mean to attempt to regain the many years I have fruitlessly spent.'

> *December 19th*, 1758: . . . through the negligence, if not the wickedness of those around me in my earlier days, and since perhaps through my own indolence of temper, I have not that degree of knowledge and experience in business, one of my age might reasonably have acquir'd . . .
> *March 1760*: . . . my natural indolence . . . has been encreas'd by a kind of indifference to the world, owing to the number of bad characters I daily see . . .

By shifting the blame on to others, he tries to relieve the bitter consciousness of failure: which is one source of that excessive 'attention to the sins of his neighbour' mentioned by Waldegrave. Indeed, George III's letters, both before and after his accession are full of it: 'the great depravity of the age,' 'the wickedest age that ever was seen,' 'a degenerate age,' 'probity and every other virtue absorb'd into vice, and dissipation'; etc. 'An ungrateful, wicked people' and individual statesmen alike receive castigation (*in absentia*) from this very young Old Testament prophet. Pitt 'is the blackest of hearts,' 'the most dishonourable of men,' and plays 'an infamous and ungrateful part'; Lord Temple, an 'ungrateful arrogant and self-sufficient man'; Charles Townshend is 'a man void of every quality,' 'the worst man that lives,' 'vermin'; Henry Fox, a man of 'bad character,' 'void of principles'; Lord Mansfield is 'but half a man'; the Duke of Bedford's character 'contains nothing but passion and absurdity'; etc. As for George II, the Prince felt ashamed of being his grandson. And on 23 April 1760, half a year before his accession, aged twenty-two he wrote to Bute: '. . . as to honesty, I have already lived long enough to know you are the only man who possesses that quality . . .'

14. See *Letters from George III to Lord Bute* (1939), edited by Romney Sedg-wick, from which all such letters are quoted. Mr. Sedgwick's edition is a masterpiece of scholarship. To mention but one aspect: from internal evidence he has succeeded in dating some 330 undated letters.

In Bute he thought he had found the tutelary spirit who would enable him to live up to his future high vocation. Here are further excerpts from the Prince's letters to him:

> *July 1st, 1756*: My friend is . . . attack'd in the most cruel and horrid manner . . . because he is my friend . . . and because he is a friend to the bless'd liberties of his country and not to arbitrary notions . . .
>
> By . . . your friendship . . . I have reap'd great advantage, but not the improvement I should if I had follow'd your advice . . . I will exactly follow your advice, without which I shall inevitably sink.

> *March 25th, 1757*: I am resolved . . . to act the man in everything, to repeat whatever I am to say with spirit and not blushing and afraid as I have hitherto . . . my conduct shall convince you that I am mortified at what I have done and that I despise myself . . . I hope this will persuade you not to leave me when all is at stake, when nobody but you can stear me through this difficult, though glorious path.

In June 1757 Leicester House were alarmed by rumours of an alliance between the Duke of Newcastle and Henry Fox, and were ascribing fantastic schemes to the Duke of Cumberland. The Prince already saw himself compelled to meet force by force or to 'yield up the Crown,'

> for I would only accept it with the hopes of restoring my much beloved country to her antient state of liberty; of seeing her . . . again famous for being the residence of true piety and virtue, I say if these hopes were lost, I should with an eye of pleasure look on retiring to some uninhabited cavern as this would prevent me from seeing the sufferings of my countrymen, and the total destruction of this Monarchy . . .
>
> *August 20th, 1758*: . . . by . . . attempting with vigour to restore religion and virtue when I mount the throne this great country will probably regain her antient state of lustre.

Was this a Prince nurtured in 'arbitrary notions,' ambitious to make his own will prevail? or a man with a 'mission,' striving after naively visionary aims? No doubt, since early childhood it must have been rammed into him, especially when he was being reproved, to what high station he was born; and disparaging comparisons are said to have been drawn between him and his younger brother. He grew up with a painful consciousness of his inadequacy: 'though I act wrong perhaps in most things,' he wrote on one occasion. Excessive demands on a child, complete with wholesome exhortations, are fit to reduce it to a state of hebetude from which it is not easy to recover. A great deal of the pattern of George III's behaviour throughout life can be traced back to his up-bringing.

He spent his young years cut off from intercourse with boys of his own age, till he himself ceased to desire it. Bubb Dodington notes in his *Diary* on 15 October 1752, that the Princess Dowager of Wales

> did not observe the Prince to take very particularly to anybody about him, but to his brother Edward, and she was glad of it, for the young people of quality were so ill-educated and so vicious, that they frightened her.

And so they did him for the rest of his life. Isolation by itself would be apt to suggest to a child that there was something wrong with those he had to shun; but this he was probably told in so many words. On 18 December 1753, Dodington records another talk with the Princess:

> I said, it was to be wished he could have more company. She seemed averse to the young people, from the excessive bad education they had, and from the bad examples they gave.

So the boy spent joyless years in a well-regulated nursery, the nearest approach to a concentration camp: lonely but never alone, constantly watched and discussed, never safe from the wisdom and goodness of the grown-ups; never with anyone on terms of equality, exalted yet oppressed by deferential adults. The silent, sullen anger noted by Waldegrave, was natural to one who could not hit back or speak freely his mind, as a child would among children: he could merely retire, and nurture his griefs and grievances—and this again he continued through life. On 3 May 1766, during a political crisis, he wrote to Bute: 'I can neither eat nor sleep, nothing pleases me but musing on my cruel situation.' Nor could he, always with adults, develop self-reliance: at nineteen he dreamt of reforming the nation, but his idea of acting the man was to repeat without blushing or fear what he had to say.

For the pious works which were 'to make this great nation happy' Bute's 'sagacious councils' were therefore indispensable. When in December 1758 Bute expressed doubts whether he should take office in the future reign, the Prince in a panic searched his own conscience:

> Perhaps it is the fear you have I shall not speak firmly enough to my Ministers, or that I shall be stagger'd if they say anything unexpected; as to the former I can with great certainty assure that they, nor no one else shall see a want of steadiness either in my manner of acting or speaking, and as to the latter, I may give fifty sort of puts off, till I have with you thoroughly consider'd what part will be proper to be taken . . .

George III adhered to this programme. On his grandfather's death he waited to hear from Bute what 'must be done.' When expecting Pitt at a critical juncture: 'I would wish to know what I had best say. . . .' With regard to measures or appointments: 'I have put that off till I hear my Dear Friend's opinion'; 'If this [is] agreeable to my D. Friend I will order it to day . . .'; 'I desire my D. Friend to consider what I have here wrote, if he is of a contrary opinion, I will with pleasure embrace it.' And when in November 1762 Bute declared he would retire on conclusion of peace:

> I had flattered myself [wrote the King] when peace was once established that my D. Friend would have assisted me in purging out corruption . . . ; . . . now . . . the Ministry remains compos'd of the most abandon'd men that ever had those offices; thus instead of reformation the Ministers being vicious this country will grow if possible worse; let me attack the irreligious, the covetous &c. as much as I please, that will be of no effect . . . Ministers being of that stamp . . .

Two years on the throne had worked little if any change in his ideas and language; nor did the next twenty. The same high claims on himself, and the same incapacity to meet real situations he was faced with: hence his continued dependence on others. By 1765 he saw that Bute could not help him, by the summer of 1766 he had written off Bute altogether. In the spring of 1765 he turned to the Duke of Cumberland, the bugbear of his young years: 'Dear Uncle, the very friendly and warm part you have taken has given me real satisfaction. . . .' [15] And to Pitt, 'the blackest of hearts': 'My friend for so the part you have acted deserves of me. . . .' [16] In July 1765 Cumberland formed for him the Rockingham Administration and presided over it a quasi-Viceroy; but a few months later Cumberland was dead. In July 1766 Chatham formed his Administration; but a few months later his health broke down completely. Still George III clung to him like a mollusc (a mollusc who never found his rock). 'Under a health so broken,' wrote Chatham, 'as renders at present application of mind totally impossible. . . .' [17] After nearly two years of waiting for his recovery, the King still wrote: 'I think I have a right to insist on your remaining in my service.' [18] Next he clung to the ineffective Grafton who longed to be relieved of office; and when Grafton resigned, the King wrote to him on 27 January 1770:

> My heart is so full at the thought of your retiring from your situation that I think it best not to say more as I know the expressing it would give you pain.[19]

Then came North. Totally unequal to the difficulties of the American crisis, in letter after letter he begged the King to let him resign. Thus in March 1788:

15. Fortescue I, no. 74.
16. *Ibid.*, no. 94.
17. *Ibid.*, no. 538.
18. Fortescue II, no. 669.
19. Grafton MSS.

> Lord North cannot conceive what can induce His Majesty, after so many proofs of Lord North's unfitness for his situation to determine at all events to keep him at the head of the Administration, though the almost certain consequences of His Majesty's resolution will be the ruin of his affairs, and though it can not ward off for a month that arrangement which His Majesty seems to apprehend.[20]

But the King would not hear of it. July 2nd, 1779: 'no man has a right to talk of leaving me at this hour. . . .' [21] October 25th, 1780: he expects North 'will show that zeal for which he has been conspicuous from the hour of the Duke of Grafton's desertion.' [22]

George III's attitude to North conformed to the regular pattern of his behaviour. So did also the way in which after a while he turned against North in bitter disappointment. By the '70s the King spoke disparagingly of Bute and Chatham; and in time his imagination enabled him to remember how on the day of his accession he had given the slip to them both. A month after Grafton had resigned, George III wrote to him: 'I . . . see anew that the sincere regard and friendship I have for you is properly placed. . . .' [23] Somewhat later his resignation changed into 'desertion.' When North resigned: 'I ever did and ever shall look on you as a friend as well as a faithful servant. . . .' [24] But incensed at the new situation he soon started attacking North, and treated him niggardly and unfairly over his secret service accounts. George III's attachment was never deep: it was that of a drunken man to railings—mechanical rather than emotional. Egocentric and rigid, stunted in feelings, unable to adjust himself to events, flustered by sudden change, he could meet situations only in a negative manner, clinging to men and measures with disastrous obstinacy. But he himself mistook that defensive apparatus for courage, drive, and vigour, from which it was as far removed as anything could be. Of his own mental processes he sometimes gave discerning though embellished accounts. Thus to Bute in 1762: 'I . . . am apt to despise what I am not accustom'd to . . .' And on 2 March 1797, to the younger Pitt when criticizing the way measures were weakened in passing through Parliament:

> My nature is quite different I never assent till I am convinced what is proposed is right, and then . . . I never allow that to be destroyed by after-thoughts which on all subjects tend to weaken never to strengthen the original proposal.[25]

In short: no after-thoughts, no reconsideration—only desperate, clinging perseverance.

20. Fortescue IV, no. 2241.
21. *Ibid.,* no. 2696.
22. Fortescue V, no. 3165.
23. March 2nd, 1770, Grafton MSS.
24. Fortescue V, no. 3593.
25. Windsor MSS.

Still it might be said: at least he broke through his indolence. Yes, indeed: from pathologically indolent he turned pathologically industrious —and never again could let off working; but there was little sense of values, no perspective, no detachment. There is a legend about a homunculus whose maker not knowing what to do with him, bid him count poppy-seed in a bag. That George III was doing with his own busy self. His innumerable letters which he copied in his own hand, or the long documents transcribed by him (he never employed an amanuensis till his eye-sight began to fail) contain some shrewd perceptions or remarks, evidence of 'very tolerable parts if . . . properly exercised.' But most of his letters merely repeat approvingly what some Minister, big or small, has suggested. 'Lord A. is very right . . .'; 'General B. has acted very properly . . .'; 'the minute of Cabinet meets with my fullest concurrence . . .'; 'Nothing can more deserve my approbation than'— whatever it was. But if a basic change is suggested, his obstinacy and prejudices appear. On 15 March 1778, in a letter to Lord North, he makes an unusual and startling admission:

> I will only add to put before your eyes my most inmost thoughts, that no advantage to this country nor personal danger can ever make me address myself for assistance either to Lord Chatham or any other branch of the Opposition. . . .[26]

As a rule he would sincerely assert, perhaps with somewhat excessive ostentation, that first and foremost he considered the good of the country. When told by Bute that it would be improper for him to marry Lady Sarah Lennox, he replied: 'the interest of my country ever shall be my first care, my own inclinations shall ever submit to it' (and he added: 'I should wish we could next summer . . . get some account of the various Princesses in Germany'—and he settled down to 'looking in the New Berlin Almanack for Princesses'). When considering withdrawal from the German War, he wrote (with a sidelong glance at the late King) about the superiority of his love 'to this my native country over any private interest of my own. . . .' He was 'a King of a free people'; 'I rely on the hearts of my subjects, the only true support of the Crown,' he wrote in November 1760. They will not desert him—

> if they could be so ungrateful to me who love them beyond anything else in life, I should then I really believe fall into the deepest melancholy which would soon deprive me of the vexations of this life.

The same note, of love for this country and trust that his subjects would therefore stand by him, continues for almost twenty years. But gradually other overtones begin to mix with it. He had become the target of virulent attacks and unjust suspicions which he deeply resented. Thus to Lord North on 7 March 1780: '. . . however I am treated I

26. Fortescue IV, no. 2221.

must love this country.' 27 And to the Prince of Wales on 14 August 1780:

> The numberless trials and constant torments I meet with in public life, must certainly affect any man, and more poignantly me, as I have no other wish but to fulfill my various duties; the experience of now twenty years has convinced me that however long it may please the Almighty to extend my days, yet I have no reason to expect any diminution of my public anxiety; where am I therefore to turn for comfort, but into the bosom of my own family? 28

And he appealed to his son, the future George IV, to connect himself only with young men of respectable character, and by his example help 'to restore this country to its former lustre'—the old tune once more. And, in another letter:

> From your childhood I have ever said that I can only try to save my country, but it must be by the co-operation of my children only that I can effect it.29

In the 1780s there is a more than usually heavy crop of bitter complaints about the age by one 'righteous overmuch': 'it has been my lot to reign in the most profligate age,' 'depravity of such times as we live in,' 'knavery and indolence perhaps I might add the timidity of the times. . . .' And then:

> I thank Heaven my morals and course of life have but little resembled those too prevalent in the present age, and certainly of all objects in this life the one I have most at heart, is to form my children that they may be useful examples and worthy of imitation . . .30

With the King's disappointments in country and son another note enters his letters. He warns the Prince—

> in other countries national pride makes the inhabitants wish to paint their Princes in the most favourable light, and consequently be silent on any indiscretion; but here most persons if not concerned in laying ungrounded blame, are ready to trumpet any speck they can find out.31

And he writes of the 'unalterable attachment' which his Electoral subjects have shown to their Princes. When George III went mad in 1788, he wanted to go back to Hanover. Deep down there was a good deal of the Hanoverian in him.

His insanity was a form of manic-depression. The first recorded fit

27. Fortescue V, no. 2963.
28. Windsor MSS.
29. *Ibid.*
30. Windsor MSS.
31. *Ibid.*

in March 1765 was of short duration, though there may have been a slight relapse in May; and a year later he wrote to Bute—

> if I am to continue the life of agitation I have these three years, the next year there will be a Council [of] Regency to assist in that undertaking.

During the next twenty-three years he preserved his normal personality. The attack in 1788 lasted about half a year: the King was over fifty, and age rendered complete recovery more difficult. His self-control weakened and his irritability increased. He was conscious of a growing weakness. Yet there was something about him which more and more endeared him to the people. He was never popular with London society or the London mob; he was much beloved in the provinces—perhaps it was his deeper kindness, his real piety, and sincere wish to do good which evoked those feelings. These appear strikingly, for instance, in his own account of his journey to Portsmouth in 1788,[32] and in Fanny Burney's account of his progress through Wiltshire in 1789.[33] He was not a politician, and certainly not a statesman. But in things which he could judge without passion or preconceived ideas, there appears basic honesty and the will to do the right thing. I shall limit myself to two examples. When in 1781 a new Provost was to be appointed at Eton, George III insisted on choosing a man 'whose literary tallents might make the appointment respectable . . . for Eton should not be bestowed by favour, but merit.' [34] And when in 1787 a new Lord Lieutenant had to be chosen for Ireland, the King wrote to the younger Pitt about the necessity

> of looking out for the person most likely to conduct himself with temper, judgement, and an avowed resolution to avoid partiality and employ the favours he has to recommend to with the justice due to my service and to the public. . . . When I have stated this Mr. Pitt must understand that I do not lean to any particular person . . . when I state that a Lord Lieutenant should have no predelection but to advance the public good I should be ashamed to act in a contrary manner.[35]

I have given here a picture of George III as seen in his letters, 'warts and all.' What I have never been able to find is the man arrogating power to himself, the ambitious schemer out to dominate, the intriguer dealing in an underhand fashion with his Ministers; in short, any evidence for the stories circulated about him by very clever and eloquent contemporaries. He had a high, indeed an exaggerated, notion of royalty but in terms of mission and duties rather than of power; and trying to live up to this idealized concept, he made unreasonable

32. Windsor MSS.
33. Fanny Burney, *Diary* (1905), vol. iv, pp. 310-11.
34. Fortescue V, no. 3455.
35. Windsor MSS.

demands on himself. Setting himself unattainable standards, he could never truly come to grips with reality: which condemned him to remain immature, permanency of inner conflict precluding growth. Aware of his inadequacy, he turned to others and expected them to enable him to realize his visionary program (this appears clearest in his relations with Bute); and he bitterly reproached them in his own mind, and blamed the age in which he lived, for his own inevitable failure. The tension between his notions and reality, and the resulting frustration, account to a high degree for his irritability, his deep-seated resentments, and his suppressed anger—for situations intolerable and disastrous for himself and others; and it may have been a contributory factor in his mental breakdowns. The desire to escape from that unbearable conflict repeatedly shows itself in thoughts of abdication which must not be deemed insincere because never acted upon (men of his type cannot renounce their treadmill). He himself did not understand the nature and depth of his tragedy; still less could others. There was therefore room for the growth of an injurious legend which made that heavy-burdened man a much maligned ruler; and which has long been accepted as history.

ESMOND WRIGHT
Parliament: Politics and Policy, 1763-1774

⟐ As yet no study has been written *in extenso* or in summary form describing the significance for the study of the American Revolution of the researches of the Namierist school. Namier himself wrote two articles on Charles Garth and devoted a short section of *England in the Age of the American Revolution* to an analysis of colonial affairs. References to the colonies can be found in the writings of John Brooke, J. B. Owen, Ian Christie, and Bernard Donoughue for various periods of the years from 1745 to 1782, and in Namier's and John Brooke's three-volume study of the membership of the House of Commons, 1754-1790. It is clear from these studies that the nature of factional politics made any sustained American policy difficult, indeed, perhaps impossible. Clearly it produced vacillation, uncertainty, and contradiction. Clearly also it produced a government that was the reverse of tyrannical. The essay that follows is an attempt to draw conclusions relevant to the causes of the Revolution from the researches of the Namierist school. ⟐

THE WORK OF Sir Lewis Namier and his associates in recent years has revised all prevailing views on the structure of British politics in the age of the American Revolution. George III, it is now clear, was not a tyrant seeking to destroy the constitution; he did not destroy the party system, for there was no system to destroy and little as yet that was recognizable as party. The government was royal and was produced by devising links between various "connections"; and in the eighteenth century, it was the government that made majorities, not majorities the government. Ministers were responsible not to Parliament but to the King, and they managed Parliament on his behalf. The King himself, unlike his Hanoverian predecessors, was genuinely interested in Britain; he was strong-willed and hard-working, young and sincerely patriotic; but he was also obstinate, short-sighted, and unforgiving.

From the moment of the King's accession in 1760, American affairs played a major part in British politics. For the first sixteen years, questions of American defense, American taxation, and American "rights" were among the chief topics of parliamentary debate. Inevitably they became involved with all the other controversial issues: the wisdom or otherwise of the peace settlement with France in 1762–63; the liberty of the subject and the free reporting of parliamentary debates, raised by the career of John Wilkes; the heavy cost of government and, especially as it seemed in a Parliament of landowners, the heavy burden of the land tax; and the "rights" of the King-in-Parliament to be the supreme lawmaking authority in the Empire. American questions could rarely be considered in and for themselves, but they were discussed almost as thoroughly in Britain as in America.

Central though American affairs were, however, any consistent approach to them by the government of the day was all but impossible. Government was too fluid, too mixed and broad-bottomed, to allow any consistent policy to emerge on any issue. All the Whig groups, whose composition was very fluid, supported the 1688 settlement; by 1763 this had involved them in the support of the *status quo* and in strong views on the sanctity of Parliament. They were worried by the American problem, but they were worried more by its disruptive effect on British politics than by any other aspect. They were often therefore short-sighted in their estimates of it. "The seditious spirit in the colonies owes its birth," said Grenville, "to the factions in this House."

One of the Whig groups, the Old Whigs, has normally been excepted from any such indictment, largely because of the role of its spokesman, Edmund Burke, the exponent of party government in its modern sense, and in his speeches of 1774–75 the exponent of a liberal imperialism toward the colonies. The researches of Professor Namier and of Professor Pares have reduced the importance of this group and of their spokesman. Their leaders were not distinguished. Rockingham was young, wealthy, honest, and of sound judgment, but no speaker and no fighter for causes; he was, says Mr. Christie, "the pilot who shunned rather than weathered the storm." The fourth Duke of Devonshire was popular

Reprinted by permission of Hill and Wang, Inc., from Esmond Wright, *Fabric of Freedom* (New York, 1961), pp. 22-34.

and equable in manner but of mediocre talents. They were not particularly skillful in parliamentary management; they refused to establish an American secretaryship, although this had long been discussed; Burke's eloquent justification of party, however prescient, was in some measure an elaborate and rather stagy defense of the Whig families, "the great oaks that shade a country." Even Lord Rockingham's administration of 1765–66, so often thought of as liberal, was a coalition government that had to include three of the King's Friends.

Nevertheless, alone among the Whig groups, the Old Whigs had something that approached a policy for America, and it had a certain discernible consistency. They opposed the taxing of the colonists not on grounds of principle but for reasons of a political tact that Burke elevated into wisdom: "things that are lawful are not always expedient"; "magnanimity in politics is not seldom the truest wisdom and a great Empire and little minds go ill together." They opposed the Stamp Act not as a measure that was illegal but as one that was unwise.

Similarly, Lord Chatham, who denied that Parliament had any power to tax America, had to head mixed administrations, and, however liberal on some issues, it was Chatham in 1766 who proposed a bill "declaratory" of Parliament's "high rights and privileges" over America. The liberal was also the imperialist, and did not see the terms as antithetical. Pitt, who became Lord Chatham in 1766, was himself in no small way responsible for the confusion of politics in the early years of George III's reign, partly by his understandable but impulsive resignation in 1761, still more by his unpredictability. Like all politicians of the day he had a following, though it was small and powerless—"square pegs who could not fit into round holes" as Dr. Brooke describes them. Pitt wielded an influence, however, that could have made, as it helped to destroy, governments. He was popular in the City and had the support of Beckford and Wilkes. If he had combined with the Whigs he could have destroyed Bute in 1762 or Grenville in 1765. But he declared himself against any combination with the Whig families who had refused to destroy French trade and seapower in 1761–62; he declared himself indeed against all connection, and particularly against its high priest Newcastle, his uncongenial bedfellow of the years of victory. For Pitt's Whiggism, like his grandfather's before him, was born of respect not for gentry but for trade; he spoke for the rising commercial classes.

He saw himself, however (in his own phrase), as "a man standing single," and this was as anachronistic in the 1760s as was Burke's apologia for party. He played fast and loose across the political checkerboard, the vain, theatrical victim of gout and of his own temperament, seeing himself, in the 1760s as in the 1750s, as the figure to whom in the end all would have to turn. There seems no reason to reverse Winstanley's judgment of some forty years ago: "Pitt failed as a domestic politician, and the early years of the reign of George III constitute the record of his failure." The latest detailed study of his 1766–68 administration, that of John Brooke, attributes its failure not to his illness nor to the weakness of his Cabinet, but to deeper political causes. "He looked with contempt upon cultivating a majority in the House of Commons. . . . He cared neither for the friendship nor enmity of politicians who thought in terms of places and patronage. . . . It was not his illness alone that wrecked the Administration; it was the mixture of grandeur and aloofness which made so great a statesman so poor a politician."

The same doubts hung at the time over Shelburne, lacking though he was in Pitt's flamboyance. "The Jesuit of Berkeley Square," he was seen by colleagues as a "secret enemy" and was never trusted, in part because of his early association with Bute; no group grew up around him. His manner was both obsequious and sarcastic; he was jealous and suspicious; he had no skill in the management of men; he had all Pitt's faults and few of his virtues; and, where India was concerned, he seems to have been open to the charge of directing his activities to the ends of personal financial gain. But of all the major politicians of his day, Shelburne alone was well informed on the American question. And he was perhaps the most consistently liberal figure in Parliament, on economic and parliamentary questions, on Wilkes, free trade, and religion. He served for a few months in Grenville's ministry as President of the Board of Trade and formulated an intelligent and coherent western policy. And in 1782 it was through his contacts with Richard Oswald and Franklin that the peace was at last signed.

It was therefore impossible for any one group to allow the American question to become the key question of policy. In any event, any such assumption would have been false to eighteenth-century politics. The task of government was administrative, not legislative. No group other than the Rockinghams had anything resembling a party "program." In a real crisis, as in 1775, parliamentary opinion tended to rally behind the King. When it finally broke with him, as in 1782, the government came close to paralysis and the King himself thought of abdication. As a result, no agreed solutions could emerge from Parliament for the baffling problems of the New World, for its frontier security, for its native population, for the financing of its defense, or for guiding its growing trade along new lines.

Only three men showed genuine concern for those problems at the legislative level: Rockingham, who held office for only one year; Pitt, whose illness deprived his country of its one possible political savior; and Shelburne, who came to power only in time to make a peace of surrender. Whatever the reason for it—an unimaginative King, an unrepresentative House, or mere faction—during the years from 1760 to 1784 Parliament was complacent about and indifferent to the American problem. The colonies, their sugar and tobacco, furs, fish and timber, their governorships and tax collectorships, their stamp distributors and Indian agents, their markets for London, Bristol, and Glasgow agents, were the spoils not of an imperial system gone awry or of a despotic King, but of a parliamentary and largely aristocratic battleground in which only a handful of men knew or cared about them. And until 1782 the association of the American cause with radicalism, with "Wilkes and liberty," and its exposition at home mainly by merchants and dissenters, by London aldermen or by somewhat suspect Irish carpetbaggers, did not enlist particular sympathy in a Parliament that was still the preserve of the Duke of Omnium.

Moreover, at a time when politics was relatively unaffected by public opinion but greatly affected by pressure groups, when West Indian planters and Indian "nabobs" were peculiarly powerful, there was no sustained American pressure group in Parliament at all. Only on repeal of the Stamp Act was there temporary accord between the West Indian and the American merchants: it did not last. A few individuals were interested in the American problem; and there were two ex-colonial governors, Thomas Pownall of Massachusetts—on this issue the ablest and most experienced of all members of Parliament, although regarded as a "wild man" and, worse, a bore—and George Johnstone of West Florida.

But they were a handful only, and they were not a united group. Those of them who showed independence and had posts to lose— like Conway and Barré—lost them in the war, to be regarded as heroes in America. By no means all Americans living in London shared their sentiments; former colonial agents as often as not came in the end to support Britain, among them Richard Jackson and William Knox. Between 1763 and 1783 only five Americans sat in the House of Commons, and of these never more than three sat at any one time. Of them, one—Paul Wentworth—was a loyalist, and another—Henry Cruger of New York—was by no means consistently pro-American. Only Barlow Trecothick, who helped to have the Stamp Act repealed, was of real help to the American cause. What was needed was a Virginia or Massachusetts cousinhood to offset Jamaica and India House. The absence from Parliament of an American "interest" in these years was the most serious political fact of all.

The role of government in the eighteenth century was thus—of necessity—small. And its powers of law enforcement were, it should be remembered, very limited. Mobs and riots were frequent occurrences. This explains much of the Revolutionary period: the ineffectivness of the mercantile system before 1763 and the bitterness aroused by the law once its enforcement was effective; the power of mobs, whether of transient soldiers and sailors in New York, angry at British press gangs, or of those who wrecked the Stamp Act and the tea duty of 1773; the effect on civil government of groups like the Sons of Liberty or the Mohawk River Indians, and the powerlessness of authority to curb them; the danger implicit in any meetings under the Liberty Pole; and the fear of a standing army and the invitation to belittle its garrisons. In the eighteenth century the line that separated a snowball fight from an outbreak of civil war, or even a revolution, was a narrow one. Violence was never far below the surface in eighteenth-century society, whether at home or overseas: except in the most disciplined or sophisticated societies it never is. And when authority is weak or hesitant, it is natural to see the right of assembly, the right of vigilante justice, and even the right to riot as expressions of a natural right.

In the circumstances of eighteenth-century parliamentary politics, then, a policy for the colonies was hard to manufacture. It was not indeed felt to be needed, except in a crisis. The administration of the colonies was the responsibility of the Privy Council and primarily of the Secretary of State for the Southern Department, acting on the advice of the Board of Trade and Plantations. The Board, which consisted of eight active and eight honorary members, examined all laws passed by the colonial assemblies and occasionally imposed a royal veto on them. Of 8563 laws submitted to it, 469 were disallowed. It drafted instructions to colonial governors, recommended appointments, and gave advice. None of its members had had colonial experience, and they invariably and exclusively reflected mercantile opinion.

In the early part of the eighteenth century the Board had declined in influence, and the Duke of Newcastle in particular had been jealous of its allegedly wide powers of patronage. There was no consistency of opinion as to its powers. The Earl of Halifax, on becoming its President in 1748, had sought to extend its authority, and began a campaign for the creation of a specifically American department. From 1752 to 1761 it had the right to appoint colonial governors and to control all ordinary correspondence with them. In 1757, with Pitt's support, Halifax was admitted to the Cabinet. He was a clear-headed imperialist and wanted the colonists taxed for their own defense. This new efficiency, again antedating 1760, along with Pitt's zest and success as Secretary of State, brought Parliament into the day-by-day matters of administration; increasingly the Commons took an interest and at times an initiative, rarely unselfish or high-minded, in colonial patronage, in the workings of the laws of trade, or in curbing American manufactures. And this parliamentary curiosity, which at home appeared a guarantee of liberty against royal or bureaucratic power, appeared in colonial eyes at best as meddling interference, and in the end as a new species of tyranny.

The Board of Trade was then intermittently powerful, but its power again declined after Halifax's retirement in 1761. The Board was never an effective and not always a sympathetic colonial office, close though its contacts were with merchants and colonial agents; whenever it proposed major expenditure, particularly for colonial defense, it met opposition from Parliament and the Treasury; it could in the last resort only advise and recommend, not enforce. "The Lords of Trade," said Governor Belcher, "are not very mighty lords; nor are they able to administer life or death."

Nor did the creation in 1768 of a third secretaryship of state, designed to be a Secretary for American Affairs, improve matters. Hillsborough was quite unqualified for the post and his powers were never precisely defined. When the office had been first proposed, Newcastle spoke of a "Secretary for the Indies." Although by 1768 it was concerned with the American colonies, it was not until Germain became its holder in 1775 that it came to rank as equal to the two existing secretaryships. What vigor there was under Hillsborough (1768–72) and Dartmouth (1772–75) came from the office of its permanent secretary. This post was held by John Pownall as Secretary of the Board of Trade from 1748 to 1768, and then as Under Secretary for the Colonies (1768–70). Unlike his brother, an ex-governor of Massachusetts, John Pownall knew of the colonies only at second hand, and he favored a policy of coercion toward them. Pownall was succeeded by William Knox, who served until the department was abolished by Rockingham's reforms in 1782. Knox had estates in Georgia as a rice-planter; he had been an agent for Georgia in London from 1762 until 1765, but lost his post because of his advocacy of the Stamp Act. He favored the creation of a colonial aristocracy and the inclusion in Parliament of representatives from the colonies. It was from Pownall and from Knox that the first drafts of bills came. The frequent changes of ministry and their fluctuating membership gave these permanent officials considerable influence.

There was, however, even after 1768, no one single agency in London wherein lay exclusive responsibility for the colonies. The Secretary of State and the Board of Trade, the Treasury, and the Surveyor and Auditor-General of the colonies, the Commissioner of Customs, the Secretary-at-War, the Admiralty and the Admiralty Courts, the Surveyor-General of the King's Woods, the Postmaster-General, the Bishop of London—all were involved. Much time was spent in consultation and discussion among them; still more was wasted in the physical effort of reaching the appropriate authority. The Admiralty alone had fifteen branches scattered in all parts of the town, from Whitehall to Cheapside; the Board sat in Whitehall, but the Navy Office was in Seething Lane, the Victualling Office in East Smithfield, the Ordnance in the Tower. Any rapid dispatch of business was unusual, almost impossible, in London, and it took a further five weeks at best, and ten weeks as normal, to pass the results on to the colonies; a similar period followed in waiting for a reply. "Seas roll and months pass between the order and the execution," said Burke.

And the documents that were dispatched were bureaucratically standardized. The instructions issued by the Board of Trade were not changed in essentials throughout its existence, from 1696 to 1782. Hillsborough, as American Secretary, insisted that all applications from any colony should come direct from the governor to him, and not through a colonial agent in London, even though that agent was Franklin. Governor Sharpe similarly told Maryland to avoid modes of transmission that were "disrespectful to the Crown." There was small awareness of the colonial growth in population, of their sense of being, in Governor Bernard's words, "perfect states, not otherwise dependent on Great Britain than by having the same King."

The result of this was that the British government was parliamentary and—as it saw itself—free at home but bureaucratic and royal abroad. Indeed, at a time when separatist feeling in the colonies was very strong, and the political structure and societies of the colonies varied, centralization was increasing—not decreasing—in London. More and more colonies were coming under the control of the Crown, even if in one or two cases governors were not appointed by the Crown. In 1752 colonial governors were reminded that they must abide by their instructions and that all colonial laws should be brought into conformity with royal instructions. The more daunting the colonial problems and the more extensive the territory to be administered, the more the need grew for plan and pattern. In the new areas acquired in 1763—Canada, the Floridas, the trans-Allegheny country—there were no representative institutions, and little information available; here was no local opinion to conciliate, and politics could be discounted. It was all too possible for Americans, for whom the pattern of government had not changed since 1660, to see themselves as protesting against a tyranny like that of Charles I; the Burke-Whig view of George III has some validity when the King is seen in an American rather than a British context. When after 1763 Parliament increasingly associated itself with the King in colonial matters, it appeared in American eyes as remote and unrepresentative, not the guardian but the enemy of liberty. The Declaration of Independence was America's Grand Remonstrance.

Before 1763 Parliament had played small part in colonial rule, either in theory or practice. There is hardly a single Act of Parliament for the colonies before 1763 that is not a trade bill. At various times, however—1701, 1706, 1715, 1722, and again in 1744 and 1748—the Board of Trade, in its efforts to establish a homogeneous system of administration, tried to extend the royal prerogative in the colonies, and brought in measures to make the private proprietary colonies royal. Parliament was slow and reluctant to interfere with colonial charters or to tighten the system, but it did authorize the transfer to the Crown of the rights of the Carolina proprietors in 1729, and it appropriated considerable sums to help establish Georgia in the 1730s. For the rest, it confined itself mainly to trade regulation. The administration of the colonies was left to the executive. It was of course more powerful in theory than in fact; the years from 1733 to 1763 were years of administrative laissez faire that came close to destroying the mercantile system.

Then why, after 1763, did Parliament suddenly concern itself, not merely with the trade, but with the actual ruling of the colonies? In part, the answer is constitutional. The departments responsible for America were now headed by members of ministries based on parliamentary combinations. Such combinations were held together by patronage, and the colonies were a rich field. For their part, too, the colonies maintained agents in London, and sometimes these agents were themselves members of Parliament, like Richard Jackson or Burke himself. Even when they were not, they brought what influence they had to bear on Parliament.

But it seems also to be true that in the years from 1756 to 1774 Parliament was becoming remarkably self-conscious. There was at last an end of Stuart threats, and an end of the reversionary problem that had bedeviled the monarchy. The winning of America and India brought more than pride; it brought to a head both a sense of the importance of the colonies and a sense of their absolute dependence on the mother country—distressingly true in the light of colonial hesitations to help the campaign against the French. The Wilkes case, the attempt to suppress the printing and reporting of debates, the concern with privilege—due as much to a parliamentary as to a royal sensitiveness—indicate the mood. In 1763 there was a new consciousness of victory and of Empire, of which Pitt was the symbol. For the first time the colonies were valued not merely for their trade or as counters in European diplomacy but as possessions; there was glory in their mere extent, and their administration could no longer be ignored. And there was, in all the factional politics of the eighteenth century, no serious questioning of the legislative authority of Parliament. Some, like Pitt, might with baffling logic hesitate to admit that the legislative power included the right to tax. But few had his doubts, even on this. The year of the Stamp Act saw the publication of the first volume of Blackstone's *Commentaries on the Laws of England*. "There is and must be in every state a supreme, irresistible, absolute and uncontrolled authority, in which the *jura summa imperii,* or rights of sovereignty, reside"; "this supreme power is by the constitution of Great Britain vested in the King, Lords and Commons."

Parliamentary sensitiveness to its own rights was very evident in Grenville's attitude to the American problem. After the repeal of his own Act, he consistently opposed all suggestions for a return to the old system of requisitions or for a revenue derived from quitrents, on the ground that all such funds would be Crown revenues, beyond the control of Parliament. British parliamentary imperialism was born in 1763. This was a different species, of course, from the jingoism that had to wait for widespread literacy and a popular press. It was in fact more dangerous because less responsible. Power over remote territories and increasingly alien peoples was now to be political as well as economic; trade could flourish by means of war; Oceania would now give law to the sea, even if those giving it were in fact a small group of men in a faction-ridden Parliament.

RICHARD W. VAN ALSTYNE

Parliamentary Supremacy
versus Independence

▣ Historians are now familiar with the stages whereby the colonies reached their decision to declare independence. With the stages whereby Britain decided to be firm—stages marked by uncertainty, intrigue, and vacillation—they are on the whole much less familiar. In the article that follows, Richard W. Van Alstyne reveals from a careful examination of the evidence how the factional politics of Westminster hindered the shaping of any clear or coherent policy. All groups in Parliament were adamant on the right of parliamentary supremacy, but all in varied ways sought to avoid a crisis. From Van Alstyne's paper Burke and the Rockinghams (with the exception of the Duke of Richmond) emerge with no credit. The North administration thought that if the storm really broke, it still had the force on the spot to curb trouble—the cardinal error. If there were any British "heroes" at this stage they are David Hartley, the later architect of reconciliation, and Chatham, always in high policy the realist. Chatham saw in the Declaratory Act of 1766 the real cause of mischief; it should be repealed. His plan was embodied in the "Provisional Act for settling the troubles of America," and he advocated constitutional reform: a standing army was necessary for the protection of the colonies but it would be under strict control; colonial assemblies would enjoy fullest rights of legislation and taxation in local government. Repeal a colony's fears and resentments "and you may then hope for her love and gratitude." Here as earlier he was the Churchill of his times, but without his great good fortune. ▣

IN ORDER to comprehend the problem which Great Britain faced with respect to the American colonies in the crucial year 1775, we must recognize and examine three separate and distinct schools of thought. The government constituted the first of these schools, and the ideas it represented came from Lord North in the Commons and the earl of Mansfield in the Lords. The king agreed, but it is a mistake to assume that he thought out the government's basic attitude; he merely reflected the mind of the government and fell in with its proposals. The Rockingham group, to which Edmund Burke and Sir George Savile belonged, comprised the second and middle school. Burke is the classic spokesman for this group, but we shall do well at the outset to

Reprinted by permission from the *Huntington Library Quarterly*, XXVI (1963), 201-215.

recognize that he did no more than follow the lead of his friend and patron, the marquis of Rockingham. Chatham, Shelburne, and Camden constituted the leadership of the third school in the Lords; and David Hartley, who owed his seat to Lord Rockingham, was its best spokesman in the Commons. Then there are two other men whose names will appear prominently in this paper, and whom it will be well to identify. They are Charles Lennox, third duke of Richmond (who was a close friend of Lord Rockingham and a loyal member of his group, but who belonged in spirit more with the Chathamites) and Augustus Henry Fitzroy, third duke of Grafton, a former member of the Rockingham Whigs and a good personal friend of Lord North and other members of the government. Silent during the first eight months of the year, he became alarmed at the tragic turn of affairs after Bunker Hill and aroused himself to vigorous opposition on the side of the Chathamites.

I shall discuss each of these schools of thought in its turn and examine its proposals for remedial action.

The government was in the process of making up its mind during the month of January. Burke asserted on January 20 that it had as yet given no sign of a clear and decisive policy, and there is no reason for believing him wrong. But on that day Chatham forced the issue by demanding the recall of the troops from Boston, and on February 1 he introduced into the Lords a comprehensive measure for settling the troubles in America. Chatham's bill asserted the supreme legislative authority and superintending power of Britain over the colonies; proposed the repeal of the Quebec Act; declared that no tallage, tax, or other charge would be levied against the Americans; made it legal for them to meet in general congress in Philadelphia on the following May 9; and stipulated that the delegates there assembled recognize the supremacy of Parliament and make a free grant to the king of a certain perpetual revenue.[1]

Lord North on his part fixed upon the principle of parliamentary supremacy. The Americans, he said, had entered "an almost universal confederacy" to resist and deny this principle. Here was the great barrier which separated and for the present disunited the two countries. The question lay within a very narrow compass: the government was determined to enforce the sovereignty of the king and Parliament. It intended to put down the rebellion, but beyond that it did not plan to persist. It would be satisfied with the "submission" of the colonies. Once that was given, they could expect their grievances to be redressed.[2]

1. *The Parliamentary History of England,* XVIII, hereafter referred to as *PH* (London, 1813), cols. 149-203; *The Correspondence of Edmund Burke,* ed. George H. Guttridge, III, hereafter referred to as Guttridge (Chicago, 1961), 101-103.

2. *PH,* cols. 221-223. North, being a courtesy peer, sat in the House of Commons. Such few of his personal papers as are still extant are in the Guildford Collection, Bodleian Library, Oxford. They are of little value; but the letters of Brownlow North, the younger half brother, to his father, the first earl of Guildford, are informative respecting personalities in the upper house and opinions expressed there. Brownlow North sat in the Lords as bishop of Lichfield, then as bishop of Worcester, finally as bishop of Winchester.

Lord Mansfield, who was chief justice, made the point even more precisely. "We were reduced to the alternative," he declared, "of adopting coercive measures, or of forever relinquishing our claim of sovereignty or dominion over the colonies . . . . [Either] the supremacy of the British legislature must be complete, entire, and unconditional; or on the other hand, the colonies must be free and independent." Thus Mansfield defined the position of the government in simple and categorical terms: either the supremacy of Parliament or an "independent American empire." The latter was inadmissible, just as secession and independence of the Confederate States were inadmissible to the Lincoln government in 1861. There was no middle ground. The imposition of the taxes, Mansfield volunteered, had been in his opinion a mistake; but it was "utterly impossible to say a syllable on the matter of expediency, till the right was first as fully asserted on one side, as acknowledged on the other." [3]

It is important to take into consideration the impressions of a younger member of Parliament who felt the crisis very keenly, but who took the side of the government. William Eden, the later Lord Auckland, was thirty-one years of age in 1775; he had been elected to Parliament the year before, though he had been under-secretary to Lord Suffolk in the northern department since 1772; and in December 1777, after the shock of Burgoyne's surrender, he recalled how he felt at the outset of the quarrel. His letter, written for the benefit of his friend Wedderburn, the solicitor general, reads as follows:

> When I first came into parliament, I found the nation actually engaging in measures of force for the recovery of colonies, which had been dependent on her from their first foundation. There was at that moment no alternative but 'War or Separation.' All retrospect to the causes of such an alternative were idle; it was necessary to take a choice; and in so doing I was not influenced either by the popular cry or by political connections. As an individual of a family possessing considerable interests both in Gt. Britain and America I was naturally indisposed to a separation evidently mischievous to both countries, but still further as an English gentleman inheriting my share of that English pride which I never wish to lose, I could not bear to see a dismemberment of the Empire without running every hazard to prevent it. Nor did I give in to these feelings under a misconception that the task we were undertaking would be an easy one. I was aware of the difficulties which existed in the one Continent and would spring up in the other

3. *PH*, cols. 269-271. As chief justice, Mansfield was not a member of the government in 1775, but it seems very likely that he was influential in formulating its policy. In a very adroit speech on the same day, Lord Shelburne drew him by charging that he had behaved unconstitutionally in mixing the executive and judicial powers together. The noble lord, records the *PH*, thereupon "rose in great passion" (col. 282).

Mansfield's private papers are probably of great value, but are unhappily still closed to scholars. They are at the family estate in Scotland.

and I should have learnt them indeed indirectly from Dr. Franklin if I had had no other access to them, for I had lived many years and still continue to live in the most intimate intercourse with a friend of that gentleman (Mr. John Lee) who had imbibed from Dr. F and from their mutual friends a strong partiality to the cause of the colonies and no inconsiderable knowledge of their natural strength and advantages. . . .[4]

The most then that the government expected was that the Americans concede the supremacy of Parliament; on this point it felt it could not yield. Beyond that, however, it was prepared to be generous. The Americans need but propose means and give assurances of their intentions to contribute a proper share of service and burden in the common defense, and Parliament would not argue its right to tax them. "Where violence is with resolution repelled," wrote the king to Lord North, February 15, "it commonly yields, and I owne though a thorough friend to holding out the Olive Branch I have not the smallest doubt that if it does not succeed that when once vigorous measures appear to be the only means left of bringing the Americans to a due Submission to the Mother Country that the Colonies will Submit. . . ."[5] "If the Americans," declared Lord George Germain, "pointing the late Acts out as a grievance, would petition for their repeal, he would stretch forth the first hand to present it; but, on the contrary, if they claimed such repeal as a right, thereby disputing the authority of the mother country, which no reasonable man ever called in question, he wished the said Acts might be enforced with a Roman severity."[6] Lord North then put these ideas in the form of a resolution, which passed the House sitting as a committee of the whole on February 20, by a vote of 274:88. Thereafter there was no real variation in the British government's policy until 1782, when under a different ministry and with great reluctance it admitted independence. The resolution is therefore reproduced in full. It reads:

That it is the opinion of this Committee, that when the governor, council, and assembly, or general court, of any of His Majesty's provinces or colonies in America, shall propose to make provision, according to the condition, circumstances, and situation, of such province or colony for, contributing their proportion to the common defence (such proportion to be raised under the authority of the

4. British Museum Add. MSS. 46,490-91, Pkt. 2. The family interests in America were probably identified with Eden's brother Robert, who was a governor of Maryland and married into the Calvert family. I am greatly indebted for this document and for the information connected with it to Ian Christie, Reader in Modern History at University College, London.

5. *The Correspondence of King George the Third,* ed. John Fortescue, III (London, 1928), No. 1595.

6. *PH,* col. 192. On Germain consult George H. Guttridge, "Lord George Germain in Office, 1775-1782," *Amer. Hist. Rev.,* XXXIII (1927), 23-43; and Gerald S. Brown, "The Policy of Lord George Germain toward the American Revolution" (unpubl. dissertation, Univ. of Minn., 1948).

general court, or general assembly, of such province or colony, and disposable by parliament) and shall engage to make provision also for the support of the civil government, and the administration of justice, in such province or colony, it will be proper, if such proposal shall be approved by his Majesty and the two Houses of Parliament, and for so long as such provision shall be made accordingly to forbear, in respect of such province or colony, to levy any duty, tax, or assessment, or to impose any farther duty, tax, or assessment, except only such duties as it may be expedient to continue to levy or to impose for the regulation of commerce; the nett produce of the duties last mentioned to be carried to the account of such province or colony respectively.[7]

Meanwhile on or about the seventh of January, Chatham, in his anxiety to avert a crisis, had had an interview with Lord Rockingham. Rightly or wrongly, Chatham believed that the Declaratory Act had been the cause of all the confusion, and he asked the cooperation of the Rockingham group in getting the measure repealed, or at least amended. But Rockingham had originated the Declaratory Act in 1766, and he now refused to go back on it. To him it was the ark of the covenant; he made more of it than did Mansfield and Lord North, who were satisfied with the abstract principle of parliamentary supremacy.[8] This had been a sore point between Rockingham and Chatham from the beginning, and the marquis showed his irritation. On this difference alone there was little, if any, possibility of cooperation between them.[9] When Chatham defended his proposed bill of February 1 in the Lords, he received no support from Rockingham; and, on a motion by Lord Sandwich, the first lord of the admiralty, the bill was voted down (61:32) on the first reading.

Nor, when the government made known its own position, did the Rockingham group rise to the occasion.[10] They were against the use of

---

7. *PH*, col. 320. In support of his resolution, Lord North declared himself in favor of the right of Parliament to tax the colonies, but would transfer the exercise of the right to the colonial assemblies (*ibid.*, col. 352). This is indeed a finely drawn distinction, yet it is the basis on which the government rested its whole policy of coercion. In the same speech Lord North said he was for leaving the colonies at liberty to contribute voluntarily to imperial defence. Parliament would retain the legal right to reject or increase these voluntary aids; but it is plain from the context that the government did not intend to exercise its "right."

8. The authorities agree that the act was a politically necessary measure in 1766 in order to appease the feeling in Parliament and secure the repeal of the Stamp Act. John Heneage Jesse, *Memoirs of the Life and Reign of King George the Third* (London, 1867), I, 329-331; Arthur S. Turberville, *The House of Lords in the XVIII Century* (Oxford, 1927), p. 324.

9. Guttridge, 90-93.

10. Rockingham's complacency and stuffy adherence to the Declaratory Act appear to justify the severe criticisms levelled at him by various writers. See, for example, John Brooke, *The Chatham Administration, 1766-1768* (London, 1956), pp. 24-26. Turberville says, however, that he "was conscientious and universally respected. Though his intellectual endowment was small, and he was more at home on the race-course than in the Council-chamber, on the other hand he had the invaluable

troops in America, but even in this respect they hung back and left the initiative to Chatham. Burke in the Commons publicly denounced Lord North's conciliatory resolution as "insidious and perplexing," but his argument reads like a sophistry; he offered no convincing reasons against the resolution, nor did he propose any alternative. "A more complete Scheme of senseless Tyranny never was devised by the pride and folly of man" was his way of dismissing the resolution, but one searches in vain for a justification of these harsh words.[11] His tone suggests that he was moved by nothing better than party passion against the government. The nearest that Burke came to a constructive proposal was his celebrated speech of March 22, 1775, on conciliation. In this address he offered thirteen resolutions proposing the repeal of the measures passed against the Americans since 1767 and leaving to the provincial assemblies the determination of their own grants and subsidies. But Burke was silent on the Declaratory Act, he evaded the issue of parliamentary supremacy, and he added nothing essential to what the ministry had already offered.[12]

Evidently the Rockingham group was caught on the horns of a dilemma. Chatham and his friends sensed the danger, however, and were prepared. Not a moment was to be lost if a civil war was to be averted, declared the earl. Assertions of the omnipotence of Parliament were futile. "Every danger and every hazard impend, to deter you from perseverance in your present ruinous measures.—Foreign war hanging over your heads by a slight and brittle thread: France and Spain watching your conduct, and waiting for the maturity of your errors;—with a vigilant eye to America, and the temper of your colonies, more than to their own concerns, be they what they may." [13] Chatham then demanded that all acts (including the Declaratory Act) upon which Parliament could take money from the Americans be repealed, and that the latter be given the right to take money only from themselves through their assemblies.

Chatham too paid his respects to the doctrine of parliamentary supremacy, but he subordinated it to the exigencies of the moment.

11. Guttridge, 118; *PH*, col. 319.

12. *PH*, cols. 478-538. Like the American patriots, Burke and Chatham denounced the government for its "tyranny"; and the epithet "British tyranny" passed down into history, a cliché repeated innumerable times and echoed even to this day by some American writers. But the inherent injustice, not to say irrelevancy, of the epithet should be noted.

13. *PH*, col. 156; and Chatham to Shelburne, Jan. 31, 1775, in the Shelburne MSS at Bowood, Calne, Wilts. Chatham was suffering constantly from gout, even to the extent of having it in his hands. Lady Chatham wrote his letters for him to Lord Shelburne.

---

capacity of inspiring loyalty in his followers, he was more successful in maintaining party cohesion than many abler men have been, and he could stand up to the King when occasion demanded it. But he was much more successful in the Cabinet than in Parliament. He was a bad and nervous speaker and seldom opened his lips in the House of Lords if he could avoid it . . ." (*House of Lords*, p. 323).

Here is the crucial point of difference between him on the one hand, and the ministry and Rockingham group on the other. Unwilling to see the line drawn on what he regarded as an unreal issue, Chatham wanted to act immediately. The alternative was civil war within the empire and a foreign war outside. The following excerpt from a letter which Chatham wrote to Baron Bridport (Admiral Alexander Hood) on June 6, 1773, is of interest: "What can France desire more, than to see her rival sinking every year, from being mistress of the world, land and sea, into the bubble of her enemies, and the scorn of nations? She will therefore leave us to pursue, unmolested, tho' not always unfrightened, our own plans of self-destruction, and let peace ruin us, without risking a war" (Bridport Papers, Vol. II, B.M. Add. MSS. 35,192).

The duke of Richmond, in the debate of February 7, 1775, joined Chatham in voicing his fears of France and Spain.[14] In the following week of February, when Lord Mansfield set forth the government's position, Lord Camden, an equally great lawyer and an associate of Chatham, tried ridicule. He concluded, he said, on "the high sounding unintelligible phrases of legislative supremacy and parliamentary omnipotence; but, for his part, they conveyed to his mind precisely such an idea, and gave equal satisfaction, as the answer given by the fine gentleman in the play, who, being charged with baseness by his friend, who told him he had eat his meat, drank his wine, and lain with his wife, made no other reply, at the end of every sentence, but, 'Sir, I wear a sword.'" Camden objected to the folly of blocking up the colonial ports to commerce, the life blood of England herself (a point on which all parties agreed), and ended on an apt quotation from Shakespeare that, without commerce, when compared with the several great powers of Europe, England was no more than a "bird's nest floating on a pool" (*PH,* cols. 273, 272).[15]

14. *PH,* col. 286. Richmond was the exception to the timidity and lack of imagination shown by the Rockingham group, but he never felt free to join the Chathamites. His private character was unexceptionable, and he was very ambitious in public life, though somewhat violent and intractable. A. S. Turberville, *A History of Welbeck Abbey and Its Owners,* II (London, 1939), 179-180, says that he was the ablest peer in the group, but he was too radical for his colleagues, who thought him unsafe and given to romantic visions. He was outspoken, and his speeches were very informative, but evidently he was condemned to play the part of a lone wolf. Consult also G. H. Guttridge, *English Whiggism and the American Revolution* (Berkeley, 1942); and D. J. Turner, "George III and the Whig Opposition (1760-1794): A Study of the Organization, Principles, Policy and Conduct of the Rockingham-Portland Whigs" (unpub. diss., Univ. of Nottingham, 1953).

Turner says that Richmond detested Chatham, and Albemarle publishes correspondence which gives the impression that friendship and cooperation between Chatham and the Rockingham group were out of the question. Jesse, *Memoirs,* while paying tribute to Chatham's abilities, criticizes him for being very pompous and full of morbid fancies.

15. *PH,* cols. 271-273. Camden in February 1766 joined with Shelburne and three other young peers in denouncing Rockingham's Declaratory Act. Turberville, *House of Lords,* p. 325.

Now let us, before going farther, review in brief these three proposed methods for dealing with the American problem. The government acted on the conviction that the doctrine of parliamentary supremacy must be maintained in the strictest and most literal sense; that, if necessary, force without stint must be invoked to uphold it. But, practically speaking, all that the Americans need do was to pay lip service to the principle, and all would be forgiven. It seems clear that the ministry did not even intend to hold out on its demand that the colonies share in the cost of imperial defense. "Submission" was all that was expected. Therein, of course, was the fallacy in the government's approach. It thought it was facing an insurrection; actually it was confronted with a revolution. Its opponents entertained large ambitions of their own and remained unmoved by the spirit of compromise even to the extent of the empty gesture of "submission."

The Rockingham group also adhered to parliamentary supremacy; it would not listen to pleas to modify or amend the Declaratory Act. Yet it would do nothing to enforce the act. It would recall the troops and adopt a passive attitude toward the rebels. This, it could be argued in retrospect, was Britain's true policy: ignore the issues and let the insurrection peter out. Like Don Quixote, the rebel leaders would find themselves in the absurd position of battling an imaginary foe. But the Rockingham group did not argue its case forcefully. It made no appeal to imaginative statesmanship, but confined itself to dissent and to admissions of discouragement. Its attitude was essentially defeatist.

The Chathamites too believed in parliamentary supremacy, as a theory. But they would not remain passive and run the risk of the Americans' rejecting conciliation. They proposed to recapture the leadership by boldly repealing all of the measures in question and then by laying upon the Americans an obligation to share in the expenses of the empire. (They did not say what they would do in case the Americans rejected this obligation; and therefore it could be argued that their position was really no better than the government's, if indeed it was as good.) But Chatham and his friends were genuinely alarmed—terrified would be more accurate. They sensed the perils of a general war, with Britain in the middle and facing hopeless odds. All this they grasped before the struggle commenced. Hence they would leave nothing to chance in healing the wounds and solidifying the empire.

On March 27, five days after Burke's conciliation speech, David Hartley tried a fresh approach, one that relegated the principle of parliamentary supremacy still farther to the background. Hartley read to the Commons the draft of a "Letter of Requisition" that he had written for the king to send to each of the provinces. Carefully phrased and practical in its approach to the common defense problem, the letter put the emphasis on the contribution of the royal navy to the security of the empire. It then proceeded to state that His Majesty regretted that "needless and imprudent discussions of speculative points, from mutual misapprehensions, have been converted into anger and animosities, which threatened the most fatal consequences." And in conclusion, it said, His Majesty wishes to see "unanimity restored . . . in one common obedience to the supreme legislature," so that they may join "to support the dignity of his crown, the just authority of parliament, the true and combined interests of Great Britain and America. . . ." [16]

Hartley's idea that the king should assume the initiative, merely reporting the results to Parliament, contained important constitutional implications: it pointed at the supremacy of the crown, rather than of Parliament, and hence provided a way of getting around the troublesome and sterile dogma of parliamentary supremacy. Lord Abingdon was to develop this concept at greater length in a pamphlet published over two years later. [17] The king would deal with his American subjects, who were not the subjects of Parliament. It was the Declaratory Act that was unconstitutional. But Hartley's motion unfortunately received scant attention. The government, of course, was not interested. Lord North condemned the proposed letters as a return to Charles I's levies for ship money, and the motion was negatived without a division. [18]

But Hartley's efforts to rouse the country to the dangers of impending war did not go unheeded. Warning of the "fatal example" of Spain in the Netherlands, he renewed the argument on May 2, when the armed clash at Lexington was still unknown. Three newspapers—the *Morning Chronicle and London Advertiser,* the *London Chronicle,* and the *Morning Post and Daily Advertiser*—printed the speech, which is worth quoting in part. Said Hartley on this occasion:

> It is next to infatuation and madness, for one moment, to suppose that we can have an American without a French and Spanish war. I am clear that they will keep off while there is any possibility of the American dispute being made up, but when once the war is begun, and neither party can withdraw, then, Sir, in spite of all those assurances which your Chief Justice gained at Paris from the French ministers, you will find them take a determined part— a part plainly pointed out by both interest and ambition. . . . Nothing but the most infantine credulity can believe the contrary; you will then find yourselves engaged in a French war, in a Spanish

16. *PH,* cols. 565-566, 567. G. H. Guttridge, *David Hartley, M. P.: An Advocate of Conciliation, 1774-1783,* Univ. of Calif. Pubs. in Hist., XIV (Berkeley, 1926), is the principal work on this brilliant, but rather eccentric figure. Like Richmond, Hartley belonged with the Rockingham group (he owed his seat in Commons to Sir George Savile), but he took positions far too strong for the group to accept.

17. *Thoughts on the Letter of Edmund Burke, Esq.* (Oxford, 1777). For a brief discussion of this pamphlet see my "Europe, the Rockingham Whigs, and the War for American Independence: Some Documents," *HLQ,* XXV (1961), 3.

18. *PH,* col. 574. Many writers assume that the differences with the colonies could not be resolved because responsible government did not then exist. See, for example, Eric Robson, *The American Revolution* (London, 1955), p. 78. But Chatham's pragmatic approach and Hartley's proposal show there was no intrinsic constitutional obstacle in the path of a settlement.

war, I think, in a Prussian war; and wars are so catching, Sir, when they spread, in I know not how many other wars likewise. . . .[19]

In its issue for July 3 the *London Evening-Post,* a strong pro-Chatham paper laboring to oust the "wicked ministers," published a "most authentic report" that the revolutionary congress had resolved on independence and were hesitating whether to form two separate republics, a northern and a southern, or to unite all the provinces in one association. The report was published in at least two other papers, the *Morning Post* and the *Gazetteer;* and it is interesting because it shows that the idea of an independent American empire, upon which Lord Mansfield had been insisting, was being taken seriously in Britain. The colonists might protest their loyalty, but their protestations were being questioned. Furthermore, the *Evening-Post* wanted to know how the ministry proposed to keep the country from becoming a province of France. France and Spain were rearming; the Americans were getting arms, ammunition, and cannon from the French; and once the colonies were lost, Britain's "commerce, opulence and splendor" would be gone forever. The shedding of blood and destruction of property in America must be stopped at all costs; France alone stood to win; and only Chatham could head off the disaster.[20]

The clash at Lexington was known in England on May 28, and the battle that occurred at Bunker Hill on June 16 became public knowledge after August 12. These events discouraged the Rockingham group. "Your accounts are most melancholy to a thinking man," wrote Richmond to Burke. "I believe our meridian is past, and we must submit to our political as to our natural old age, weakness, and infirmity." [21] Neither Burke nor Rockingham held out much hope for peace. They admitted that the country as a whole was on the side of the government, that even the merchants who had been in opposition were now taking a different view: government contracts and an "incredible increase" in the Polish and Russian markets accounted for the change, and the

19. From the *Morning Post and Daily Advertiser,* May 5, 1775, B.M., Burney Coll. It was also reported in the papers that speculators in the city were offering ten guineas against a hundred that war with France or Spain would break out within twelve months, but that few of the underwriters would insure at that price. Sentiment in the city was strongly opposed to the government in this matter.

Burke, having learned by May 28 of the battle of Lexington, privately expressed his belief that "All our prospects of American reconciliation are . . . over." Guttridge, 160-162. But neither he nor Lord Rockingham seem to have taken into account the danger of a general war. Richard Champion, the merchant of Bristol who had close contacts in America, notably with Willing, Morris & Company of Philadelphia, was their source of information on American events.

20. *London Evening-Post,* July 3 and 11, August 12, 1775.

21. Guttridge, 170. And Rockingham, upon learning on June 23 of the fall of Ticonderoga, expressed his conviction that "the whole of the continent is enraged and will unite or rather is united in the determination of resistance" (*ibid.,* p. 172).

mercantile world now regarded the American war "not so much as their Calamity as their rescource." [22] The Whigs saw but one possibility: if they could keep Parliament from committing itself to the war, they might yet force an end to the hostilities. This was a forlorn hope, but it was agreed that the group would meet in London about the middle of October, well before the opening of the fall session, and draw up a memorial to His Majesty to be introduced into Parliament after the first day. If the memorial failed to pass, as they feared, they would follow an earlier proposal of Burke's to absent themselves from Parliament whenever American affairs were being debated. Their role, as men of high rank and fortune, concluded Lord Rockingham, was to step forward "to face a torrent, not merely of ministerial or court power, but also of almost general opinion." [23]

We turn back now to study the government's policy of employing force to bring about "submission." On French interest in the quarrel the government was well informed, but it was complacent toward the possible dangers. Having been told that the French had ordered nineteen ships of the line, in addition to frigates, to be fitted out at Brest, Lord Suffolk, the secretary of the northern department, saw no reason for alarm. "We have had so much concurrent intelligence of this sort that I suspect it is not void of foundation," he wrote Gower, April 20, 1775. "But what is the object? When there is not the smallest dispute existing between France and us, is France disposed to hostilities against us?" [24] Spanish rearmament aroused more interest: Spain was thought to be preparing an attack on Portugal and suspected of bidding for French support. So the embassy in Paris was instructed to caution Vergennes, the French foreign minister, against encouraging the Spaniards.[25] On July 12, 1775, Horace St. Paul, who was temporarily in charge of the Paris embassy, wrote his first report on French shipments of contraband to America. Goods to the value of 32,000,000 livres had been sent via Santo Domingo. By September the government was sure the rebels were being constantly supplied with arms and ammunition from France and the West Indies. Three hundred casks of gunpowder and five thousand muskets complete with bayonets were reported shipped from the ports of Bayonne, St.-Malo, and Bordeaux on the first of the month. But no effort was made to stop this trade beyond asking Vergennes to prohibit the port officers from allowing the shipments. No formal complaint was filed at Versailles, and no orders were issued

22. Burke to Rockingham, Aug. 23, 1775, Guttridge, 189-196. Parliament, of course, was not in session during the summer months, a circumstance which afforded Rockingham some relief.

23. Rockingham to Burke, Sept. 24, 1775, Guttridge, pp. 214-217.

24. Granville Papers (second Earl Gower and first marquis of Stafford), London, Public Record Office (hereafter referred to as P.R.O.), 29/1, Bundle 1775-1796.

25. St. Paul to Rochford, No. 12, May 3; Rochford to St. Paul, No. 7, May 12; St. Paul to Rochford, No. 20, May 24, 1775. P.R.O., State Papers 78/296.

to British naval officers to watch vessels entering or leaving French ports.[26]

But, where the Americans alone were concerned, the government was confident that it could cope with their rebellion. Lord North advised the king on July 26 that the war had grown to such an extent that it would have to be treated as a foreign war.[27] Lord Dartmouth wrote to General Gage in Boston to say that it was hoped the rebellion could be confined to New England—that the middle colonies would prove more reasonable and accept the conciliatory resolution of February 20.[28] But regardless of this possible split in the rebel ranks, it was resolved to go ahead. Either the colonies must be given up altogether, or they must be made to submit to the will of Parliament. The king put the question very simply and straightforwardly in a letter to Lord North on July 26. He wrote:

> I am clear as to one point that we must persist and not be dismayed by any difficulties that may arise on either side of the Atlantick; I know I am doing my Duty and therefore can never wish to retract; the Resolution proposed by the House of Commons is the utmost that can be come into; and if people will have patience this must in the end be obtained.[29]

26. *Ibid.*, St. Paul to Rochford, No. 31, July 12; Rochford to St. Paul, Nos. 11, 12, 19, and 21, July 21 and 27, Sept. 15 and 29, 1775. See also Rochford to Dartmouth, Sept. 19, 1775, enclosing a four-page letter received from a person who had lived in France for many years. The letter gives intelligence regarding French and Spanish plans to take advantage of the rebellion, describes shipments of military stores sent the rebels from the French West Indies during the preceding seven years, and charges that French agents were freely dispersed throughout the American colonies for the purpose of inflaming the minds of the people. Dartmouth Papers, I, 383 (Hist. MSS. Comm., 11th, 14th, and 15th Reports). There was nothing "secret" about French aid to the Americans, nor did the British depend upon "spies" for their intelligence, Samuel Flagg Bemis, Carl Van Doren, and other writers to the contrary notwithstanding. This is a subject which will receive attention in a subsequent study.

27. *Correspondence of George III*, No. 1682.

28. Clarence Edwin Carter, *The Correspondence of General Thomas Gage with the Secretaries of State 1763-1775*, II (New Haven, 1933), 199-202.

29. *Correspondence of George III*, No. 1683. Evidently His Majesty had considered the possibility of trouble with the Bourbon powers, but had characteristically dismissed it from his mind. For an instructive treatment of the diverse views of historians regarding the king see Herbert Butterfield, *George III and the Historians* (London, 1957). Richard Pares perhaps comes closest to a balanced judgment, though his comment seems a bit unkind. He writes: "George III was, in many ways, the spiritual ancestor of Colonel Blimp; yet there was something almost admirable in his rigidity, and it showed to best advantage in war." *King George III and the Politicians* (Oxford, 1953), p. 69. Charles R. Ritcheson, *British Politics and the American Revolution* (Norman, 1954), is also very informative in his discussion of the many personalities involved in this tangled story; and for a stimulating reexamination of the whole problem of the Revolution see Robson, *passim*.

These views comprised the background to the decision to issue a royal proclamation announcing a state of rebellion in the colonies. There seemed no alternative: not only had battles been fought, but the Americans had assumed the offensive by the invasion of Canada. The king was impatient over the delay in framing the proclamation; and it was agreed that in spite of the difficulties a considerable army should be recruited and dispatched to America to be ready for action in the spring of 1776.

III

Consequences

THE CONFEDERATION PERIOD

RICHARD B. MORRIS

The Confederation Period and the American Historian

Professor Morris' survey of some recent writing on the period of confederation poses many of the issues that were the result of the Revolution: Whig élite *versus* the "masses," frontier *versus* coastal settlements, federalism *versus* unitary government, the character of the new government itself. The Whigs were, he believes, divided "on almost all issues except that of political independence from Great Britain. . . . The imposition of a vitalized federalism and the tightening of the bonds of union precipitated a greater revolution in American life than did separation from England."

PLAUTUS TELLS US that "one eyewitness is worth ten hearsays," but I am not sure that he would have left us this counsel if he had lived during the Confederation period of American history. In this era the eyewitnesses themselves failed to see eye to eye. In fact, the two opposing views of the post-Revolutionary years which are held by historians of the twentieth century can be traced directly to the Founding Fathers. The first we might call the Washington-Madison-Hamilton approach, accepted by most historians of the post-Revolutionary generation, and developed by George Bancroft, John Fiske, John B. McMaster, and with some reservations by Andrew C. McLaughlin. The other is the approach of certain Antifederalist leaders, an approach adopted by Henry B. Dawson, by J. Allen Smith, by the early Charles A. Beard, and by the more recent Merrill Jensen.

If one could read the minds of the majority of the Founding Fathers in 1787—and an abundant and ever-increasing quantity of first-hand documentation makes this a less formidable effort than it seems on its face—he might be very much surprised indeed that any issue should have arisen in historiography about the years of the Confederation. The majority of the Founders saw a clear drift toward anarchy culminating in a crisis. Constantly needled by such correspondents as Henry Knox and

Reprinted by permission from the *William and Mary Quarterly,* XIII (1956), 139-156.

David Humphreys, Washington's alarm at the weaknesses of the Confederacy was deepened as the disorders in Massachusetts in the fall of 1786 seemed to portend a crisis for the nation. "I predict the worst consequences from a half-starved, limping government, always moving upon crutches and tottering at every step," he wrote. On August 1, 1786, he asserted: "I do not conceive we can long exist as a nation without having lodged somewhere a power which will pervade the whole Union in as energetic a manner as the authority of the State governments extends over the several states." On October 22 he wrote David Humphreys: "But for God's sake tell me what is the cause of all these commotions? . . . I am mortified beyond expression that in the moment of our acknowledged independence we should by our conduct verify the predictions of our transatlantic foe, and render ourselves ridiculous and contemptible in the eyes of all Europe." Nine days later he wrote Henry Lee, "To be more exposed in the eyes of the world, and more contemptible than we already are, is hardly possible." [1] On November 5 he told James Madison, "We are fast verging to anarchy and confusion!" [2]

Others than the New England Federalists, who were closest to Shays' Rebellion and understandably perturbed, shared Washington's views about the state of the nation. Henry Lee declared: "We are all in dire apprehension that a beginning of anarchy with all its calamitys has approached, and have no means to stop the dreadful work." [3] In December of 1786 Madison wrote Jefferson of "dangerous defects" in the Confederation.[4] During the fall of 1786 John Jay kept writing Jefferson that "the inefficacy of our Government becomes daily more and more apparent," and intimated that the Shaysites had more "extensive" objectives than the immediate redress of grievances.[5] Edmund Randolph, who oscillated between Federalism and Antifederalism, wrote Washington in March of 1787, "Every day brings forth some new crisis"; and he expressed doubt whether Congress could survive beyond the current year.[6] No one at the Constitutional Convention was more explicit than Randolph in spelling out the defects of the government, which he considered "totally inadequate to the peace, safety, and security of the Confederation" and which he repeatedly denounced for its "imbecility." [7]

For the classic contemporary view of the alarming weaknesses of the Confederation we must turn to *The Federalist*. Therein Hamilton, a con-

1. *The Writings of George Washington from the Original Manuscript Sources, 1745-1799,* ed. J. C. Fitzpatrick (Washington, 1931-44), XXVIII, 502; XXIX, 27, 34.

2. *Ibid.,* XXIX, 51.

3. Henry Lee to George Washington, Oct. 17, 1786, *Letters of Members of the Continental Congress,* ed. E. C. Burnett (Washington, 1921-33), VIII, 486,

4. *The Papers of Thomas Jefferson,* ed. Julian P. Boyd (Princeton, 1950-   ), X, 574.

5. *Ibid.,* p. 489.

6. *The Writings of George Washington . . . ,* ed. Jared Sparks (Boston, 1834-37), IX, 243 n.

7. *Records of the Federal Convention of 1787,* ed. Max Farrand (New Haven, 1911-37), I, 19, 24, 25.

sistent viewer-with-alarm during this period, attacks the Confederation government as inefficient, asserts that the country had "reached almost the last stage of national humiliation," speaks disparagingly of "the present shadow of a federal government," views the Confederacy as dying, and urges ratification of the Constitution to prevent anarchy, civil war, and "perhaps the military despotism of a victorious demagogue." [8] It would be easy to pile up assertions in similar vein from the pens of Knox and the two Morrises.

These Federalist worthies were in general agreement that the weaknesses of the Confederation could be attributed to financial muddling by the states; to English dumping; to the loss of the British West Indian market; to paper money; to stay laws; to state tariffs; but, above all, to a lack of coercive power by a central authority. Observers in charge of foreign affairs, notably Jay and John Adams, felt that this was the most critical spot in the American system of government. "I may reason till I die to no purpose," declared Adams in June 1785. "It is unanimity in America which will produce a fair treaty of commerce." [9]

In eloquence, prestige, and even in numbers among the leadership the Federalist view of conditions had impressive support, but it was far from universally held. George Clinton, the bête noire of the nationalist leaders, was quoted as intimating that the calling of a Constitutional Convention was "calculated to impress the people with an idea of evils which do not exist." [10] At the Convention, Gunning Bedford of Delaware expressed a complacent view of the government of the Confederacy, and at the Pennsylvania ratifying convention Antifederalists under the leadership of William Findley, Robert Whitehill, and John Smilie asserted that the people along with the legislature had been frightened into consenting to a state convention by unfounded talk of impending anarchy.

Thus there was a division of opinion in 1787 about conditions in the Confederation, and there never has ceased to be down to the present day. More recent writers who look at the Confederation through Antifederalist spectacles are buoyed up by the fact that Franklin and Jefferson were not as disturbed about conditions as other contemporaries. Yet Jefferson, as he was passing through Boston on his way to France, found "the conviction growing strongly that nothing could preserve the confederacy unless the bond of union, their common council, should be strengthened." [11] It is perhaps especially significant that when Franklin, Jefferson, and Robert R. Livingston expressed in writing a more roseate view of conditions than other Founding Fathers, they were making these observations to foreigners—to Frenchmen or to Englishmen. They were seeking to reassure friends and well-wishers of America abroad that this country was not headed for a collapse. Such assertions must be discounted as skillful

8. See especially *Federalist* 1, 15, 16, and 85.

9. Adams to Jay, June 26, 1785, *Works of John Adams*, ed. C. F. Adams (Boston, 1850-56), VIII, 276.

10. *Advertiser*, New York, July 21, 1787.

11. Jefferson to Madison, July 1, 1784, *Jefferson Papers*, VII, 356.

propaganda. In France, for example, Jefferson reassured Démeunier that the United States was in no danger of bankruptcy and that, with certain minor exceptions, "the Confederation is a wonderfully perfect instrument." [12] Similarly, when Franklin wrote to M. Le Veillard on March 6, 1786, that "America never was in higher prosperity," [13] commodity prices had steadily dropped—they were to decline thirty per cent between 1785 and 1789; farm wages were shrinking and were to fall to a low of forty cents a day by 1787; mortgage foreclosures and judgments for debts in central and western Massachusetts had reached an all-time high; and in the Valley of Virginia, as Freeman Hart has pointed out, executions more than doubled between 1784 and 1788.[14] In fact, the only economic index that showed an upturn was that for foreign trade, for in commerce the worst of the depression set in a bit earlier than in other lines and showed a more complete recovery by 1788. Again, when Livingston wrote Lafayette in April 1787 that commodity prices and wages were higher than before the war, he was evading the real issue of how far they had dropped since the coming of the peace.[15]

This double standard of correspondence—one line for Americans, the other for foreign well-wishers—is revealed in the writings of that arch-pessimist, George Washington. It is true that he was somewhat more candid with his old friend Lafayette, whom he wrote on August 15, 1786, that he chose to remain silent on domestic affairs "since I could not disguise or palliate, where I might think them erroneous." [16] Yet two weeks earlier he had written two letters which are very nearly contradictory to each other. On August 1 he wrote the Chevalier de la Luzerne a reassuring letter to counteract reports of the American situation circulating in Europe. "In short," he concluded his picture of domestic America, "the foundation of a great empire is laid, and I please myself with a persuasion, that Providence will not leave its work imperfect." On the same day, however, he wrote John Jay, then Secretary for Foreign Affairs, expressing the doubt that the nation could exist much longer unless stronger powers were lodged with the central government.[17]

Even the younger generation, men who could scarcely be accused of strong Federalist attachments, accepted the Federalist view of the glaring weaknesses of the Confederation. Consider, for example, Andrew Jackson, who was admitted to practice law the year the Constitutional Con-

12. *Jefferson Papers*, X, 14 ff.

13. *Complete Works of Benjamin Franklin*, ed. John Bigelow (New York, 1887-88), IX, 300-301.

14. Freeman H. Hart, *The Valley of Virginia in the American Revolution* (Chapel Hill, 1942), pp. 123-125. For evidence from the court records of sharply mounting indebtedness in central and western Massachusetts, see R. B. Morris, "Insurrection in Massachusetts," in *America in Crisis*, ed. Daniel Aaron (New York, 1952), p. 24. On the steady upsurge of insolvency in Connecticut during the entire Confederation period, see *Public Records of the State of Connecticut (1776-1796)*, eds. C. J. Hoadly and L. W. Labaree (Hartford, 1894-1951), VII, xv, xvi.

15. R. R. Livingston Papers, Bancroft Transcripts, New York Public Library.

16. Washington, *Writings*, ed. Fitzpatrick, XXVIII, 521.

17. *Ibid.*, pp. 501, 502.

vention met in Philadelphia. In his Proclamation against Nullification Jackson declared in 1832: "But the defects of the Confederation need not be detailed. Under its operation we could scarcely be called a nation. We had neither prosperity at home nor consideration abroad. This state of things could not be endured, and our present happy Constitution was formed, but formed in vain if this fatal doctrine prevails." [18]

Jackson's view of the Confederation period was the view of the nationalist commentators on the Constitution and of the nationalist historians. It was expounded by James Wilson and Nathaniel Chipman, by Nathan Dane, and most notably by Joseph Story and George Ticknor Curtis, who gave formal expression to the views of Daniel Webster. In his *History of the Origin, Formation, and Adoption of the Constitution,* first published in 1854, Curtis begins by declaring: "The Constitution of the United States was the means by which republican liberty was saved from the consequences of impending anarchy. . . ." Paraphrasing the Founding Fathers, Curtis saw the Confederation as "a great shadow without the substance of a government. . . ." He saw the whole period as replete with "dangers and difficulties," full of "suffering and peril." [19]

Curtis' view of the Confederation interlude was fully shared by the nationalist historians writing in the generation or two following the adoption of the Constitution. Most distinguished of this group, George Bancroft—whose literary career spans the period from the Age of Jackson to the Age of Chester A. Arthur—put off writing about the post-Revolutionary era until the closing years of his life. His *History of the Formation of the Constitution of the United States of America* was not published until 1882. As might be expected, Bancroft viewed the period from a nationalist or continental point of view. He stressed the "helplessness" of Congress, whose "perpetual failures" he considered "inherent and incurable." To Bancroft "no ray of hope remained" but from the convention summoned at Annapolis.[20] Nevertheless, he treats the Massachusetts debtors with sympathy and understanding, approves of Bowdoin's lenity toward the Shaysites, and reviews the economic decline which set in at the start of the period in sober language, in sharp contrast with the more intemperate treatment of the insurrection by his contemporary Richard Hildreth, who had surveyed the period many years earlier.[21]

Perhaps the historian who coined the term "critical period" to describe the Confederation interlude was William Henry Trescot. In his rather temperate and fair-minded *Diplomatic History of the Administrations of Washington and Adams,* published in 1857, he asserted: "Indeed, it would be more correct to say, that the most critical period of the

18. *Compilation of the Messages and Papers of the Presidents, 1789-1902,* ed. J. D. Richardson (Washington, 1903), II, 643.

19. George Ticknor Curtis, *History of the Origin, Formation and Adoption of the Constitution of the United States* . . . (New York, 1854), I, xi, 233, 234, 330.

20. George Bancroft, *History of the Formation of the Constitution of the United States of America* (New York, 1885), I, 262-266.

21. *Ibid.,* pp. 274-275; Richard Hildreth, *The History of the United States of America* (New York, 1848-51), III, 472-477.

country's history embraced the time between the peace of 1783 and the adoption of the constitution in 1788." [22] This point of view was adopted by Frothingham, by Schouler, and by von Holst. The last-named spoke of "the contemptible impotence of Congress. . . ." This was strong language, but Washington had used it before him.[23]

The classic exposition of the Federalist approach is found in John Fiske's *The Critical Period of American History, 1783-1789*. His title has fastened upon an epoch in American history a popular nomenclature that dies hard. The first edition appeared in 1888, not too long after the appearance of Bancroft's *Last Revision*. The title and theme of the book were suggested by the fact of Tom Paine's stopping the publication of the "Crisis," on hearing the news of the treaty of peace in 1783. Now, Paine said, "the times that tried men's souls are over." Fiske does not agree with Paine. The next five years, he contends, were to be the most critical time of all. Fiske used the term "critical" first to settle the question whether there was to be a national government or a group of small city-states. Secondly, he used the term to describe what he regarded to be the utter incompetence of the states and the federal government to deal with the problem of postwar reconstruction. To Fiske the drift "toward anarchy" was only checked by the eleventh-hour ratification of the federal Constitution.[24]

It has become the fashion of latter-day historians to criticize Fiske's scholarship. McLaughlin concedes that "there are not many errors in fact in the book," but insists that "as an authority the work is altogether without scientific standing, because it is little more than a remarkably skilful adaptation of a very few secondary authorities, showing almost no evidence of first-hand acquaintance with the sources." [25] Yet McLaughlin himself shows surprisingly little acquaintance with the sources when he describes economic conditions in the Confederation and gives the reader a string of generalizations entirely unsupported by statistical evidence or other business documentation. But the issue is not whether Fiske used first-hand sources, but whether he produced a valid synthesis. As one who has conducted graduate seminars for some time, I am not unaware of the

22. William Henry Trescot, *The Diplomatic History of the Administrations of Washington and Adams: 1789-1801* (Boston, 1857), p. 9. Long before Trescot, however, Richard Henry Lee, a leading Antifederalist, wrote, Oct. 8, 1787: "I know our situation is critical, and it behoves us to make the best of it." "Letters of the Federal Farmer," Letter I, in *Pamphlets on the Constitution of the United States,* ed. P. L. Ford (Brooklyn, 1888), p. 280.

23. Richard Frothingham, *The Rise of the Republic of the United States* (Boston, 1910. First published in 1872), pp. 583 ff.; James Schouler, *History of the United States of America under the Constitution* (revised ed., New York, 1894), I, 13 ff.; H. von Holst, *The Constitutional and Political History of the United States,* trans. John J. Lalor and Alfred B. Mason (Chicago, 1889-92), I, 37.

24. John Fiske, *The Critical Period of American History, 1783-1789* (Boston and New York, 1888), pp. 55-57, and Chap. IV, *passim.*

25. Andrew C. McLaughlin, *The Confederation and the Constitution, 1783-1789,* in *The American Nation: A History,* ed. Albert Bushnell Hart, X (New York and London, 1905), 319-320.

fact that a good many people saturate themselves in the primary sources but are utterly unable to interpret them intelligently. Whether or not William Macdonald's appraisal of Fiske's book as "the best comprehensive account of the period" [26] still stands today, John Fiske's approach to the era had an enormous impact both upon the public and upon fellow historians. John Bach McMaster adopts it without reservations. In his *History of the People of the United States* he refers to the "disaffected," meaning the Shaysites, "associating for evil purposes," as opposed to "the better-minded," equally active in forming societies "for good purposes." [27] His treatment might well have been written by George R. Minot, clerk of the Massachusetts lower house, whose contemporary account of Shays' Rebellion betrays the fears of the conservative element as to the broader implications of the insurrection. [28] McMaster excoriates Clinton and New York for particularist tendencies. Save for Rhode Island, no state behaved worse than New York, McMaster contends.[29]

Other writers, while generally accepting the nationalist synthesis of the period, have approached the Confederation years in a somewhat more objective spirit than did Fiske and most of his predecessors. In the editor's introduction to Andrew C. McLaughlin's volume in the old *American Nation* series, Albert Bushnell Hart expresses doubt whether Fiske's "critical period" was "really a time of such danger of national dissolution as people then and since have supposed." He views the McLaughlin volume as showing "a more orderly, logical, and inevitable march of events than has commonly been described." [30] McLaughlin sees little or no justification for the constant lament about poverty in this period. "Some tribulation there was," he concedes, "but that the country was forlorn, destitute, and poverty-stricken is far from the truth." He sees indications of an upturn in trade by 1786. However, on the constitutional and diplomatic aspects of the period there is little difference between McLaughlin and Fiske. Referring to the humiliating relations with the Barbary states, McLaughlin asserts: "All this, like everything else one touches during the dismal period, discloses the helplessness of the confederacy." Toward the Shaysites he is far less sympathetic than Bancroft. "The vicious, the restless, the ignorant, the foolish—and there were plenty of each class— were coming together to test the strength of the newly established government of Massachusetts." The result, as he sees it, was "nothing short of civil war," but its virtue was that it disclosed the dangers, helped to bring about a reaction, discredited extreme democratic tendencies, and thereby aided the men who sought to inject vigor into the union.[31] Thus, those who were led by the editor of the series to believe that they were going

26. William Macdonald, in *The Literature of American History: A Bibliographical Guide . . .* , ed. J. N. Larned (Boston, 1902), p. 156.

27. John Bach McMaster, *A History of the People of the United States, From the Revolution to the Civil War* (New York, 1883-1913), I, 313.

28. *History of the Insurrection in Massachusetts in 1786 . . .* (Worcester, 1788).

29. *History*, I, 369-370.

30. McLaughlin, *The Confederation and the Constitution*, p. xv.

31. *Ibid.*, pp. 71, 107, 156, 161.

to read a revisionist book were to find that it was essentially conventional in interpretation. Similarly, Edward Channing, in his *History of the United States,* published some years after McLaughlin, stresses the "helplessness" of the existing government and its failure to win respect either at home or abroad, but finds evidence of a business upthrust before the new Constitution went into operation.[32]

The Antifederalist or pro-democratic interpretation (and I need hardly say that the two terms are not necessarily equated) was perhaps first, among nineteenth-century historians, expounded by Henry B. Dawson, a learned military historian of the American Revolution, who also devoted himself to studying the role of the masses in that war, and had a penchant for picking controversial issues which he fought with relish and passion. In an article in the *Historical Magazine* in 1871, Dawson attempted to refute John Lothrop Motley, who, in a celebrated letter to the London *Times* written during the Civil War, had asserted that the Confederation was a period of "chaos," in which the absence of law, order, and security for life and property was "as absolute as could be well conceived in a civilized land." These were reckless and false accusations, Dawson charged. He traced their origin to distinguished men of the Confederation period who had spread them "for selfish or partisan motives." He accused these leaders of having "nullified the established law of the Confederacy and violently and corruptly substituted for it what they styled the Constitution of the United States." Dawson had made extreme and curiously unbalanced charges but failed to substantiate them. The significance of the attack, however, lies far less in the kind of evidence adduced than in its formulation of the notion that the Federalists conspired to falsify the true conditions of the period in a deliberate effort to create panic and undermine the government of the Confederation. Oddly enough, the criminal statistics Dawson cites for New York State not only are inconclusive regarding lawlessness, but point directly opposite to what Dawson believed. They indicate that in New York City and County there were almost twice as many indictments between 1784 and 1789 as there were for the first five years under the new federal government.[33] Concerning law and order, Dawson may very well have been on the right track, but somewhere along the path he lost the scent.

Despite the intemperate character of his attack, Dawson had touched off certain doubts as to the reportorial objectivity both of the Founding Fathers and of later historians. These were again raised in 1907, when J. Allen Smith, in his *The Spirit of American Government,* attacked on a second front, contending that the Constitution was the result of a counter-revolution. To him the Declaration of Independence spelled sweeping changes in the American form of government, changes manifest in an omnipotent legislature and the overthrow of the system of checks and

32. Edward Channing, *A History of the United States* (New York, 1916-26), III, 491, 414-415, 426-427.
33. Henry B. Dawson, "The Motley Letter," *Historical Magazine,* 2nd Ser., IX (Mar., 1871), 157 ff.

balances which had been derived from the English constitution, with its characteristic blending of monarchical, aristocratic, and democratic elements. To Smith the chief feature of the Articles of Confederation was the entire absence of checks and balances, the vesting of all power in a single legislative body, unchecked by a distinct executive or judiciary. The fact that the power which was vested in the continental legislature was ineffectual did not disturb him. His main point, though, was that such democratic changes had been wrought by radical forces and that the conservatives, once they had a chance to assess the situation, set about, in more or less conspiratorial fashion, to redress the balance. The Constitutional Convention was called, according to Smith, not only to impart vigor to the government but to institute an elaborate system of constitutional checks. The adoption of this system he calls a "triumph of a skillfully directed reactionary movement." [34] The idea that the adoption of the Constitution was the result of a struggle among interest groups was pressed by Arthur F. Bentley in *The Process of Government* (1908), in language which stemmed from Madison's *Federalist* 10, and in a more naked form by A. M. Simons' *Social Forces in American History* (1911).

The most significant amplification of the Smith-Bentley-Simons approach came in 1913 from the pen of Charles A. Beard. In his *An Economic Interpretation of the Constitution of the United States* Beard concedes that "interpretative schools seem always to originate in social antagonism," but he prefers the road which explains proximate or remote causes and relations to the so-called "impartial" history which surveys outward events and classifies and orders phenomena.[35] Beard was profoundly influenced by the Turnerian school, which substituted for the states'-rights interpretation of our history a recognition of social and economic areas, independent of state lines, which acted as units in political history. For the period of the Confederation the most important Turnerian contribution was Orin G. Libby's *Geographical Distribution of the Vote of the Thirteen States on the Federal Constitution,* an original and searching study published as far back as 1894. Beard found that nationalism cut across state lines, that it was created by a welding of economic interests of creditors, holders of personalty—especially public securities—, manufacturers, shippers, commercial groups, and speculators in western lands. While this majestic formula helped explain why people were Federalists, it has failed dismally in explaining differences between Federalists and Antifederalists. Recent studies by Robert Thomas of the property interests of members of the ratifying convention in Virginia have failed to turn up any significant differences between the two parties either in the kind and quantity of their property-holdings or in their relative status as creditors or debtors. On the other hand, Jackson T. Main asserts that the Virginians

---

34. J. Allen Smith, *The Spirit of American Government: A Study of the Constitution, Its Origin, Influence, and Relation to Democracy* (Chautauqua, 1911), p. 37.

35. Charles A. Beard, *An Economic Interpretation of the Constitution of the United States* (New York, 1949), pp. 3-4.

who favored greater centralization were found in pro-creditor areas, the Northern Neck and much of the Tidewater, while the opposition came from the debtor Piedmont. After 1785, Main contends, the Shenandoah Valley counties, which had previously voted with the Piedmont on most issues, now supported a grant to Congress of power over commerce. But the picture is at best hardly clean-cut or conclusive.[36]

Beard suggested that general social conditions were prosperous and that the defects of the Articles did not justify the "loud complaints" of the advocates of change. In short, Beard found that the "critical period" was really not so critical after all, but, drawing upon Dawson's article, "a phantom of the imagination produced by some undoubted evils which could have been remedied without a political revolution." [37] Save for a quotation from Franklin, Beard fails to document this crucial generalization.

Lest anyone should carry away with him the view that Beard opposed the Constitution, as did J. Allen Smith, it might be well to point out that in his *Supreme Court and the Constitution,* published the previous year, he praised the Constitution and furnished historical precedents for judicial review. In later years he drew further and further away from any monolithic economic interpretation of the period. Although his *Rise of American Civilization* adhered to the approach of his *Economic Interpretation,* as did Parrington's treatment in *Main Currents in American Thought,* Beard by 1935 completely repudiated economic determinism. In *The Republic* (1943) he considered the adoption of the Constitution as the alternative to military dictatorship. In his *Basic History of the United States* (1944) he defended checks and balances as curbs on despotic powers, whereas in his earlier *Rise of American Civilization* he insists that checks and balances dissolved "the energy of the democratic majority." [38] In *The Enduring Federalist,* published in 1948, he refers to the Congress of the Confederation as "a kind of debating society," and describes conditions in the Confederation period in language which would have gratified Fiske and perhaps shocked Bancroft.[39] In short, by the end of his career, Beard, the confirmed nationalist and isolationist, had moved a long way from the Beard of pre-World War I days.

But it is the unreconstructed Beard who still captures the imagination of our younger scholars. Today the chief disciple of J. Allen Smith and the early Beard is Merrill Jensen. In two significant books, *The Articles of Confederation,* published in 1940, and a more amplified treatment of the same problem, *The New Nation,* which appeared in 1950, Professor Jensen expounds learnedly and at length the argument that the Federalist

36. Robert E. Thomas, "The Virginia Convention of 1788: A Criticism of Beard's *An Economic Interpretation of the Constitution," Journal of Southern History,* XIX (1953), 63-72. Jackson T. Main, "Sections and Politics in Virginia, 1781-1787," *William and Mary Quarterly,* 3rd Ser., XII (1955), 96-112.

37. Beard, *An Economic Interpretation of the Constitution,* pp. 47-48.

38. Charles A. Beard and Mary R. Beard, *The Rise of American Civilization* (New York, 1930. First published in 1927), I, 326.

39. Beard, *The Enduring Federalist* (New York, 1948), pp. 27-30.

party was organized to destroy the kind of democratic government and economic practice made possible by the Articles of Confederation.[40] Jensen sees the Articles as a constitutional expression of the philosophy of the Declaration of Independence, the Constitution as a betrayal of those principles. To Jensen the Articles were designed to prevent the central government from infringing upon the rights of the states, whereas the Constitution was designed to check both the states and the democracy that found expression within state bounds. As Jensen sees it, the Confederation government failed, not because it was inadequate, but because the radicals failed to maintain the organization they had created to bring about the American Revolution. He speaks of the radicals as having won *"their war,"* but the fact remains that it was as much the war of the conservatives; probably a good deal more so.

Mr. Jensen finds conspiracy and betrayal at various levels. He suggests that the conservatives might well have betrayed the diplomatic objectives of the Revolution were it not for the integrity of Jay and Adams. He deplores the fact that radical leaders of the Thomas Burke–Richard Henry Lee–Sam Adams vintage quit the field and left it to what General Horatio Gates, scarcely an objective or disinterested patriot, called "the rapacious graspers of power and profit." Gates was one grasper of power who just missed the brass ring. Mr. Jensen sees this revolutionary group outnumbered by 1781, and worn down by defeat. Then from 1781 to 1783 the government revolved around Robert Morris and his satellites, for all practical purposes a dictatorship in Mr. Jensen's eyes. But when we look more closely at these counterrevolutionaries, the sharp line between radicals and conservatives seems to fade away. Who was more radical than Alexander McDougall in Sons-of-Liberty days? Yet it was he who headed a delegation of officers to Congress in the winter of 1783. Perhaps Hamilton was not far wrong when he defended the Morris faction as not only "the most liberal," but as "the men who think continentally." The issue does not seem to have been one between radicals and conservatives, but between extreme particularists of the Clinton stripe and continental nationalists of varying shades and degrees.

Mr. Jensen is most effective in recounting the constructive steps taken in the Confederation period to repair federal and state finances. He points out that the Confederation actually managed to reduce the principal of its debt, and praises the states for their role in paying the national debt. Mr. Jensen points to the rapid amortization of state debts as evidence of the ability of the states to put their financial houses in order without much help from a central government. There is no doubt whatsoever that the states had now largely assumed the debt-funding function that the federal government had proven incapable of shouldering. Dr. E. J. Ferguson's studies of the assumption of the federal debts by the

40. *The Articles of Confederation: An Interpretation of The Social-Constitutional History of the American Revolution, 1774-1781* (University of Wisconsin, 1940. Second printing with additional foreword, 1948). *The New Nation: A History of the United States During the Confederation, 1781-1789* (New York, 1950).

states reveal the considerable progress that was made in that direction in the Confederation period.[41] But, in terms of more recent ideas of economic planning, it would now seem that states like Massachusetts made the mistake of a too rapid amortization of the state debt, thereby initiating a sharp deflationary thrust. Even a conservative like Governor Bowdoin urged in 1786 a more gradual plan of amortization than that which the property-conscious legislature had enacted.

In short, the Beard-Jensen approach has served to present the Confederation period in a more constructive light, to give greater recognition to signs of economic expansion in the period and to the stabilizing role of the states, particularly in financial matters. As Allan Nevins has pointed out, when the new federal government went into effect, in no state was the debt appallingly high, and in some it was already low.[42] Mr. Jensen is doubtless correct in arguing that in most states the forces of law and order never lost the upper hand. In New York that arch-Antifederalist George Clinton personally led the troops of the state against the insurrectionary Shays. In most cases—and Maryland is an excellent example—the disgruntled elements confined their efforts to obtaining relief in a legal manner through legislative action.

In truth, the real difference between the nationalist and Antifederalist schools of historiography turns neither on the extent of the depression nor on the amount of anarchy in the "critical period," but springs from a deep divergence in interpreting the American Revolution and the issues for which it was fought. Mr. Jensen sees the radical party in the Revolution as comprising the town masses and the frontier groups. As he views it, the radicals fought for an internal revolution; those conservatives who reluctantly supported the war merely wanted independence from England. In fact, this school of historiography depicts the American Revolution as essentially a civil war among the Whigs. In this version there seems to be little or no room for Tories, for redcoats, or for Hessians. This formula fails to explain why New York City and Philadelphia were hotbeds of Loyalism, why the regulators of Carolina and the levelers of upstate New York were Tories, or why debtors and creditors, hard-money men and paper-money men, suffrage expansionists and suffrage restrictionists were arrayed on the same side. It fails to explain the prominent role of the Whig conservative elite in bringing about the Revolution or to lay the foundation for understanding why in so many areas the radicalism of the leadership was that of the Gironde, not the Mountain.[43]

41. E. J. Ferguson, "State Assumption of Federal Debt During the Confederation," *Mississippi Valley Historical Review*, XXXVIII (1951), 403.

42. Allan Nevins, *The American States During and After the American Revolution* (New York, 1927), p. 541.

43. For examples from New England, see Lee N. Newcomer, *The Embattled Farmers: A Massachusetts Countryside in the American Revolution* (New York, 1953); Oscar Zeichner, *Connecticut's Years of Controversy, 1750-1776* (Chapel Hill, 1949). Robert E. Brown, *Middle-Class Democracy and the Revolution in Massachusetts, 1691-1780* (Ithaca, N. Y., 1955), demonstrates that in Massachusetts the property qualification for voting did not bar the majority of adult males from

In the last analysis the view that the course of the Confederation period was determined by a counterrevolutionary movement, which, through the instrumentality of the Constitutional Convention, nipped democracy in the bud, hinges upon one's ideas about the American Revolution. Unless one is ready to accept the thesis that the group that started the war were libertarians and democrats and were supplanted by a conservative authoritarian party, one cannot give uncritical adherence to the Smith-Beard-Jensen approach to the Confederation period. The facts simply will not support the argument that the democratic forces originally seized control of the movement in the states. Even in the short run, these forces were unsuccessful in every state save Pennsylvania and Georgia. In New Jersey, then as now hospitable to democracy, the Constitution, as Mr. McCormick has demonstrated,[44] was welcomed by all classes because it promised needed financial relief. In that state a western conservative coalition brought about deflationary policies, but not until the very end of the period under review. But the counterrevolution, if the halting of the leftward swing of the pendulum deserves that appellation, was gradual and mild. States like Delaware and Maryland, as John A. Munroe [45] and Philip Crowl [46] have shown us, did not have a counterrevolution, because there never was the kind of democratic upthrust that characterized the early Revolutionary years in Pennsylvania.

The failure of the so-called democratic forces, as Elisha P. Douglass has recently restated for us,[47] is a tribute to the vigorous Revolutionary leadership of the Whig conservative forces and their awareness of the fundamental issues at stake. It was the Whig conservatives, not the regulators in North Carolina or the back-country insurgents in Massachusetts, who took the lead in the movement toward independence. Only where the Whig elite seemed timorous and unwilling to move from protest to revolution did the democratic and back-country forces have any chance of seizing power. That was the case in Pennsylvania, where the conservatives had abdicated their political leadership, and to a lesser degree in Georgia, where the story still remains to be spelled out and where the democratic victory was by no means as clear-cut as in Pennsylvania.

The Burke-Bryan-Lee-Clinton forces that comprised the so-called "democratic" party in the Revolutionary years—just what did they stand for? What kind of democracy did they want? The touchstone of their democracy seems to have been an advocacy of a unicameral legislature, a

44. Richard P. McCormick, *Experiment in Independence: New Jersey in the Critical Period, 1781-1789* (New Brunswick, 1950).

45. *Federalist Delaware, 1775-1815* (New Brunswick, 1954).

46. *Maryland During and After the Revolution* (Baltimore, 1942).

47. *Rebels and Democrats* (Chapel Hill, 1955).

taking part in elections. He opposes the view of an "internal revolution" on the ground that democracy was already established. It is unlikely, however, that a re-examination of the nature and extent of the franchise and other so-called democratic indices in most of the remaining twelve states will support his concluding speculation that the "common man . . . had come into his own long before the era of Jacksonian Democracy."

popularly elected judiciary, and a weak executive—and very little else. In some respects the Whig conservatives held more advanced views than did the radicals. Judged by present-day standards the majoritarians were not always liberal. Back-country enthusiasts of the Great Awakening, they were by no means as ready to tolerate non-Protestant religious beliefs as were the deistically-minded Whig leaders. In fact, some of the most revealing evidence presented by Mr. Douglass is that which indicates that left-wing Protestants of Pietist or evangelical inclinations were fundamentalists in outlook and often basically conservative on political issues. It was they who tried to curb the political rights of non-Protestants, and in Pennsylvania it was the so-called radicals who enacted a law restricting freedom of expression. No, the majoritarians did not always act in democratic ways, nor did they seem always willing to abide by the will of the majority. Witness the shocking abuse of power by the radicals in Pennsylvania who established the state constitution by fiat and did not dare submit it to the people. In fact, they went so far as to require the people to take an oath to support the constitution as a prerequisite to exercising the franchise.

Much has been made of the distrust of the masses held by the Whig conservatives, of the views of men like Jay that "the mass of men are neither wise nor good." But many of the Antifederalists shared similar views. Take Samuel Chase, who, as Philip Crowl has shown us, was instrumental in framing Maryland's ultraconservative constitution, and is alleged to have been unstinting in his praise of the aristocratic features of that document, particularly of the electoral college for choosing senators. His desertion to the Antifederalist camp is perhaps best explained by his financial reverses, but he did not linger in it too long. In the federal Convention the Antifederalist John F. Mercer had opposed allowing the people to participate, declaring, "The people cannot know and judge of the characters of Candidates. The worst possible choice will be made." [48] Elbridge Gerry, who refused to sign the Constitution, asserted that "the evils we experience flow from the excess of democracy" and expressed concern at "the danger of the levilling [sic] spirit." [49] In New York the bulwark of Antifederalism was the landowner, with his rural isolation, his dread of the federal impost, and his jealousy of sharing political power. True, he was supported in his opposition to the Constitution by tenants and small farmers, but the Antifederalist leaders of that state had little faith in the people. At the New York Convention George Clinton criticized the people for their fickleness, their tendency "to vibrate from one extreme to another." It was this very disposition, Clinton confessed, against which he wished to guard.[50]

48. *Records of the Federal Convention of 1787,* ed. Max Farrand (New Haven, 1911-37) II, 205.

49. *Ibid.,* I, 48.

50. *Debates in the Several State Conventions on the Adoption of the Federal Constitution, . . . Together with the Journal of the Federal Convention . . . ,* ed. Jonathan Elliot (Philadelphia, 1881), II, 359.

The Antifederalists were not poured out of one democratic mold,[51] any more than the Federalists represented a unitary point of view about how to strengthen the central government. As Robert East has demonstrated,[52] there was a wide breach between the Bowdoin-Adams kind of federalism in Massachusetts and the Cabot-Pickering stripe of particularism, with its strong sectional and anti-Southern overtones. There was an even wider gulf between the democratic nationalism of Franklin and the authoritarian nationalism of Hamilton.

On the pro-democratic side of the Federalist ledger must be credited the position of the Whig conservatives in support of certain basic human rights which they conceived as fundamental and not subject to change at the caprice of majority rule. Fortunately for the evolution of American democracy, the principles of the conservative revolutionaries and their so-called democratic opponents were largely complementary to each other. Although almost everywhere the radicals were defeated in their efforts to seize the machinery of Revolution, the liberative effects of the war proved a deterrent to the kind of social revolution which would have enshrined class hatreds and ensured violent reaction.[53]

Yes, the American Whigs were divided in the years of the Revolution on almost all issues except that of political independence from Great Britain. Since diverse and even divergent interests forged the Whig alliance, it was only to be expected that the victory of the patriots would settle no single social or economic issue except freedom from British mercantilist controls, hardly an unmixed blessing in the years of the Confederation. Despite the efforts of J. Franklin Jameson to consider the American Revolution as a social movement, the fact is that the great internal social reforms lay ahead. As Harrison Gray Otis once wrote to a friend of Revolutionary days: "You and I did not imagine when the first war with Britain was over that the revolution was just begun." [54] Similar sentiments were expressed by Dr. Benjamin Rush on an earlier occasion. In his "Address to the People of the United States on the Defects of the Confederation" Rush declared: "The American war is over; but this is far from being the case with the American Revolution." [55]

Indeed, the imposition of a vitalized federalism and the tightening of the bonds of union precipitated a greater revolution in American life than

51. The reader is referred to the provocative article by Cecelia M. Kenyon, "Men of Little Faith: The Anti-Federalists on the Nature of Representative Government," *William and Mary Quarterly,* 3rd Ser., XII (1955), 3-43.

52. "The Massachusetts Conservatives in the Critical Period," in *The Era of the American Revolution,* ed. R. B. Morris (New York, 1939), pp. 349-391.

53. "Was there ever a revolution brought about, especially so important as this, without great internal tumults and violent convulsions!" Sam Adams asked rhetorically. *The Writings of Samuel Adams,* ed. H. A. Cushing (New York, 1904-08), III, 304.

54. Samuel Eliot Morison, *The Life and Letters of Harrison Gray Otis* (Boston and New York, 1913), I, 49.

55. Reprinted in H. Niles, *Principles and Acts of the Revolution in America* (Baltimore, 1822), p. 402.

did separation from England. To those who view the adoption of a system of republican federalism as constituting a more thoroughgoing break with the political system of the past than did that earlier severing of the tenuous bonds of empire—and there is impressive evidence in the Confederation interlude of our history to substantiate this interpretation—the Federalists, not the Antifederalists, were the real radicals of their day.

CONSEQUENCES FOR THE UNITED STATES

WILBUR H. SIEBERT

The Dispersion of the American Tories

▣ For the now independent states, the consequences of their separation from Britain were profound, whether seen as political, economic, or social. For one thing, a quite large minority—an intellectually and socially important minority—went into or were already in exile: the Loyalists. If one accepts Louis Hartz's view that the United States inherited and did not have to fight for its non-feudal status, one can do so only by minimizing the role of the Loyalists, as most American historians have done.* Though the reference is confined to a footnote, R. R. Palmer has reminded us recently of the scale of the Loyalist migration, and there is now a considerable, though uncoordinated, literature on them.† Perhaps the leading scholar of Loyalist migration was the late Wilbur H. Siebert. ▣

NORFOLK AND CHARLESTON, Savannah and St. Augustine, Philadelphia and New York, Boston, Penobscot, Fort Niagara and Detroit were, during their days of occupation by the British, the most important centers to which were drawn, as by powerful magnets, those elements of the colonial population which were forced out of their various localities by the intolerance and conflict of a struggle that was marked by the characteristics of civil war both in the populous sections and in the back country. The list of such centers might be greatly lengthened by including those Canadian towns and villages that were near enough to our northern frontier to be used by the English as military posts and magazines, and by the same token were accessible to numbers of fugitive adherents of the crown whose zeal found vent in joining loyalist regiments. But the loyalist regiments in Canada would have filled but slowly, if they had depended entirely on voluntary enlistments. From various posts recruiting officers were sent into the enemy's country to bring in Tory groups to be armed and employed on marauding and rescue expeditions. In these ways not less than ten corps of American loyalists, several of which reached

* Louis Hartz, "American Political Thought and the American Revolution, *American Political Science Review,* XLVI (1952), 342.

† R. R. Palmer, *The Age of the Democratic Revolution* (Princeton, 1959), and see Bibliography: The Loyalists.

Reprinted from the *Mississippi Valley Historical Review,* I (1914), 185-197.

a maximum of five hundred or six hundred men, were formed and maintained throughout the Revolution in what was called the Northern or Canadian Division.

Large numbers of these recruits proceeded northwards by way of the Hudson River and Lake Champlain to one or another of the chain of posts along the Richelieu. Not all loyalists, however, followed this direct course: many entered Canada along routes, of which there were five in general use, running from the Hudson to points between Oswego and Montreal, the refugees being quartered at various places on both sides of the river St. Lawrence. Not infrequently the recruiting agents led in women and children with the men, some arriving, we are told, "in a state of nakedness and great want." In other instances families were brought in under flags of truce, a system that was in operation on Lake Champlain from the fall of 1778 if not earlier, and was regularly employed throughout the remainder of the contest. As the British were in control of the lake, their vessels and bateaux were in constant requisition for the conveyance of aggregations of families from Pointe au Fer, Mill Bay, Skenesborough, Crown Point, and other convenient places to St. John, north of the lake, whence they were sent under guidance to various localities in the province of Quebec to join husbands and fathers from whom they had been separated for longer or shorter periods. Sometimes these fatherless groups braved the severities of the winter season in order to reach the goal of safety and loyalty where fugitive or exiled kindred already awaited them.

Many of these refugees were from Charlotte and Tryon counties and the city of Albany in New York state, while a smaller proportion came from New England. Not a few—probably no less than 1800—had enlisted under Burgoyne, but had been left at the catastrophe to look after themselves. In truth, Burgoyne blamed his Tory contingent for his defeat, and completely ignored it in his articles of capitulation. This deliberate neglect was partly remedied by the Tories themselves, for, the night before the surrender at Saratoga, some of them decided to make their escape, and struck out through the woods or followed the Indian paths to Canada. Others, however, awaited the formal capitulation, and consequently did not find another opportunity of getting to the desired haven for weeks or months afterward. As Burgoyne carried with him blank commissions under which to enroll new regiments of refugees, and as he detached Baum's men in order to fill these regiments, his treatment of the loyalists must be regarded as reprehensible to the last degree.

Later on, expeditions were sent out for the express purpose of rescuing parties of loyalists from hostile communities. At least three such expeditions were authorized by Governor Haldimand for the year 1780. Two of these were led by Sir John Johnson who delivered 150 loyalists from the Mohawk Valley on his first incursion but was thwarted by the Americans on his second, the Tories being confined in the forts while the danger lasted. The third expedition, under Majors Carleton and Houghton, succeeded in bringing in a number of families from south of Lake

George, in whose train others followed, including one group of "about 230 souls." [1] These and the other expedients of border warfare produced results as unmistakable as they were dreadful: they finally reduced the border lands to a state of desolation. A year and a half before the close of the war it was estimated that Tryon County alone had lost two-thirds of its inhabitants, of whom 613 were reported as having deserted. Of those remaining, 380 were widows with a proportionate number of fatherless children. The number of farms left uncultivated was placed at 12,000.[2] In March, 1783, the single district of Montreal, which lay just north of New York state, contained its maximum number of refugees (not including enlisted loyalists), namely, 1,700, who were distributed at 17 posts and magazines within the district. During the following summer, fleets of transports sailed up the river St. Lawrence on their way from New York City to Quebec, bearing over 1,300 more. Seven hundred of the latter were sent on to Sorel, a fortified place at the mouth of the Richelieu, where they remained until lands could be assigned them for permanent settlement. This took place during the year 1784. A census of that year shows that approximately 5,500 disbanded troops and loyalists received grants in the province of Quebec. Of these about one-fourth were settled east of the St. Lawrence, that is, at 3 posts on the Richelieu, and on the eastern and southern shores of the Gaspé Peninsula. Most of the others, or about 3,000 married and single men, were sent up the St. Lawrence, being assigned lands in a series of townships laid out for them west of Montreal in what is now the province of Ontario. The residue either scattered among the older communities or, despite the opposition of Haldimand, located on seigniorial lands along the Vermont frontier. Immigration continued during the subsequent years, the English population in Lower Canada reaching about 20,000 by 1791, due chiefly to the influx of loyalists.

The process of segregating this element from New Hampshire, Vermont, and eastern New York, which was performed by the military posts of Lower Canada, was duplicated for the back country by Fort Niagara and Detroit. At Fort Niagara this process began soon after Captain John Butler arrived there from Montreal in November, 1775, accompanied by several other refugees from Tryon County. As a devoted loyalist, an experienced leader of war parties, and an interpreter at Indian councils, Butler was well qualified to transform Niagara into a hotbed of Toryism, to help win the active support of the Six Nation Indians, and conduct operations against the border settlements. From among the loyalists who took shelter at the fort and those brought in by his emissaries, he began the organization of a corps of rangers, which the authorities at Quebec decided should consist of 8 companies. Despite losses and occasional

1. See the author's paper on "The American Loyalists in the Eastern Seigniories and Townships of the Province of Quebec," in Royal Society of Canada, *Transactions*, 1913.

2. F. W. Halsey, *The Old New York Frontier, 1614-1800* (New York, 1901), 313.

desertions, he had 6 full companies enrolled by December, 1778. Two months later (February 12) over 1,300 persons were drawing rations at Fort Niagara, of whom 445 were Indians and 64 were members of "distressed families," chiefly from the Mohawk Valley. After Sullivan's raid up the Genesee River, the number of savages at the post increased to more than 5,000 (September 21, 1779), and as Sullivan had destroyed 40 Indian villages with their fields of maize, 3,000 of these aborigines found themselves homeless and dependent on Niagara for clothing and provisions all winter. A scarcity of supplies, the severity of the season, and starvation brought the only relief possible to many. Another consequence of Sullivan's raid appears to have been the approximate completion of Butler's Rangers, notwithstanding the earlier casualties in every company. If space permitted, I might tell further of the constant arrival of fugitives at the fort from various quarters, including the Ohio country. Suffice it to say that on October 1, 1783, there were 2,000 troops, loyalists, and Indians at Niagara, of whom about one-half were loyalists.[3]

This number probably did not include the inhabitants of a refugee settlement which had been begun 3 years before by Haldimand's instructions on the west side of the Niagara River. That settlement was still small, numbering scarcely more than a hundred persons at the beginning of December, 1783.[4] In June of the following year, Butler's regiment was disbanded and the little colony opposite the fort suddenly gained a population of 620 rangers and others.[5] By the end of another twelvemonth the increase amounted to 20 per cent more, or a total of 770.[6] Meanwhile, before the close of the year 1784, most of the Six Nations, or Iroquois Confederacy, had removed to the reservation which had been set apart for them along the Grand River. This lay west of the Niagara colony, its settlers numbering about 1,000, not counting a few disbanded soldiers who made their homes among the Indians. Another reservation, situated on the north side of Lake Ontario near Cataraqui (now Kingston), was occupied by a part of the Mohawk tribe.

For the expanse of country at the west end of Lake Erie, Detroit served the same purposes during the period as Fort Niagara at the east end: it was the center of tribal gatherings, the asylum of Tory refugees, and the source of successive raids into Ohio, Kentucky, and Virginia. In March, 1777, Sir Henry Hamilton, the lieutenant governor at Detroit, was empowered to raise as many loyalists and savages as possible to send out against the neighboring communities. From this time may be dated the embodiment of the corps known as the "Detroit Volunteers," which gained leadership on the arrival, in 1778, of Simon Girty, Matthew Elliot, and Alexander McKee, all of whom were fugitives from Fort Pitt. Girty

3. E. Cruikshank, *Butler's Rangers and the Settlement of Niagara* (Welland, 1893), 27 *et seq.*; F. H. Severance, *Old Trails on the Niagara Frontier* (2d ed., Cleveland, 1903), 56 *et seq.*
4. Canadian Archives, B. 169: 1.
5. Canadian Archives, B. 168: 38-41.
6. *Ibid.*

in particular was the instigator of war parties in which the Wyandot and other tribes coöperated with the royalists in harrying the frontier and gathering in adherents of the crown. When peace returned the colonization of the region east of the Detroit River followed. The officers commanding the king's ships on Lake Erie were soon authorized to transport free of expense such disbanded loyalists as chose to settle at the mouth of the river just named. At the same time McKee, Girty, and a few others, including Captain William Caldwell of Butler's Rangers, secured from the Ottawa Indians deeds to Colchester and Gosfield townships (known as "The Two Connected Townships") on the lake front and opened them to colonization. Under the rule that grants of this sort could be made only by the crown, the Indians were induced to reconvey these districts to the Canadian government; and in 1788, Major Mathews, who had been sent from Quebec to Detroit for the purpose, laid out the two townships in 109 lots, and confirmed the original squatters in their possessions, although the final adjustment was not reached until five years later. During this period a land board, whose members were chiefly American loyalists, was in control, carrying on surveys on Lake Erie and the Detroit and Thames rivers, correcting conflicting claims and making grants. Those who were to have participated in the formation of "The New Settlement" in the townships on the lake were to have received provisions and tools, like loyalist settlers elsewhere; but long delays discouraged many, and the promoters of the settlement were forced to witness the return of perhaps a hundred or more to the states. Others, who had drawn lots in The Two Connected Townships, preferred to locate on the River Thames, where the soil was of a better quality. Thus, the land board of the district of Hesse had plenty to do in dealing with the accumulation of nearly 300 petitions that were before it in 1791. The New Settlement began about five miles east of the Detroit River and extended for a distance three times as great along Lake Erie. The region next to the river remained for a time unsettled, partly because of its marshy character and partly on account of doubtful claims. In January, 1793, however, Lieutenant Governor Simcoe and his council took action constituting this tract the township of Malden and granting it to McKee, Elliot, and Caldwell, while at the same time confirming the possession of those settlers who had already made improvements there.[7]

In the spring of 1791, when Patrick McNiff, deputy surveyor at Detroit, laid out four townships on the River Thames, two on each side of the stream, he found twenty-eight families already there. These people appear not to have been molested, presumably on account of their previous adherence and services to the crown, and by February, 1793, the land board had granted certificates for all the lots surveyed in this region, extending to two and one-half townships in length. Among those who found homes here and in The New Settlement was a considerable group of Butler's men. Other refugees took up lands along the Detroit and St.

7. A. Fraser, *Third Report of the Bureau of Archives for the Province of Ontario,* 1905 (Toronto, 1906), 222, 223.

Clair rivers, and in localities nearby. The trials of these people in obtaining lands is illustrated by the experience of Frederick Arnold, who chose lots for himself and his son on the Thames at the time of the survey, but testified before the land board in the fall of the same year (1791) that these lots had been occupied by others. He also testified that he had brought in twenty-five families in 1784, none of whom had yet been able to "procure an establishment on the King's waste lands" and were threatening to return to the states.[8]

Another movement of loyalists into the Lake Erie region that can be definitely traced resulted in the colonization of Long Point. As early as September, 1792, Lieutenant Governor Simcoe proposed a plan for a military settlement here, stating that those to be brought in should be brave and determined loyalists. Although this project was approved by the British government several years later, it was frustrated by Governor General Dorchester who objected on the score of the needless expense involved. Meantime, a few squatters, mostly loyalists, had wandered in and, finding the region to their taste, had cleared farms for themselves to which they were not able to secure legal title. It was not, indeed, until Simcoe had departed for England (in 1796) that proclamations were issued inviting settlers into this district, and appealing especially to the United Empire loyalists. The immigrants who responded were chiefly of this class from Lower Canada and New Brunswick, the great majority having lived in the latter province for a decade or longer. Some came by land, following the Indian trails; but most of them came in open boats, coasting along the northern shores of Lake Ontario and Lake Erie. If courage and determination were deemed necessary qualifications for the pioneers of Norfolk County, surely these qualities cannot be denied to the forty-seven families who are known to have made the long and hazardous journey to Long Point between the years 1792 and 1812 and to have distributed themselves throughout five of its townships.[9]

Before 1783 there had been but little settlement in Upper Canada; but the closing year of the Revolution witnessed the arrival in this section of 10,000 loyalists; during 1784 this population doubled, and by 1791 it was estimated at 25,000. The records of the land office of Ontario indicate that no less than 3,200,000 acres had been granted to this class of people who had settled in Upper Canada before 1787.[10] It is, of course, significant that in 1791 Parliament passed the Constitutional Act separating the western province from the old province of Quebec.

If now we turn to those towns on the Atlantic coast which the British held for longer or shorter periods, we find that they also were the asylums of refugees, a fact made clear as they were successively evacuated. There were, to be sure, flights of individuals and families in considerable numbers from these coast towns from 1774 on. When Judge Samuel Curwen, a refugee from Salem, Massachusetts, arrived in London in

8. Fraser, *Third Report Bureau of Archives*, 152.
9. Ontario Historical Society, *Papers and Records*, 2: 43-47, 68, 69.
10. Fraser, *Third Report Bureau of Archives, passim.*

July, 1775, he found—to use his own words—"an army of New Eng-landers" already there. A month later he wrote to another fugitive from Massachusetts, who with wife and children had gone to Halifax, that the "army" of exiles in London were "lamenting their own and their country's unhappy fate." [11] Evidently, then, the English metropolis was already a city of refuge for many American loyalists, and Halifax was beginning to shelter some of the same class. Only seven months later, however, the capital of Nova Scotia was to experience such a visitation of refugees as London itself had probably not yet experienced; for when Howe's fleet sailed from Boston in March, 1776, it was accompanied by over eleven hundred hapless exiles. As Lieutenant Governor Oliver had carefully estimated the number of loyalists under his charge towards the end of the previous January at "upwards of 2,000," we may fairly sup-pose that many anticipated the evacuation by an earlier departure to Nova Scotia, to Penobscot, or to Great Britain. Three weeks after the arrival of the Boston contingent in Halifax, Oliver wrote to Lord George Germain of the colonial office describing the distressing situation of his protégés in Nova Scotia, forced as they were to pay "six fold the usual Rent" for miserable lodgings and "more than double the former price for every Necessary of Life." Such relief as could be had came only from the abundant supply of fish in the harbor and the issuance of fuel and pro-visions to loyalists as well as soldiers. The result was that many of the principal refugees applied to Howe forthwith for a passage to Europe at the expense of government, and were promised the first transport that could be spared for the purpose.[12] Ample evidence shows that various companies of Bostonians sailed from this port for England at different times, their successive arrivals being recorded by Curwen and by Hutchin-son, the refugee governor of Massachusetts, from early in June to near the close of July, 1776.[13] Philadelphia, at its evacuation, witnessed the departure of almost three times the number carried by Howe to Halifax. So great was the concourse of inhabitants which withdrew from this place that the fleet in the Delaware could accommodate none of the evacuating troops, who took up the line of march for New York City. The fleet sailed for the same destination, which was already the mecca of persecuted loyalists, northern and southern, and remained so throughout the war.[14]

For some time William Knox, a Georgia loyalist who was under-secre-tary in the colonial office in London, had cherished the plan of establish-ing a separate province for these proscribed fellow countrymen of his; and at length, in September, 1778, General Clinton was ordered to secure a

11. Samuel Curwen, *Journal and Letters* (G. A. Ward, ed.—New York, 1845), 31, 34.

12. R. Frothingham, *History of the Siege of Boston* (Boston, 1849), 311, 312; Lieutenant Governor Thomas Oliver to the Earl of Dartmouth, Public Record Office, Colonial Office, 5.21:297; Lieutenant Governor Oliver to Lord George Germain, Halifax, April 21, 1776, *ibid.*, 5.21: 159.

13. Siebert, *The Flight of American Loyalists to the British Isles* (Columbus, 1911), 6, 7.

14. *Ibid.*, 8, 9.

post on the Penobscot River as the first step to that end. In the follow-ing June and July, the post was duly established and soon became, in the picturesque language of the Massachusetts leaders, a "viperine nest" which they tried to destroy, though without success. The fortress attracted Tories and their kindred from Maine and Massachusetts, became crowded to overflowing, and a village of substantial cottages, with wharves and stores, sprang up under its shadow. When the contest ended, Massachu-setts was able to obtain by the unyielding diplomacy of her son, John Adams, what she had not secured by military siege: Penobscot was sur-rendered by the British, and a hundred and fifty families, together with part of the garrison, were removed to Passamaquoddy Bay, there to be joined by various associations of loyalists from New York and elsewhere. As most of these groups were still within disputed territory, a boundary question arose which was not solved for many years.[15] Knox's scheme of a loyalist province failed, it is true, but it is also true that the people who were its beneficiaries participated in the settlement and organization of a greater loyalist province a little to the eastward of the one proposed, namely, the province of New Brunswick.

At the time when Passamaquoddy was settled, New Brunswick was still a part of Nova Scotia, and as such shared with that province in the great immigration from New York. According to the official enumeration of the British commissary general, dated November 24, 1783, 29,244 persons sailed from that port for various parts of Nova Scotia.[16] Of this number about 12,000, including 11 royalist corps, settled north of the Bay of Fundy; and before another year elapsed succeeded in having that region erected into an independent province. Meanwhile, the remaining or penin-sular portion of Nova Scotia gained 17,300 colonists, all from New York, besides 5,000 or more from other quarters. Their settlements, of which upwards of a score may be counted, took form chiefly along the southern shore of the peninsula; and a large part of the lumber, with which they built their habitations, was supplied by the industry and com-mercial enterprise of their fellow exiles at Passamaquoddy Bay.

Only a few hundreds of the southern loyalists went to the maritime provinces. The early reverses which the British suffered in Virginia sent Governor Dunmore and numbers of his sympathizers aboard the shipping at Norfolk in December, 1775. After a delay of nearly eight months the crowded vessels set sail for various destinations, one for Glasgow, others for England, and still others for Antigua, Bermuda, and East Florida. About the same time refugees from the Carolinas and Georgia began find-ing their way into the two Floridas, many taking service in the provincial

15. S. F. Batchelder, *The Life and Surprising Adventures of John Nutting, Cambridge Loyalist* (Cambridge, 1912); G. A. Wheeler, *Castine, Past and Present, the Ancient Settlement of Pentagöet, and the Modern Town* (Boston, 1896), 311-313; Maine Historical Society, *Collections*, ser. 2, vol. 1: 395-400; W. F. Ganong, "A Monograph of the Evolution of the Boundaries of the Province of New Brunswick," in Royal Society of Canada, *Transactions*, ser. 2, vol. 7, sec. 2.

16. Fraser, *Second Report of the Bureau of Archives for the Province of Ontario, 1904* (Toronto, 1905), 11.

regiments there. At length, in July and December, 1782, the evacuations of Savannah and Charleston, respectively, took place. Three months after the former event a census showed that the population of East Florida had been nearly doubled by the influx of 3,340 whites and blacks from Georgia, exclusive of those who had arrived before the evacuation. Simultaneously with this census, numbers of loyalists, military and civilian, began embarking from Charleston for St. Augustine, among these being the North and South Carolina regiments and a body of merchants and planters. Then, on December 14, came the formal evacuation of Charleston, with the result of the sudden trebling of the population of East Florida; and by May, 1783 (according to the figures of General McArthur, who was in command in that province) it quadrupled, reaching a total of 16,000, of whom McArthur estimated 5,400 were whites and 9,600, blacks. In the meantime, the merchants who had come in were accommodated with houses in St. Augustine, the planters were placed on unoccupied lands in the country, and a little town sprang up at the bluff on St. John's River. As provisions and tools were badly needed the authorities exerted themselves to furnish these supplies.

Thus far, in considering the withdrawal of the British from Charleston and Savannah I have accounted for less than half of the numbers who left these two ports, for in each case less than half went to East Florida. Of the 7,000 who sailed from Savannah, Governor Wright, other officers, and part of the garrison disembarked at Charleston; General Alured Clark and part of the British regulars sailed for New York, and the remainder —loyalists and their Negroes—proceeded to Jamaica. Of the 9,121 persons, white and black, who left Charleston (not counting the troops) nearly 3,900 embarked for Jamaica; 470, for Halifax, and smaller numbers for St. Lucia, England, and New York. The Georgians and Carolinians who settled in Jamaica were joined by other refugees from Honduras and the Mosquito Coast, from Pensacola and St. Augustine, from New York City, and after 1785 from Shelburne in Nova Scotia. The fact that Jamaica made a gain of 11,500 white inhabitants alone between the years 1775 and 1787 is explained in no small degree by the continual inflow of American loyalists during that period. Several of the smaller islands of the British West Indies (St. Lucia, St. Christopher, Antigua, and probably others) experienced accessions that were relatively large for them.

The conquest of West Florida by the Spanish in May, 1781, resulted in the departure of many of its provincial defenders to New York City and of a few to Jamaica, as already mentioned. After the treaty of Versailles, by which both East and West Florida were ceded to Spain and the Bahamas were obtained in exchange, the loyalists in the eastern province were left only the choice between submitting to Spanish rule and preserving their fealty by withdrawing to a British possession. What was more natural, then, than that the Bahamas should be regarded as the true Land of Canaan by the thousands awaiting a second or even third expatriation in East Florida. But this did not prove to be the case. The loyalists did not propose to pass through the ordeal of another general exodus without adequate knowledge of their destination in advance. Meanwhile, two shiploads departed for England. At length, in the fall of 1783, Lieutenant Wilson of the engineers was dispatched from St. Augustine to make the round of the Bahama Islands and report on their availability for colonization. His report was reassuring: it ascribed their uncultivated condition to the indolence of the inhabitants, who it declared contented themselves with whatever nature produced by her unaided efforts. The opportune arrival of some government transports (September 12) started the movement, and from that time a steady stream of refugees poured into the Bahamas, unoccupied lands being granted them free of quit rents for ten years. Upwards of fifteen hundred persons from St. Augustine engaged to settle on Great Abaco Island, and we know that an almost equal number embarked at New York for the same place in August and September, 1783. New Providence, Cat, Long, and Crooked islands, and doubtless others, profited by this migration; but it is difficult to arrive at a correct estimate of the total increase of the Bahama population due to this movement. A committee of the House of Assembly of the islands reported in 1789 that the increase for the years 1784 and 1785 amounted to twelve hundred loyalists and thirty-six hundred colored people, the latter brought in by the former; but we are not informed how many came in during 1783. Perhaps it is safe to say that the Bahamas gained between six thousand and seven thousand of both races as the result of the exodus from the mainland.[17] It has been estimated that before 1783 England received about two thousand from New York alone; [18] but it should not be forgotten that other American ports, both northern and southern, together contributed certainly no less a number before the war closed, and that needy Tories from over the sea continued to seek financial relief in London for some years after the war. In this paper only casual reference has been made to the political and other effects of the dispersion of the American loyalists. Without attempting to discuss this subject at the present time, it must suffice to say merely that the accession of these people marked an epoch in the history of Jamaica and the Bahamas, the maritime provinces, and Lower and Upper Canada. Their work was essentially that of sturdy pioneers and political organizers; and, while their strain lasts, England need have no fears concerning the loyalty of her American provinces.

17. Siebert, "Legacy of the American Revolution to the British West Indies and Bahamas" (Ohio State University, *Bulletin,* 17, no. 27 [Columbus, 1913]).

18. A. C. Flick, *Loyalism in New York during the American Revolution* (New York, 1901).

FREDERICK B. TOLLES
The American Revolution Considered as a Social Movement: A Re-evaluation

▣ The removal of the Loyalists left the country to the direction of its Whig leaders and to the debate over who should rule at home, the issues debated so vividly by the Progressives. Robert E. Brown has contended that in Massachusetts, at least, no political revolution was necessary.* And Frederick B. Tolles submitted to searching criticism the treatise of John Franklin Jameson, *The American Revolution Considered as a Social Movement* (1926), in which he had contended that many social consequences were the result of the revolution. ▣

SOMETIMES a single essay, a monograph, or a series of lectures makes historiographical history. It was so in 1893 when Frederick Jackson Turner read his paper on "The Significance of the Frontier in American History." It was so again in 1913 when Charles A. Beard published his *Economic Interpretations* [sic] *of the Constitution.* And it was so in 1925 when J. Franklin Jameson delivered his four lectures at Princeton on "The American Revolution Considered as a Social Movement."

At first glance the comparison with Turner and Beard may seem strained. We are accustomed to think of Jameson as a scholar's scholar, a kind of indispensable historical midwife—curator and editor of manuscripts, director of other men's research, editor of the *American Historical Review*—not as a pathbreaker, an innovator. But this is to do him less than justice. *The American Revolution Considered as a Social Movement* stands as a landmark in recent American historiography, a slender but unmistakable signpost, pointing a new direction for historical research and interpretation. Before Jameson, the American Revolution had been a chapter in political, diplomatic, and military history, a story of Faneuil Hall and Lexington, Independence Hall and Valley Forge, Versailles and Yorktown. After Jameson, it became something different, something greater—a seismic disturbance in American society, a sudden quickening in the American mind.

The American Revolution, like the French, Jameson believed, was accompanied by social and cultural changes of profound significance.

---

* Robert E. Brown, *Middle Class Democracy and the Revolution in Massachusetts, 1691-1780* (Ithaca, 1955).

Reprinted by permission from the *American Historical Review*, LX (1954), 1-12.

The stream of revolution, once started, could not be confined within narrow banks, but spread abroad upon the land. Many economic desires, many social aspirations were set free by the political struggle, many aspects of colonial society profoundly altered by the forces thus let loose. The relations of social classes to each other, the institution of slavery, the system of landholding, the course of business, the forms and spirit of the intellectual and religious life, all felt the transforming hand of revolution, all emerged from under it in shapes advanced many degrees nearer to those we know.

No more than Turner's or Beard's was Jameson's notion wholly new. Just a year earlier, in his massive volume on *The American States during and after the Revolution,* Allan Nevins had devoted fifty pages to the task of demonstrating in impressive detail that "a social and intellectual revolution" occurred between Lexington and Yorktown. Nearly twenty years before, Carl Becker had described the Revolution as a twofold contest: for home-rule on the one hand, for "the democratization of American politics and society" on the other. As far back as 1787, Benjamin Rush had perceived that the American revolution was bigger than the American war, that the real revolution was in "the principles, morals, and manners of our citizens," and that, far from being over, that revolution had only begun.

Jameson's view of the Revolution was not new, but no one hitherto had marshaled the evidence so compactly, conveyed it so lucidly, or argued from it so persuasively. Perceptive historians immediately greeted his little volume as a gem of historical writing—"a truly notable book," Charles A. Beard called it, ". . . cut with a diamond point to a finish, studded with novel illustrative materials, gleaming with new illumination, serenely engaging in style, and sparingly garnished with genial humor."

The influence of this little book with the long title has grown steadily. A year after its publication, the Beards summarized its thesis in their widely read *Rise of American Civilization.* Jameson's emphasis on social factors harmonized perfectly with the intellectual and political climate of the 1930's. In 1940, after the author's death, a second edition appeared, and in 1950 a third—an unusual tribute to a set of academic lectures. With the passage of a quarter-century, the book has achieved the standing of a minor classic. One will find hardly a textbook that does not paraphrase or quote Jameson's words, borrow his illustrations, cite him in its bibliography. The notion of the Revolution as a social upheaval has achieved the final seal of acceptance: it has been taken over by the historical novelists—by such writers as Kenneth Roberts and Howard Fast, to name two rather unlikely bedfellows.

Jameson, one suspects, had no idea he was writing a classic. His aim was simply to challenge American historians by opening new windows on the Revolutionary era, suggesting new directions for future research, throwing out tentative hypotheses for others to test. Over the past quarter-century historians have risen to his challenge with a flood of articles, monographs, academic dissertations, and full-dress histories bearing on one or another of his propositions. But the average textbook-writer, one is tempted to believe, has not got beyond Jameson. The time has come to go back and ask how Jameson's original thesis stands up in the light of all this detailed research; what modifications, if any, must be made; what further extensions, if any, are possible.

Jameson disposed his arguments under four rubrics—the status of persons, the land, industry and commerce, thought and feeling. If we recognize, as he did, that such divisions are purely arbitrary, we may adopt his procedure.

American society, he suggested, was measurably democratized during the Revolution. The upper stratum, the old colonial aristocracy, was largely liquidated—by banishment, voluntary exile, or impoverishment. New groups rose to the surface to take their places. "In most states the strength of the revolutionary party lay most largely in the plain people," and the social changes which they brought about naturally tended "in the direction of levelling democracy." Broadening of the suffrage elevated "whole classes of people . . . in their social status," and the revolutionary philosophy of liberty wrought improvements in the condition of the most debased class in America—the Negro slaves.

Recent studies of individual states and regions seem to suggest that Jameson was too sweeping when he equated colonial aristocrats with Loyalists and implied that this group was erased from American society. In eastern Massachusetts it was perhaps true that "a majority of the old aristocracy" emigrated. But in the central and western part of the state the oldest, most respected families chose the Whig side and remained to perpetuate their local rule in the days of the early Republic. In New Hampshire, except around Portsmouth, society had never been highly stratified, and the Tory emigration bore away few outstanding individuals. In Connecticut, where "the native aristocracy of culture, wealth, religion, and politics" tended to be loyal to the crown, at least half of the Tories never left the state. Others were welcomed back even before the war was over. Within six months of the peace treaty, New Haven was openly extending an invitation to former Loyalists to return, and President Ezra Stiles of Yale College was grumbling about efforts "silently to bring the Tories into an Equality and Supremacy among the Whigs." In New York and Philadelphia, many prominent merchants—perhaps the majority—were Loyalists, or at least "neutralists," and they stayed on in such numbers as to give a definite tone to postwar society, politics, and business in these important centers. In Maryland, the "internal" Revolution turns out to have been a struggle between one group of aristocrats—planters, merchants, lawyers—and another; the "plain people" took little part in the conflict and the resultant social shifts were minimal. In Virginia, of course, most of the "F.F.V.'s" were Whigs, and their control of politics was to continue through the days of the "Virginia dynasty."

In the North Carolina back country it was the "plain people"—the old Regulators—who were most stubbornly Loyalist. Clearly Jameson's generalizations about the fate of the old aristocracy must be qualified.

What about the new democracy of the Revolutionary period? Unquestionably a sense of dignity and importance came to the common man—the small farmer, the town artisan—as a result of his revolutionary activities and the limited extension of the suffrage. But before we can say with assurance how democratic the new society was, we must answer the prior question: how undemocratic was the old? No one will dispute the fact that provincial society was stratified, that class distinctions existed, that political and social equality were hardly dreamed of. A recent brilliant study of electoral practices in colonial Massachusetts raises, however, some questions. By means of ingenious statistical methods and samplings of contemporary opinion, the author of this study has shown rather convincingly that, in the Bay Colony at least, practically all adult males had the vote. Massachusetts society before 1776, he concludes, was "very close to a complete democracy." And he hints of further revisions to come. "As for the 'internal revolution' in other colonies," he says, "—perhaps we should take another look. There is more than a hint in the records that what applies to Massachusetts applies without too much change to other colonies as well."

Though the Negro slave received some indirect benefits from the Revolution, the indentured servant, Jameson found, received none. Nor has subsequent research uncovered any important evidence that he overlooked. While he was dwelling on the negative side, Jameson might have mentioned another large dependent class that gained nothing in status as a result of the Revolution. Even before independence was declared, that doughty feminist Abigail Adams was writing to her husband in Congress: "By the way, in the new code of laws which I suppose it will be necessary for you to make, I desire you would remember the ladies and be more generous and favorable to them than your ancestors." Her husband wrote back as much in earnest as in jest: "Depend on it, we know better than to repeal our masculine systems." It was to be nearly three quarters of a century before the Declaration of Independence would be revised by a group of determined ladies at Seneca Falls to read: "All men and women are created equal." Both negative and positive evidence, then, suggests that the Revolution made less difference in the status of persons in America than Jameson believed.

The doctrine that underlies Jameson's second lecture is, quite explicitly, economic determinism: "political democracy," he says flatly, "came to the United States as a result of economic democracy." The movement for manhood suffrage which reached its fruition in Jacksonian America, he maintains, was rooted in a peculiarly American type of land tenure—the system of small holdings or what he chooses to call "peasant proprietorship." This system the Revolution fixed upon the nation when it swept away the royal restrictions, the archaic manorial laws and usages which had encumbered the land throughout the colonial period. There was, he makes clear, "no violent outbreak," no bloody massacre of land-lords as in France a decade later. Still, "in a quiet, sober, Anglo-Saxon way a great change was reflected in the land system of America between the years 1775 and 1795." Specifically, the changes were of three sorts: the discontinuance of quitrents and of the king's right to mast-trees, the abolition of primogeniture and entail, the confiscation and distribution of the Tory estates.

The importance of the quitrents and the king's "broad arrow" was probably more symbolic than real. Jameson himself admitted this: payment of quitrents, he pointed out, was "largely evaded"; the law giving the king's surveyors the right to reserve the tallest, straightest pine trees for the Royal Navy "was not rigorously enforced." Still, no historian will deny the importance of an emotion-laden symbol, and Jameson insists, quite rightly, that the quitrent and the king's "broad arrow" were symbols of an obsolete and alien feudalism, that until they were done away with, private property was not private property.

There is high authority, of course, for attaching great significance to the abolition of primogeniture and entail in Virginia—the authority of Thomas Jefferson. But these gestures too, it now appears, were more important in the realm of symbol than of economic reality. In point of fact, neither primogeniture nor entail operated to any important degree in Virginia. Recent research has shown that most estates in the Old Dominion were not entailed but could be freely alienated. And primo-geniture was mandatory only if the property-owner died intestate. Most Virginia planters were careful to make wills. By their wills they often distributed their property among all their sons, and sometimes even their daughters. So Jefferson, in the words of his most authoritative biographer, "did not destroy the country gentry as a group with the blows of his mighty ax, and there is insufficient reason to believe that he wanted to." What he did was merely to "remove legal vestiges of Old World aristoc-racy." The sweeping conclusion reached by a recent student of this prob-lem in Virginia may well apply to other colonies: "No radical change of custom in devising estates resulted from the abolition of primogeniture and entail."

On the confiscation of Loyalist lands much has been written of late years. The evidence has not been canvassed for all the states, but a definite conclusion seems to be emerging that considerably less diffusion and democratization of landownership resulted from the breakup of these estates and their disposition in small parcels than Jameson supposed.

The most intensive study has been centered on the southern counties of New York, where the DeLanceys, the Bayards, the Philipses held sway in colonial times over their vast baronies. When the revolutionary New York government seized the estates and sold them off, some of the land, to be sure, went to former tenants and other landless individuals. But the bulk of it was bought up by wealthy patriots and merely augmented the domains of rival families like the Livingstons, Schuylers, and Roose-velts. "While it is true," concludes the author of this study, "that the disposal of the loyalist estates effected a greater diffusion of ownership, it is questionable whether it went far toward a radical redistribution of landed wealth and a new social and economic order."

The same thing seems to have been true in Maryland, where wealthy Whig planters and speculators bought up a large proportion of the desirable Tory lands in Baltimore and Frederick counties. Nor is the story greatly different in western Massachusetts or New Hampshire. The South Carolina confiscation law, in the opinion of a contemporary, was actually "so framed that a man who wants land has no chance to get any," for the state required security which only the wealthy landowner could provide.

The case of North Carolina is instructive. The authority on the Loyalists of that state, noting that the confiscated lands were sold in plots averaging two hundred acres, concludes with Jameson that the confiscations "tended to make the Revolution economic and social as well as political." From his own evidence, however, one could draw the equally justified inference that many a wealthy patriot took advantage of the bargain prices to increase his holdings and consequently his social status. The largest Tory estate was that of the great speculator Henry McCulloh —some 40,000 acres. Of the ninety purchasers of McCulloh's lands thirty-four bought more than one tract. Some acquired as many as ten or fifteen, thereby creating estates as large as 5,000 acres. Robert Raiford purchased parcels from five different Tories and put together an estate of more than a thousand acres. The 3,600-acre estate of Thomas Hooper passed almost intact to John McKinsey. Before a final generalization can be made about the social effects of the confiscations in North Carolina, we need to know more about the previous economic status of the purchasers.

The largest estate to be confiscated in America, as Jameson pointed out, was that of the Penn family. By the Divesting Act of 1779 the Pennsylvania legislature assumed control of twenty-one and a half million acres— all the ungranted lands which by royal charter had belonged to the proprietors. But this proprietary land, from which the Penns had never received any income, was comparable, surely, to the ungranted crown lands which fell into the hands of the other commonwealths. Much more significant is the fact that the private manors, the "proprietary tenths," of the Penns, amounting to more than 500,000 acres, together with the quitrents on them, were specifically "confirmed, ratified and established for ever" in the hands of the Penn family—and this by the most "radical" of all the revolutionary legislatures!

Clearly, there are two ways of reading the evidence concerning the confiscation and sale of Loyalist lands. Jameson, who was arguing a thesis, chose to stress the "democratizing" effects. But there were other social consequences of an opposite tendency—the aggrandizement of certain individuals and families already well entrenched, the opportunities opened for speculation—and we shall not understand all the social results of this great sequestration of lands until we assess these as well.

In particular, until someone has studied the social effects of land speculation in the Revolutionary and post-Revolutionary era as Professor Paul

W. Gates has done for a later period, we shall not know whether the operations of the speculators hastened or delayed settlement, encouraged or hindered the system of small holdings. Meanwhile, we may note that Professor Abernethy considers the Virginia land office act of 1779 (drafted, incidentally, by Thomas Jefferson) "a colossal mistake," a blow to economic democracy, and a retarding influence on settlement because it played into the hands of speculators and thus *prevented* the diffusion of land in small holdings. By this act, he says, "democracy was defeated in Virginia at the moment when it might have had its birth."

Land speculation was, of course, a form of business enterprise. And business enterprise, it is now clear, took a sharp spurt as a direct result of Revolutionary conditions. That Jameson should have perceived and stressed this in 1925 is sufficiently remarkable. His chapter on "Industry and Commerce" undoubtedly opened the eyes of many American historians to the economic facts which, as everyone now recognizes, are as crucial in the history of a war as the political, diplomatic, and military facts.

Some of the new economic paths which the Revolution opened, turned out to be blind alleys. Postwar interest in the improvement of agriculture, reflected in the sudden popularity of farmers' societies, proved to be short-lived and relatively ineffectual. In some regions the wartime growth of manufacturing, which Jameson noted, was choked off by the postwar flood of cheap British goods, which he neglected to mention.

But in other ways enterprise burgeoned and flourished under wartime and postwar conditions. Opportunities for quick gains in privateering and profiteering, the opening of new markets, the expansion of the credit system, the injection of new supplies of specie into the economy as a result of foreign borrowing, the rise of new business groups around men like Jeremiah Wadsworth, William Duer, Robert Morris, the very idea (a new one for Americans) of large-scale business association—all these were constructive economic forces generated by the Revolution. Especially important were the rise of banking and the spread of incorporation. In the words of one economic historian, the Bank of North America, which opened in Philadelphia in 1782, "was identified with the American Revolutionary 'settlement,'—as the Bank of England was with that of the Glorious Revolution."

The same scholar gives us some revealing statistics on the chartering of business corporations: "In contrast with the half-dozen American business charters granted in the entire colonial period, eleven were issued in the United States between 1781 and 1785, twenty-two between 1786 and 1790, and 114 between 1791 and 1795." Economic facts of this order have led one writer to treat the American Revolution as "the triumph of American mercantile capitalism." Whether or not one wishes to adopt this view, it is clear, as Jameson dimly perceived, that the Revolution loosed potent new forces in the American economy. How these forces were related to the social and political democracy which Jameson saw as products of the Revolution remains to be studied.

When he turned from the hard facts of economic history to the impalpable realm of "thought and feeling," Jameson was less at home. Yet even here he opened vistas which a generation of intellectual and cultural historians have explored with profit. The greater part of his final lecture is concerned with the effect of independence on the churches—with disestablishment and the separation of church and state, with the reorganization of the churches on a national basis, with the wartime decline of religious life and the postwar spread of liberal theologies. Subsequent research has added little to Jameson's account of these matters, except to fill in details. What Jameson did—and it was no trifling achievement—was to bring American church history within the purview of American historians—to take, as it were, the first steps toward giving this neglected orphan child a home and a standing within the family of historical disciplines.

Certain of his insights, naturally, have proved more fruitful than others. His *obiter dictum* to the effect that military men can never again play the part in public life that they played after the Revolution falls strangely on our ears, who have known the proconsulate of MacArthur, the foreign ministry of Marshall, the Presidency of Eisenhower. Curiously, Jameson found little evidence of educational advance in the Revolutionary era, except for the founding of new colleges. Had he taken a broader view of education, he might have recognized a number of important developments directly or indirectly related to wartime experience: the improvement of medicine (including dentistry) and of medical education; the emergence of civil engineering from military engineering; the founding of Judge Tapping Reeve's "law school" at Litchfield, Connecticut, in 1784; the diffusion of scientific knowledge through the revived activity of the American Philosophical Society and the founding of the American Academy of Arts and Sciences; the popularity of pamphleteering as a form of mass education; and—not least important—the informal education, the widening of horizons, that resulted from wartime mobility, from the fact that, for the first time, many Americans rubbed elbows—and minds—not only with Europeans but with other Americans. The school of intellectual and cultural historians which has sprung up in the last quarter century has made much of the "intellectual democracy" and the "cultural nationalism" which Jameson vaguely perceived as concomitants, in the realm of "thought and feeling," of the American Revolution.

The danger here as elsewhere is that the historian, misled by his enthusiasm for the concept of "revolution," will posit too abrupt a set of changes, will pay too little attention to the evidences of historical continuity. Jameson himself did not altogether avoid this pitfall. For example, he wrote that "Joel Barlow's *Vision of Columbus,* or President Stile's celebrated election sermon on *The United States Elevated to Glory and Honor,* could not possibly have been written twenty years earlier." If he meant by this that the idea of the United States as an independent nation was not entertained in the 1760's, the statement is obviously correct, though hardly startling. If he meant that before 1775 no American felt or expressed love for the land, pride in its people, confidence in its future, he was just as obviously wrong. For one finds strong feelings of American patriotism in a pre-Revolutionary poem like Freneau and Brackenridge's "The Rising Glory of America," written in 1771, in the sermons of Samuel Davies and Jonathan Mayhew in the 1750's, even in Judge Samuel Sewall's proud paean to his beloved Plum Island, Crane Pond, and Turkey Hill as far back as the last decade of the seventeenth century. Indeed the points at which the supports to Jameson's thesis seem weakest—where for example he argues for sharper changes in the political and social status of individuals than can be justified on the evidence —are precisely those points at which he overlooked or underestimated dynamic forces already present in the society of late colonial America.

Still, a historian who fashions so useful a conceptual tool, who popularizes so fruitful a hypothesis, who enlarges so notably our understanding of a significant era in American history, can be forgiven a few oversights, a few overstatements. Basically, the "Jameson thesis" is still sound, and, what is more important, still vital and suggestive, capable of still further life, still greater usefulness. Jameson, after all, did much more than give us a new approach to the American Revolution. He formulated and cogently applied to a particular period an important general thesis—"the thesis that all the varied activities of men in the same country and period have intimate relations with each other, and that one cannot obtain a satisfactory view of any one of them by considering it apart from the others." For this he deserves homage as one of the founders of American social and cultural history.

MERRILL JENSEN
Democracy and the American Revolution

In 1957 the editors of the *Huntington Library Quarterly* published an Early American History Number which allowed Merrill Jensen and Clarence L. Ver Steeg to restate the democratic case that there *was* a basic change in the political balance of power and that, whether or not it was a "social" revolution, it had certainly profound economic consequences. Professor Ver Steeg confesses that he is but raising questions, "requiring answers that only a thorough investigation can provide." The study of the Revolution and its domestic consequences, endlessly being investigated, has no answers that are likely to be final.

THE HISTORIAN who ventures to talk about democracy in early America is in danger because there are almost as many opinions as there are writers on the subject. The Puritans have been pictured as the founders of American democracy, and it is vigorously denied that they had anything to do with it. Some have seen in Roger Williams the father of American democracy, and others have denied that he was a democrat, whatever his putative progeny may be. The conflict is equally obvious when it comes to the American Revolution, and the problems of solution are far more complex than they are for the seventeenth century. The difficulty is compounded, for all too often men's emotions seem to become involved.

It is sometimes suggested that we avoid the use of the word "democracy" when discussing the sevententh and eighteenth centuries. It seems to me that this is a flat evasion of the problem, for the Americans of those centuries used the word and they meant something by it. Our task, then, is not to avoid the issue but to try to understand what they meant, and understand what they meant in the context of the times in which they lived. What we must not do is to measure the seventeenth and eighteenth centuries in terms of our own assumptions about what democracy is or should be. This is all the more important since many of us do not seem to be too clear about our assumptions, even for the century in which we live.

A number of years ago I took the position that "in spite of the paradoxes involved one may still maintain that the Revolution was essentially, though relatively, a democratic movement within the thirteen American colonies, and that its significance for the political and constitutional history of the United States lay in its tendency to elevate the political and economic status of the majority of the people." And then, with a somewhat rhetorical flourish which I have sometimes regretted but have not as yet withdrawn, I went on to say that "the Articles of Confederation were the constitutional expression of this movement and the embodiment in governmental form of the philosophy of the Declaration of Independence." [1] One thing can be said for this statement at least: reviewers read it and quoted it, some with raised eyebrows, and some with approval, whether or not they said anything at all about the rest of the book.

During most of the present century historians have assumed that democracy was involved somehow or other in the American Revolution. They have assumed also that there were conditions within the American colonies that were not satisfactory to at least some of the American people. The causes of internal discontent were various, ranging all the way from religious to economic differences. The discontent was of such intensity that in certain colonies it led to explosive outbreaks in the 1760's such as the Regulator movements in the Carolinas, the Paxton Boys' uprising in Pennsylvania, and the tenant farmer revolt in New York, outbreaks that

Reprinted by permission from the *Huntington Library Quarterly*, XX (1957), 321-341.

1. Merrill Jensen, *The Articles of Confederation: An Interpretation of the Social-Constitutional History of the American Revolution, 1774-1781*, reprint with new foreword (Madison, Wis., 1948), pp. 15, 239.

were suppressed by the armed forces of the colonial governments and with the help of British power.

Most historians have agreed also that the individual colonies were controlled politically by relatively small groups of men in each of them, allied by family, or economic or political interests, or by some combination of these. The colonial aristocracies owed their position to many things: to their wealth and ability, to their family connections and political allies, and to the British government which appointed them to office. As opposed to Britain, they had won virtual self-government for the colonies by 1763. Yet in every colony they were a minority who managed to maintain internal control through property qualifications for the suffrage, especially effective in the growing towns, and through refusal or failure to grant representation in any way proportional to the population of the rapidly growing frontier areas. Probably more important than either of these was the fact that in most colonies the aristocracies manned the upper houses of the legislatures, the supreme courts, and other important posts—all by royal appointment. Beyond this, their control extended down through the county court system, even in Massachusetts. In short, colonial political society was not democratic in operation despite the elective lower houses and the self-government which had been won from Great Britain.[2]

This is a brief but, I think, fair summary of a widely held point of view concerning the political actualities at the beginning of the revolutionary era.

This view has been challenged recently. A writer on Massachusetts declared that "as far as Massachusetts is concerned, colonial society and the American Revolution must be interpreted in terms something very close to a complete democracy with the exception of British restraints." It was not controlled by a wealthy aristocracy. There was little inequality of representation, and property was so widely held that virtually every adult male could vote.[3] The assumption that Massachusetts was an idyllic democracy, united in the fight against British tyranny, will be somewhat surprising to those who have read the letters of Francis Bernard and the diary of John Adams, not to mention the history of Thomas Hutchinson, and, I suspect, would be even more surprising to those gentlemen as well. Elsewhere, this writer has implied that what was true for Massachusetts was probably true for other colonies and for the United States after the Revolution.[4]

2. *Ibid.*, ch. iii, "The Internal Revolution"; Leonard W. Labaree, *Conservatism in Early American History* (New York, 1948); and Robert J. Taylor, *Western Massachusetts in the Revolution* (Providence, 1954), as examples. For methods of local control see Charles S. Sydnor, *Gentlemen Freeholders: Political Practices in Washington's Virginia* (Chapel Hill, 1952).

3. Robert E. Brown, "Democracy in Colonial Massachusetts," *New England Quarterly*, XXV (1952), 291-313, and at length in *Middle Class Democracy and the Revolution in Massachusetts, 1691-1780* (Ithaca, N. Y., 1955).

4. Robert E. Brown, "Economic Democracy Before the Constitution," *American Quarterly*, VII (1955), 257-274.

On the other hand it is asserted that democracy had nothing to do with the Revolution. Such an assertion made in connection with Pennsylvania is a little startling, for ever since C. H. Lincoln's work of more than a half century ago, down to the present, it has been held that there was a democratic movement in Pennsylvania during the revolutionary era. Not so, says a reviewer of the most recent study. He declares that "the attribution of democratic motivations and ideas to eighteenth century colonists is a common fault among many historians of the colonial period. . . ." He argues that the struggle in Pennsylvania before 1776 was one between "radical and conservative variants of whiggism," which he defines as one between "those who held privilege most dear and those who valued property above all." The Pennsylvania Constitution of 1776 itself was not democratic, but a triumph of "colonial radical whiggism." [5]

It is clear that a considerable diversity of opinion prevails. It is also clear that the time has come to set forth certain propositions or generalizations which seem to me to have a measure of validity.

First of all, a definition of democracy is called for. And just to face the issue squarely, I will offer one stated at Newport, Rhode Island, in 1641 when a meeting declared that "the government which this body politic doth attend unto . . . is a democracy or popular government; . . . that is to say: It is in the power of the body of freemen, orderly assembled, or the major part of them, to make or constitute just laws, by which they will be regulated, and to depute from among themselves such ministers as shall see them faithfully executed between man and man." That such an idea was not confined to Newport was shown six years later when the little towns in Rhode Island formed a confederation, the preamble of which states: "It is agreed, by this present assembly thus incorporate, and by this present act declared, that the form of government established in Providence Plantations is democratical; that is to say, a government held by the free and voluntary consent of all, or the greater part of the free inhabitants."

These are simple but, I think, adequate definitions. I will go even further and offer as a theoretical and philosophical foundation for democracy the statement by Roger Williams in the *Bloudy Tenent* of 1644. After describing civil government as an ordinance of God to conserve the civil peace of the people so far as concerns their bodies and goods, he goes on to say: "The sovereign, original, and foundation of civil power lies in the people (whom they must needs mean by the civil power distinct from the government set up). And if so, that a people may erect and establish what form of government seems to them most meet for their civil condition. It is evident that such governments as are by them erected and established have no more power, nor for no longer time, than the civil power or people consenting and agreeing shall betrust them with. This is clear not only in reason, but in the experience of all com-

5. Roy N. Lokken, review of Theodore Thayer, *Pennsylvania Politics and the Growth of Democracy, 1740-1776* (Harrisburg, 1953), in *William and Mary Quarterly*, XII (1955), 671.

monweals where the people are not deprived of their natural freedom by the power of tyrants." [6]

The central issue in seventeenth-century New England was not social equality, manhood suffrage, women's rights, or sympathy for the Levellers, or other tests which have been applied. The central issue was the source of authority for the establishment of a government. The English view was that no government could exist in a colony without a grant of power from the crown. The opposite view, held by certain English dissenters in New England, was that a group of people could create a valid government for themselves by means of a covenant, compact, or constitution. The authors of the Mayflower Compact and the Fundamental Orders of Connecticut operated on this assumption, although they did not carry it to the logical conclusion and call it democracy as did the people in Rhode Island. It is the basic assumption of the Declaration of Independence, a portion of which reads much like the words of Roger Williams written 132 years earlier.

The second proposition is that colonial governments on the eve of the Revolution did not function democratically, nor did the men who controlled them believe in democracy. Even if we agree that there was virtually manhood suffrage in Massachusetts, it is difficult, for me at least, to see it as a democracy. In 1760 the government was controlled by a superb political machine headed by Thomas Hutchinson, who with his relatives and political allies occupied nearly every important political office in the colony except the governorship. The Hutchinson oligarchy controlled the superior court, the council, the county courts, and the justices of the peace; with this structure of appointive office spread throughout the colony, it was able to control the house of representatives elected by the towns. For six years after 1760 the popular party in Boston, led by Oxenbridge Thacher and James Otis, suffered one defeat after another at the hands of the Hutchinson machine. The popular leaders in the town of Boston tried everything from slander to mob violence to get control of the government of the colony but it was not until after the Stamp Act crisis that they were able to win a majority of the house of representatives to their side. Even then, men like James Otis did not at first realize that the Stamp Act could be turned to advantage in the fight against the Hutchinson oligarchy.[7] In terms of political support between 1760 and 1765, if Massachusetts had a democratic leader, that man was Thomas Hutchinson, a charge to which he would have been the first to issue a horrified denial.

The third proposition is that before 1774 or 1775 the revolutionary movement was not a democratic movement, except by inadvertence. The pamphleteers who wrote on political and constitutional questions, and the

6. *English Historical Documents*, IX, *American Colonial Documents to 1775*, ed. Merrill Jensen (London and New York, 1955), pp. 168, 226, 174.

7. See Ellen E. Brennan, *Plural Office Holding in Massachusetts 1760-1780* (Chapel Hill, 1945), and "James Otis: Recreant and Patriot," *New England Quarterly*, XII (1939), 691-725.

town and county meetings and legislatures that resolved endlessly between 1763 and 1774, were concerned with the formulation of constitutional arguments to defend the colonies and their legislatures from interference by parliament.

The colonial theorists wrote much about the British constitution, the rights of Englishmen, and even of the laws of nature, but they accepted the British assumption that colonial governments derived from British charters and commissions. Their essential concern was with the relationship that existed, or ought to exist, between the British government and the colonial governments, and not with the relationship between man as man, and government itself. Such writers showed no interest in domestic problems, and when it was suggested that the arguments against taxation by parliament were equally applicable to the taxation of underrepresented areas in the colonies, or to dissenting religious groups, such suggestions were looked upon as being quite out of order.

The same indifference was displayed in the realm of political realities. The ardent leaders of the fight against British policies showed no interest in, or sympathy for, the discontent of back-country farmers or religious groups such as the Baptists. Instead, they temporarily joined with their political enemies to suppress or ignore it. Such sympathy as the discontented got, they got from the British government, or from colonial leaders charged with being tools of the British power.

The fact is that the popular leaders of the revolutionary movement had no program of domestic reform.[8] Instead, their program was a combination of a continuous assault on the local officeholding aristocracies and an ardent attack on British policies; and in the course of time they identified one with the other. It is sometimes difficult to tell with which side of the program the popular leaders were more concerned. In Massachusetts, for instance, before 1765 they were so violent in their attack on Hutchinson that they prevented Massachusetts from joining the other colonies in making formal protests against British legislation.

The fourth proposition is related to the third. It is that although the popular leaders in the colonies showed no interest in internal political and social change, they were still able to build up a political following, particularly in the seacoast towns. They were superb organizers, propagandists with a touch of genius, and possessed of an almost demonic energy in their dual fight against the local political aristocracies and British policies. After a few false starts such as that of James Otis, who at first called the Virginia Stamp Act Resolves treason,[9] the popular leaders took an extreme stand on the subject of colonial rights. The political aristocracies might object to British policies, as most of them did, but considering what they owed to British backing, they displayed an

---

8. For example, see Irving Mark, *Agrarian Conflicts in Colonial New York, 1711-1775* (New York, 1940); *The Carolina Back-Country on the Eve of the Revolution,* ed. Richard J. Hooker (Chapel Hill, 1953); and Elisha Douglass, *Rebels and Democrats* (Chapel Hill, 1955).

9. Brennan, "James Otis: Recreant and Patriot," p. 715.

understandable caution, a caution that made it impossible for them to pose as patriotic leaders.

The popular leaders were also willing to take extreme measures in practical opposition to British policies, ranging all the way from mob violence to non-importation agreements forced upon unwilling merchants. And with ever more force and violence they accused Americans who did not agree with them or their methods of knuckling under to British tyranny and of readiness to sell the liberties of their country for a little pelf. In the course of this campaign they appealed to the people at large. Men who normally could not or did not take part in political life, particularly in the cities, were invited to mass meetings where the rules of suffrage were ignored and where they could shout approval of resolutions carefully prepared in advance by their leaders. In addition, the mob was a constant factor in political life, particularly in Boston where it was efficiently organized. Mobs were used to nullify the Stamp Act, to harass British soldiers, to hamper the operations of the customs service, and to intimidate office holders.

All these activities on the part of the disfranchised, or the hitherto politically inactive, accustomed men to taking part in public affairs as never before; and it gave them an appetite for more. From the beginning of the crisis in 1774 onward, more and more "new men," which was the politest name their opponents called them, played an ever more active role, both on the level of practical politics and on the level of political theory. They began writing about and talking about what they called "democracy." And this was a frightening experience, not only to the conservative-minded leaders of the colonies, but to many of the popular leaders as well.

For instance, when a New York mass meeting gathered in May 1774 to answer the letter of the Boston Town Meeting asking for a complete stoppage of trade with Britain as an answer to the Boston Port Act, the people talked about far more than letter writing. One alarmed observer wrote: "I beheld my fellow-citizens very accurately counting all their chickens, not only before any of them were hatched, but before above one half of the eggs were laid. In short, they fairly contended about the future forms of our government, whether it should be founded upon aristocratic or democratic principles." The leaders had "gulled" the mob for years, and now, said Gouverneur Morris, the mob was waking up and could no longer be fooled. The only salvation for the aristocracy of New York was peace with Britain at almost any price.[10]

Another witness to the stirrings among the people was John Adams. Unlike Gouverneur Morris, he never wavered in his belief in independence, but at the same time he was constantly concerned with the danger of an internal upheaval. Years later in his "Autobiography," he recalled as vividly as if it had happened the day before an event that took place while he was home in Massachusetts in the fall of 1775. While there he

10. Gouverneur Morris to [John] Penn, May 20, 1774, in *English Historical Documents*, IX, 861-863.

met a man who had sometimes been his client. "He, though a common horse jockey, was sometimes in the right, and I had commonly been successful in his favor in our courts of law. He was always in the law, and had been sued in many actions at almost every court. As soon as he saw me, he came up to me, and his first salutation to me was, 'Oh! Mr. Adams, what great things have you and your colleagues done for us! We can never be grateful enough to you. There are no courts of justice now in this province, and I hope there never will be another.' " Then Adams goes on: "Is this the object for which I have been contending? said I to myself, for I rode along without any answer to this wretch. Are these the sentiments of such people, and how many of them are there in the country? Half the nation for what I know; for half the nation are debtors, if not more, and these have been, in all countries, the sentiments of debtors. If the power of the country should get into such hands, and there is great danger that it will, to what purpose have we sacrificed our time, health, and everything else? Surely we must guard against this spirit and these principles, or we shall repent of all our conduct." [11]

In May of 1776, with the talk of independence filling the air and the Virginia convention planning to draft a constitution, old Landon Carter of Virginia wrote to Washington bewailing the "ambition" that had "seized on so much ignorance all over the colony as it seems to have done; for this present convention abounds with too many of the inexperienced creatures to navigate our bark on this dangerous coast. . . ." As for independence, he said, "I need only tell you of one definition that I heard of Independency: It was expected to be a form of government that, by being independent of the rich men, every man would then be able to do as he pleased. And it was with this expectation they sent the men they did, in hopes they would plan such a form. One of the delegates I heard exclaim against the Patrolling Law, because a poor man was made to pay for keeping a rich man's slaves in order. I shamed the fool so much for it that he slunk away; but he got elected by it." [12]

One could go on endlessly giving examples like these from the hectic days between 1774 and 1776, examples of the fear among leaders of all shades of opinion that the people would get or were getting out of hand. Meanwhile there was an increasing amount of political writing in the newspapers, writing which was pointing in the direction of independence and the creation of new governments in America. More than a year before *Common Sense,* a piece which appeared first in the *Pennsylvania Packet* declared that "the history of kings is nothing but the history of the folly and depravity of human nature." "We read now and then, it is true, of a good king; so we read likewise of a prophet escaping unhurt from a lion's den, and of three men walking in a fiery furnace without having even their garments singed. The order of nature is as much

11. John Adams, "Autobiography," *The Works of John Adams,* ed. Charles F. Adams (Boston, 1856), II, 420-421.

12. *American Archives,* ed. Peter Force, 4th ser. (Washington, 1837-1846), VI, 390-391. May 9, 1776.

inverted in the first as it was in the last two cases. A good king is a miracle." [13]

By early 1776 the debate over future governments to be adopted was in full swing. Disliking intensely the ideas of government set forth in *Common Sense,* John Adams drafted his *Thoughts on Government.* His plan was modeled on the old government of Massachusetts, with an elective rather than a royal governor, of course, but it certainly contemplated no radical change in the political structure.[14] John Adams was no innovator. He deplored what he called "the rage for innovation" which had appeared in Massachusetts by June of 1776. The projects, said he, are not for repairing the building but for tearing it down. "The projects of county assemblies, town registers, and town probates of wills are founded in narrow notions, sordid stinginess, and profound ignorance, and tend directly to barbarism." [15]

There was equal alarm in the south at demands for change and new governments. Among those who sought to defend the old order was Carter Braxton. In a long address to the Virginia convention he praised the British constitution and declared that it would be "perverting all order to oblige us, by a novel government, to give up our laws, our customs, and our manners." The spirit or principles of limited monarchy should be preserved. Yet, he said, we daily see it condemned by the advocates of "popular governments. . . . The systems recommended to the colonies seem to accord with the temper of the times, and are fraught with all the tumult and riot incident to simple democracy. . . ." Braxton declared that democracies would not tolerate wealth, and that they could exist only in countries where all the people are poor from necessity. Nowhere in history could he find an example of a successful democracy. What he proposed for Virginia was a three-part government with a house of representatives elected by the voters for three years. The house, in turn, would choose a governor to serve during good behavior and a council of twenty-four to hold their places for life and to act as an upper house of the legislature.[16] Braxton in Virginia, like John Adams in Massachusetts, hoped to make the transition from dependence to independence without any fundamental political change.

But change was in the air, and writer after writer sought to formulate new ideas about government and to offer concrete suggestions for the theoretical foundations and political structures of the new states to be.

13. *English Historical Documents,* IX, 816-817.

14. *Works of John Adams,* IV, 189-200.

15. To John Winthrop, Philadelphia, June 23, 1776, in Mass. Hist. Soc. *Collections,* 5th ser. (Boston, 1878), IV, 310. This was in reply to a letter of John Winthrop, written on June 1, in which he reported to Adams on the various schemes afoot in Massachusetts. *Ibid.,* 305-308.

16. *The Virginia Gazette* (Dixon and Hunter), June 8, 1776. This had been printed earlier in pamphlet form. For similar ideas see the letter of William Hooper, North Carolina delegate to the Continental Congress, to the North Carolina Provincial Congress. October 26, 1776, in *The Colonial Records of North Carolina,* ed. W. L. Saunders, X (1890), 866-869.

In 1775, on hearing that congress had given advice to New Hampshire on the establishment of a government, General John Sullivan offered his thoughts to the revolutionary congress of his colony. All government, he wrote, ought to be instituted for the good of the people. There should be no conflicting branches in imitation of the British constitution "so much celebrated by those who understand nothing of it. . . ." The two houses of the legislature and a governor should all be elected by the people. No danger can arise to a state "from giving the people a free and full voice in their own government." The so-called checks upon the licentiousness of the people "are only the children of designing or ambitious men, no such thing being necessary. . . ." [17]

In the middle colonies appeared an address "To the People of North America on the Different Kinds of Government." After defining monarchy, aristocracy, oligarchy, and democracy, the anonymous writer said: "Popular government—sometimes termed democracy, republic, or commonwealth—is the plan of civil society wherein the community at large takes the care of its own welfare, and manages its concerns by representatives elected by the people out of their own body."

"Seeing the happiness of the people is the true end of government; and it appearing by the definition, that the popular form is the only one which has this for its object; it may be worth inquiring into the causes which have prevented its success in the world."

This writer then undertakes to explain the failure of former democracies. First of all, he says that past republics tried democracy too late and contained within them remnants of aristocracies and military cliques which disliked it. A second cause was that men did not have adequate knowlelge of representation and that their large and tumultuous assemblies made it possible for unscrupulous men to charge all troubles to the constitution. A third cause of failure has been the political writers who from ignorance or ulterior motives have tried to discredit democracy. "This has been carried to such a length with many, that the mentioning a democracy constantly excites in them the idea of anarchy; and few, except such as have emancipated themselves from the shackles of political bigotry and prejudice, can talk of it with patience, and hearken to anything offered in its defence." Such are the causes of the destruction of former republics, but the Americans have the best opportunity ever open to mankind to form a free government, "the last and best plan that can possibly exist." [18]

In "The Interest of America," another writer says that new governments must soon be created in America and that "the good of the people is the ultimate end of civil government." Therefore, "we should assume that mode of government which is most equitable and adapted to the good of mankind . . . and I think there can be no doubt that a well-regulated democracy is most equitable." The annual or frequent choice of magistrates is "most likely to prevent usurpation and tyranny; and

17. John Sullivan to Meshech Weare, Winter Hill [Mass.], December 11, 1775, in *American Archives*, IV, 241-242.

18. *American Archives*, V, 180-183. [March 1776.]

most likely to secure the privileges of the people." Legislatures should be unicameral, for a plurality of branches leads to endless contention and a waste of time.[19]

In New England, where the revolutionary congresses of Massachusetts and New Hampshire were controlled by leaders along the seacoast, there was a growing discontent among the people of the back-country counties. Out of it came one of the clearest democratic statements of the times: "The People are the Best Governors." The author starts with the premise that "there are many very noisy about liberty, but are aiming at nothing more than personal power and grandeur." "God," he said, "gave mankind freedom by nature, made every man equal to his neighbor, and has virtually enjoined them to govern themselves by their own laws." Representatives in legislatures should have only the power to make laws. They should not have the power to elect officials or to elect councils or senates to veto legislation. Only the people have this power. If there must be senates, they should be elected by the people of the state at large and should have only advisory powers. Representation should not be according to taxable property, for "Nature itself abhors such a system of civil government, for it will make an inequality among the people and set up a number of lords over the rest." Representation according to population also has its difficulties. The solution is for each town to have one representative, with more for larger towns if the legislature thinks fit. So far as property qualifications for representatives are concerned, there should be none. "Social virtue and knowledge . . . is the best and only necessary qualification of the person before us." If we have property qualifications "we root out virtue; and what will then become of the genuine principle of freedom?" "Let it not be said in future generations that money was made by the founders of the American states an essential qualification in the rulers of a free people." The writer proposed annual elections of a one-house legislature, of a governor, and of the judges of the superior court. The people in the counties should elect annually all their own officials—judges, sheriffs, and others—as should the inhabitants of the towns. And in all elections "any orderly free male of ordinary capacity" should have the right to vote if he has lived in a town for a year.[20]

From such discussions one may sum up certain of the essential ideas. (1) They agree that the "good" or the "happiness" of the people is the only end of government. (2) They agree that "democracy" is the best form of government to achieve that end. (3) They show a distrust of men when in power—a distrust shared with far more conservative-minded writers of the times.

As to details of government there are variations, but they do agree on fundamentals. (1) The legislatures, whether one or two houses, are to be elected by the people. (2) Public officials, state and local, are to be elected by the people or by their representatives in the legislatures. (3)

19. *Ibid.*, VI, 840-843. [June 1776.]

20. Reprinted in Frederick Chase, *A History of Dartmouth College and the Town of Hanover, New Hampshire* (Cambridge, 1891), I, Appendix D, 654-663.

There should be annual elections. (4) Some argue for manhood suffrage, and one writer even advocated that tax-paying widows should vote. (5) There should be freedom of religion, at least for Protestants; in any case, freedom from taxation to support established churches.

One may well ask: did such theoretical discussions have any meaning in terms of practical politics, or were they idle speculations by anonymous writers without influence? The answer is that they did have meaning. I have already cited the discussion of the principles of government in New York in the spring of 1774, and the litigious jockey in Massachusetts in 1775 who hoped that the courts would remain closed forever. These are not isolated examples. By the end of 1775 all sorts of organized activity was under way, ranging in place from North Carolina to New Hampshire, and from militia groups to churches.

In North Carolina the defeat of the Regulators in 1771 had not ended discontent but merely suppressed it. By September 1775 Mecklenburg County was instructing its delegates in the provincial congress to work for a plan of government providing for equal representation and the right to vote for every freeman who supported the government, either in person or property. Legislation should not be a "divided right"; no man or body of men should be "invested with a negative on the voice of the people duly collected. . . ." [21] By November 1776, when North Carolina elected a congress to write its first state constitution, Mecklenburg County was even more specific in its instructions. It told its delegates that they were to endeavor to establish a free government under the authority of the people of North Carolina, and that the government was to be a "simple democracy, or as near it as possible." In fixing fundamental principles, the delegates were to "oppose everything that leans to aristocracy or power in the hands of the rich and chief men exercised to the oppression of the poor." [22]

In the middle colonies militia organizations made demands and suggestions. Pennsylvania was in turmoil, with the assembly controlled by the opponents of independence and the revolutionary party working in large measure through a voluntary militia organization called the Associators. In February 1776 a committee of privates from the Philadelphia Associators told the assembly "that it has been the practice of all countries, and is highly reasonable, that all persons . . . who expose their lives in the defense of a country, should be admitted to the enjoyment of all the rights and privileges of a citizen of that country. . . ." All Associators should be given the right to vote.[23]

In June the committee of privates again protested to the legislature. This time they denied the right of the assembly to appoint two brigadier generals for the Associators as recommended by the Continental Congress. The privates declared that since many of them could not vote, they were

21. *Colonial Records of North Carolina*, X, 239-242. [Sept. 1775.]
22. Ibid., 870, a-f. [Nov. 1776.]
23. Votes and Proceedings of the Assembly, Feb. 23, 1776, in *Pennsylvania Archives*, 8th ser. [Harrisburg, 1935], VIII, 7406.

not represented in the assembly. Furthermore, many counties where the Associators were most numerous did not have proportional representation. And for that matter, since many members of the assembly were members of a religious profession "totally averse to military defense," they could not possibly be called representatives of the Associators.[24]

While such ideas were being expounded in Pennsylvania, some militia in Maryland were proposing a new constitution. There was a growing discontent in Maryland with the revolutionary convention which was opposed to independence, and whose members were appointing one another to military posts. Government by convention should stop, said one writer, and regular government be instituted.[25]

Late in June 1776 deputies from the militia battalions in Anne Arundel County met and proposed a constitution to be submitted to the people of the county. They started out with the declaration that the right to legislate is in "every member of the community," but that for convenience the right must be delegated to representatives chosen by the people. The legislature must never form a separate interest from the community at large, and its branches must "be independent of and balance each other, and all dependent on the people." There should be a two-house legislature chosen annually "as annual elections are most friendly to liberty, and the oftener power reverts to the people, the greater will be the security for a faithful discharge of it." All provincial officials, including judges, should be elected annually by joint ballot of the two houses. All county officials should be chosen annually by the people of each county. Nothing is said of property qualifications for either voting or office-holding. So far as taxes are concerned, "the unjust mode of taxation by poll" should be abolished, and all monies raised should be according to a fair and equal assessment of people's estates.[26]

In New Jersey the revolutionary congress, like that in other colonies, was trying to prevent change and was maintaining the land qualification cannot conceive the wise author of our existence ever designed that a certain quantity of earth on which we tread should be annexed to a man for voting for its members. But the complaints grew so loud that it was forced to yield. One petition in 1776, for instance, declared that "we to complete his dignity and fit him for society. Was the sole design of government either the security of land or money, the possession of either or both of these would be the only necessary qualifications for its members. But we apprehend the benign intentions of a well regulated government to extend to the security of much more valuable possessions—the rights and privileges of freemen, for the defense of which every kind of property and even life itself have been liberally expended." [27]

24. Ibid., 7546-47. June 14, 1776.

25. "An American" in "To the People of Maryland," *American Archives*, VI, 1094-96.

26. Ibid., 1092-94. June 26-27, 1776.

27. Richard P. McCormick, *The History of Voting in New Jersey . . . 1664-1911* (New Brunswick, 1953), pp. 66-68.

In Massachusetts the Baptists were quick to draw a parallel between the fight for civil liberty against England and their own fight for religious liberty. Baptists were being jailed for refusal to pay taxes to support churches. Their leader, the Reverend Isaac Backus, put Sam Adams squarely on the spot in January 1774. "I fully concur with your grand maxim," wrote Backus, "that it is essential to liberty that representation and taxation go together." Hence, since the representatives in the Massachusetts legislature have only civil qualifications, how can they levy ecclesiastical taxes? "And I am bold in it," Backus goes on, "that taxes laid by the British Parliament upon America are not more contrary to civil freedom, than these taxes are to the very nature of liberty of conscience. . . ." He hopes, he says, that Adams will do something about it so that a large number of peaceable people "may not be forced to carry their complaints before those who would be glad to hear that the legislature of Massachusetts deny to their fellow servants that liberty which they so earnestly insist upon for themselves. A word to the wise is sufficient." [28]

Samuel Adams was not interested in liberty of conscience, particularly for Baptists, and he did not reply. But Backus pursued him to the first Continental Congress in Philadelphia where a four-hour meeting was held in Carpenter's Hall one night. The Massachusetts delegation met with the Baptists, but with a large audience present, among whom were the Quaker leaders James and Israel Pemberton, and members of congress like Joseph Galloway. The Backus diary gives a picture of Sam and John Adams quite literally squirming as the Baptists cited the facts of religious life in Massachusetts.[29] One can well imagine with what delight Galloway and the Pembertons looked on as the Massachusetts delegation vainly tried to wriggle out of a dilemma produced by the contradiction between their theory and their practice.

The Declaration of Independence was taken seriously by many Americans, or at least they found its basic philosophy useful in battling for change in the new states. Nowhere was this done more neatly than in Grafton County, New Hampshire. The Provincial Congress was in the control of eastern leaders and they refused to grant representation that the western towns thought adequate. In calling elections in the fall of 1776, the Congress grouped various towns together for electing representatives and told them that the men they elected must own real estate worth £200 lawful money. Led by professors at an obscure little college at Hanover, the people of Grafton County went on strike. They refused to hold elections, and town after town met and passed resolutions. The whole procedure of the Congress was unconstitutional. No plan of representation had been adopted since the Declaration of Independence. By the Declaration, said Hanover and two other towns in a joint statement, "we conceive that the powers of government reverted to the people at

28. To Samuel Adams, Jan. 19, 1774, in Alvah Hovey, *A Memoir of the Life and Times of the Rev. Isaac Backus* (Boston, 1859), pp. 195-197.
29. *Ibid.*, ch. xv.

large, and of course annihilated the political existence of the Assembly which then was. . . ." Six other towns joined together and declared it to be "our humble opinion, that when the declaration of independency took place, the Colonies were absolutely in a state of nature, and the powers of government reverted to the people at large. . . ." Such being the case, the Provincial Congress has no authority to combine towns, each of which is entitled to representation as a corporate entity. And it has no right to limit the choice of representatives to the owners of £200, said the people of Lyme, because "every elector in free states is capable of being elected." [30]

It seems clear, to me at least, that by 1776 there were people in America demanding the establishment of democratic state governments, by which they meant legislatures controlled by a majority of the voters, and with none of the checks upon their actions such as had existed in the colonies. At the same time there were many Americans who were determined that there should be no changes except those made inevitable by separation from Great Britain.

The history of the writing of the first state constitutions is to a large extent the history of the conflict between these two ideals of government. The conflict can be exaggerated, of course, for there was considerable agreement on structural details. Most of the state constitutions worked out in written form the structure of government that had existed in the colonies, all the way from governors, two-house legislatures, and judicial systems, to the forms of local government. In terms of structure, little that is revolutionary is to be found. Even the much maligned unicameral legislature of Pennsylvania was only a continuation of what Pennsylvania had had since the beginning of the century.

The significant thing is not the continuity of governmental structure, but the alteration of the balance of power within the structure, and in the political situation resulting from the break away from the supervising power of a central government—that of Great Britain.

The first and most revolutionary change was in the field of basic theory. In May 1776, to help bring about the overthrow of the Pennsylvania assembly, the chief stumbling block in the way of independence, Congress resolved that all governments exercising authority under the crown of Great Britain should be suppressed, and that "all the powers of government [be] exerted under the authority of the people of the colonies. . . ." John Adams described it as "the most important resolution that ever was taken in America." [31] The Declaration of Independence spelled it out in terms of the equality of men, the sovereignty of the people, and the right of a people to change their governments as they pleased.

Second: the Revolution ended the power of a sovereign central gov-

30. *American Archives,* 5th ser. (Washington, 1848-1853), III, 1223-24, and Chase, *History of Dartmouth,* I, 426-433.

31. *Warren-Adams Letters,* I (Boston, 1917), 245; in Mass. Hist. Soc. *Collections,* Vols. 72, 73.

ernment over the colonies. Britain had had the power to appoint and remove governors, members of upper houses of legislatures, judges, and other officials. It had the power to veto colonial legislation, to review cases appealed from colonial supreme courts, and to use armed force. All of this superintending power was wiped out by independence.

Third: the new central government created in America by the Articles of Confederation was, in a negative sense at least, a democratic government. The Congress of the United States had no power over either the states or their citizens. Hence, each state could govern itself as it pleased, and as a result of some of the new state constitutions, this often meant by a majority of the voters within a state.

Fourth: in writing the state constitutions, change was inevitable. The hierarchy of appointed legislative, executive, and judicial officials which had served as a check upon the elective legislatures was gone. The elective legislature became the supreme power in every state, and the lower houses, representing people however inadequately, became the dominant branch. The appointive houses of colonial times were replaced by elective senates, which in theory were supposed to represent property. They were expected to, and sometimes did, act as a check upon the lower houses, but their power was far less than that of pre-war councils.

Fifth: the office of governor underwent a real revolution. The governors of the royal colonies had, in theory at least, vast powers, including an absolute veto. In the new constitutions, most Americans united in shearing the office of governor of virtually all power.

Sixth: state supreme courts underwent a similar revolution. Under the state constitutions they were elected by the legislatures or appointed by governors who were elected officials. And woe betide a supreme court that tried to interfere with the actions of a legislature.

What such changes meant in terms of political realities was that a majority of voters within a state, if agreed upon a program and persistent enough, could do what it wanted, unchecked by governors or courts or appeals to a higher power outside the state.

There were other areas in which changes took place, although they were only beginnings. A start was made in the direction of ending the property qualification for voting and office-holding. A few states established what amounted to manhood suffrage, and a few years later even women voted in New Jersey although that was stopped when it appeared that woman suffrage meant only a means of stuffing ballot boxes. A few states took steps in the direction of representation according to population, a process as yet unsolved in the United States. A large step was taken in the direction of disestablishing state churches, but on the whole one still had to be a Protestant, and a Trinitarian at that, to hold office.

In connection with office-holding, there is one eighteenth-century American idea that is worthy of a whole study by itself, and that is the concept of rotation in office. Many Americans were convinced that office-holding bred a lust for power in the holder. Therefore there must be frequent, if not annual, elections; and there must be a limitation on the time one might spend in certain offices. There is probably no more remarkable self-denying ordinance in the history of politics than the provision in the Articles of Confederation that no man could be a member of Congress more than three years out of any six. I have often been accused of wanting to go back to the Articles of Confederation, which is nonsense, but there are times when I do wish that this one provision might be revived in the twentieth century.

What I have done in this paper is to set before you some of the reasons for believing that the American Revolution was a democratic movement, not in origin, but in result. Certainly the political leaders of the eighteenth century thought the results were democratic. Whether they thought the results were good or bad is another story.

CLARENCE L. VER STEEG

The American Revolution Considered as an Economic Movement

HISTORIANS for a generation or more have been so sensitive to economic influences during the Revolutionary period that a modern scholar places his reputation in jeopardy if he fails to take account of such forces, regardless of what phase of political, social, or cultural life he is investigating. Although this sensitivity did not have its birth with the notable works of Charles A. Beard, they assuredly stand as an unmistakable landmark. The results, in the main, have been good. Our perspective of the Revolutionary generation has broadened, our understanding deepened; and the main stream of events has often been magnificently illuminated.

In contrast, historians have tended to neglect the other side of the coin, giving relatively little, if any, attention to the influences that political, social, and cultural forces might have had upon economic development. Even studies embracing what are normally considered "economic" subjects—such as the role of merchants, the course of trade, the change in the land systems—have almost invariably been oriented toward a distinct vantage point: What effect did a change in land policy have upon social structure? How did the course of trade affect diplomatic policy? How significant was the position of the merchant in the formulation of political decisions? As illuminating as such studies have been, the results have given us only a partial view, for we have yet to answer the questions

Reprinted by permission from the *Huntington Library Quarterly*, XX (1957), 361-372.

which arise when economic developments are approached from the reverse, and what many economists would call the proper perspective. Did the modification of political institutions affect the economy? Did political action influence economic change? Were social theories produced that modified the actions of merchant and planter capitalists? Did American society by its very structure circumscribe or direct the course of economic change? How significant was the American Revolution generally upon the rise of capitalism in America? If historians are to assess the impact of the American Revolution upon the whole of American life, these questions and others of equal importance need more precise answers than we now possess.

To illustrate the lack of balance in current historical writing, one need only compare the emphasis given by scholars to the social rather than the economic consequences of the Revolution. Numerous monographic and more general works covering the period could be cited to support this point, but textbooks in United States history give as reliable a testimony as one would wish. Whereas none would be considered complete without its section neatly entitled "Social Impact of the Revolution," or something similar, followed by appropriate paragraphs of description and analysis, no textbook examined by the writer has a similar section devoted to the economic impact. Indeed, it is rare when the possibility of economic results is so much as mentioned. The textbooks in American economic history offer little more. A chapter on the Revolution is seldom included. When it is, too often its focus is "economic causation"; in fact, most economic histories are organized in such a way that one would scarcely realize that a Revolution had taken place. Let it be quickly said that this comparison casts no reflection whatsoever on the textbook writers; the texts, quite properly, merely show the trend of scholarship. Although individual scholars, treating isolated subjects, have sometimes attempted to evaluate the economic effect of the Revolution, no major attempt has been made to bring together the existing material, much less to strike out into unexplored areas where fresh insights and new material would provide the ingredients for a solid synthesis. The only possible exception in the literature of the Revolution is Evarts B. Greene's helpful chapter on "The War's Economic Effects" in his *The Revolutionary Generation, 1763-1790* (New York, 1943). Greene gives a useful summary of some of the scholarship, but his approach is rather limited. Furthermore, Greene's chapter has never caught the attention of scholars; it has not been a departure point for new investigation.[1]

What becomes increasingly obvious, therefore, is that this significant

1. It will be interesting to see whether or not the volume in Rinehart's series on the *Economic History of the United States,* covering the period 1776-1815, will grapple with this problem or whether it will be a straight narrative. There are three places where a summary of the general economic development for these years can be found: Edward Channing, *History of the United States* (New York, 1912), III, ch. iii; Clarence L. Ver Steeg, *Robert Morris, Revolutionary Financier* (Philadelphia, 1954), ch. iii, stressing the period up to 1781; and Merrill Jensen, *The New Nation* (New York, 1950), pp. 179-244, stressing the Confederation period.

theme, the impact of the Revolution upon the course of economic develop-ment, rates a thorough book-length study. This article can be little more than an introduction to an exciting historical problem. Its primary pur-pose is to focus attention upon the importance of the theme in terms of an area for research and in terms of a more complete understanding of the Revolutionary epoch. It will also attempt to indicate possible ap-proaches to the problem, to make a preliminary assessment of some of the existing material, and, on occasion, to suggest additional theses that might help to define the problem. Part of the following discussion, there-fore, will view familiar material from a somewhat different perspective, while other parts will suggest areas that seem to deserve more elaborate consideration if historians are eventually to make a realistic evaluation, and to see the Revolution in its fullest context.[2]

One of the most obvious, but largely overlooked, changes brought by the Revolution, carrying with it the broadest economic implications, was the new relationship between the rights of private property and mineral rights or, to use a broader term, natural resources. A careful study of this transition has never been made, but it is clear that whereas mineral rights in colonial times resided with the sovereign, to be granted or reserved as circumstances dictated, the Revolution saw such rights brought eventually within the the purview of private property. The control of natural resources, therefore, was secured more firmly by private enterprisers.

It will be recalled that the charters of most colonies, though granting the rights to minerals and mines, contained a clause reserving the fifth part for the crown. This figure was more than a token; it represented an acknowledgment that the crown, when it disposed of land, possessed the power to grant or retain natural resources under the soil. That such grants were made at all merely indicates that the crown did not believe such resources existed in quantity and, in consequence, it could be generous with an added "inducement" to colonization. As a result, there was some mining activity in the majority of colonies before the Revolution. It is interesting, however, to speculate how magnanimous the crown would have been in granting any mineral rights if precious metals, the priority minerals of the seventeenth and eighteenth centuries, had suddenly been discovered in the colonies; given the basic mercantile position of the mother country it is safe to say that its terms would have been somewhat less liberal.

From the point of view of this article, it is significant that the sov-ereign right of the central government over mineral resources, though retained as a matter of form, apparently was not preserved in substance. So far as my investigation goes, there seems to be no discussion of this point in the exhaustive debates that took place on the land question dur-ing the Revolution. The Land Ordinance of 1785, it is true, reserved "one-third part of all gold, silver, lead, and copper mines" for the

2. Because of the exploratory nature of this article, only a few citations have been made.

national government, but if a scholar relies on the standard monographs on the national land system, nothing seems to have come of it. Although the problem requires more exhaustive study, it would seem that one of the legacies of the Revolution, established almost by default, made an incalculable impact on American society where the command of critical natural resources—coal, iron ore, oil and gas, precious metals, and many others—has been a key factor.

Two of the basic elements in eighteenth-century economic life, farming and land policy, were also greatly influenced by the Revolution. Quite naturally, the celebrated Land Ordinance of 1785 comes immediately to mind, for it was largely responsible for "institutionalizing" the basic productive unit in Midwestern agriculture, the family farm. What this meant for the course of economic development is significant; interestingly enough, arguments are still raging as to the merits of the established family farm as compared with a much larger unit, seemingly more suitable to the complex economy of modern times. The Land Ordinance is only the most obvious of more subtle changes from the land practices of the colonial period, some of them procedural and others substantive, depending upon the region studied. Moreover, the stimulus given to land speculation by some of the interstate and international business groups—an area in which additional research would clarify many issues—is of great importance in itself.[3]

Farming, at least in two regions, the South and New England, underwent a profound change. That historian of agriculture, Lewis C. Gray, whose discriminating analysis and careful judgment commands respect if not always agreement, goes so far as to assert: "For the South it [the American Revolution] was also a great economic Revolution."[4] He particularly emphasizes that general farming, as distinguished from the production of staples in certain areas, was stimulated; and he stresses the importance of the new internal lines of communication and trade. Gray has received additional ammunition from Professor Lawrence Harper who has traced the relative production of specific staples. Indigo, for example, ceased to be produced soon after the Revolution, not so much because indigo failed to enjoy the British subsidy of colonial times, but rather because the British subsidy after the Revolution, applying as it did only to producers within the empire, resulted in a price advantage that the South could not meet.[5] It is also well to remember that the

3. Payson J. Treat's standard monograph, *The National Land System, 1785-1820* (New York, 1910), ch. ii, makes some comparison between colonial land systems and that evolved after the Revolution. It is entirely possible, however, that the "New England influence" on the national land system has been overstated. It was a thesis that was given wide currency before new research revised some previously accepted assumptions on eighteenth-century New England land policy.

4. Lewis C. Gray, *History of Agriculture in the Southern United States to 1860* (New York, 1941), II, 613.

5. Lawrence A. Harper, "The Effect of the Navigation Acts on the Thirteen Colonies," in *The Era of the American Revolution,* ed. R. B. Morris (New York, 1939), pp. 24-25, and n. 61.

damage caused by the fighting—the crops and livestock destroyed, and the wasted fields—meant that the South needed time to rebuild its plantation economy, especially in South Carolina and Georgia. Indeed, the desperate search for new staples to replace the loss of indigo, together with the limited geographical area where rice could be produced, helps to explain the renewed interest in cotton, which had been experimented with for a century previous to independence but never produced in quantity.

Although the New England farmer generally was not asked to face the ravages caused by military engagements, the Revolution had a profound effect upon New England agriculture. The decisive change that occurred when its customary marketing outlets were eliminated, especially those to the West Indies, was not immediately apparent, for until 1780 war-born markets took up the slack. With the sharp cutback in wartime markets starting late in 1781, and with no comparable peacetime markets to replace them, the New England farmer suffered a blow from which he never fully recovered. It is highly probable that the despair and discontent of agrarian New England in the 1780's is largely explicable in terms of the economic consequences of the Revolution.[6]

Trade, as well as agriculture and land policy, was never the same as a result of the Revolution. In some areas it was greatly broadened; in others it was sharply restricted. Furthermore the lines of trade were modified and mercantile connections were altered to meet the new circumstances. Although this effect of the Revolution has received some attention, more exacting studies are needed before it can be adequately measured.

The opening of the China trade, for example, was a direct consequence of the Revolution. In colonial times, the British imperial system made any notion of such a trade an unattainable dream. With the elimination of the British restrictions, this new vista was opened; and the business enterprisers of the new republic, anticipating its promise of rich rewards, rushed to exploit it. It matters not that their hopes were, in part, built upon illusions, for these illusions were quickly dispelled. What is significant is that the Asiatic trade introduced new products, created new demands, and, in some respects, educated this country's merchants in new trading techniques. William B. Weeden's apt statement deserves to be quoted; he asserts that the Revolution marked a break where one passes "from the Peter Faneuils, the negro and rum dealers of the middle century, to the Derbys, Perkinses, Thorndikes. . . . These men brought the far Eastern world home to its new counterpart in the West." [7] The influ-

6. There is some difference of opinion among scholars who have recently surveyed this problem. Oscar and Mary Handlin's *Commonwealth; A Study of the Role of Government in the American Economy: Massachusetts, 1774-1861* (New York and London, 1947), pp. 1-52, is a good evaluation for the whole New England economy. Percy Bidwell and John Falconer's *History of Agriculture in the Northern United States to 1860* (Washington, 1925), is of no help.

7. William B. Weeden, *Economic and Social History of New England, 1620-1789* (Boston and New York, 1890), II, 821-822.

ence of this trade, of course, was not confined to New England. It was a Pennsylvanian, Robert Morris, who was mainly responsible for outfitting the first American ship to Asiatic waters, and it was a New Yorker, John Jacob Astor, whose career was built upon the rewards of this trade.

Whereas the Pacific trade was opened, the Caribbean trade was sharply reduced. Many factors were responsible, not the least of course being the British and French imperial systems, which automatically established a barrier against commodities from the new nation. Where the West Indies had served as an important market for fisheries, livestock, lumber, rum, and other goods during the colonial period and had acted as the crucial entrepôt during the War of Independence itself, it was suddenly closed to American products. How significant this result was for the economy of the new country has often been suggested, but it is a theme that still requires more elaborate and precise investigation.[8]

When trade is basically modified, it is axiomatic that mercantile connections are modified as well. As the most casual reading of the recently published volumes on eighteenth-century merchants will testify, the impact of the Revolution was profound. Some trading connections were completely changed; in others the nature of the trade itself was altered; in still other cases, a particular merchant or merchant group either won or lost its relative position in the trading community. The Pepperrells of Piscataqua, remaining loyal to Britain, abandoned American shores; the Browns of Providence, though they maintained their important position in the trading community, modified their business connections and adjusted their manufacturing interest to suit the new era; in New York City, James Beekman, whose business was seriously crippled during the Revolution when he was forced to flee from New York City to escape the British, found after the war that the pattern of trade relationships he used with success before 1776 was no longer applicable; Robert Morris, whose relative position within the mercantile community had improved so significantly that he could properly be called the Prince of Merchants, found it not only necessary after 1783 to establish a new network of business partnerships to adjust to the times, but also advantageous to expand his business operations and diversify his investments.[9]

General business organization, as well as the careers of individual merchants, was influenced by the Revolution. Robert East's indispensable book has demonstrated the intricate connections between business groups during the Revolution; but he was primarily interested in their political and to some extent social impact.[10] Using some of the identical material,

8. Merrill Jensen believes that there was less disruption to the West India trade than most scholars have asserted (*op. cit.*, pp. 198-199).

9. Byron Fairchild, *Messrs. William Pepperrell: Merchants at Piscataqua* (Ithaca, N. Y., 1954). James B. Hedges, *The Browns of Providence Plantation: Colonial Years* (Cambridge, Mass., 1952), pp. 285-286, p. 306. Philip L. White, *The Beekmans of New York* (New York, 1956), pp. 441-530; Clarence L. Ver Steeg, *Robert Morris, Revolutionary Financier* (Philadelphia, 1954), ch. x.

10. *Business Enterprise in the American Revolutionary Era* (New York, 1938), *passim*.

it is possible to reverse the coin and see the results upon economic life: the rise of multiple partnerships and the beginnings of the corporate structure; the expansion of business groups to include every major marketing center; and the modification of these connections to meet new trade and business opportunities. When the Revolution so profoundly affected so many of its most representative mercantile leaders and the structure of business generally, how can it ever be said that it had little impact upon the economic development of the United States or the rise of commercial capitalism in the young republic!

A discussion of trade during the Revolution inevitably leads to the subject of interstate commerce, especially of course to the fact that its control was placed within the framework of the national government. This subject has become so commonplace that there is a tendency to dismiss it without relating its significance to the rise of commercial capitalism. During the first six decades of the eighteenth century one of the key signs of economic maturation and of developing commercial capitalism was the increased specialization that occurred within the colonies. Each region—New England, the Middle Colonies, and the South—was producing commodities for market that were best suited to its resources. This specialization, among other things, stimulated intercolonial trade. When the Revolution placed its blessing upon this development by giving control of interstate commerce to the national government (the Articles of Confederation in allocating this power to the individual states were actually running counter to the colonial experience and, it should be added, to reality) the consequences were so significant as to be almost incalculable. An unlimited, unfettered, internal market not only stimulated the fruition of commercial capitalism, but also laid down the basic pattern that was to provide an expanding market for the industrial America that would eventually emerge.

The problem of money and money supply and its relation to economic development is a theme that runs through American history, but we still need an evaluation of the effect of the financial experience and policies of the Revolution upon the economic development of the nation. For a nation based upon a money economy, the mere act of transfer, shifting the financial problems from Britain to the United States, is obviously important for the direction of economic development, but scholars have yet to study the finances in this context.

There are, however, other promising approaches, one of which could focus around the concept of an expanding economy. It is possible, for example, that the extensive use of paper money—far outreaching any colonial experience—stimulated general economic activity, although this thesis requires a more precise examination before it can be accepted. Moreover, a number of alert minds during these formative years explored the relationship between national credit and an expanded national economy—Peletiah Webster, Robert Morris, Gouverneur Morris, and Alexander Hamilton, to cite the most obvious. Still another part of the story is the creation of commercial banks, made possible only by the act of Independence. Although the Bank of North America, chartered in 1781, was first, it was quickly imitated by banks in Massachusetts and New York and plans were laid to create others. The critical role played by these institutions is a matter of record, particularly in their credit experience and their role in the expansion of the economy. Without question, such ideas, practices, policies, and institutions in financial affairs—the result of the Revolution—played a significant role in the economic development of the period; indeed, it is possible that careful study and analysis will find that not nearly enough stress has been placed on their far reaching effects.

Another area requiring further research is manufacturers.[11] At first glance this plea may appear unnecessary, for numerous historians assert that manufacturing was greatly extended, often supporting such claims with some specific illustrations. What is overlooked, however, is how often historians are merely quoting each other. The few basic economic studies that have included a section on manufacturing—so far as the writer knows, no single monograph on manufacturing in the Revolution exists— are sadly in need of revision. In addition, scholars have failed to distinguish between an increase in production and an increase in total "plant" capacity, a crucial feature of the industrial expansion in the First and Second World Wars. It is logical to assume that the demand for guns, wagons, tents, clothing, and other articles brought an expansion in total productive capacity, but the evidence is not conclusive; nor is there so much as a well-informed estimate as to the degree of expansion.

Another factor that remains virtually unnoticed is the expansion of foreign investments in the United States during and after the Revolution. Before independence, quite naturally, neither French nor Dutch capital was invested in American enterprise; almost immediately upon the outbreak of war, however, key figures in both countries appeared to exploit the opportunities opening up in the new nation. In France such great names as that of Chaumont were prominent; in Holland, the Willinks and the Van Stapenhorsts. Some of the investment was purely speculative —the "investments" in currency, for example. In other cases, it was geared to more lasting enterprises, such as the French financial backing given to several new commercial houses. It can also be assumed that foreign investment in American securities must have played some part in capital formation during this period, but there has not been so much as a scholarly guess as to how significant a part. More important, the question of British investment has been neglected. Leland Jenks's fine study of the migration of British capital to the United States begins too late to throw much light on the Revolutionary epoch, with the result

11. It is of interest to note that J. Franklin Jameson, *The American Revolution Considered as a Social Movement* (Princeton, 1926), spends an entire chapter on "Industry and Commerce," although it is difficult to see how he relates it directly to social change, except to state that the "Revolution brought ultimate benefit to the agriculture, the manufacures, and the commerce of the United States of America" (p. 114). The focus of this article, in contrast, is upon those areas where the Revolution may have altered the direction or emphasis of economic development.

that our information is less than sketchy for the prewar as well as the immediate postwar period. Although historians have not given the entire subject of foreign investment its due, and in consequence we cannot speak of the results with confidence, it most certainly is an area of almost limitless possibilities.

Another promising approach, but one that has attracted little attention, is to use material normally discussed in terms of social history. The abolition of primogeniture and entail is a case in point. In most discussions the social consequences of these acts are emphasized: making the stratification produced by a set land system more flexible and thereby encouraging democratization. Seldom, if ever, is the abolition of primogeniture and entail considered in terms of its economic impact, a perspective of equal, if not greater, importance. To encourage a flexible land system where more efficient producers using up-to-date techniques can thrive, in contrast to a static system that settles for the status quo, is surely a matter of some importance. Indeed, it is instructive that historians have recently discovered that the abolition of primogeniture and entail in Virginia had minor social significance and that support for this act was more universal than had been assumed.[12] It might well be another way of saying that these acts were more important for economic than for social results. More study is needed before a final conclusion can be drawn, but it is evident that a number of topics customarily considered in a social context will be rewarding avenues of exploration for the historian evaluating the economic consequences of the Revolution.

In fact, the number of essential questions requiring answers that only a thorough investigation can provide is a bit overwhelming. Historians have acknowledged that recent depressions, that of the 1930's in particular, have brought about some profound changes, but they have yet to appraise the lasting effect of the immediate postwar depression upon the course of economic development. Historians have written about the rise of the port of Baltimore, when the British blockade of Philadelphia brought new opportunities to its Maryland neighbor, but they have yet to assess the total effect of the Revolution upon the marketing centers of the new nation, including New York City. Historians have noted the decline of fisheries in New England, the change that took place in whaling, and the move from the outports of Massachusetts to Boston, yet they have been slow to determine whether or not the economy of one region of the nation received a more durable impress from the Revolution than did the others. Historians talk about American society with confidence, but they have never asked whether it contained within itself certain special characteristics that would decisively determine the course of economic life in the New Nation.

These considerations re-emphasize not only the importance of the theme but also the vast number of questions that will need to be asked—

12. A choice example is to trace the increasing firmness with which this new thesis is accepted in the works of Irving Brant, Dumas Malone, and Nathan Schachner on Madison and Jefferson respectively.

and, if possible, answered—if we are to assess the full impact of the Revolution. Although this article is merely an introduction rather than a *summa* and any conclusions are, at best, tentative, the evidence concerning the economic consequences of the Revolution is impressive. It is entirely possible that when scholars have completed their investigations, they will conclude that the American Revolution is of greater importance for its economic consequences, where the surface has scarcely been scratched, than for its social consequences, where the research in the Revolution has been concentrated in recent decades. To use the celebrated phrase of that pioneer in the field, J. Franklin Jameson, as a model, a phrase that has made scholars acutely conscious of the social aspects of the Revolution—the time seems overdue for historians to recognize and develop the idea of "The American Revolution Considered as an Economic Movement."

CONSEQUENCES FOR THE WORLD

LOUIS GOTTSCHALK

The Place of the American Revolution in the Causal Pattern of the French Revolution

🔲 The belief that there is a causal relationship between the American and the French Revolutions has long been an axiom among historians. French troops were involved after 1778, decisively so at Yorktown; French money was invested almost from the outset; in French salons Franklin presented a favorable if quite fanciful portrait of the American as a natural man; Lafayette returned to France imbued with notions of *le gloire* compounded of vaguely democratic sentiments, great respect for Washington, and immense enthusiasm for Lafayette. Yet a direct relationship is distressingly hard to establish. This subject has recently been given a renewed emphasis partly because of our own familiarity with revolutions in our now revolution-conscious world, and also because of the theses of R. R. Palmer, who has stressed that the age of the French Revolution should be studied rather in terms of a Democratic Revolution of the West.* Between 1768 and 1789 Europe itself was in turmoil—in Geneva, in Ireland, in the Netherlands, even, in prospect at least, in Britain. And this became a world reality after 1789. The leading American student of the French Revolution and the biographer of Lafayette is Louis Gottschalk. 🔲

. . . THE PRINCIPLE of liberty and the proposition that all men are created equal were inherited by the people of the United States from a long tradition. That tradition had Biblical origins; its genealogy can easily be traced by the brilliant pattern it weaves through the history of British and European political philosophy and constitutional practice. Its collateral American lines reached maturity in the constitutions of the separate states (some of which came even before the Declaration of Independence), the

* *The Age of the Democratic Revolution*; "The World Revolution of the West," *Political Science Quarterly*, LXIX (1954), 1-14.

Reprinted by permission from the *Publication of The American Friends of Lafayette*, No. 2 (1948), 495-510.

Declaration of Independence itself, and in the first ten amendments of the federal constitution.

It is sometimes believed that it was because of the principles for which the Americans fought and which they had incorporated in their widely admired Declaration of Independence that the government of France joined with the young American nation to fight against the tyranny symbolized by the British army and its Hessian mercenaries. That belief, however, contains sentimental overtones that do not ring true. That the ideals of "life, liberty and the pursuit of happiness" had a significant influence in determining French foreign policy before 1778, if it is true at all, is true only in small part. How little truth there is in it can be shown by citing the outstanding contemporary French writers on political theory, the very people whose purpose it should have been to promote the ideals of liberty among the French.

Take, for example, Beaumarchais. He was one of the writers in the period before the French Revolution largely responsible for the spread of the idea of liberty in France. He was greatly interested in American independence, and was influential in forming the American policy of the French minister of foreign affairs, the Comte de Vergennes. Yet from the letters that Beaumarchais wrote to the minister before 1778, it is clear that he did not intend the ideal of liberty to have the foremost part in that policy. He made the more practical plea that the independence of the American colonies from England would redress the world's commercial balance and would be to the political advantage of the French empire.

And Turgot, also a minister of the king and justly reputed to be one of the outstanding economic reformers of his day, was still less a champion of American freedom. When the minister of foreign affairs sent around a memorandum asking for opinions as to whether the French government should take part in the War of American Independence, Turgot replied: "It seems to me that the most desirable outcome from the viewpoint of the two crowns [the French and the Spanish] would be that England overcome the resistance of her colonies." He went on to say that a long-drawn-out war between the British and the American insurgents would be to the advantage of France. A similar point of view was presented by the Abbé de Mably, generally considered one of the most radical political theorists of the day, in an essay entitled *Notre Gloire ou Nos Rêves*. Its short, hard-headed considerations regarding the welfare of France were more typical of the attitude of French writers *before* the Declaration of Independence than the sentimental championing of American liberties.

It is sometimes said that many French soldiers came to America before 1778 to fight on behalf of the ideal of liberty. That is supposed to be particularly true of the Marquis de Lafayette. But it can be shown—I have spent many hours and written many pages in the effort to show —that as a matter of fact Lafayette's interest in political ideals, if it existed at all before 1776, was not very keen. Its vigorous growth came only *after* he had enlisted in the American service, and was not a cause of his doing so. It was less spiritual motives—such as escape from frustration, desire for glory, and hatred of the British—that led to his heroic behavior. What was true of Lafayette was *a fortiori* true of other European soldiers who volunteered their services to the American army, and was still more true of those soldiers who went as part of the French army, following the formal Franco-American alliance, to fight under Rochambeau on the side of Washington. The attitude of the French people before or shortly after the Declaration of Independence [that] was known to them is well summed up by Morellet, another of that group of writers of the eighteenth century Enlightenment called "the *philosophes*." In a letter to the British minister Shelburne dated January 5, 1777—i.e., shortly after news of the Declaration of Independence had reached France—Morellet declared that many partisans of America in Paris were less friendly to American liberty than hostile to Great Britain.

Offsetting this prevalent attitude, however, was that of other Frenchmen who thought of America as fighting the cause of mankind. After Benjamin Franklin got to France, he reported a general feeling that America was fighting for the liberty of all in fighting for her own. Franklin, however, is not the best of witnesses in this regard. Naturally he encountered the most pro-American elements, and the less friendly persons he met were not likely to express themselves freely in his presence. And yet Franklin's testimony enables us to note that the news of the Declaration of Independence, which had arrived in France just about a month ahead of him, marked a significant change in French public opinion. While before the end of 1776 the prevailing attitude toward the American rebellion was Anglophobe, by the beginning of 1777 it had become Americanophile.

For a time after 1776—that is to say, between 1776 and the signing of the treaty of alliance of 1778—the official policy and the opinion of a large part of the population was for the most part Anglophobe and not libertarian. Between 1776 and 1778, the pro-American party in France published a periodical entitled *Les Affaires de l'Angleterre et de l'Amérique*. This periodical appeared to be published in the Belgian city of Antwerp. At any rate, that city was indicated on the title page as its place of origin. It probably was printed and published in Paris, but in order to avoid the censorship authorities, who apparently still were unfriendly to American ideals, it was made to appear to come from a foreign country. This newspaper has often been cited as showing the popularity of republican principles in France before 1778, but recent investigation shows that it endeavored to soften the impact of republican principles against a cushion of anti-English arguments rather than to propound republican principles directly and positively. There was at the same time in Paris also a pro-English, anti-American propaganda intended to counteract that of the friends of America. This English propaganda, organized under the guidance of Isaac De Pinto, played upon the widespread antipathy in France to rebellion and reproached the Americans as insurgents.

The Alliance of 1778 changed the picture thoroughly, making official France outwardly, and the greater part of the French people sincerely, friendly to America as well as hostile to England. That alliance was largely, however, the result rather of the fear that the American colonies might become reconciled to the mother country, thereby re-establishing English supremacy upon the seas and overseas, than of France's interest in the ideals set forth in the Declaration of Independence. The English historian W. E. H. Lecky has well summed up the French attitude of that day. The French, he said, were not moved by American liberty, but they were greatly concerned with American independence. After 1778, however, the spirit of liberty grew in France and cemented the friendliness of the people of France toward the people of the United States.

As a general rule, American history textbooks give the impression that what went on in the thirteen transatlantic British colonies from 1778 to 1783 was the major phase of the War of the American Revolution. Nevertheless, to most contemporaries outside of America, that was only a small part of a much bigger war—one that may indeed be called a "world war," if by that phrase is meant a struggle fought all over the world. Only a portion of the total forces involved were engaged in what is now the eastern part of the United States and Canada. Others fought in the West Indies, South America, Africa and Asia, and on the high seas. The total number of land forces under arms in the United States seldom, if ever, reached more than 40,000 on either side. In only one instance did Washington command more than 16,000 men, and that was at Yorktown, where nearly half of them were French. A bigger army in France had constituted one of the most serious threats of invasion that England had ever had to face before 1940, and in Spain another army nearly as large had besieged Gibraltar and invaded Minorca. The fleets that fought in the East and the West Indies sometimes numbered more men than were engaged in the most decisive land battles of the American phase of the conflict.

Eventually nearly every country of Europe was involved directly or indirectly in the War, which was only another in a century-long series that France had been fighting against England for world hegemony. Since the Treaty of 1763, the French had made a vigorous effort to fan the ill-feeling between the American colonies and their mother country into a flame that could be quenched only with blood. After rebellion started, it would probably have resulted in reconciliation between the colonies and England if the French had been willing that it should end in a peaceful manner. Not only did they form an alliance with the United States, they also brought in the Spanish and the Dutch. Before peace was made, a formidable coalition of world powers was lined up against England instead of merely thirteen under-populated colonies.

France also put a great deal of effort and money into the thirteen colonies themselves. True, the forces sent there were small compared to those sent elsewhere. Likewise, the fleets that sailed there went usually on side-trips from their campaigns in the West Indies. But the visit of one of those fleets proved to be the means by which Cornwallis was cut off from aid or retreat, and the half-army that Rochambeau placed under Washington at Yorktown (after agreeing to wait no longer for the other half to come) was the deciding factor in winning that decisive encounter.

Though France, Spain, Holland, and the United States formed quite a strong coalition, they were not the only countries involved in the war. Practically every other big European state was included in a league of "armed neutrality," organized to fight England "short of war" (to use a phrase not then current). They resisted her on the high seas, seeking to refute the contention that she ruled the waves and that the oceans were not free. Thus, Russia, Prussia, the Holy Roman Empire, the Scandinavian countries, Portugal and the Two Sicilies became indirectly involved in the War of American Independence. The separated German states also became interested in its outcome, since Austria and Prussia were carrying on a little war of their own—the so-called "Potato War" (1778-79)— which remained localized and bloodless because England and France, allies of Prussia and Austria respectively, were busily engaged in fighting each other in America and elsewhere. Thus another important aspect of European history during the eighteenth century—the struggle for leadership in the Holy Roman Empire—was for a while affected by what went on in America.

Nor did the war end when the American phase of it was decided. Yorktown was fought in 1781, but peace was not made until 1783. Several things that occurred in the meantime had a greater influence than the victory at Yorktown on what that peace would be. For example, France was decisively defeated in the West Indies waters, and it became obvious that the siege of Gibraltar would not succeed. These failures rather than Yorktown determined the outcome for the Spanish, the Dutch, and the French. They determined also that Britannia would continue to rule the waves, even though she lost her thirteen Continental colonies.

Thus it happened that, from the military and diplomatic point of view, the Revolutionary War was much more than a war for American independence. Although time was to show that the establishment of a sovereign American federation was perhaps the most important result of that war, to contemporaries the future of the United States appeared to be only one among many issues that had induced the big powers to become involved in the struggle. It is even conceivable that if the Battles of Lexington and Concord had not made the American rebellion the immediate occasion of that struggle, England and France might have engaged about the same time anyway in another round of their hundred-year contest for control of the seas and of the colonies beyond the seas. In that event, it is also conceivable, the strategy on both sides might have been much the same as it actually was, except perhaps for the campaigns on the North American continent.

In other words, the War of the American Revolution was a conflict in which France played the major part on the allied side and the American states a minor one. To Frenchmen the capture of small islands like Grenada and Dominica and naval defeats like the Battle of the Saints in the West Indies were no less important and roused no less enthusiasm or distress than Yorktown. When victory finally was won, Frenchmen rejoiced not so much because the United States was independent as because England had been humbled, her empire torn asunder, and her control of trade and the seas jeopardized.

In 1783, the "Second Hundred Years' War" looked as if it were over and had ended in a decision favorable to France. The conflict was not over, however. The very effort France had made to win the latest bout left her too much exhaused to reap the expected rewards. Exhaustion soon combined with other complications to lead to domestic collapse. Eventually the struggle was renewed, with revolutionary ideologies as one of the weapons in this fight, and came to a close only with the decisive defeat of Napoleon Bonaparte and France.

In preparing that collapse of France with its subsequent revolutionary ideology, the American Revolution played a part that has not always been properly understood, though generally recognized. A few years ago I tried to show that unrest alone is insufficient to create a revolution. In addition, I maintained, there must exist a sense of solidarity among the restless; and they must also have leadership and some program of reform. Even with all these, however, my argument continued, revolutions have been known to fail if they met with effective conservative resistance; and hence it follows that revolutions succeed not so much because the revolutionaries are strong as because the vested interests are weak—or, to use Hegelian terms, not so much because antithesis is irresistible as because thesis has collapsed.

The French Revolution, for example, could hardly have come about without the American Revolution. Unrest, the factor for which one naturally looks first in analyzing the causes of a revolution, would perhaps have been no less pronounced in France if the American Revolution had not occurred. It was caused by many age-old social, economic, political, religious, intellectual, and other provocations, with which the fate of America had very little association. But one important source of dissatisfaction was definitely connected with the American Revolutionary War. While popular uneasiness had been rife for decades, it did not come to a head until the French treasury was threatened with bankruptcy. That danger was in large part due to French sacrifices in the American Revolution. The French had given and loaned great amounts of money to America. They had also made loans to other allies. They had sent huge armies and fleets to every quarter of the globe. The war is generally estimated to have cost France 2,000,000,000 livres. The program of economy and reform that France's comptroller-general, Turgot, had embarked upon before the war had had to be abandoned. Not only were Turgot's sympathizers disillusioned, but also, when the war was over, France's accumulated debt had reached about 4,000,000,000 livres. Meanwhile the cost of living had gone up distressingly.

It is difficult to translate the significance of a 4,000,000,000 livre debt for France of the 1780's into terms that would be intelligible to a twentieth-century American audience. In the first place, our attitude toward national indebtedness has changed, and many, if not most, of us no longer think that having an unfavorable trade balance or being a debtor rather than a creditor nation is necessarily disastrous if the national economy is otherwise sound. In France of the 1780's, however, Adam Smith and his ideas of free trade as the true basis of the wealth of nations were not yet well known, and if the Physiocrats were more renowned, their emphasis was rather upon the virtues of a healthy domestic agriculture than upon those of vigorous international trade and exchange. Hence all but a few in France felt that a large national debt would ruin the country's credit; and that feeling did more to make their fears come true than the logic of the actual situation.

In addition, correctly to appreciate the differences between our reactions and theirs to such a situation, we must make allowances for the differences in population, national income, natural resources, and the comparative price index. France in that day had about one-sixth or one-seventh of the population of the United States of today, and her national income probably was proportionately less, because the chief enterprise was still a relatively primitive form of agriculture. Modestly estimated, a four-billion-livre debt weighed about as heavily on France in the 1780's as a debt of around twenty-five billion dollars would have weighed on the United States of the prewar period of the 1930's. Even in the present day of astronomical national debts, that is a staggering sum if allowance be made for the inflationary trends since the 1930's. The debt and the rising cost of living could not alone have brought on the French Revolution, but they were major contributing factors in the accumulating unrest. Both were in large measure directly attributable to French participation in the American Revolutionary War.

What is more important, general awareness that dissatisfaction was widespread throughout France, with a resultant solidarity among the dissatisfied, became much more marked after the 1770's. That too was attributable in large measure to French participation in the American Revolutionary War. To be sure, France was an absolute monarchy; the press was censored, and writers were sent to prison for the expression of heterodox opinions. The French had nevertheless been the allies of a confederation that believed in republican institutions. Several of those confederated states had constitutions containing bills of rights guaranteeing civil and political liberty. It became desirable for absolutist France to tolerate—in fact to build up—among its people a sympathy with the republican institutions of America, its ally.

It was now the patriotic duty not only of French writers to promote the interest of French people in the American nation but also of the censors not to interfere unnecessarily with their doing so. For example, in 1778 a collection was published of the constitutions of the states and the Declaration of Independence, which was dedicated to Benjamin Franklin and was referred to as "the code of liberty." In 1783 a much more impressive work reinforced the pro-American impact. It contained, besides the constitutions of the thirteen states, other significant American documents, although it was called *Les Constitutions des Treize États de l'Amérique*. It was of special significance that this work was published by the king's official printer. That meant, as was later pointed out when a French Revolutionary assembly issued the famous Declaration of the Rights of Man and of the Citizen, that a declaration of rights actually had been promulgated in France by royal consent several years earlier.

Another reason for the rapid spread of American ideals of liberty in France before the French Revolution was the personal popularity of Benjamin Franklin. He was petted by the ladies and feted by the aristocracy; he was lionized by the court and eulogized by poets, scientists and journalists; and he was envied by Arthur Lee and John Adams. The effect, direct or indirect, of Franklin's personal charm, his wide correspondence, and the writings about him was that the people of France often thought of all Americans as being made more or less in his image. The thought was probably far from true, but it did Americans no harm that their allies tended to think so.

Another channel for the favorable impact of American ideals upon French popular psychology was the impression made upon the soldiers who went from France to fight in the War of American Independence. Lafayette went back to France a worshipper of Washington and, for the most part, an uncritical admirer of American institutions. The Abbé Robin, who had been a chaplain with Rochambeau's army, wrote a book about his experience that spoke of the Americans as if they were a nation of new Arcadians. Chastellux, who already had a great reputation as a *philosophe* and was third in command to Rochambeau, wrote a volume on his journeys through America that induced its readers to believe that American institutions were ideal and the American people admirable. And a number of young men who, like Lafayette, were to become leaders in the forthcoming revolution in France—men like Alexandre de Lameth, Mathieu Dumas, the Comte de Ségur, the Vicomte de Noailles, and that Saint-Simon who became the founder of the famous school of socialist utopians in the nineteenth century—all stated in later years that they had imbibed their first ideas of liberty from their contact with Americans during the Revolutionary War. These people wrote, spoke, and made orations about the American people, American institutions, and American principles. They fondly nurtured idealizations of which they would brook no criticism. They flocked to the defense of the Americans whenever American virtues were questioned by others, like Deux Ponts, Moré, Biron, and Armand, who had hardly less right to speak of the American people than they. And the people of France, it proved, preferred to believe those who eulogized rather than those who disparaged America. The occasional book that criticized the United States won very little audience, whereas books like those of Chastellux and Robin received an enthusiastic welcome; and Lafayette became the most popular Frenchman of the day in France as well as America.

Another factor that led to the spread of American ideals in France was the active propaganda of French agents, both diplomatic and unofficial, in America. Crèvecoeur's famous *Letters from an American Farmer* spread broadcast a roseate picture of the United States in vastly different English and French editions. Foremost among the official propagandists was the Chevalier de La Luzerne, the French minister in Philadelphia. La Luzerne subsidized Americans, including Thomas Paine, to write things about America for circulation in France. Paine, according to La Luzerne, proved too lazy to write a reply to a critique of America by an illustrious *philosophe,* the Abbé Raynal, and La Luzerne satisfied himself by carefully going over the French translation of Carver's *Voyages through the Interior Parts of North America* and helping the translation to win approval in France.

So the king's government, on the one hand, promoted interest in American institutions, while, on the other, it opposed freedom in order to uphold absolute monarchy. This predicament arose largely because there was a war going on and France wanted to win it. Money had to be advanced and armies raised if it was to be won, and those things could not easily be done without popular support. The predicament was solved by weakening the royal censorship to the point where, in the famous "flood of pamphlets" of 1788, it practically collapsed.

Thus the 1770's marked a new era in the propagation of the ideas that formed the intellectual foundations of the French Revolution. The change was noticeable in two ways. In the first place, ideas of reform became common property, and no longer belonged exclusively to the literate classes. In the second place, they became concrete rather than abstract. The outstanding students of French public opinion during this period, like Daniel Mornet, find that before the 1770's the *philosophes* had appealed only to a limited audience, consisting almost exclusively of those who could afford to buy the very expensive books produced by the high publication costs of that day, and that they had dealt with mankind in broad general terms. But after the 1770's, as the appeal of the *philosophes* became more popular and was spread more widely than before—through conversations, law courts, sermons, masonic lodges, and club meetings, as well as books, it became more specific. The demand was now not alone for the general reform of mankind in accordance with "the laws of Nature and of Nature's God" but also for practical and immediate changes in French government and institutions. Even the authors of utopias tended to turn from picturing purely imaginary states to describing what an ideal France might someday be; and although none of them spelled *nature's* backward, one of them did spell *Paris* backward to make the name of his ideal city.

Madame d'Houdetot, a friend of Franklin, wrote to him that America had now provided the *philosophes* with "an example and a hope." In other words, America had become a case of Philosophy teaching by Example. In much the same way that speculative socialists of more recent times, unable to make a great impression upon the popular mind if they talked merely of what might be, found that, when they had an actual example in Russia, they could more easily bring about political pressure and effect political action, so the *philosophes,* the political theorists of the eighteenth century, once they could point to a living illustration of the Rights of Man in America, rallied behind them the type of person that could not grasp principles but could visualize the force of political reform in action. Old writers now began to write about American institutions rather than the abstract Rights of Man and the welfare of mankind in general. Condorcet, Raynal, Chastellux, Turgot and Mably were only a few of the figures among the recognized *philosophes* who turned their attention to America, writing critiques of the American constitutions and innovations. A set of new writers who would probably have developed into another generation of *philosophes* if their energies had not been diverted by the French Revolution also became leaders in the new American vogue. Men like Mirabeau and Brissot, not to mention Condorcet and Lafayette again, wrote about the new America, holding it up as an example of what a good state ought to be. France, they thought, could hardly become a republic; it was too big to be anything but a monarchy. Yet otherwise it might follow the American model profitably.

The attention these writers received was heightened by the controversies in which they engaged with Americans like Adams, Jefferson, Livingston, Mazzei and Barlow, and by translations of more sober historical and anthropological writings of American students like Filson, Carver and Ramsay. French journals carried articles on America—sometimes by Americans. Abbé Raynal's popular *History of the Two Indies* in the original edition of 1775 gave only twenty pages to the United States but in that of 1780 almost one hundred and fifty. Thus war, diplomacy and propaganda united to produce a general awareness of the existence of a restless spirit in France.

France had, however, long been restless. Nearly every decade since Louis XIV's death had witnessed a revolutionary crisis. But the repeated crises that had flared up to the danger point had in the end died down without producing catastrophe. One reason for the ineffectiveness of these outbursts was that they had had no enterprising leadership. The American Revolution now helped to supply that deficiency. An actual, though far from exhaustive, count has been made of Frenchmen who took a leading part in both the American and the French Revolution. There were thirty-eight of them, including Lafayette, the Lameth brothers, the Rochambeaus (father and son), Duportail, Estaing, Dumas, Ségur, Jourdan, Gouvion, Noailles, Custine, Beauharnais, Montmorency-Laval—

to mention only those who were conspicuously friendly to the French Revolution in its initial stages. Of these, as we have noted, several admitted that they owed much of their interest in revolutionary ideas to America. How far the American Revolution was a factor in training men, like Brissot, Condorcet, Dupont, Marat and Robespierre, who were not soldiers, for their roles in the French Revolution can be only a matter of conjecture. It would be rash to believe that such men, but for the American development, would not have become revolutionary leaders. Yet they followed American affairs and watched the republican experiment with keen interest, as their writings and speeches make abundantly clear.

Thus the American Revolution helped to provide leaders for the French Revolution and made it possible for unrest to result in more effective demands for reform. It did more than that, however. It also furnished a model, a program, and a political philosophy for those leaders. As we have already seen, the French philosophers no longer had to talk about abstractions like natural law, natural institutions and natural morality derived from a hypothetical Common Sense or Reason. They no longer had to seek in the wilds of America or Asia for the theoretical Child of Nature. In live Americans like Benjamin Franklin they now found an impressive exemplar of a people who had actually achieved a life and a society that a philosopher might embrace. Across the Atlantic, as anyone who was not willfully blind could see, vigorous states prospered with governments based upon the Rights of Man.

To be sure, the *philosophes* deceived themselves somewhat. Franklin fell a little short of being a paragon, and the United States of being Arcadia. Yet it was more convincing to cite concrete cases than to point to sublimated primitives or to hypothetical societies. The American Arcadia, if not examined too critically, fully justified the speculations of the philosopher, Why could not Arcadia be located also in France?

With such queries political propaganda in France took on a more specific, pragmatic and effective form. The illiterate on the café terrace of the smallest village could grasp what the new generation of *philosophes* was saying as readily as the learned in the salons of the capital. Lafayette was not alone in noting that liberal ideas spread rapidly throughout France after the American Revolution. Talleyrand remarked that subsequent to the victory over England America became "the sole topic of conversation" among the aristocracy; and the English agriculturist Arthur Young observed in his travels in France in 1787 "a strong leaven of liberty, increasing every hour since the American revolution."

No man's testimony in this regard can be more convincing than Thomas Jefferson's. As American minister to France, he was sympathetic with the reform party, particularly with Lafayette, who had no secrets from him, and he knew more about the American Revolution than any other man in France. When the French Revolution was unmistakably on its way, he wrote the well-known English liberal Dr. Richard Price his interpretation of how it had come about: "Though celebrated writers of this and other countries had already sketched good principles on the subject of government, yet the American war seems first to have awakened the thinking part of this nation in general from the sleep of despotism in which they were sunk. The officers too who had been to America were mostly young men, less shackled by habit and prejudice, and more ready to assent to the dictates of common sense and common right. They came back impressed with these. The press, notwithstanding its shackles, began to disseminate them; conversation, too, assumed new freedom; politics became the theme of all societies, male and female, and a very extensive and zealous party was formed, which may be called the Patriotic party, who, sensible of the abusive government under which they lived, longed for occasions of reforming it."

Yet, if my theory of the causes of revolution is right, provocations, crystallized public opinion, popular leaders, and a program of reform, even when they occur together, do not make a revolution unless the conservative forces are too weak to resist change effectively. Here, too, the American contribution was significant. The royal debt, by weakening the French treasury, made revision of the fiscal system inescapable. Furthermore, although there was still very little republicanism in France after the American Revolution, many more among the influential circles than before favored thoroughgoing reform of the monarchy. Important, too, in creating weakness of the conservative forces was the fact that aristocratic officers who had returned from the war in America could no longer be counted upon to obey if ordered to shoot down opponents of the government. An "American faction" also grew up in the parlements, and a "liberal aristocracy" at court, with Lafayette foremost among them. The same conditions that provided leaders for the revolutionaries created disaffection among the conservatives at the very time when the conservatives should have presented a united front if the Old Régime were to be preserved.

It goes without saying that the conditions which together made reformers willing to risk revolution and conservatives unable to resist it— a combination which makes revolution inevitable—naturally did not come exclusively from the American shore. The American Revolution had less effect on the French peasants, who formed about three-fourths of France's population, or on the city workers, or on the lower clergy than on the upper classes, except as its influence seeped down from the aristocracy and the middle class or as it was reflected in general agitation, fiscal difficulties and the rising cost of living. But upon the aristocracy and the middle class that influence was great. And the French Revolution at the outset was a movement of the aristocracy and the middle class.

On the eve of the French upheaval, Baron Friedrich Melchior de Grimm, though himself a friend of the *philosophes,* intimated that Frenchmen might well regret America if they stopped to think. "Her liberty has cost France nearly two billions," he wrote. ". . . That costly glory will serve only to hasten a revolution the outbreak of which all the nations of Southern Europe would seem well advised at least to put off, if the force of circumstances should make it inevitable." Louis XVI himself recognized that the American Revolution was the source of his troubles. The French Revolution had just begun when Sultan Tippoo of Mysore asked for French aid in driving the English out of India. Louis XVI, hesitating to comply, commented dryly: "This occasion greatly resembles the American affair, of which I never think without regret. On that occasion they took advantage somewhat of my youth, and today we are paying the penalty for it. The lesson is too vivid to be forgotten."

It is now about half a century since Lord Acton gave his deservedly famous lectures on the French Revolution at Cambridge University. I can find no better words to end my argument than those he used to begin his lecture on "The Influence of America":

> The several structures of political thought that arose in France, and clashed in the process of revolution, were not directly responsible for the outbreak. The doctrines hung like a cloud upon the heights, and at critical moments in the reign of Louis XV men felt that a catastrophe was impending. It befell when there was less provocation, under his successor; and the spark that changed thought into action was supplied by the Declaration of American Independence. It was the system of an international extra-territorial universal Whig, far transcending the English model by its simplicity and rigour. It surpassed in force all the speculation of Paris and Geneva, for it had undergone the test of experiment and its triumph was the most memorable thing that had been seen by men.

W. R. BROCK
The Effect of the Loss of the American Colonies upon British Policy

For Britain the loss of the American colonies was fundamental. It wrecked North's Administration and produced a revival of factional intrigue—from which some strange alliances like that of Fox and North were one result; the King talked of abdication; in the end only the emergence of Pitt restored stability and continuity to government. Nor did the loss of the American colonies have any constructive effect on the character of the Empire. Some suggestions have been made that in the agenda of the Carlisle Mission of 1778 a beneficent liberal spirit is evident, in which the notion of parliamentary supremacy was to be quietly bypassed and the shape of a new Commonwealth system can be detected.* In fact the Old Colonial System lived on. If there was a certain retreat from Grenville's unfortunate schemes, Lord Sheffield's views were quite as influential after 1783 as Lord Shelburne's, and Knox and Jenkinson, the backroom boys, still largely ran the machinery of state. The new constitution for a Loyalist-peopled Canada was strikingly less "democratic" than that of the United States in 1787. It was to the closeness of trade ties rather than the conversion of Britain to any political liberalism, and to the realistic outlook of Alexander Hamilton, however unpopular it might be at home, that effective Anglo-American cooperation was due.   ▣

I. Problems of an Empire in Ruins

(1) COULD GREAT BRITAIN SURVIVE? Two weeks after Yorktown, but before the news of that disaster had reached England, George III wrote to Lord North that "The dye is now cast whether this shall be a great Empire or the least dignified of European States." [1] England had not fought the war of the Revolution to secure a paltry revenue or to establish legalistic points, but because it was held that the British power could not survive without the supremacy of Parliament over the whole Empire. Great as this power had become, modern history was littered with the records of states which had grasped at greatness without the will or resources to maintain it. Dwarfed in Europe by the population of France and overseas by the possessions of Spain, Britain was engaged in a continuous struggle for survival; whether she could survive after the loss of the American colonies was the first and greatest problem which confronted her statesmen.

(2) THE COMMERCIAL PROBLEM. The conventional explanation of Britain's greatness rightly stressed the importance of sea-power, which was not reckoned by the strength of the Royal Navy alone. In time of war much of the actual fighting was carried on by merchantmen commissioned as privateers, and the Royal Navy counted upon trained merchant seamen to man its ships.[2] It was, therefore, a cardinal point of British policy to encourage shipping, and the great instrument was the Navigation Act, designed to secure for British shipping a monopoly of

* C. R. Ritcheson, "Anglo-American Relations, 1783-1794," *South Atlantic Quarterly,* LVIII (1959), 364-380; "The American Revolution: Its Influence on the Development of the British Empire," *Parliamentary Affairs,* IV (1950-1951), 245-260.

Reprinted by permission from the Historical Association (London) *Aids for Teachers* Series, No. 3 (1957).

1. *Correspondence of Geo. III* (ed. Fortescue), V, p. 297.

2. As an example of private contribution to naval strength Lord Hawkesbury stated that Liverpool equipped 120 privateers, manned by 8754 men, between August 1778 and April 1779 (*Parlt. Hist.* XXXI, 136).

trade with the colonies, a decided advantage over foreigners in the home ports and as large a share as possible in the world's carrying trade. In 1783 Lord Sheffield, one of the ablest defenders of this policy, proclaimed that, "The Navigation Act, the basis of our great power at sea, gave us the trade of the world; if we alter that act, by permitting any state to trade with our islands, or by suffering any state to bring to this country any produce but its own, we desert the Navigation Act and sacrifice the marine of England." [3] But the great problem of 1783 was whether this policy could be maintained when one of the foreign states was made up from former colonies which had grown within the imperial system, contributed a very substantial part to our pre-war merchant marine, supplied the British West Indies with provisions, conducted extensive carrying trades in the Atlantic area under the British flag, and provided an important market for British manufactures. It could be argued either that the principles of the Navigation Act were more necessary than ever to protect British power against a new rival, or that the loss of the colonies made necessary a relaxation of these principles in order to feed British colonies and to protect British markets.

The loss of the colonies had split the single cloth from which the old colonial policy had been made, and brought into the arena of practical politics Adam Smith's distinction between a policy of opulence and a policy of defence. The shipping interest and entrepôt merchants who wished to preserve a monopoly of colonial produce were ready recruits for the policy of defence, while manufacturers and export merchants stressed the importance of the American market and the need to allow Americans to earn the money to pay for British goods. Consumers were, as usual, inarticulate, but they may be presumed to have favored any policy which lowered the price of goods. Lord Sheffield admitted that, "in point of commerce, it is clear that the easier the means of exchange of commodities the better; that if the foreigners find it more convenient to carry in their own ships what we want, we have a chance of buying cheaper; and by tempting the free arrival of all foreign ships in our ports, we facilitate their taking out our commodities. But the great object of the Navigation Act is naval strength; it therefore sacrifices these commercial speculations to strengthen our marine." [4] Here, in essence, is the conflict between welfare and national security which still plagues the countries of the world.

(3) ANGLO-AMERICAN RELATIONS. Upon a solution of these questions of commercial policy might depend much of the future of Anglo-American relations. The highest hopes were expressed by the author of a pamphlet of 1783, who may have echoed the opinions of Lord Shelburne: "It was a part of true policy to pursue the measures which tended to restore a

3. Lord Sheffield, *Observations on the Commerce of the United States,* 3rd ed. p. 214.
4. Lord Sheffield, *Observations on the Commerce of the United States,* 3rd ed. p. 214.

cordial friendship, and which, perhaps, might at length be productive
of a federal union between the two countries." [5] Others believed that
Great Britain had much to lose and little to gain by such a conciliatory
policy, and many British statesmen were influenced by a low estimate
of the future power of the United States. "We might as reasonably dread
the effects of combination among the German as among the American
States, and deprecate the resolves of the Diet, as those of Congress,"
exclaimed Lord Sheffield.[6] It was argued that an unyielding defence of
British interests would divide the United States and perhaps induce some
former colonies to return as supplicants to the old allegiance.[7] Against
this David Hartley, who was employed in 1783 to negotiate on commercial questions with the American commissioners, believed that British
intransigence would cement the union and turn a potential friend into a
bitter enemy; "I have often," he wrote in 1785, "met with this sentiment
amongst Americans: viz, If we have not close commercial connections
with Great Britain we shall have war. This seems to be the secret touchstone of their thoughts." [8]

(4) COLONIAL GOVERNMENT. The problem of economic policy was
closely linked with that of colonial government. The author of the
pamphlet already quoted wrote, "If we are so wise as to profit by experience, and send liberal laws to our remaining colonies, instead of troops,
bad governors and machiavellian systems, we shall be freed from the
burden of transmitting large sums thither, which we can no longer afford,
and shall receive considerably from thence in return, by the necessary
balance of our commerce." [9] But if British interests prevented the colonies from resuming or developing trade with their American neighbours,
colonial autonomy must be set within narrow limits. Even if imperial
self-sufficiency, never realised in practice, had to be abandoned in theory,
it was still possible to think of colonies as instruments of imperial strategy. The attempt to create a central financial system for the Empire,
inaugurated by the Stamp Act, had been finally abandoned in 1778 when
Parliament gave up its right to levy internal taxes upon the colonies, but
this, if anything, made British statesmen more ready to count the commercial or strategic values of colonies to set against their cost. William
Knox, a former under-secretary who was much consulted on commercial
policy in 1783, made it a principle that "It was better to have no colonies

5. *Considerations on the Provisional Treaty with America.* London, 1783, by
Andrew Kippis, D.D. p. 23.
6. Sheffield, *op. cit.,* p. 198.
7. For what it is worth, Bancroft, a former British Agent in America, gave it
as his opinion that if British policy "extended towards a recovery of the Sovereignty
of the now United States, or towards a dissolution of their Confederation . . . .
these ends will be best promoted by an adherence to the system of excluding
American vessels from the British plantations and American shipping from the
advantage of being sold and employed in this Kingdom." (P.R.O., F.O. 4.3.90).
8. P.R.O., F.O. 4.3.131.
9. Andrew Kippis *op. cit.,* p. 79.

at all than not to have them subservient to the maritime strength and commercial interests of Great Britain." [10] Inland colonies could find little place in this conception, and Sheffield believed that "it was not in the interest of England to raise colonies of farmers in a country which could only produce the same articles as England did." [11] The consensus of opinion seemed to be that England's future lay in the East, but that existing colonies should be used to some purpose. Such a policy necessarily required that ultimate political control should remain at Westminster.

II. *The Debate Over Commercial Policy*

(1) AN ARGUMENT OVER MEANS NOT ENDS. It is a mistake to regard the controversies of 1783 as a contest between the children of light and the children of darkness: on the one side can be found free trade sentiments which were to triumph in the nineteenth century and expressions of friendship for America which appeal to the twentieth, but on the other were able men who sincerely believed that Britain might be ruined by mistaken generosity and whose arguments were by no means negligible. What is remarkable is the extent to which men of the second rank prevailed over their leaders in a time of political instability; the makers of the new policy were not Shelburne, Fox or Pitt, but William Knox, a former junior minister, William Eden, a careerist not yet at the height of his power, Lord Sheffield, a wealthy landowner and political amateur, and Charles Jenkinson, long regarded as the organiser of the "secret influence" of the Crown. One explanation of the defeat of those who wished for free intercourse with America lies in the fact that, as Eden remarked in Parliament, "there never existed any difference of opinion as to the object in view . . . to gain . . . as great a share of the American commerce as could be gained without imminent risk, or actual disadvantage to the naval strength of Great Britain." [12] It was an argument over means not ends.

The American treaty commissioners at Paris hoped to negotiate a commercial agreement which would give Americans the privileges which they enjoyed as colonists, and Pitt introduced a bill which embodied Shelburne's free trade ideas and which would have given the Americans everything which they could want. It was obviously to the advantage of the United States, as a new nation in a world of closed economic systems, to open as many doors as possible, but no one expected them to pay for colonial privileges by a colonial exclusion from foreign markets. David Hartley, whom Fox sent as negotiator to Paris, believed that the American proposals would "in effect reunite the two countries

10. W. Knox, *Extra-Official State Papers*, II, p. 54.

11. *Parlt. Hist.* XXIX, p. 404.

12. *Parlt. Hist.* XXIII, 729.

together as one people;" [13] but might they not equally well give the Americans a competitive advantage which would enable them to dominate the commerce of the Atlantic? If they threatened to become the Dutch of the New World, ought not Great Britain to employ against them the same weapons with which she had broken the Dutch stranglehold over the carrying trade? Pitt's bill was attacked in Parliament by Eden and in print by Sheffield, whose extremely able work, *Observations upon the Commerce of the United States,* maintained that "the system of sacrificing permanent interests from a temporary impatience to induce or enable the Americans to trade with us—the system of courting them, lest their trade should take another course, and of treating the Navigation Act as obsolete, impolitic or useless, cannot be attributed to anything but ignorance, levity, or treachery." [14]

(2) THE WEST INDIAN TRADE. The crux of the problem was the West Indian trade, which had been so great an element in the commercial prosperity of the former colonies and to which the United States now attached pre-eminent importance. That the islands would have to receive their food from the mainland was hardly questioned, for the idea that they might be supplied from British North America was no more than an aspiration, and it was equally certain that some West Indian produce would have to be given in exchange; the vital question was whether this trade should be carried in American ships. It was widely believed that if the Americans did not carry this point they would retaliate against British ships and imports. It was a powerful part of Sheffield's argument to dispel these fears, and, as he remarked in a later edition of his work, "Every day's experience shews that this country, from the nature and quality of its manufactures, and from the ascendancy it has acquired in commerce, will command three fourths of the American trade. The American merchants solicit a correspondence and beg for credit, because they feel their own want of capital, they know our traders are more liberal, and our goods cheaper and better, than any in Europe." [15] The result of the Shelburne-Pitt bill was not, therefore, to carry the day for free intercourse, but to rouse a storm which could not be ignored.[16] "The more I have enquired upon this subject," wrote Fox to Hartley, "the more I am convinced that the prejudices on this matter (if that be the name they deserve) are so strong that such a measure as a relaxation of the Act of Navigation in this instance can never be taken but upon a full and solemn Parliamentary enquiry." [17] Parliament was unwilling to commit itself

13. P.R.O., F.O. 4.2.56.

14. Sheffield, *op. cit.,* 229.

15. *Ibid.,* 263.

16. It does not appear that the men who have been mentioned as defenders of the Navigation Acts were interested parties. Sheffield is often referred to as the "spokesman" of the shipping interest, but he does not seem to have been directly concerned with shipping. He did, however, stimulate ship-owners to take an active part by petition to Parliament and interviews with ministers.

17. P.R.O., F.O. 4.2. June 10, 1783.

and authorised the King in Council to issue orders for the temporary regulation of trade; renewed from year to year until 1797, this delegation of authority meant that vital problems during a crucial period were settled by executive action.

The first Order (14th May 1783) showed the Government to be fully aware of the need to promote direct trade between Britain and America, for it opened British ports to American ships on very favourable terms, and gave to exports to the United States the same bounties and drawbacks as to those destined for British colonies. But Americans could bring to Great Britain only the produce of the United States, and the sale of American ships (which had always formed an important part of colonial remittances to Great Britain) was discouraged by adherence to the rule of the Navigation Act that foreign built ships would not be treated as "British," even if owned and manned by British subjects. The West Indian trade was regulated by an Order of July 2nd, framed by William Knox, which allowed trade in the manufactured products of the United States and the principal products of the West Indies, except cotton, but confined this trade in both directions to British ships. Knox believed that he had saved British sea-power; but he had done so by unilateral action on a subject under negotiation, and offended the Americans not only by its matter but also by its manner.

The main initiative in commercial policy now passed to Charles Jenkinson, successively Lord Hawkesbury and Earl of Liverpool, who headed a Privy Council committee of enquiry in 1783 and became, in 1786, President of the newly constituted Board of Trade. Jenkinson was one of the best-informed men of his age on commercial matters and he was also a firm believer in the Navigation Act, which he re-codified in the light of changed circumstances; under his guidance shipping prospered, and a firm resistance was offered to any concessions in favour of America. As Jenkinson held office until 1804, the decisions of 1783 fixed the pattern of imperial policy and of Anglo-American relations for a generation ahead and cast a long shadow over the nineteenth century.

III. *The Problem of Colonial Government*

(1) CANADA. UNITED EMPIRE LOYALISTS AND PITT'S CANADA ACT, 1791. British statesmen would have been happy to make no innovation in colonial government, but the Loyalist settlements in British North America soon presented a problem which could not be avoided. Everyone wished to do what was right for the hardly used Loyalists, and justice combined with commonsense to demand that they be given the representative institutions to which they were accustomed. The Canada Act of 1791 was introduced by Grenville, its principal author, with the statement that "we are now about to communicate the blessing of the English constitution to the subjects of Canada, because we were fully convinced that it was the best in the world." And Pitt hoped "they were all agreed to give to Canada a

free constitution in the English sense of the word." [18] The apparent liberality of these sentiments implies neither a recognition of a right to self-government nor a relinquishment of the attempt to impose imperial interests upon colonial societies.

Some time previously Grenville had circulated to his colleagues a paper which forms an interesting commentary upon the loss of the colonies and its political lessons.[19] He argued that "the revolt of those provinces is not justly ascribed to a communication of the British constitution, which, in fact, they never enjoyed; but that, as their form of government differed essentially from that of Great Britaain, so the points in which that difference consisted were those which operated to produce their separation from the Mother Country." In the former colonies "no care was taken to preserve a due mixture of the monarchical and aristocratical parts of the British constitution"; weak executive authority had been brought into direct conflict with elected assemblies and "to the want of an intermediate power, to operate as a check, both on the misconduct of Governors and on the democratical spirit which prevailed in the Assemblies, the defection of the American provinces may perhaps be most justly ascribed." The remedy proposed was to make the upper house, or Legislative Council, a nominated body from which a hereditary aristocracy might, in course of time, be created. At the same time this Council would not imitate the old colonial councils in having executive functions, and a new executive council would act as the Governor's "cabinet." Lord Chancellor Thurlow was more dubious about the effect of transmitting the blessings of the English constitution to the colonies, and placed more emphasis upon the need to rely upon governors to maintain imperial interests. "If political liberty," he wrote, "be established in a colony, the sovereignty which, following that principle, must be distributed in certain proportions among the people, will also be established there; and the immediate effect of that will be an habitual independent attention to a separate interest." [20] He believed that "the share of the Crown in the sovereignty is certainly not enough by itself to create dependence," but institutions ought to be shaped "so as to preserve the greatest degree of habitual influence possible in the executive branch of government; that being . . . the only point of contact between this mother and her colonies." Thus British statesmen accepted, as an inescapable fact, that colonies must have representative institutions, but were puzzled to discover how this might be reconciled with imperial interests; this was to remain the classic problem of colonial government.

18. *Parlt. Hist.* XXIX, 657 and 404.

19. This document is printed from the Colonial Office papers in Harlow and Madden, *British Colonial Developments.* It is unsigned, but Grenville's authorship seems to be established by his letter to Thurlow and by Thurlow's reply, in Hist. MSS. Comm. *Dropmore Papers,* I, 497, 504, and cf. Manning, *British Colonial Government,* 328, note 37.

20. *Dropmore Papers,* I, p. 504ff.

The hope of creating a colonial aristocracy proved fanciful, because it was conceived without knowledge of conditions in a mobile and expanding society, but in other respects the Canada Act of 1791 set a pattern for colonial government in which strong governors, buttressed by whatever influence the Crown could command, faced bi-cameral legislatures to which they were not responsible. This pattern is remarkable for the inevitable friction which it occasioned between governors and legislatures, between imperial interests and local autonomy, and between economic behaviour determined in London and the natural tendency of economic life to flow in the easiest channels. Yet the system also contained a great element of flexibility, for there was nothing to prevent the governor from choosing his executive councillors from the legislature, and for men who wished to follow the British model this might be, in the long run, a natural course of action. If constitutional practice in the modern Dominions duplicates, with necessary modifications, that of Great Britain, it is because the lessons of the Revolution learned in England were not those learned in America. The Canada Act and the American constitution, so nearly contemporary in time, mark a definite divergence between the two types of Anglo-Saxon constitutionalism.

(2) IRELAND. Paradoxically, at a period when the British government was trying to create a Canadian aristocracy, it was running into difficulties in the one country where an anglophile aristocracy was part of the established order of things. The autonomy which Ireland had won between 1779 and 1782 gave power to a minority within a minority— to those Protestants who were qualified to vote—yet it became apparent that Protestant ascendancy must pursue a genuinely Irish policy: this would mean the encouragement of domestic manufactures and, perhaps, free trade outside the Empire. The prospect was alarming to many English interests. Manufacturers were persuaded that their sales would suffer in Ireland (though their spokesmen had, at first, been prepared to take on all comers in an open market), but the driving power behind the agitation against economic independence for Ireland were the shippers who feared that every Irish sloop crossing the St. George's Channel would carry a cargo of tropical produce brought to Ireland by American or other foreign ships, and the West India interest which feared that foreign sugar would flood the British market by the same means. In 1785 Pitt, who had at first wished to exempt Ireland from the Navigation Act in return for a contribution to imperial defence, was persuaded to incorporate in his act safeguards for imperial economic interests, and thus converted a measure which would have been passed with enthusiasm by the Irish Parliament into one which was bitterly resented. The unfortunate and naked fact was that British interests could only be protected by the influence of the Crown, administered by the Lord Lieutenant, and designed to create a Parliamentary majority. In 1785 influence was not strong enough and Pitt's measure was rejected. Perhaps Thurlow had Ireland in mind when he commented upon Grenville's enthusiasm for a

colonial aristocracy with the observation that, "If placed in hands unequal to it, [it] will only be despised; but if lodged with families of permanent consideration will grow . . . into an independent interest." [21] So long as the Empire was conceived as a defence mechanism for established British interests, no British government would admit the implications of autonomous units under a single sovereign. It would be unjust to blame the statesmen of the day for thinking of the Empire in that light, but it is right to recognise that their outlook severely limited the scope of political experimentation. From the British point of view the need to annihilate Irish independence by union with England was implicit in the situation even before the Irish peasantry were infected from France with the spirit of revolution.

IV. The Consequences of the Decisions Taken After the Loss of the American Colonies

(1) IMMEDIATE SUCCESSES. In the short run all the cards seemed to fall as the defenders of the Navigation Act had predicted. At the end of the eighteenth century Great Britain could look with satisfaction upon a greatly increased merchant marine and vastly increased exports. Moreover, much of the increase of shipping had apparently been at the expense of the Americans (though recently the latter found new employment in carrying staple crops to Europe from the West Indian islands belonging to foreign belligerents). The exigencies of the war had made necessary some breaches in the walls of the imperial system by permitting trade in American ships under licence, but the principles of the Navigation Act were still accepted as normal and necessary.[22] If Great Britain was not exactly winning the war with France, at least she had saved herself from the total decline which many expected in 1783.

(2) THE UNITED STATES FAILS TO RETALIATE. British policy had been most unpopular in the United States, and after the inauguration of the new national government in 1788 retaliatory measures against Great Britain were confidently expected and strongly urged by a powerful party. Yet, though the retaliatory policy won successes in the House of Representatives—even extending to the passage of a non-intercourse bill early in 1794—these measures were opposed by Washington and Alexander Hamilton, and consistently lost in the Senate, where Hamilton's

21. *Dropmore Papers*, I, p. 504ff.

22. In 1800 the old argument with the West Indies was still going on. The shortage of shipping had made necessary the admission of American ships to Island ports to bring in provisions and lumber and to take out molasses and rum, but when Barbados asked permission to let them also take away sugar and coffee, this was too much for the Lords of Trade presided over by Lord Liverpool: it would "give the American States a share in the Trade and Navigation of those islands, from which His Majesty's European Dominions derive so great a benefit . . . It would have the effect of subverting the wise Regulations and Restrictions of the Navigation Act," P.R.O., B.T. 5.12.191ff.

friends prevailed. The realists who guided American destinies knew that, though the United States were politically independent, they remained economically dependent upon Great Britain, and the shippers and merchants who were most directly affected by British policy were the strongest supporters of their government's endeavours to avert a breach. Britain took the major part of American exports, provided an overwhelming quantity of imports, and through generous credit, provided the new nation with much of its working capital. Hamilton believed that America could attain prosperity and strength by using the contributions of Great Britain, and in the long run this belief was to be justified; in the meantime, however, it meant a somewhat tame acceptance of British restrictive policy. In 1794 the treaty negotiated by Jay gained only the admission of very small American ships to the West Indies, but this was of little value to American ship-owners who wanted the West Indian trade, not as an extension of the coasting trade, but as a stage in the round-about voyages of ocean-going vessels. The Senate found the British concession so unsatisfactory that it refused to ratify this clause.

(3) THE FULL BALANCE SHEET LESS FAVOURABLE. Yet there were signs also that the reckoning with the United States was not complete and that the instruments of imperial strategy were not strong enough to accomplish the tasks which they had been set. In 1784 Sir Guy Carleton told the Committee of the Privy Council that "The struggle now to be decided involves a very important question, whether the United States or the remaining British colonies in America shall engross the benefits arising from a trade between the Continent and the Islands—if the former shall succeed, their cause and interest, political as well as commercial, must increase; and in like manner, if the Loyalists prevail, they will contribute proportionately to their own and to the national strength and prosperity." [23] But by 1800 there was no doubt whose cause, "political as well as commercial," was dominant in the New World, and so far from becoming the instruments by which British commercial prosperity might be maintained, the Islands and the British North American colonies were dependent upon the United States for essential supplies. Moreover, there was a growing suspicion that the rise of British trade and shipping might be caused by industry's response to foreign demand, particularly in the United States, rather than by the maintenance of old restrictions. The argument was to continue far into the nineteenth century, with the unwritten alliance between American agriculture and British industry gradually forcing Great Britain along the road to free trade. In the broader field of imperial relationships the record was not impressive. The problem of reconciling imperial interests with local autonomy was no nearer solution in 1800 than it had been in 1774. Irish self-government had been abandoned in favour of union with Great Britain. In British North America a half century of political tension lay ahead. The West Indies were doomed to decline, discontent, and (except in Bar-

23. P.R.O., B.T. 6.81.79ff. Quoted by G. S. Graham, *British Policy and Canada,* 71.

bados) to the loss of their old representative institutions. Yet one should not ask too much of statesmen or even of nations: faced in 1783 with the task of saving British power from what seemed to many a total wreck, the men of this generation had been understandably reluctant to concede too much; preoccupied with immediate tasks, they had neither the leisure nor the inclination to look into the remote future, and their immediate success may well palliate their failure to rebuild the Empire on a new model.

QUADRANGLE PAPERBACKS

American History

Frederick Lewis Allen. *The Lords of Creation.* (QP35)
Lewis Atherton. *Main Street on the Middle Border.* (QP36)
Thomas A. Bailey. *Woodrow Wilson and the Lost Peace.* (QP1)
Thomas A. Bailey. *Woodrow Wilson and the Great Betrayal.* (QP2)
Charles A. Beard. *The Idea of National Interest.* (QP27)
Carl L. Becker. *Everyman His Own Historian.* (QP33)
Ray A. Billington. *The Protestant Crusade.* (QP12)
Allan G. Bogue. *From Prairie to Corn Belt.* (QP50)
Kenneth E. Boulding. *The Organizational Revolution.* (QP43)
Gerald M. Capers. *John C. Calhoun, Opportunist.* (QP70)
David M. Chalmers. *Hooded Americanism.* (QP51)
John Chamberlain. *Farewell to Reform.* (QP19)
Alice Hamilton Cromie. *A Tour Guide to the Civil War.*
Robert D. Cross. *The Emergence of Liberal Catholicism in America.* (QP44)
Richard M. Dalfiume. *American Politics Since 1945.* (NYTimes Book, QP57)
Chester McArthur Destler. *American Radicalism, 1865-1901.* (QP30)
Robert A. Divine. *American Foreign Policy Since 1945.* (NYTimes Book, QP58)
Robert A. Divine. *Causes and Consequences of World War II.* (QP63)
Robert A. Divine. *The Illusion of Neutrality.* (QP45)
Elisha P. Douglass. *Rebels and Democrats.* (QP26)
Felix Frankfurter. *The Commerce Clause.* (QP16)
Lloyd C. Gardner. *A Different Frontier.* (QP32)
Edwin Scott Gaustad. *The Great Awakening in New England.* (QP46)
Ray Ginger. *Altgeld's America.* (QP21)
Ray Ginger. *Modern American Cities.* (NYTimes Book, QP67)
Ray Ginger. *Six Days or Forever?* (QP68)
Gerald N. Grob. *Workers and Utopia.* (QP61)
Louis Hartz. *Economic Policy and Democratic Thought.* (QP52)
William B. Hesseltine. *Lincoln's Plan of Reconstruction.* (QP41)
Granville Hicks. *The Great Tradition.* (QP62)
Dwight W. Hoover. *Understanding Negro History.* (QP49)
Stanley P. Hirshson. *Farewell to the Bloody Shirt.* (QP53)
Frederic C. Howe. *The Confessions of a Reformer.* (QP39)
Harold L. Ickes. *The Autobiography of a Curmudgeon.* (QP69)
Louis Joughin and Edmund M. Morgan. *The Legacy of Sacco and Vanzetti.* (QP7)
William Loren Katz. *Teachers' Guide to American Negro History.* (QP210)
Burton Ira Kaufman. *Washington's Farewell Address.* (QP64)
Edward Chase Kirkland. *Dream and Thought in the Business Community, 1860-1900.* (QP11)
Edward Chase Kirkland. *Industry Comes of Age.* (QP42)
Adrienne Koch. *The Philosophy of Thomas Jefferson.* (QP17)
Gabriel Kolko. *The Triumph of Conservatism.* (QP40)
Walter LaFeber. *John Quincy Adams and American Continental Empire.* (QP23)
Lawrence H. Leder. *The Meaning of the American Revolution.* (NYTimes Book, QP66)
David E. Lilienthal. *TVA: Democracy on the March.* (QP28)
Arthur S. Link. *Wilson the Diplomatist.* (QP18)
Huey P. Long. *Every Man a King.* (QP8)
Gene M. Lyons. *America: Purpose and Power.* (QP24)
Jackson Turner Main. *The Antifederalists.* (QP14)
Ernest R. May. *The World War and American Isolation, 1914-1917.* (QP29)
Henry F. May. *The End of American Innocence.* (QP9)
George E. Mowry. *The California Progressives.* (QP6)
William L. O'Neill. *American Society Since 1945.* (NYTimes Book, QP59)
Frank L. Owsley. *Plain Folk of the Old South.* (QP22)
David Graham Phillips. *The Treason of the Senate.* (QP20)
Julius W. Pratt. *Expansionists of 1898.* (QP15)
C. Herman Pritchett. *The Roosevelt Court.* (QP71)
Moses Rischin. *The American Gospel of Success.* (QP54)
John P. Roche. *The Quest for the Dream.* (QP47)
David A. Shannon. *The Socialist Party of America.* (QP38)
Andrew Sinclair. *The Available Man.* (QP60)
John Spargo. *The Bitter Cry of the Children.* (QP55)
Bernard Sternsher. *The Negro in Depression and War.* (QP65)
Richard W. Van Alstyne. *The Rising American Empire.* (QP25)
Willard M. Wallace. *Appeal to Arms.* (QP10)
Norman Ware. *The Industrial Worker, 1840-1860.* (QP13)
Albert K. Weinberg. *Manifest Destiny.* (QP3)
Bernard A. Weisberger. *They Gathered at the River.* (QP37)
Robert H. Wiebe. *Businessmen and Reform.* (QP56)
William Appleman Williams. *The Contours of American History.* (QP34)
William Appleman Williams. *The Great Evasion.* (QP48)
Esmond Wright. *Causes and Consequences of the American Revolution.* (QP31)

QUADRANGLE PAPERBACKS

European History

William Sheridan Allen. *The Nazi Seizure of Power.* (QP302)
W. O. Henderson. *The Industrial Revolution in Europe.* (QP303)
Raul Hilberg. *The Destruction of the European Jews.* (QP301)
Telford Taylor. *Sword and Swastika.* (QP304)
John Weiss. *Nazis and Fascists in Europe, 1918-1945.* (NYTimes Book, QP305)

Philosophy

F. H. Bradley. *The Presuppositions of Critical History.* (QP108)
William Earle. *Objectivity.* (QP109)
James M. Edie, James P. Scanlan, Mary-Barbara Zeldin, George L. Kline. *Russian Philosophy.* (3 vols, QP111, 112, 113)
James M. Edie. *An Invitation to Phenomenology.* (QP103)
James M. Edie. *New Essays in Phenomenology.* (QP114)
James M. Edie. *Phenomenology in America.* (QP105)
Manfred S. Frings. *Heidegger and the Quest for Truth.* (QP107)
Moltke S. Gram. *Kant: Disputed Questions.* (QP104)
E. D. Klemke. *Studies in the Philosophy of G. E. Moore.* (QP115)
Lionel Rubinoff. *Faith and Reason.* (QP106)
Paul Tibbetts. *Perception.* (QP110)
Pierre Thévenaz. *What Is Phenomenology?* (QP101)

Social Science

Nathan Glazer. *Cities in Trouble.* (NYTimes Book, QP212)
George and Eunice Grier. *Equality and Beyond.* (QP204)
Charles O. Lerche, Jr. *Last Chance in Europe.* (QP207)
David Mitrany. *A Working Peace System.* (QP205)
Martin Oppenheimer and George Lakey. *A Manual for Direct Action.* (QP202)
James Parkes. *Antisemitism.* (QP213)
Fred Powledge. *To Change a Child.* (QP209)
Lee Rainwater. *And the Poor Get Children.* (QP208)
Clarence Senior. *The Puerto Ricans.* (QP201)
Arthur L. Stinchcombe. *Rebellion in a High School.* (QP211)

DATE DUE

DATE DUE			
FEB 8			
FEB 2 '73			
E H			
MAY 10 1983			
MAY 21 1983			
JAN 7 '85			
JAN 7 '86			
MY 8 '91			
NOV 1 5 1996			
MAY 1 9 1997			
GAYLORD			PRINTED IN U.S.A.